Gardening made easy . . .

Written not for those who want to win prizes at exhibitions but for those who want beautiful gardens for their own delight, this book has become the great stand-by for gardeners in hundreds of thousands of homes. It covers the whole range of normal small-garden activities, from the initial stages of layout and design through planning, planting, propagation, greenhouse management, the gardener's enemies, a programme for each month's work and appendices full of valuable information.

Writing as one giving advice to a friend, the author sets out to save the reader from the back-aches and disappointments which beset the amateur and he does so in simple language unencumbered with technical jargon. He avoids the confusion of listing innumerable choices, and gives instead a careful selection of the flowers, fruit, and vegetables which he has found most rewarding.

A special feature which will be of great assistance is that, as an amateur, the author is able to recommend particular nurseries and proprietary products of merit.

There is a very full index, sixteen pages of photogravure plates, and many line-drawings showing exactly the way in which certain jobs should be done. It is the ideal book for the gardener who has no time to become involved in technicalities.

The cover illustration is taken from a photograph by Harry Smith of azaleas in the author's garden.

Currently available by the same author in PAN books

SPRINGBOARD TO VICTORY:
Battle for Kohina

'Written simply and colloquially and with immense gusto by a practical gardener of excellent taste.'— LORD MORTON in *Journal of the Royal Horticultural Society*.

'Packed with so much useful information on every aspect of the small garden that it can take its place with the best of professional textbooks.'—*House and Garden*.

'One of the best general books on gardening I have studied for a very long time.'—*Country Life*.

'An excellent buy for the would-be-good small gardener.'—*New Statesman*.

THE SMALL GARDEN

C. E. LUCAS PHILLIPS

Extensively revised
by the author

PAN BOOKS LTD : LONDON

By arrangement with
WILLIAM HEINEMANN LTD
LONDON

First published 1952 by Wm. Heinemann Ltd.
First published by Pan Books Ltd. 1956,
33 Tothill Street, London, S.W.1

330 33031 4

2nd Printing 1957
New Edition (Revised) 1961
4th Printing 1962
5th Printing 1963
New Edition (Revised) 1965
7th Printing 1966
New Edition (Revised and Re-set) 1969

For
B. J. L. P.
conjugi dilectissimæ

Printed in Great Britain by
Richard Clay (The Chaucer Press), Ltd.,
Bungay, Suffolk

CONTENTS

	PAGE
PREFACE	12
GARDENERS' JARGON	13
PRESENTATION	17

Limited Objective—On Dogmatism—Pest No. 1—On Becoming a Fan—Roses by Other Names—Unorthodox Authorship.

PART I: FUNDAMENTALS

CHAPTER
I FIRST STEPS	25
Lay-out	25
Aspect	27
Design	28
II THE PLANT	30
Root and Branch	30
Elemental Needs	31
The Blossom	33
Tender and Hardy	34
The Span of Life	35
III MOTHER EARTH	36
Top Soil and Sub-soil	36
Types of Soil	37
Chemical Elements	39
Organic Foods	40
Inorganic Foods	45
Lime	47
IV THE GARDENER'S ARMOURY	51

CHAPTER		PAGE
V	GARDEN OPERATIONS	56
	Cultivation in General	56
	Drainage	58
	Digging	61
	Ridging	64
	Manuring	64
	Weeding	65
	Watering	67
	Staking	68
	Mulching	69
	Planting	70
VI	BE FRUITFUL AND MULTIPLY	73
	Propagation Generally	73
	Plants from Seed	74
	Cuttings	81
	Root Cuttings	86
	Leaf Cuttings	86
	Layers	87
	Division	87
VII	PRUNING	89
VIII	PATHS AND TERRACES	97
IX	THE SMALL GREENHOUSE AND OTHER GLASSWORKS	102
	General Management and Uses	102
	What to Grow	107
	The Frame	112
	Cloches	113
	Soil Heating	114

PART II: FLOWERS

	INTRODUCTORY	117
X	ANNUALS AND BIENNIALS	118
	Bedding	121
	The Best Annuals and Biennials	122

CHAPTER		PAGE
XI	HERBACEOUS AND MIXED BORDERS	135
	The Use and Misuse of Border Plants	135
	A Selection of Perennials	140
	Second Eleven	156
XII	ROCK GARDENS AND STONEWORKS	159
	The Lure and the Hazard	159
	The Rock Garden Proper	160
	Dry Walls and Banks	164
	Moraine and Scree	166
	What to Plant	166
	Some Second Choices	176
	Rock Garden Paths and Pavings	177
	Plants for Dry Walls	178
	For Herbaceous and Mixed Borders	179
XIII	BULBS AND THEIR KIND	180
	Bulbs in General	180
	Bulbs Indoors	184
	A Selection of Bulbous Plants	186
XIV	ROSES	203
	First Words	203
	The Shapes and Forms of Roses	203
	The Breeds of Roses	204
	Cultivation	206
	Planting	207
	After-care	208
	Pruning	209
	The Rose's Enemies	215
	Propagation of Roses	216
	Lay-out and Display	217
	Varieties to Choose	217
XV	FLOWERING SHRUBS AND SMALL TREES	221
	Introductory	221
	Small Trees	224
	Flowering Shrubs, mostly deciduous	227
	Winter-flowering Shrubs	237
	Shrubs for Lime-free Soils	237
	Evergreens	241
	Dwarf and Carpeting Shrubs	243
	Second Eleven	244
	Conifers	246

CHAPTER			PAGE
XVI	CLIMBING AND WALL PLANTS		248
XVII	HEDGES AND EDGES		256
	What to Plant		259
	Brief List of Hedging Plants		262
	Renovating Old Hedges		264
XVIII	SOME SPECIALITIES		266
	Carnations and Pinks		266
	Clematis		270
	Chrysanthemums		274
	Irises		279
	The Heather Family		282
XIX	THE LAWN		286

PART III: FOOD

XX	FRUIT		293
	Introductory		293
	Situation and Soil		294
	Planting		295
	Shaping		295
	Pruning		297
	Spraying		300
	Selections and Cultural Notes		301
XXI	SIMPLE VEGETABLES AND HERBS		
	Introductory		328
	General Cultivation		329
	Special Family Needs		331
	Rotation of Crops		334
	Lay-out		335
	Frames and Cloches		336
	Selections		336

PART IV: KNOW YOUR ENEMY

INTRODUCTORY			361
XXII	FRIEND AND FOE		362
	Friends		362
	Enemies in General		364
	Remedies in General		366

CHAPTER		PAGE
XXIII	THE ENEMY IN DETAIL	369
	Soil and General Pests	369
	Plant Pests	371
	Fungus Diseases	374
	Physiological Ailments	375
XXIV	THE MEDICINE CUPBOARD	378

PART V

THE YEAR'S WORK	381

APPENDICES

1. Some Memoranda	393
2. Flower-pot Sizes	393
3. Seed and Potting Composts (John Innes)	394
4. The North Wall and Border	394
5. Some Plants for Dry Soils	395
6. Some Plants for Moist Soils	396
7. Town Gardens	396
8. Some Good Nurseries	398
INDEX	401

ILLUSTRATIONS IN PHOTOGRAVURE

(between pages 96 and 97)

Rose 'Golden Wings'   *Arthur Hunt*
Clematis 'W. E. Gladstone'   ,,   ,,
Lily 'Enchantment'   ,,   ,,
Lily 'Thunderbolt'   ,,   ,,
The ground-hugging rose R. *paulii*
    'Rosea'   ,,   ,,
Rose 'Sarah van Fleet'   ,,   ,,
Magnolia grandiflora   *Harry Smith*
Achillea 'Gold Plate'   *Bernard Alfieri*
Red Hot Pokers (*Kniphofia*)   *Harry Smith*

(between pages 208 and 209)

Anemone blanda   *Reginald A. Malby*
Anemone pulsatilla (*Pulsatilla vulgaris*) ,,   ,,
Dicentra spectabilis   ,,   ,,
Campanula pusilla 'Miss Willmott'   ,,   ,,
Alstrœmeria Ligtu hybrid   ,,   ,,
Liatris pycnostachia   ,,   ,,
An Astilbe   ,,   ,,
Echinacea 'The King'   ,,   ,,
A row of young trees of the columnar
    cherry 'Amanogawa'   *John Green-Wilkinson*
Lilium testaceum   *Reginald A. Malby*
Leocojum vernum   ,,   ,,
A spray of *Rosa moyesii*   ,,   ,,
Hibiscus syriacus   ,,   ,,
A young Witch Hazel   ,,   ,,
Buddleia alternifolia trained as a
    standard   ,,   ,,
A perfect example of how to clip a
    hedge of *Lonicera nitida*   ,,   ,,
A hedge of *Berberis stenophylla* in
    flower   ,,   ,,

(between pages 320 and 321)

A sturdy, wind-resistant annual
mallow, *Lavatera trimestris* *Harry Smith*

A sea-holly, the white-collared
Eryngium alpinum   „ „

Hypericum olympicum in the author's
rock garden   „ „

One of the herbaceous borders „ „

The Canary ivy at the front door „ „

The multiple sprays of the Canadian
lilac '*Virgilia*'   *Bernard Alfieri*

Verbascum broussa, completely clad in
white felt   „ „

The author displays his cordon
redcurrants   „ „

*Line drawings can be readily traced through the
Index*

PREFACE TO THE FIFTH (1969) EDITION

IN each successive edition of this book since its first issue in 1952 I have been obliged to make a great many revisions in order to keep it reasonably up-to-date. Every year new flowers and vegetables, new chemicals and new techniques in horticultural methods make their appearances. Indeed, so much has happened in our world in the past few years that all editions earlier than this one are to some extent obsolete. Moreover, one's own experience broadens and one's opinions change.

The amendments in this edition are very much more extensive than in any previous revision, and many passages have been completely rewritten. In order to keep the price of the book down to a modest figure, however, I have retained the original method of writing plant names, which was acceptable at the time of the first edition, and I have also, in most instances, retained the older horticultural names of those plants that have been the victims of the botanist's passion for changing them. However, in most nurserymen's catalogues you are still much more likely to find them under the old names than under the new ones.

On the whole, I have tended to be somewhat conservative in my choices of varieties of flower, fruit, and vegetable. There are many good new ones (and some not so good), but all the varieties I have chosen, whether old or new, are thoroughly reliable. As the following pages show, I often regard new varieties with a slightly sceptical eye.

C. E. LUCAS PHILLIPS

September 1968

THIS very brief dictionary of gardening terms is included 'by special request' as a means of ready reference. It can't hope to be complete, but numerous other definitions are given in the text and can be dug out by means of the Index. Terms specially used in pruning are in Chapters VII and XX. A bare minimum is included of the Latin and Greek terms most commonly used in plant names, and these are in italics. Of adjectives, the masculine form only is given. Thus *albus* is *alba* in the feminine and *album* in the neuter; *officinalis* is both masculine and feminine, but *officinale* in the neuter. *n* = noun; *v* = verb.

ACID SOIL. Soil with a low lime content.
ALBUS. White.
ALKALINE SOIL. Opposite to acid.
ANTHER. The pollen-bearing part of the stamen.
-ANTHUS. Flower; as in Polyanthus and polyantha, many-flowered; or macrantha, large-flowered.
ATRO-. Deep in colour, as in atropurpurea.
AXIL. The angle between a stem and a branch; hence axillary.

BED OUT, *v*. To plant out a whole flower-bed according to a set scheme with plants already well advanced in growth; e.g. 'geraniums' for summer bedding, or wallflowers for spring bedding.
BOLT, *v*. To run to seed prematurely, as of lettuces.
BRACT. Rudimentary leaves at the base of a flower.
BRASSICA. For our purposes, a vegetable of the cabbage family.
BREASTWOOD. On wall-trained fruits, shoots that grow outwards from the wall; also called 'fore-right' shoots.
BUD, *n*. There are flower- or fruit-buds, and wood- or growth-buds; horticulturally, the term is used not only of a well-developed bud, but also from the moment when there is a tiny mark or swelling on the stem.

A shoot showing: *a*, terminal or extension bud; *b*, leaf axil; *c*, axillary bud. Important in Sweet Peas, Chrysanthemums, Tomatoes, etc.

BUD, *v.* To propagate a desired variety by inserting a bud of that variety into a suitable root stock.

CALCAREOUS. Chalky, of soil.

CALYX. The circlet or whorl of sepals that enclose a flower-bud before it opens.

CHAMÆ-. Close to the ground, as in Chamæcyparis, False Cypress.

CHLOROSIS. Loss of green pigment (chlorophyll) in foliage.

CHRYS-. Golden.

COCCINEUS (pronounced 'Koksineus'). Scarlet.

COLLAR. The junction of stem and root.

COMPOST. Has two meanings—a special mixture of soil components made up for pots or seed-boxes; and decomposed organic matter from a 'compost heap' used as manure.

CORM. A bulb-like swelling of a stem underground, e.g. Gladiolus and Crocus.

COROLLA. The whole circlet or whorl of petals in a flower.

CROCK. A piece of broken flower-pot, or other stony material in lieu, laid in the bottoms of pots or seed-boxes for drainage.

CULTIVAR. Orthodox term for the named variety of a species, occurring in cultivation, not the wild; same thing really as 'variety'.

CUTTING. A portion cut from a living plant from which a new plant can be grown; usually a small stem or branch; but sometimes a root or leaf.

DEAD-HEAD, *v.* Gardeners' colloquialism for removing spent flowers from a plant.

DENTATUS, DENTICULATUS. Toothed.

DISBUD, *v.* Usually, to remove a certain number of small flower buds below or around the main one so that it may develop to its best.

DRILL, *n.* A tiny trench, maybe only ¼-in. deep, made in the soil for sowing seed.

EYE. A rudimentary bud.

FASTIGIATE. Tall, slender, columnar, the branches erect.

FIBROUS. Of roots; thin, hair-like roots, more or less dense. 'Fibrous loam' is old turf with plenty of dense grass roots.

FL. PL. = FLORE PLENO. Double-flowered. *See* 'Single'.

-FOLIUS. Leaved, as in longifolius, long-leaved.

FRUTICOSUS. Shrubby.

FULGENS. Shining, glowing.

GLABROUS. Smooth, hairless.

GLAUCOUS. Sea-green.

HARDEN OFF, *v.* To accustom a non-hardy plant, raised under glass, to outdoor conditions gradually.

HEAVY SOIL. One preponderating in clay.

HEEL IN, *v.* To make a rough trench, put the plants in semi-erect, and cover their roots with soil as temporary protection until ready to plant; or, as with spent Tulips and other bulbs that have to be got out of the way, to allow them to complete their cycle of life.

HUMUS. *See* Chapter III.

INFLORESCENCE. The method in which flowers arrange themselves on a stem, whether 'solitary' (one flower per stem, as in the pansy), or in a 'spike', a 'raceme' (a spike on which each floret has a short stem, as in the lupin), a domed 'umbel' (several flowers

14

springing from one point, as in the polyanthus), a flattish 'corymb', etc. These terms are often used inexactly.

JAPONICUS. Japanese.

LATI-. Broad, as latifolius, broad-leaved.

LEGUME. A plant that forms its seeds in pods, as in peas, beans, Lupin, Laburnum, Broom.

LIGHT SOIL. One predominating in sand.

LOAM. A blend of clay, sand, and humus.

MACRO-. Large or long, e.g. macrocarpus, large-fruited, and macrantha, large- or long-flowered.

MICRO-. Small.

MULCH, *v.* To cover the soil with leaves, grass-mowings, manure, etc., either to conserve moisture, or to provide a food for the plants, or both (Chapter V).

MULTI-. Many.

NANUS. Dwarf.

'NEW WOOD.' A shoot (branch or twig) that has sprouted and grown in the current season.

NODE. The joint on a stem, often slightly swollen, from which a leaf-stalk will sprout or has sprouted.

NURSERY. A small reserved part of the garden, especially the kitchen garden, in which young plants are reared; it has a seed-bed and a pricking-out bed.

OFFICINALIS. Commercial, medicinal.

'OLD WOOD.' A shoot that grew last year or earlier.

'OPEN' WEATHER. Weather in which the soil is neither frost-bound nor saturated with rain.

PAN. A shallow pottery vessel in which seed is sown, often in preference to a seed-box; also a hard, compressed sub-stratum of soil.

PERENNIAL. A plant that lives on from year to year (Chapter II).

PERI-. Around; e.g. perianth, the roundish combination of calyx and corolla in a Narcissus and other plants.

PERSICUS. Persian.

-PHYLLUS. Leaf, e.g. microphyllus, small-leaved.

PINCH, *v.* To nip out, commonly with the finger-nails, the growing point of a plant or one of its shoots.

PISTIL. The female organ of a flower including stigma, style, ovary.

POLY-. Many, e.g. polyanthus, many-flowered.

POT ON, *v.* To move a plant from a small pot into a larger one as it grows.

PRÆCOX. Early, precocious.

PRICK IN, *v.* To work fertilisers etc. into the top inch or two of soil with hoe or fork.

PRICK OUT, *v.* To transplant seedlings from their seed-bed or box into another bed or box, at wider spacing to allow healthy development.

REPENS, REPTANS. Creeping.

RHIZOME. A prostrate, fleshy stem, emitting roots below and leaves above, most familiar in flag irises; sometimes an underground stem. Pronounced 'ryzome'.

RUNNER. A prostrate shoot thrown out by some plants, which roots

15

at several points and forms new plants, e.g. strawberry, ground ivy, 'couch' grass.

SAX-. Rock-loving, as in saxifrage and the adjective saxatile.

SCABER. Rough.

SCHIZ-. Split. Pronounced 'skyz'.

SCION. A cultivated variety of a tree, shrub, etc., that has been grafted or budded on to a different root stock, often of a wild species, as in roses, fruit trees, lilac, etc.

SEED-BED. Any strip or patch of soil specially prepared for the sowing of seed, whether in the nursery or the open ground.

SELF-COLOURED. Of one colour throughout.

SEPAL. One of the leaf-like members that collectively form a calyx.

SERRATA, SERRATE. With saw-edged leaf.

SERRULATA, SERRULATE. Finely saw-edged.

SESSILIS. Sessile, stalkless.

SINENSIS, *SINO-*. Chinese.

SINGLE. A flower that has only one ring of petals, as in the wild brier or dog rose, and the common buttercup. Cf. single and double Chrysanthemums, Asters, etc.

SOUTH WALL. That side of a wall which faces South.

SPECTABILIS. Showy.

SPIT. The depth of one spade in digging.

SPUR. A fruit-bud or cluster of several on fruit trees (Chapter XX).

STAMEN. The whole male organ of a flower.

STANDARD. Of trees, an erect stem without branches below a certain height.

'START', *v*. To start a plant into early growth before planting out, e.g. Dahlia and Begonia, by planting it under glass.

STENO-. Narrow, e.g. stenophylla, narrow-leaved.

STIGMA. The sticky part of the pistil or female organ of a flower; it receives the pollen.

STOCK. The rooted growth, often of a wild species, on which a cultivated scion is grafted or budded.

STOP, *v*. To remove the growing tip of a plant to induce branching.

STRICTUS. Erect and slender.

SUB-. Semi, as in subsessile, subserrulata.

SUCKER. A shoot springing from the root formation of a plant, usually noxious, as in the Rose and Lilac, where a cultivated variety is budded on other stock; but in the raspberry and blackberry they are the normal means of multiplying.

TAP-ROOT. A thick tapering root growing straight downwards.

TILTH. Cultivation. A 'fine tilth', as of a seed-bed, is soil worked down to small, loose, fine crumbs, or particles.

TOMENTOSUS. Woolly.

TRANSPIRATION. The giving-out of moisture by a leaf.

TUBER. A fleshy underground stem, as in the Dahlia and potato.

VEGETATIVE propagation. The raising of plants by cuttings, budding, division, etc., not by seed.

VULGARIS. Common.

WHORL. A ring or circlet of petals, leaves or sepals springing from the same level on a stem.

16

PRESENTATION

LIMITED OBJECTIVE—ON DOGMATISM—PEST NO. 1—
ON BECOMING A FAN—ROSES BY OTHER NAMES—
UNORTHODOX AUTHORSHIP

WHY another garden book, I asked, when there were so many good ones already? Because, they answered, there is nothing that just meets our need—a short and simple book, yet reasonably complete, for those of us who have only small gardens, as most of us understand the term, who have no time or inclination for mixing ounces of this or that per square yard, but who would like, with small resources, to turn out a garden in which we can take pleasure and pride.

This, then, is a book by an amateur for amateurs; by an amateur who, starting in complete ignorance some forty odd years ago, made his first attempt at gardening by sowing sweet pea seed six inches deep under an elm tree, and who had to contend with the problems of catching the 8.30 am daily. Remembering my own early tribulations, therefore, I have designed this book for those who have little or no experience, but who do at least know which end of a hoe is which. It will also, I hope, be a help to those who have passed their novitiate and are anxious to make progress in the craft, and to all who wish to grow, for their own delight, good roses or clematis or peas, and to make their gardens, however small, an integral part of their homes, as full of pleasure and of practical usefulness as their houses.

Space (which means money—your money) has obliged several limitations. Therefore do not look in here for any guidance on how to grow for exhibition—no legendary beans or parsnips, no solitaire roses of splendid size and substance.

17

Nor, unfortunately, will there be anything about heated green-houses, orchids, cacti, large trees or water-gardens. And in the lists of flowers and vegetables I have omitted anything 'precious' or unduly difficult, and have, moreover, been highly selective in all these lists, aiming, in the first place, at dealing with the better of the usual things that most people will want to know about and 'look up', and, secondly and specially, at pointing to some worthwhile and unhackneyed things which, though not in the least 'rare' to a horticulturist, are for some reason seldom seen in small places but ought to be, for their merits as well as their ease.

What has been more difficult than selection has been compression. Each of these chapters is a fit subject for a whole volume, some of them for several volumes. Besides having to shun that friendly discursiveness that makes gardening books agreeable, I have also had to omit all those qualifications, those ifs and buts, that books on gardening ought to contain but seldom do. For in gardening, as in law, dogmatism and downright mandamus ought to be guarded against. The doctors of gardening, on some matters, disagree as much as others. Listen to them, if you ever have the chance, on lilies! One man's experience is not another's. Moreover, soil, climate, situation and aspect have such infinite variations that what is right treatment in one instance is not necessarily right in another, and the local knowledge of the old hand may be worth more than many written words. That, with the utmost respect, is one of the qualifications to be put upon what we hear from experts in the non-technical Press and on the Air, who are even more tethered for space and time than I, and who would be the first to agree that you should not too far dogmatise, for example, on the pruning of apples and roses. You can only guide. Every gardener finds his own way of doing things and where I have found a particular method good I advocate it. I am convinced, for example, that, where things are permanently planted, we worry the soil too much. And there are many popular misconceptions about roses. Labour-saving has been much in my mind, and, as compared with technical books, I have simplified appreciably in matters of fertilisers, insecticides and so on. Where orthodoxy is safest for the apprentice, however, I have followed that path.

What is a 'small' garden? The City Magnate would have an idea quite different from his clerk's. There are the pocket-handkerchief gardens of cottage and town house, and the rather larger gardens of the suburbs and the country. I have borne in mind a limit of about an acre, but with special consideration for the suburban garden of less than half that size. The limitation, of course, applies in no way to cultural requirements, and what is good for the rose and the daffodil in the cotter's plot is equally good for the Magnate's demesne.

Most people who possess anything like an acre, or half of it, contribute weekly to the support of a gentleman known as Jobbing Gardener. You are warned of the danger that he may prove to be Garden Pest No. 1. I have come across a few good ones and, very rarely, one or two very good ones, who have been brought up on the staff of some big establishment or who have taken the trouble to train themselves properly. If you have one of these, reward him well. Usually, however (leaving aside those who are just downright bad or bone-idle), Jobbing Gardener's ability is limited to keeping the place tidy, trimming the hedges (often wrongly), making a bonfire, mowing the lawn and, sometimes, the raising of the simpler vegetables. Such a man should not be allowed on any kind of flower-bed except to weed it. Put a pair of secateurs or any kind of pruning tool into his hand and he is likely to become 'the blind Fury with th' abhorred shears that slits the thin-spun life'.

I hope that these pages will help you to be independent of him, and that the bug of gardening will bite you 'good and proper', urging you to aim at perfection in the production of flower, fruit, and herb. Adventure forward on your own. But remember that real gardening is sometimes hard work. If you are no longer young, don't overdo it, though personally I have always found it a happy slavery, overcoming even the lure of golf. Learn all you can from living examples. Go to Kew Gardens, the Royal Botanic Garden in Edinburgh, Harlow Car at Harrogate, and Roath Park in Cardiff and visit the better

19

nurseries. Haunt all the flower shows that you have time for, but don't go by looks alone, for the beauty that allures you on the bench may not be hardy, may grow too big, may fear lime or be otherwise fastidious. Collect all the catalogues you can and compare one with another, though not all nowadays are informative on cultural needs and many are plastered with too much colour at the expense of factual information. Good examples of really good catalogues are those of Jackman, Notcutt, Hillier, Sunningdale, and John Scott; for roses, those of Harkness, Cocker, Le Grice, and Murrell; of heathers, John Letts.

You will get great benefit also from joining the Royal Horticultural Society and the specialist society of any particular flower that appeals to you, such as the Royal National Rose Society, the Alpine Garden Society, the Scottish Rock Garden Club, and those dedicated to the Delphinium, Sweet Pea, Iris, Dahlia, etc. RHS Fellowship give you free admission to their numerous shows and to their gardens at Wisley in Surrey, where you may learn a lot and where many specialists are at your service.

I have included in this book most features that my friends exhorted me to cover, such as a glossary and a cultural calendar. What I have *not* been able to do, or only in part, is to avoid 'those awful Latin names'. It's not so easy. I'll explain why, and end up by describing the 'system' I am using for this book.

Consider *Salvia superba*, one of our best perennials, clad in greyish foliage, and muted violet flowers.

Seeing this plant in a lady's border one day, I remarked: "Your sages look well."

"Sages?" she replied. "My dear man, those aren't sages, they're salvias." (Yes, she was that sort.)

Well, what *is* one to do? The horticulturist is so often blamed for using Latin names, yet here was I howled down for using the English one. For salvia is sage. My hostess thought that sage was just something you put into stuffing, which is *Salvia officinalis*, and which the border variety somewhat resembles. If, on the other hand, I had used the term 'salvia', she might have supposed me to be referring to that brilliant pillar-box-red bedding plant which startles the optic nerve in August, and which is *S. splendens*. That, indeed, is what 'salvia' means to most people.

Most of us, I am sure, would prefer to use English names, many of which have a native charm and euphony. Sweet William, Canterbury Bell, Larkspur, Love-in-a-mist, Columbine and many another are delectable. Not all, however; Sneezewort and Fleabane make no appeal to me, and Venus's Navel-wort is a thought too intimate. Three kinds of trouble can arise from 'popular' names. One occurs when there is more than one sort of sage or marigold, a second when there is more than one popular name for the same plant, and a third when we find the same popular name being given to different plants. The 'Bluebells of Scotland' are not those of England. The *Nigella* may indeed be Love-in-a-mist, but it may also be Devil-in-the-bush. (Is there a difference?) 'Winter cherry' may mean the red-fruited pot plant of Christmas time (*Solanum capsicastrum*), or it may mean the *Physalis* with scarlet bladders (also called Cape gooseberry!), or it may mean, and should only mean, the real cherry tree that blooms in winter.

Everyone knows the large white 'daisy' that flowers so abundantly in the border. It is called by many names—Shasta Daisy, King Edward Daisy, and several other variants—and sometimes these names are used for other plants as well. Therefore the only safe thing to call it, at any rate when ordering from a nurseryman, is *Chrysanthemum maximum*.

Another pair of misleading popular names are 'sun rose' and 'rock rose'. Both are applied indifferently, even in nurserymen's catalogues, to either the Helianthemum or the Cistus, though, since 'helios' means the sun, there is no excuse for confusion.

More troublesome are those instances where the authentic botanical name for one plant is popularly applied to another. Nasturtium, which legally is a name for water-cress, doesn't matter a great deal, but other instances definitely lead to confusion. A glaring one is 'geranium'. The real Geranium is a hardy perennial with deeply cut foliage and dainty blossoms,

21

often blue or mauve, spreading widely and densely and used in the herbaceous border and rock garden. The more effulgent creature used for summer 'bedding out' or window-sill pots is no 'geranium' at all, but a *Pelargonium*. If we so miscall it, what shall we call the true Geranium?

Likewise, *Syringa* is the authentic name for Lilac, and not for that white-flowered bush of spicy fragrance which is properly *Philadelphus*. An odd confusion. By all means call *Syringa* Lilac, but don't call *Philadelphus* 'syringa'.

Another little oddity is 'japonica'. This word, of course, merely means Japanese, and we have a long and varied list of plants called so-and-so japonica. Popular taste, however, has attached the name specifically to the Japanese Quince. So inconsistent are we, indeed, that we have often abandoned a perfectly good English name in favour of a foreign one, as in Cranesbill, Mullein, Meadow Saffron, Meadow Rue, Stonecrop. And there is also, of course, a long, long list of importations from abroad that have never had any English names—*Chrysanthemum, Dahlia, Rhododendron* and a host of others. So why make a fuss about other Greek or Latin names?

So far the weight of argument has been mainly in favour of the classicists. The purpose of the botanical name is, of course, to identify every plant precisely all over the world, so that there shall be no confusion, and that you, Reader, may be sure of getting exactly what you want from the nursery. On the other side of the House, we argue that botanical names are so constantly changed by the erudite people that order these matters, nearly always to something even more tortuous to the tongue than the old name, that there is a great deal of confusion, and a lot of alternative names are bandied about. Nurserymen very frequently use invalid ones. Thus it would save a lot of bother if, generically, we called the 'japonicas' Japanese Quinces, and the true Geranium by its good English name Cranesbill. Moreover, no one, I hope, will ever be coerced into calling the Sweet Pea, Sweet William, Canterbury Bell, Daffodil, and other dear delights by any other names.

A nodding acquaintance with the method of forming these plant names is necessary for understanding garden literature.

We may ignore the higher botanical classifications, dealing only with names as they appear in catalogues. First in the name-group comes the genus, then the species, a sub-division of the genus, then, maybe, sub-divisions of the species known as varieties, often having fancy names in English or French.

Thus, to take an example, we have the genus *Rosa*, the rose. Of this one of the species is *R. centifolia*, the rose of a hundred 'leaves' (our ancestors called petals 'leaves'). Of this in turn there is a variety called *R.c. muscosa*, which is the hundred-leaved rose with mossy sepals. Note that the genus and species are abbreviated after first mention. Plants named after persons, either by right of discovery or merely for compliment, are written as in *Berberis darwinii*, Darwin's barberry, or in *Syringa vulgaris* 'Madame Lemoine', a variation, named after Mme Lemoine, of the common species of lilac. Many are named after a country or town (with no capital letter), as in *Berberis japonica*, the Japanese barberry and in *Cytisus kewensis*, the broom raised in Kew Gardens.

You pronounce all these names in a simple Anglicised manner, not *à la* modern Latin, since thousands of them are not Latin but Greek, or mixtures of the two, or sometimes Arabic (as in *Berberis*), Chinese, or even Red Indian.

Now for the method I shall normally employ in this book for plant nomenclature. With respectful apologies to the ortho-dox, the rule as far as possible will be convenience, suitability and normal usage among laymen. Those names of plants will be used which seem to be the most in common use. Snowdrop and Hollyhock will be found under those names, but Snap-dragon under Antirrhinum. Moreover, I shall use English names, even if not in common use, when it seems good to encourage them. Thus, generically, I shall write Cranesbill and Japanese Quince, but when it is necessary to identify a particular species or variety, then the forms will be *Geranium dalmaticum* and *Chænomeles superba*. Many orthodox names, in addition to those used in the text, will be found in the index.

Furthermore, knowing how newcomers to gardening are vexed by them, I shall not normally put the names of plants in italic type and shall not repeat their generic and specific names in initials unless clarity demands. Nor will capital letters be employed by any laws of logic or consistency, but only of suitability and convenience. And, as explained in my Preface, I have usually stuck to the older (and better known) names of plants, to avoid giving an awful number of synonyms.

Another departure from orthodoxy in which I am indulging is to quote freely the names of proprietary articles, such as fertilisers and toxins for pests and diseases. It is no service to one's reader who is not a chemist to exhort him to spray his roses with colloidal cuprous oxychloride. You wouldn't, I apprehend, make any such suggestion to your neighbour over the garden wall. Nor would any such synthetic 'jewels five words long' inspire anything but a stare from the assistant of Blank & Son, local 'ironmonger and horticultural sundriesman'. So I shall feel no shame about giving free advertisements, but of course there are many other good articles besides those that I mention, and new ones are always coming out.

In like manner I do not hesitate to recommend certain nurseries, especially those who deal in certain species or varieties not found in every catalogue.

CHAPTER I
FIRST STEPS

LAY-OUT—ASPECT—DESIGN

Lay-out

THE first task in any new garden is planning and design. The two are closely interrelated, planning or lay-out being part of the practical craft and management of gardening, and design the art of it. I shall have room for only a few general suggestions later on about design, which is perhaps the most fascinating of any garden exercise, but not really one to tackle at the beginning of a novitiate. Lay-out is less difficult.

A garden may be new in the sense of being a vacant plot of ground, but more often the 'new' house is an old one with an existing garden. In both places the problems of lay-out are the same, but old gardens too often have their paths and trees in the wrong places, and the impress of neglect is manifest on many sides. Whatever the condition, formulate a clear and permanent plan, even if your bank manager allows you to execute it only in stages.

First, a clear purpose. Is the garden to be a pleasaunce only, 'to weave the garlands of repose', or shall fruit and vegetables predominate, or shall there be something of all? Space may govern one's decisions. In an inviolate acre wonders can be done, but in smaller suburban gardens something usually has to be sacrificed. Economic brutalities are an impulse to grow at least some vegetables in any garden that is not more than a pocket handkerchief, but the kitchen plot needs far more time and labour than any other part of the garden, apart from the æsthetics of the matter. In any restricted space potatoes are the last thing to grow, for they are relatively uneconomic, so is the mere odd row or two of peas. Selection of

25

vegetables needs care, and we shall consider it fully in the appropriate chapter.

In no garden, however, omit fruit, especially the small bush fruits. Gooseberries, raspberries, and so on are as easy as anything, are good economics, take up very little space when properly laid out, and are acceptable to the eye, or should be; apples and pears, though sorely tortured and of little profit in most private gardens, have at least some decorative value, while cherries are very much at home on house walls. Says Thomas Tusser, of Elizabethan days:

> The Gooseberry, Respis, and Roses, all three
> With strawberries under them trimly agree.

Apportion the space, therefore, according to such broad considerations. The first things actually to be sited, however, are those to which as a rule last thought is given—namely, what I call the workshops of the garden. These are the greenhouse and frames, the tool-shed, compost bins, bonfire, and perhaps chicken-house. The greenhouse must go in the sun, the compost heap in the shade, and the bonfire must not give offence to oneself or neighbours; but, if you possibly can, group all these things together. They are closely complementary to each other, and if well placed will save an awful lot of trapesing to and fro.

If you decide to grow vegetables at all, do not stint them for space. Ten rods (roughly 300 square yards) is supposed to be sufficient ground for providing a family of four with enough vegetables for about nine months; a useful guide in calculation. Your small fruits can well share the kitchen garden if space compels, using fences or walls for loganberries, blackberries and tomatoes, and for gooseberries and red currants grown as cordons; but your apples and pears, unless grown as cordons or espaliers, ought to be kept out, for you can *not* grow acceptable vegetables under spreading trees. Given enough space, all or nearly all fruits are better in a small orchard apart. In the typical small garden, rather narrow and long, all these comestibles must of course go at the end furthest from the house, but in plots that have breadth of frontage use a side strip instead, so that the pleasure garden may benefit by the utmost length available.

If you wish to acquire merit and praise, one small but important detail is to site your beds for herbs—parsley, mint, and so on—and perhaps some lettuces, as close as possible to the door of the kitchen, so that the genius thereof can pop out quickly for a plucking.

Aspect

So much for apportionment and lay-out on broad general lines. But there is one factor that may have a decisive influence on the garden as a whole or parts of it—Aspect.

Observe the points of the compass fairly carefully. Note that the term 'south wall' means the side of it that *faces* south, and that the other side of it is consequently a north wall. Much of a gardener's skill is revealed by how he handles aspects. A south wall, or even a fence or hedge, is of precious value for sheltering anything on the doubtful side of hardiness, whether tomatoes or Ceanothus; but a north wall, so often a place of gloom, does, as I shall show, also offer unexpected opportunities for adornment and use. On the other hand, an open northerly or easterly aspect is exposed to strong and biting winds, and nothing of flower, fruit, or vegetable may be grown there that is not resistant to them. Normally, therefore, you must begin by reserving the sunniest parts of the garden for whatever you decide to make your main show—herbaceous border, rose garden, carnation beds, etc.—and for vegetables and fruit. For roses, other than ramblers or climbers, the site reserved should be out in the open, not closely shut in by walls, fences or high hedges. If there is a wall facing S, SW, or SE, don't waste it by running a path close to it, but make there the widest border that you can.

The cosiest wall, after the south one, is a SW wall. There is a special catch about east and SE walls not usually discovered without experience—namely, that right up to the end of May the early morning sun will beam upon blossom or fruitlet encrusted with frost, and, by sudden thawing, rupture them. Whereas on a SW or west wall the thaw is gradual.

Large trees, or even those of medium size, may also strongly influence lay-out. If they are retained for their own merit and virtue—and no good tree should be committed to the axe without strong cause—face the fact that very little will grow beneath it, certainly no vegetables or fruit.

Design

Now a word or two about design, but only, I am afraid, a few pointers.

Design should be studied from the windows of the principal living-rooms overlooking the garden. The view as a whole is the thing. Length of perspective is much to be desired, and one or two focal points to which the eye is instinctively directed will help to form a basis for design—a seat, a sun-dial, a prominent tree, a distant feature. There may also be a wish to screen oneself from neighbours or to hide some hideous feature outside one's own domains; usually the answer is trees.

Trees, lawns, and paths are the dominant features in creating a garden atmosphere. Paths should be as few as possible, be decorative in themselves, and go direct from A to B. If a straight line imposes too severe a strain, create some justification for a curve, by placing a bush or pool or other artifice that the path must avoid. Trees, in their turn, especially those in the background and on the perimeter, provide the architectural element of the garden's design, and turf is the stage for its coloured drama.

Surprise is a factor as important in garden design as in war. Some sudden twisting in a path, a hedge tactically sited, disclosing unexpectedly some embowered place, a retired rose-garden, a pool, give charm and variety to the otherwise commonplace.

> Let not each beauty ev'ry where be spy'd,
> Where half the skill is decently to hide;
> He gains all points, who pleasingly confounds,
> Surprises, varies and conceals the Bounds.

Garden and house being one, the house itself must be included in the design. If the style of the house permits, some sort of paved terrace, however small, will give an architectural unity to the whole. The style of house may also dictate whether the garden shall be formal—of geometrical outline, maybe embellished with a sunken enclosure—or naturalised, simulating a slice of nature. The latter course is seldom practicable in small places, and a mort of skill and judgment is needed to save any such attempts from looking sham. In the very wee plot of a town house, an all-paved garden, if it suits the style of house, is often a happy answer, enamelled with rock plants and adorned with trees in tubs. But whatever the *motif*, avoid fussiness and too much fragmentation. Simple and bold effects are best. Shun all bearded gnomes, giant frogs, and reflective storks. Shun oddities and beds of horrid shape.

Factors that may influence design are the nature of the soil, the climate, and the nature of the site. Their importance is felt more when we come actually to consider what is to be grown, but it is convenient to mention them here. The merits of soils are dealt with in Chapter III, and climate is often related to it. It is no use attempting to grow in the Midlands or in Aberdeen the more tender flowers, fruits and vegetables that may flourish in Cornwall or even Ayrshire (for parts of Scotland are bathed by the Gulf Stream, and are much milder than more southerly latitudes). The sea is also a mellowing factor, but creates its own problems of violent, salt-laden winds. Obviously, also, Norfolk is less suitable than Wales for plants that require abundant summer moisture. Therefore, 'consult the genius of the place in all', and don't be satisfied merely to copy stereotyped notions.

Related to both these factors is site—whether hill-top or valley, meadow, heath, or woodland. The top of a hill will be windswept and perhaps acid, but will be more free of frost than a valley bottom, and, in spite of previous teaching, you can often grow peaches there in the open. In marshy bottoms Brooms will fail, but some Spiræas and Primulas flourish. In large towns the impregnation of the atmosphere by sooty chemicals will tax the functioning of the leaf-organs of many plants—a study that we shall come to immediately in the next chapter.

CHAPTER II

THE PLANT

ROOT AND BRANCH—ELEMENTAL NEEDS—THE BLOSSOM—
TENDER AND HARDY—THE SPAN OF LIFE

Root and Branch

THE plants that adorn our gardens or feed our bodies have
come to us from all over the world, and gay strangers from
China and Peru, Persia and Africa, mingle cheerfully with our
own natives. The tomato and potato go into the same pot as
our coastwise cabbage and seakale. The Foxglove and the
Heather dwell at peace with the Rhododendron and the
Dahlia. Their origins are as mixed as their nationalities—
stony mountain-top, lush meadow, chalky down, shadowy
woodland, the dry and open moor, and many other diverse
conditions.

These mixed origins have through the ages caused many
plants to evolve special characteristics to ensure their survival,
conditioned by more or less heat, more or less water, more or
less lime, and so on. The cactus and the water-lily, the buttercup basking in the sun, and the ivy creeping in the shade bear
witness to a wonderful adaptability. Yet, if we except such
freaks as the mushroom, all plants clamour in common for certain essentials. It is the gardener's business, if he hopes to be
successful in his occupation, to know a little about both these
diversities and these common factors, which form what I call
the social science of plant life, so that he shall not torture
woodland Cyclamens in roaring sun or Brooms in water-laden
hollows, and so that he shall intelligently practise the simple
arts of planting and propagating.

30

The plant derives its health and nourishment principally through two organs—the root and the leaf.

Through its roots it obtains its food from the soil, which it absorbs in the form of soluble salts, i.e. through the agency of water. The root may be a 'tap' root—a thick member growing straight downwards, as in the Lupin and the Dandelion and the Carrot. Or the root may branch and re-branch in the same manner as the leaf-system above ground; of such nature are 'fibrous' roots, as in the rose and many others. These are the methods by which the plant explores for its food. Absorption is not, however, by the larger visible roots, but by minute, almost invisible root-hairs which form as a fine down near the tips of the roots. Thus it is important to damage the roots as little as possible when transplanting and to lift them with a 'good ball of soil'.

Through its leaf, which is pitted with an immense number of tiny pores, the plant performs a much more involved and indeed mysterious process. It transpires or sweats, getting rid of the water in its system; it breathes, taking in those gases it needs and rejecting others; and, through the agency of the vital green substance known as chlorophyll, it transmutes the elements of the air into carbohydrates, its energy food.

From this much-simplified outline of plant processes, we see that there are five elementals for healthy growth, and some important lessons emerge for the practical gardener.

Elemental Needs

First, like human beings, plants need *air*; therefore they must not be overcrowded. Competition is a law of nature's life.

Secondly, *light*, in order that the leaves may absorb the radiant energy of the sun. A film of dirt on the leaf or the obscurity of overhanging trees restricts light radiation. Most plants require light all day, but many have conditioned themselves to living in the diffused light of partial shade, notably plants with large, thick, extra-green leaves such as the Rhododendron and the Laurel. A very few are accustomed to even deeper shade. The riddle of the shady border or corner to be

31

found in nearly every garden is often a tough one to solve, but there are several degrees of shade. There is the 'high' or 'dappled' shade in which Rhododendrons, Camellias, and most Lilies rejoice; the oblique shade cast by a building, wall, or fence which we can embellish with many delights—Pyracantha, Camellia, Clematis, Winter Jasmine, several Roses, etc.; and the more extreme problem of the dense shade immediately beneath a large tree, for which there are few enlivening themes except in the leafless days of early spring, when many of the bulbous plants will gaily enamel the bare earth.

Third and fourth needs are *heat* and *water* in varying degrees according to the source of origin of the plants. These need not be emphasised, but what is less obvious is that the process of transpiration may be critically affected by excessive heat, by wind, and by a dry atmosphere. All these may cause the plant to transpire faster than it can take in water by the roots; and it then droops, just as a man droops in the tropics if he drinks less than he sweats. It is for this reason that the gardener must: (*a*) keep the atmosphere of his greenhouse damp in hot weather; (*b*) when raising new plants from cuttings, protect them with shade and with a 'close' atmosphere that checks transpiration; and (c) transplant all large subjects when transpiration has ceased altogether or is at its lowest. Thus deciduous shrubs are planted in winter, when they have shed their leaves, and evergreens either at the same time in mild climates or in mid-April in others, when the soil is thoroughly moist but the temperature high enough to promote rapid new root growth though not high enough for fast transpiration.

Here again many plants have specially conditioned themselves. The cactus, with thick, fleshy stem and leaves reduced to mere needles, is an extreme example of a plant conditioned to prolonged drought and heat. Less extreme examples are our own Gorse and Broom, Stonecrop and House Leek. These can 'drown' in water-logged ground, just as shade lovers can die from sunstroke if planted in intense light. At the opposite extreme of the scale are the water-lilies and their kind.

Last, the *soil* must be the right one for whatever is grown, which means that the gardener must choose the right families of plant. There is no collectivism or communism in the vegetable world. But whatever the classification of the soil—sandy or marly, acid or alkaline, and so on—the essential constituents for healthy life should be present, and in the right proportion and balance. A pronounced deficiency may cause a premature discoloration of the leaf, which is thus prevented from doing its job. By no means all plants like a rich diet, but we may say that the HCF is a medium loam, dark in colour and slightly on the acid side. This is dealt with more fully in the next chapter.

The Blossom

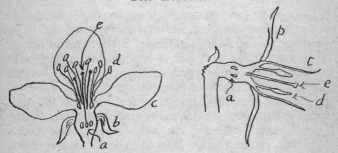

Sectional sketches of Apple Blossom and Daffodil, showing: *a*, ovary; *b*, sepal; *c*, petal; *d*, anther; *e*, stigma; *p*, perianth; *t*, trumpet-shaped corolla.

I have no room for a chapter on botany, and would urge those who have not learnt this subject to get a small elementary book about it. But, to make other chapters intelligible, I must say a brief word about the blossom.

Flowers vary greatly in their construction, but in a normal one there will be several 'whorls', or rings, of different members. Immediately below the bud may be a ring of rudimentary leaves called bracts, which, in some flowers, as in the Poinsettia, form the chief object of beauty rather than the flowers, but usually they are insignificant.

The bud itself is encased in a ring of protective sepals, collectively called the calyx. This likewise may be the plant's decorative feature, as in the Clematis and Anemone, which

33

have sepals but no petals. Within the calyx is normally a further ring, this time of petals, known collectively as a corolla. A term that is used of the Narcissus in particular is 'perianth', which is a calyx and corolla joined together, forming the round shield behind the trumpet.

Within the corolla appear the creative organs of the plant. The male organ is collectively known as the stamen, crowned with an anther loaded with brightly coloured pollen. The more complicated female organ is known collectively as the pistil, its most prominent part being the stigma, and when the male pollen falls upon the stigma, germination takes place and a seed is formed.

Many plants carry separate male and female blossoms, as in sweet corn, and others bear males on one plant and females on another. In general, self-fertilisation is abhorrent to nature. Thus if the Holly fails to berry, it is not because of any occult prescience about the approaching winter, but merely because the female flower has not been successfully pollinated by a nearby male. Similarly, many fruit trees, especially the sweet cherries and many popular apples (including Cox's Orange Pippin), are self-sterile and need a close companion of another brand to form their fruits. Even when both male and female organs are carried in the same flower there is often a device to forestall self-fertilisation.

Tender and Hardy

Besides these quiddities, plants have diversities of even greater general importance to the practical gardener.

One such diversity is in their resistance to frost, and in this characteristic we classify them thus:

A 'tender' plant is one that at all times requires warm and genial conditions; we shall have few dealings with them here.

A 'half-hardy' plant may stand fairly low temperatures, or possibly a light ground frost, such as Antirrhinums.

A 'hardy' plant is one that can stay outdoors all its life, enduring hard frosts, some more than others. This is all that 'hardiness' means in this country. It does *not* mean that you can treat the plant roughly, stick it anywhere without proper cultivation, and leave it to fend for itself. This misconception explains why thousands of pounds' worth of good seed is wasted every year, especially in 'hardy annuals', by those who imagine that the seed has merely to be broadcast lightheartedly anywhere. One has only to contrast, say, Clarkia carelessly sown on untilled soil with the same plant thinly sown on well-dug, manured soil, to realise both how poor and how splendid this ill-used flower can be. Of only very few plants is it true that they thrive in poor and rough conditions.

The Span of Life

Our next classification for garden purposes is according to the span of life.

An *annual* is a plant which germinates from seed, flowers, dies, and reproduces its seed again all in one year or season. It may be hardy, half-hardy, or tender. Most vegetables are annuals, and there are annual forms of several longer-lived flowers, such as the annual Chrysanthemum, the annual Lupin, and the annual Delphinium (which includes Larkspur). We gardeners also in practice treat as annuals some plants that by nature would live longer, e.g. Antirrhinum.

A *biennial* is a plant that germinates from seed this year, and blooms and dies next year. Sweet William, Wallflowers, and Canterbury Bell are examples. Here again there are hardy ones and others.

A *perennial* has a continuous life over a period of years, and it may be hardy or otherwise. A very large group, varying from the Oak to the Violet. A *herbaceous* perennial is one which hibernates by shedding all its upper growth in winter, stem and leaf alike, right down to ground level, but retains life in its roots and crown. This class includes all the popular families that dwell in the 'border', from the Delphinium downwards, as well as the humble rhubarb.

Another special category of perennial is the large and assorted congregation of *bulbs* and their kind, such as the Daffodil and the Dahlia.

CHAPTER III

MOTHER EARTH

TOP SOIL AND SUB-SOIL—TYPES OF SOIL—CHEMICAL
ELEMENTS—ORGANIC FOODS—INORGANIC FOODS—LIME

Top Soil and Sub-soil

WHAT goes on underground?

Since plants imbibe their food through their roots, this en-
quiry should be the first and constant concern of the gardener,
to an extent far greater than most of us realise. Earth is the
mother of all, and her children's health depends on her own.
Understand your soil and keep it in good heart and sweet
temper. This is the beginning of wisdom. Project your
thoughts underground, and ponder what is happening around
the roots and whether the feeding and physical condition and
drainage of the soil are adequate and balanced. 'Whoever
begins a garden,' said Sir William Temple as far back as 1685,
'ought in the first place, and above all, to consider the soil,
upon which the taste of not only his fruits, but his legumes
and even herbs and salads, will wholly depend.'

Over most of the land formations of the earth the forces of
nature have since times of pre-history gradually manufactured
a thin film of soil compounded partly of pulverised rock surfaces and partly of the decayed vegetable and animal wastes of
countless centuries. This film we call top soil or fertile soil.
It is not a lifeless mass, but teems with tiny organisms, which
we may refer to as bacteria. Among them are bacteria whose
purpose is to transmute the elements that are in the earth into
soluble forms which plants can imbibe through their roots.

Thus the ammonia contained in dung is converted by degrees into nitrates.

To retain fertility, top soil needs aeration by some means, as by digging, and it needs replenishment in some degree with animal and vegetable wastes. Thus when we put dung or decayed vegetable matter into the earth we are feeding the soil, whereas artificial or chemical fertilisers merely feed the plant. We say of a soil, therefore, that it contains, or does not contain, a high proportion of organic matter—that is to say, matter which has originated from some order of creation having the organs of life and growth.

Below this thin film of top soil there is a sub-soil. It may be only an inch or two below the surface, as on chalky downs, or it may be some feet below. Relatively it is a stolid and inert mass, and its lack of organic matter is shown by its lighter colour. For this reason sub-soil should not be brought to the surface, except by the experienced hand who knows how to deal with it, but should be kept at its proper level. Builders are notorious authors of this infamy. It can, however, be made fertile by creating those conditions that will encourage the bacteria to explore it, namely, by letting in air and digging in organic matter. When therefore we speak of a 'good depth of soil' we mean one that has been deeply worked by man or nature, and unobstructed by rock, gravel, chalk, water, and so on.

Types of Soil

We should accordingly look first of all at the physical structure of soil. The main classes of soil ingredients for our purpose, in addition to a certain amount of air and of water, are: sand, clay, lime (as in chalk, oolite, limestone), and humus.

To be useful to man's husbandry two or more must be blended together. Thus chalk and clay together form marl, famous for making a hard, enduring cricket pitch. Sand, clay, and humus form loam, the essential type of soil needed for nearly all crops. The characteristics of these soil constituents which it is important for the gardener to understand are briefly these:

37

Sand, being composed of relatively large, rough, and loose particles, holds air (and therefore warmth) but not water. It makes a soil 'light' and easily workable, but it has no food value and its properties are purely physical or mechanical. Soils containing too much sand 'dry out' quickly, and are said to be 'hungry', needing frequent feeding with organic matter. There are a great many types of sand; builder's sand is of little use to the gardener, who wants it sharp and rough, and 'sharp, silver sand' is a commodity he will constantly need, especially for potting and for raising seedlings.

Clay, by contrast, is a tightly bound mass of tiny particles. There are several types of it, including the boulder clay of the North and the yellow clay of London. It holds water too much and obstructs the passage of air. It is cold, stiff, sticky, and stubborn to the spade. When really dry it becomes brick-like and cracks. But it is chemically active and itself provides plant food. Clay and sand together thus balance and correct each other's faults. Soils preponderating in clay are called 'heavy'.

Lime is a very versatile factor and is sufficiently important to have a section to itself, but we may note here that chalk alone requires large quantities of organic matter to bring it to fertility.

Humus is the precious element, so elusive of easy definition, that is the product of the decomposition of vegetable and animal (i.e. organic) matter. It is the heart and soul of a soil, which, without it, would be an aggregation of lifeless mineral particles. You can, however, have too much of it, as man can of rich foods, and a few families of plants prefer a spartan diet poor in humus. Humus darkens and warms the soil.

Peat is vegetable matter long decayed in waterlogged conditions. The peats that are used for horticultural purposes are 'acid', and therefore palatable to plants that dislike lime. Peat is by no means the only or the best form of acid soil, but it has a great many horticultural uses. It holds moisture in the manner of a sponge without clogging drainage, is a marvellous conditioner of clay soil, provides a soft, easy root-run for young plants and is an essential component of most 'composts' for pots and boxes. For general purposes one uses a 'granulated' peat of medium grade, but other grades are available for special purposes.

We see from the above brief classification, therefore, that in all types of soil we require as a rule ample humus, that the best soil for general purposes is a well-balanced loam and that certain plants (called 'calcifuges') regard lime with marked distaste. A special form of loam that will be often referred to is 'fibrous' loam, which is a loam containing many fine fibrous roots in decay, as of old turf—a grand plant food.

Chemical Elements

As important as the physical properties of a soil are its chemical qualities. The principal are: nitrogen, phosphates, potash, and calcium.

There are several others, but they are matters for the specialist, and should not be monkeyed with. The importance of these four is that they need constant renewal in cultivated soil. The qualities in them that we should specially note are:

Nitrogen improves foliage, making the plant large and leafy and a lush green. Therefore it is specially good for 'greens', and in the young period of plant life generally. It is apt to be deficient in regions of heavy rainfall, especially on the tops of hills (as is lime).

Phosphates are specially valuable for root crops and roots generally, and for the ripening of seed.

Potash is noted for its effect on fruit, and is also good for foliage, which becomes scorched at the edges under a potash deficiency.

Calcium is the element found in limestone and chalk; it is a plant food and promotes the decomposition of vegetable matter.

The important thing in a soil's chemical make-up, as in its physical structure, is correct balance, though not always a balance in the same proportions. An excess of nitrogen may be as harmful as a deficiency of potash (a subject dealt with shortly in Part IV). We come now, therefore, to the means by which any such unbalance, or wastage, in the soil's condition can be made good. The deficiency may be on nature's part, as when there is a lack of lime, or it may be caused by the exhaustion of one of the soil elements by a particular crop. In cultivated places a certain amount of wastage is always going on, for the soil is being eaten by what grows in it, though certain plants provide valuable secretions in the soil, such as peas and lupins, which develop nitrogen-bearing nodules on their roots.

The chief method by which nature herself corrects this wastage is by leaf-fall and other forms of decay, returning to the soil what came out of it. I am not going to indulge in any fanciful or pseudo-psychical transports on a subject essentially earthy but which some writers have made so delightfully esoteric, nor shall I disparage the virtues of chemical fertilisers, but I do insist that the basis of all good feeding is the liberal return to the soil of a certain amount of organic waste. We will therefore consider these first before going on to the inorganic foods, after which we will look at the versatile properties of lime separately.

Organic Foods

Compared with the chemical fertilisers, the organic ones are slow in action but enduring in effect. Most have also a physical or structural use to the soil, as well as their convertible chemical values. The outstanding ones for general use are old turves, animal manures, 'compost', and leaf mould; and bonemeal is a commodity the gardener should never be without.

'Manure' generally, but not always, means animal dung. The best are those of the cow, horse, and pig, but the droppings of poultry, sheep, goats, and rabbits are also valuable. They vary greatly in merit. The dung of the corn-fed hunter and of the brewer's dray horse have greater value than that of the tradesman's nag. That of cake-fed cows is better than that of pasture-fed cows. Moreover, animal manures may also bring with them the seeds of weeds, insect pests, blow-fly grubs, and a smell.

Horse manure is best for heavy (clay) soils, cow and pig manure for light (sandy) soils. A mixture of the three is particularly good. For most purposes all animal manures should be 'short', referring to the length of the straw or other litter with which they are mixed. They should also be partially rotted. Fresh manures liberate excess acids harmful to plant life. A raw, stiff clay is the exception; fresh horse manure with plenty of long straw is then an advantage, as the tubes of straw help to aerate and open-up the compacted mass of soil. Heavy clays are similarly benefited, we may note, by digging in vegetable matter while still undecomposed, such as pea and bean haulm, fallen leaves, and soft, non-woody flower stems, especially in the lower 'spit' of the soil.

Animal manures should not be left standing out in the open for any length of time. Their vitality is thus washed out by rain or evaporated by sun. If manure has to be kept in the open, stack it into a ridged or pointed pile, firmly compacted, and cover it with a large sheet of black Polythene in a shady place; stand it on a bottom sufficiently solid to prevent the loss of its valuable liquids by seepage. Manure may also be 'composted' either by itself or mixed with other refuse.

The method of applying manure to the ground is dealt with in Chapter V.

Poultry Manure is best used in the compost heap, where it is of great value. If used separately, apply it to the ground dry, partially or wholly decomposed, preferably in spring. Used raw, it tends to burn. Keep it under cover and dry. It is deficient in potash.

Good animal manure is notoriously difficult to get nowadays in urban areas, but 'composted manure' of various brands can be bought in bags; I think they all contain lime, so should not be used for lime-haters. Of other forms of organic manure, the following are valuable:

Dried Blood. Nitrogenous; quick-acting; not cheap. Reserve it for the more precious plants. Two oz per square yard in spring or early summer.

Bonemeal. Mostly phosphatic. Good for almost everything; use it widely. Apply in autumn or winter on the surface at about 4 oz per square yard. Bone flour is quicker-acting and more quickly exhausted.

'Compost.' The compost heap or pile has attained special favour because of the increasing difficulty of obtaining animal manures. Volumes have been written about it and fierce battles waged by the advocates of one system or another. We are even told that what seems a mere heap of decomposing refuse must be in tune with the Infinite. I fear that many people make it only into a mess.

The word 'compost' is itself ambiguous, for it also means a composition, or mixture, of soils for potting and seed-boxes. The compost heap is really, in fact, a decomposition heap, for it is made up mainly of vegetable and animal wastes in the process of decay. It is a humus factory. The only thing that is new about it is the notion of applying some special agent, uncouthly called an activator, for the purpose of hastening decomposition.

I shall not attempt to examine the numerous methods. It is far better to advise the busy amateur to buy one of the inexpensive proprietary activators and follow the manufacturer's directions. There are several good ones, such as Fertosan, Q.R. ('Quick Returns'), Garotta, Adco. I have used them all, and found all good. The well-known Indore method and the Ministry of Agriculture system require no proprietaries.

The general idea is to heap up different types of refuse in an orderly manner. Heat must be generated. Thus the heap should hold a certain amount of air and not be too squashed, and it should be moist but not too wet. Exposure to sun, drying winds, and heavy rain are all alike to be avoided. Build the pile therefore in natural or artificial shade, such as the north side of a large tree, and keep it covered during the making with a sheet of black Polythene. There should be free circulation of air round the sides, so don't build it against a wall, and the base should be plain earth or brick rubble, not anything impermeable. Several small heaps are better than one big one, for the heap must be built up quickly—within periods of not more than a fortnight in summer and not more than six weeks in autumn or winter. In fact the small villa garden hardly contains enough material, other than grass, to make orthodox composting worthwhile and grass alone simply makes a squashy mess; but what can be done, with good but not best results, is to collect stuff gradually and then make a proper heap all in one day.

The stuff that can go into the heap comprises: (*a*) any soft vegetable matter from flower or kitchen garden, hedgerow or common, especially nettles, *green* bracken, pea and bean haulm, lawn mowings; (*b*) household refuse such as egg-shells, fruit and vegetable peelings and pods, fish waste, vacuum cleaner contents, tea leaves; (*c*) the dung of horse, cow, pig, chicken, etc., preferably mixed with straw; (*d*) bonfire and wood ashes. Do *not* use: hard-wooded stuff such as rose prunings or twigs; virulent or tough weeds such as dandelion, dock, couch grass, and ground elder; coal ashes or cinders: sawdust; nor any leaves except those of flowers, weeds, vegetables, or privet prunings, and especially no thick leaves or those of conifers. (See under *Leaf-mould*.)

The vegetable matter should be well mixed up; grass mowings especially should be mixed with other components, or they will make a thick, slimy blanket, obstructing air. Bash cabbage-stumps with a heavy implement or underfoot, and roughly break up into short lengths the semi-woody stems of herbaceous plants. Separate animal matter from the activator by a layer of vegetable matter. Makers of some activators claim that it is unnecessary to turn the heap once made, but it is usually best to do so at least once, bringing what was formerly on the outside into the centre.

Test when the material is ready by taking out a spadeful. When completely decomposed it will be black-brown, slightly moist, friable, and crumbly, slightly sweet-smelling, and bearing no recognisable trace of the original structure of leaf, grass, or stem. Such material is dug into the top spit only of the soil. Really well-made compost, in which all weed seeds are destroyed, can be used as a top dressing.

Fish Wastes. Available in various forms. Best to get a proprietary 'fish manure' such as Eclipse, and use it in early spring according to manufacturer's directions. It is a very good, balanced food. Apply it as you would an artificial.

Green Manure. This means a crop of some quick-growing plant dug straight into the ground while growing. Quickest and cheapest is mustard, which may be sown in August for autumn digging. Rape and annual lupin should be sown before the end of July. Not a complete food.

Hoof and Horn Meal. Used as for dried blood, and valuable for potting and for brussels sprouts. Slow.

Hops. Available in two commercial forms. 'Spent hops', which are the residue from brewings, have limited food value but are excellent for improving the texture of heavy soils. Dig in liberally at, say, 1 cwt for 15 sq yd after weathering for a few months. It is not so easy to obtain as formerly. 'Hop manure', in which the hops have been chemically treated, is a first-class plant food for all purposes in which manure or compost are advocated. Easy to handle and to store and very economical. Ideal for amateurs' use. Apply to the top spit only in early spring according to maker's directions.

Leaf-mould. A valuable source of humus, good for all soils and essential for potting. Lightens heavy soils and helps light soils retain moisture. Specify only oak or beech leaf-mould if buying.

To make it oneself, again use only oak, beech, or hawthorn. Stack in autumn under alternate thin layers of soil until June, then 'turn' the heap and treat with an activator, preferably Q.R. in this instance.

Leaves of annuals, herbaceous, and other small plants go into the compost bin. Leaves of roses, large fruit trees, conifers, and thick-leaved plants such as Laurel should be burnt. Leaves of other trees and shrubs take a long time to decompose and in small places are also better burnt.

Liquid Manure. A valuable means of feeding plants while in growth, either in the ground or in pots. Fill a small sack or sandbag with rotted, not fresh, animal manure, add a trifle of soot and suspend it in a tub or tank of water. When the resultant solution is of a deep tawny hue, draw off a small quantity, dilute it to the colour of straw and apply through a watering-can when the soil is moist. 'Maxicrop', 'Liquinure', and 'Sangral' are good and convenient proprietaries.

Seaweed. One of the oldest manures known and specially rich in potash and salt. The best is the kind with long, broad ribbons or streamers and crenellated edges. Next best are the 'bladder' seaweeds that children like to pop. The smaller, bushy kinds, often coloured, are of least value. Weed thrown up early in the year is better than summer or autumn weed, and dried weed is more valuable than wet. Use fresh at about 1 cwt per 6 sq yd, or less than half that quantity dry. Dry it under cover, not in the open. You can also compost it.

Top Spit or turf-loam is decayed turf from old pastures, or from one's own lawn, full of fibrous roots. Quite first-class for almost all purposes. Gives substance to a light soil and porosity to a heavy one. One can scarcely use too much of it. Stack it upside down, with thin layers of animal manure between the turves if available. For Rhododendrons and other calcifuges order lime-free turf-loam.

Wood Ashes from household fires, if unmixed with coal, and bonfire ashes provide some potash. The richest is from hard wood and from slow burning. Useless if left out in the rain. Collect as soon as cool enough to handle and keep in a very dry place. Of most value on heavy clays and peats; other soils it may make sticky. Apply lavishly in spring. Particularly good for tomatoes and onions.

Inorganic Foods

The majority of these are what are called artificial or chemical fertilisers. They are quick-acting, easy to handle, carry no pests, and in experienced hands can be nicely adjusted to the needs of a particular crop. But their effect is not enduring, they feed the plant only and not the soil, they have as a rule little physical or mechanical influence on soil structure. Many are caustic to foliage, should therefore not touch any portion of the plant and should be applied when there is little wind. Their best use is as a supplement to organic foods, and they are of particular value in the vegetable garden.

45

The artificials are pretty strong meat. The golden rule in their application therefore is 'little and often'. The easiest method of application, except those of granular form, is through a dredger or giant pepper-pot, easily made out of any cylindrical tin. The granular form, however, is the more convenient, for it does not blow about in the wind, and, if it touches foliage, generally rolls off. Nearly all artificials are applied in spring and summer, and they have merely to be 'pricked' into the top inch of soil with a fork or hoe.

Be particularly careful to store all chemical fertilisers in a really dry place and raised off the floor, so that there is ventilation beneath.

The chief artificials are:

Sulphate of ammonia, which provides nitrogen; superphosphate of lime, which provides phosphate; sulphate of potash, which provides potash.

There are many others. With one or two exceptions, however, I don't advise anyone who is not experienced, or who is not a chemist, to use any of these or other chemicals singly, nor to do his own mixing. They are tricky things. Nitrate of soda, for instance, makes sticky soils stickier, and sulphate of ammonia makes acid soils more acid. Moreover, there is always a danger of the soil's essential balance being upset. Therefore, whatever the experts of the Press or the Air may say, it is far sounder for the amateur to buy only proprietary fertilisers, of which there are many excellent brands. For general use he should get a 'complete' or balanced fertiliser made by a good firm such as Fison's, or old friend Clay, while the 'National Growmore', though devised for the vegetable garden, is good for flowers, too. For special purposes likewise there are excellent preparations to be had, such as Tomorite for tomatoes, and Tonk's formula for roses. It is only for exhibition that you need to fiddle about with odd ounces of nitro-chalk or whatnot.

The following, however, need special mention:

Basic Slag is a by-product of blast furnaces in the manufacture of steel, and combines phosphates with lime. If finely ground, it is a valuable fertiliser where the need might be to convert an acid soil to a limy one for vegetables, fruit, and certain flowers. In contrast to other artificials, it is slow-acting and should be applied in the autumn at about 5 oz per square yard.

Soot. Its fertilising value depends on how much sulphate of ammonia it contains. Darkens and so warms the soil. Good general stimulant with wide uses, especially for onions. Used fresh, is a repellent for slugs and other soil pests, but should not be applied to growing crops till at least three months old. Like wood ashes, it is almost useless if it is allowed to get wet. 'Soot-water' is also useful, and is made in the same way as liquid manure. Never use soot from an oil-fired boiler.

Agricultural Salt (sodium chloride) is often advocated for asparagus, seakale, and beet, and is good for light soils. Use cautiously at 1 oz per square yard as it is also a weed-killer. Seaweed is better. Never use on potatoes. Not to be confused with sodium chlorate, most deadly of all vegetation poisons.

Ashes from the kitchen boiler may conveniently be mentioned here, for, though not a fertiliser, they have several garden uses. One is to lighten heavy soils, another is for covering bulbs in pots and bowls intended for indoors, and for 'plunging' potted plants; but their most valuable use is as a deterrent to slugs on the crowns of specially susceptible plants, such as Delphiniums and the winter Iris stylosa. Before any such uses, however, they must be thoroughly 'weathered' for some three months to wash out all traces of sulphur and other elements.

Lime

Lime occupies a mid-way position between the organics and the artificials. It has several interesting properties, and its correct management is of great importance. It has both mineral and chemical qualities. It has a marked physical effect on the structure of heavy soils. It provides a plant food in a form of calcium. It cures club root in cabbages and allied plants. It promotes the decomposition of organic matter. It

47

breaks down sticky clay to loose crumbs. It encourages worms, so should be used more sparingly on lawns than elsewhere. In excess its effects are harmful, and to a fairly wide range of plants, headed by the Rhododendron, it is highly distasteful and even poisonous. The general run of plants, however, either relish it positively or at least tolerate it, and in the vegetable garden it is an essential. In strength it is a useful repellent of slugs and some other soil pests.

THE ACIDITY FACTOR

A special quality of lime is to 'correct acidity'. This is a common phrase that rather begs the question; to the layman, it means simply adding lime to a soil deficient in lime. And here we come to the heart of the matter, for, as may be inferred from the first section, the lime requirements of all soils are not the same.

A soil may be already well endowed with lime by nature, as in the locality of limestone hills or chalky downs, and even far away from such features it may have been spread by glacial action. If so, you can do nothing to take the lime away, should you want to do so, except in small pockets, and even then it may seep back. If, on the other hand, the soil is not naturally rich in lime, its requirements by way of man-made application will depend on what you want to grow in it, and if you want to grow rhododendrons, camellias, pieris, or the summer heathers you will use none at all.

Soils that are short of lime are termed *acid*—a term that will constantly recur in this book—and those that are well supplied are alkaline. Degrees of acidity vary greatly. They are measured by what is known as the pH symbol, followed by an indicative figure. There is nothing abstruse about it. Neutrality in a soil is represented by pH 7; figures below 7 represent increasing degrees of acidity, figures above it the opposite. For general garden purposes in this country best results come from a neutral or slightly acid pH reading—say from 6·5 to 7. Below 5·5 acidity is so pronounced as to cause a 'sour' soil; in such a condition it smells unpleasant and becomes green, slimy, and mossy, and a heavy dressing of lime is at once called for.

48

The amateur can test the acidity of his soil quite simply by one of the inexpensive outfits sold in garden shops. The methods often recommended of using hydrochloric acid, or litmus paper, tell you very little and are not much use. Your County Horticultural Officer will give you a more detailed analysis if you send him about a pound of soil from root level, but there may be variations in different parts of the garden.

THE APPLICATION OF LIME

As lime has a chemical action, it should *never be used at the same time as any other soil dressing, especially animal manures*. With animal manures and sulphate of ammonia, in particular, it causes the loss of nitrogen. Apply it at least a month before or three months after manuring and at least fourteen days before chemicals; keep it similarly well clear of the application of any soil fumigant (Part IV) and of soot. A convenient rule is to manure in autumn and to lime about February, but a better practice still, especially in the kitchen garden, is to do the operations in different years as described in Chapter XXI.

Except as shown below, lime is applied by merely spreading it on the surface. Clays and peats absorb it easily, and can therefore take large but infrequent dressings. In areas of heavy rainfall, however, and on thin sandy soils, dressings should be relatively more frequent but less in quantity.

FORMS OF LIME

For carnations, many rock and other plants lime can supplied in permanent form by limestone chips or dust. Another very valuable form in the flower garden and the orchard is old lime-mortar rubble; but, with the modern building practice of using cement instead of lime-mortar, it is now as difficult to get as horse manure. A good substitute is ground chalk, preferably in small lumps, or ground limestone as sold for poultry grit. These forms of lime should be applied at root level, and renewed as surface dressings (for plants that need it) every few years.

For more widespread dressing lime is available in several other forms.

Quicklime, or 'burnt lime', or 'lump lime', is the form in which it comes from the kiln. When water is poured over it, it disintegrates into a powder, and is then known as slaked lime or hydrated lime. Much the best thing, unless your soil is a light one, is to get the quicklime (if you can) and slake it yourself. It is thus more potent and mordant and is damaging to slugs. Quick and freshly slaked limes are caustic to foliage and should be used only when the ground is vacant, but commercial forms of 'hydrated' lime, which is what most small gardeners use, are reasonably safe except for young plants. On light soils the form known as carbonate of lime is to be preferred, being less easily washed through.

All these have different values, and, to sum up, the amount of lime a soil needs depends on (*a*) its degree of acidity; (*b*) whether it is light or heavy; (*c*) the form of lime used, and (*d*) what you want to grow. Comparative scales are available, but for those who are happiest with a simple rule of thumb, a good one for vegetable and fruit gardens is to use 5–6 oz per square yard every third year.

Flower gardens in good health, however, rarely need any, except for flag irises, carnations, clematis, and a few other plants.

CHAPTER IV

THE GARDENER'S ARMOURY

So far we have not put spade or hoe to ground, and before doing so in the next and following chapters we ought to see what tools are needed for the job, with a few words on their correct usage.

Buy the best tools that you can afford, of good steel and strong ash; it is better to make do with a few high-quality ones than a multitude of second-rate articles that break in one's hand.

Keep all tools clean and sharp. Stop work ten minutes before the tocsin sounds for tea, wash or scrape all earth off the tools, and finally clean with an old brush or cloth. A tool that is unlikely to be used for some time should be wiped with a slightly oily rag. Nearly all tools, moreover, should be kept sharp—spades and hoes as well as edging irons and shears—though not, of course, to the same degree. Keep a good stone and file in the tool-shed, and once a year send away all tools having a knife edge to an experienced grinder.

These are the more necessary tools:

The spade is the most important of all garden weapons. Get a size suited to your strength, but have a blade with a flange on the top edge to protect your boots. There is no room to examine the various methods of handling this weapon, except to say that the best and least fatiguing is with the left or lower hand palm downwards, acting merely as a fulcrum, while the right hand is used as a lever. Specially useful for many tasks is a long-handled spade such as is used in the East, for it reduces the pangs of 'gardener's back' and is grand for throwing spadefuls from one spot to another, especially in the tough job of trenching.

Forks are of two kinds—a potato fork with broad tines for lifting crops, and one with finer, round tines for digging. Here again a long-handled digging fork is a blessing.

Hoes are several and various. Most widely useful is the Dutch hoe, having its blade in almost the same plane as the shaft, and available in blades of different widths, from 1 in.

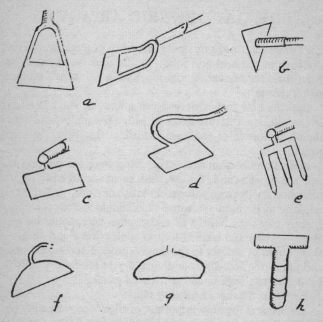

Some Hoes and a Dibber: *a*, Dutch hoe (this shape, narrow-necked, is best); *b*, triangular; *c*, draw hoe, close-coupled; *d*, swan-necked; *e*, Canterbury; *f*, onion hoe; *g*, hoes should not get round-pointed, as this; *h*, a dibber marked off in inches.

upwards; the well-equipped garden will have several. The correct action is, walking backwards, to slide the blade to-and-fro just below the surface, using both the 'leading' and the 'trailing' edges, as the RAF would say, in order to slice off weeds just below their crowns.

Next come 'draw' hoes, with the blade either close-coupled

to the shaft or set on a swan-necked shank. With these you work forward, using a chopping or drawing motion. Used also for drawing a 'drill' or minute trench in which seed is sown, and for earthing-up potatoes.

A special form of draw hoe is the Canterbury hoe, having three short prongs instead of a blade. Valuable for breaking down the upper crust of stiff, heavy soils, using swinging blows as you work forward.

Most gardeners have their pet tools, and mine is an onion hoe, which is a swan-necked hoe with semi-circular blade, preferably on a short handle. With this you can work extremely close to onions or other plants without damaging them, and you also have a free hand. Keep it sharp, especially the points, which should never become rounded. The narrow-bladed ones are usually best. Another favourite of mine is the little triangular hoe, better for making seed drills than the draw hoe.

A rake of an iron comb type, available in different widths, is a vital tool for working surfaces to a fine tilth, especially when making seed-beds, and for removing stones. The proper action is both backwards and forwards, pushing as well as pulling, with long strokes.

A 'Springbok' rake has springy metal teeth for scarifying or aerating turf; and wide wooden rakes are for gathering up leaves and for levelling soil that has been rough-dug.

Trowels, which are used for planting small things, are best short-handled, and they *must* be strong, preferably with a curved shank, and of stainless steel if you can run to it. When using a trowel, remember always to make the hole a little wider and a little deeper than the roots of the plant it is to hold. There are special trowels for rock work and for bulb-planting.

The dibber, simple though it is, is a tool to be handled with care. Use only one with a rounded point, or an air-pocket may be left beneath the seedling. In unskilled hands it is a menace to the infant plant. Use it only for big planting jobs, otherwise a trowel. Usage—make the hole, put in the seedling with the other hand, then make a slanting jab with the dibber 2 in. from the plant and lever the soil forward so that the seedling is properly embedded. *See* sketch, page 77. Firm lightly with

53

toe or knuckle. To help in planting at correct depths, mark the dibber off in inches.

A 'garden line' is essential for sowing seed, for transplanting seedlings in straight lines in the garden, and for many other jobs. It is easily home-made with two short pegs and strong cord, but the skirret type, with a revolving centre pin, is a great help. As you draw the hoe along it in making a 'drill', the trick is to keep a foot on the line, or it will belly out. A measuring rod of some sort goes with it.

'Cultivators' also need caution. The usual type has five springy prongs on swan-necks. Use only for rough work on unplanted land, otherwise it simply tears up roots. Not necessary.

The turfing-iron is a large, heart-shaped blade for lifting sods. Cut parallel lines in the turf with an edging-iron a foot apart or as needed, slide the turfing-iron forward under the turf between the lines about 1 in. deep, and roll up the sod like a Swiss roll. Only occasionally needed and can sometimes be hired from a nursery. A spade can be used instead but it is harder work.

Of wheelbarrows, the old-fashioned wooden sort, fitted with extension pieces for loads of leaves and grass, is still best, and pneumatic tyres will save damage to lawns and paths. Avoid small iron horrors with handles so close together that your legs will not go between.

Watering-cans are available in several sizes and shapes. The Haws type with long neck and several interchangeable roses is particularly valuable, especially in the greenhouse. For pot-plants in the home get a miniature can with very thin spout and no rose. When using any can, be careful not to wash out a hole in the soil. Always keep the rose on unless there is a very good reason for leaving it off. Be awfully careful to wash out very thoroughly any can that has been used for weed-killer; and preferably keep a special one for this purpose and put a dab of red paint on it.

Hoses should be made of corrugated rubber or of the new plastic. Get also a reel on which to wind the hose for easy transport and to save wear. Standpipes at tactical points in the garden are a great help when hosing. Some sort of sprinkler is also a necessity. *See* Chapter V for usage.

Mowers are numerous in make and design. I can only say get the best you can afford; a good small one is better than a large cheap one. Those with rollers back and front are best, and of course a motor-mower is highly desirable, together with a little transporting cradle on rubber tyres.

Rollers for lawns are better light than heavy. About 2 cwt is a good weight, but for paths something heavier may be needed.

Syringes will be needed for spraying liquid insecticides and fungicides. They must be capable of delivering a fine mist, and if the purse will run to it, get one that works continuously, either from a knapsack on your back or from a bucket. It is essential also that the syringe should have a bent nozzle capable of being pointed upwards to spray the under-surfaces of leaves.

For applying insecticides and fungicides in powder or dust form bellows are used instead. They are cheap, unless you like to treat yourself to the sort that requires one hand only.

Other tools that may be needed are hand shears for clipping hedges and awkward spots of grass, long-handled edging shears for cutting the whiskers of a lawn, a crescent-shaped edging-iron for trimming grass edges, besoms, a daisy-grubber, a crowbar for handling rocks and making holes for posts, a heavy rammer and mattock for making paths and steps, and other tools for specialised jobs. Weapons for pruning are dealt with in the chapter on that subject.

I have dealt here only with basic tools. There are a good many fancy gadgets on the market, but not all are as good as they claim to be. There are also electric hedge-trimmers and grass-cutters, and a whole new range of small motor-driven machines that plough, hoe, sow, and mow, and are sometimes fitted with power take-offs for hedge-trimming, etc. Whether you treat yourselves to one of these will depend on your pocket and whether the size of your garden justifies the expense.

CHAPTER V

GARDEN OPERATIONS

CULTIVATION IN GENERAL—DRAINAGE—DIGGING—
RIDGING—MANURING—WEEDING—WATERING—STAKING—
MULCHING—PLANTING

Cultivation in General

GOOD cultivation and management of the soil are to the garden as diet, grooming, and exercise are to the horse or greyhound. Much depends on the beast itself, but the trainer must fit him for the stakes.

Cultivation begins with drainage, a *sine qua non*; in most established gardens it exists satisfactorily already (but by no means always), and if that is so, this chapter's next section, which is unlikely to arouse any transports of delight, can be skipped. After that, cultivation primarily implies digging, feeding, hoeing, weeding, and the creation of those conditions that will intimidate pests and perplex the agents of disease. Good mechanical cultivation of the soil will indeed by itself alone go far, without manuring and even with imperfect drainage. Listen to the No-Digging Brigade with the attention expected from an open-minded people, but remain sceptical. Remember that soils differ enormously from one another, and what may be acceptable treatment in one garden may be quite unsuitable for another.

The normal round of the cultural year is to dig the ground in autumn with the spade, manuring as necessary, to fork it over lightly in early spring, maybe adding lime, then to sow and plant. Afterwards, during the growing season, there is frequent hoeing to harass the weeds, fertilising perhaps, and of course various other chores. This is certainly the outline routine for the kitchen garden, and for the flower garden, too, when new beds have to be made or when crops of annuals or biennials have to be put into the line and replaced on becoming casualties. A virtue of autumn digging—in which the soil should always be left in large lumps or clods, not broken down —is that frost is able to bite in deep; and frost, working on particles of soil moisture as it does on water-pipes, will burst and crumble a heavy soil into fine tilth more efficiently than man can do. Newly-broken and neglected soils of obstinate clay may have to be 'ridged'. Afterwards, by the ordinary laws, east winds should come in early spring and with their harrowing breath drive off the surface moisture, leaving the soil in the condition most fit for sowing seed—moist below but dry and of a fine tilth on the surface—with the expectation of sun to come. If it could only be so always!

Circumstances may forbid this normal routine—a mort of rain in autumn, or occupation of the new house at the wrong time of the year. If so, the preliminary digging can be done at any time of year while the soil and weather are suitable, but a substantial period, say normally six weeks, dependent on rain and the nature of the soil, should elapse before other operations, so that the soil may settle. Never dig a soil when it is sodden, nor when it is frost-bound, but a light surface frost is no objection.

In established beds where some sort of perennial plant is already growing—herbaceous borders, rose-beds, shrubbery, orchard—the procedure is different. Here there is no autumn digging with the spade. And here, for the moment, I touch my hat to the Anti-Diggers, and say that there need be no worrying of the soil when plants are already rooted. A mere scratching of the surface, as by hoeing, raking, or the lightest possible pricking over with the fork of the top inch only, is all that should be tolerated, and even that is usually unnecessary. Any deeper disturbance serves merely to tear up roots and to disturb or mutilate Lilies and other bulbs. I writhe, as the roots themselves must do, when I see Jobbing Gardener driving spade or fork deep into someone's rose-bed. What *is* valuable

57

autumn rather than digging, is the practice of mulching—
loosely blanketing the soil with leaves or other organic matter
in decay.

The same goes for spring and summer. The roots of many
plants grow close to the surface. Only the hoe should be used,
and then only for slaughtering weeds or for preventing the
concreting or cracking of heavy clays in long dry spells. Heavy
soils admittedly need more working than light ones, but normally hoeing for weeds is sufficient for preserving a surface tilth,
and I doubt whether there is much scientific backing for the
'dust mulch' one reads of so much. Here again, thick mulching
with leaves or peat is the thing; this alone will keep down quite
a lot of weeds.

Of course, keep all beds, and indeed the whole garden,
physically clean. Gather cabbage and other leaves, sticks,
twigs, and prunings and all refuse. All are breeding places for
slugs, bugs, bacteria, and other fifth columnists.

Now for the various garden operations *seriatim*. There are
variations of method, and most experienced gardeners have
their own little dodges, but those that I describe are the usually
accepted ways.

Drainage

The first necessity of good cultivation. To all normal garden
plants a waterlogged soil is fatal. The soil must, of course, be
capable of holding such moisture as plants need—and some
need a lot—and this we provide for by ensuring that plenty of
decayed or decaying organic matter is incorporated. But excess
water must be able to drain away. In most existing gardens
today there is little that need be done, but in new ground, or
in major operations such as terracing, a drainage operation is
likely to be necessary.

Pools of water lying on the surface for protracted periods
after rain show a need for drainage; but often the necessity is
less obvious. Tests should be made in any new garden by
digging holes about 3 ft deep in different parts of the garden,
and if the level of water—or 'water table'—appears to remain

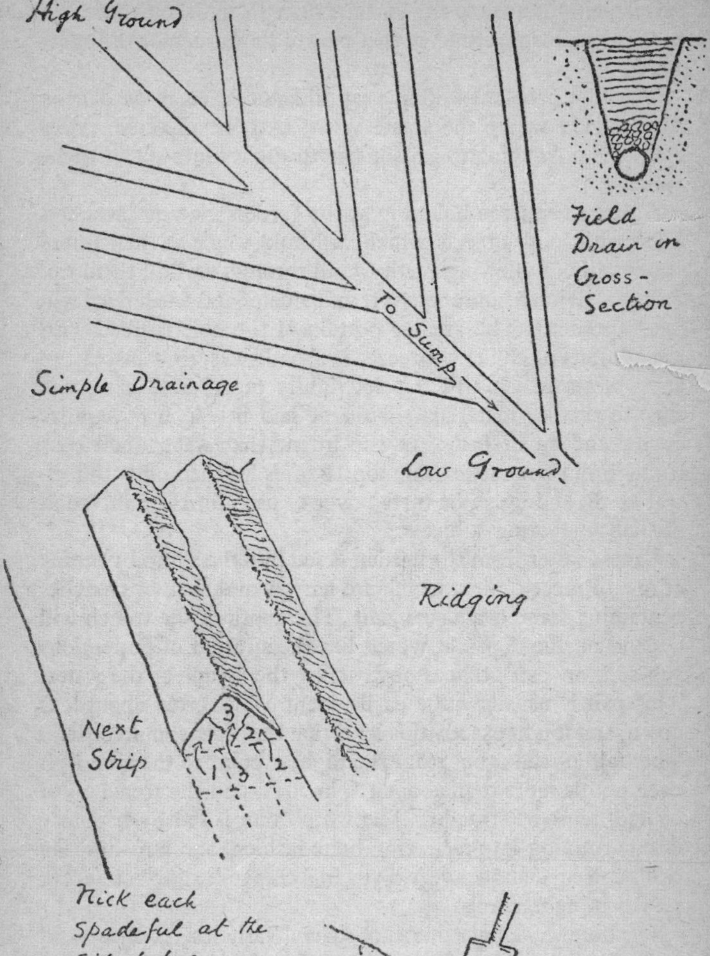

High Ground

Field
Drain in
Cross-
Section

To Sump

Simple Drainage

Low Ground

Ridging

Next
Strip

3
1 2
1 2
3

Nick each
Spadeful at the
Side before
lifting, so that it
comes out clean.

Drainage, ridging, and a digging trick.

permanently nearer to the surface than 18 in., then there is a need for drainage, either in that part of the garden or throughout it.

The first problem—often very difficult in small gardens—is to decide where the waste water is to be directed. Very often the only thing to be done is to dig a sump-pit or soakaway.

A sump is a large hole dug at the garden's lowest level and filled with loose objects which will hold water in their interstices without allowing earth to fall through and fill them up. For a small job a hole about 6 ft in diameter and 6 feet deep will meet the need. The greater portion of the hole is filled with large lumps of clinkers, breeze, broken bricks, tin cans, etc.—any objects which will not set tightly together. Nearer the surface smaller materials should be laid in—such as angular stones and small brick, to the intent that water shall pass through but not earth. The top 12 in. is finished off with topspit earth, and it can be turfed over or used for the cultivation of shallow-rooting subjects.

Excess water from the garden is fed into the sump by means of one or more drains, which are narrow and shallow trenches containing some drainage agent. The depth of the trench will depend on the depth at which lies the stratum of impervious sub-soil, or 'pan', that is obstructing the escape of the water. This pan is usually quite easily identifiable, often about 2 ft down, and it is at exactly this level that the drain should be laid. The 'fall' of the drain from the highest point to the sump-pit need not be more than about 1 ft in 50 ft, and the trenches, of course, must be straight. The main drain is fed by tributary drains running into it herring-bone fashion, and a main drain will be needed about every 5 yds in a clay soil, and about every 10 yds in lighter soils.

Of drainage agents there are several varieties. A cheap and very effective method for a small job is to lay a course of twiggy faggots, preferably of hazel, in the bottom of the trench, 6 to 12 in. thick, according to the depth of the trench, cover with turves laid upside down, and fill with top soil.

A second method is to use clinkers or coarse rubble on the

same principle as in the sump, graduating them from coarse to fine before filling in.

The best, but most expensive, method is to use earthenware field drains, which are short lengths of pipe laid simply end-to-end. They are embedded all round with a few inches of clinkers to prevent soil from silting up the pipes.

Digging

Four kinds of digging operations have to be tackled—plain surface digging, trenching, bastard trenching, and ridging. There is also, of course, mere forking, which may be needed on vacant ground in spring, and is certainly required after lifting one crop of vegetables or flowers and before replacing it with a new crop, but this needs no description.

To simplify matters, here are three canons that apply to all these tasks when they are something more than a small or casual job:

First, keep the top spit at its proper level; never bury it, nor bring a lower spit to the top (though the expert can and sometimes does). On the other hand, each spadeful, after it is lifted out, should be roughly turned over with a twist of the wrist.

Secondly, work methodically row by row in clean, straight lines. If the plot is broad, divide it into strips.

Thirdly, at the head or start of each plot or strip take out an initial trench (of variable width) across the breadth of the job, and wheel the spoil away to the tail end of the plot. When one has dug through to the end, a vacant trench will confront one, and into this goes the spoil from the first trench. In deep trenching both top and second spits are wheeled away, but must be kept separate.

PLAIN DIGGING

This is a turning-over of the surface soil one spit deep (10 in.). Make the initial trench about 15 in. wide, then dig out the next row of soil and throw it forward into the empty trench —and so on, row by row. If manure is to be applied, lay it in

61

the bottom of the initial trench, but in subsequent rows throw it on the sloping surface of the spoil in the previous row, so that it is distributed throughout the spit but with none exposed on the surface. Dig in all young unflowered weeds without tap-roots, but remove all flowered or seeded weeds and search to the uttermost extremity for tap-rooted ones, couch grass and other abominable 'underground movements'.

BASTARD-TRENCHING, OR 'DOUBLE DIGGING'

Proceed as in plain digging, but fork over the bottom or second spit of each trench. Drive the fork down and turn the soil over. Bastard-trenching is almost invariably accompanied by manuring, and the manure should go into both spits, subject to what crop you will be growing.

TRENCHING

In this operation the soil is disturbed to the depth of three spits. It is hard work, and should be undertaken by less robust people in small doses, but it is of great and lasting value, especially in the vegetable garden or where permanent and deep-rooted plants requiring good drainage and plenty of bottom food are to be established. Manuring always accompanies it. The 'drill', illustrated on the next page, is as follows:

(*a*) At the head of the plot take out the usual initial trench or trough of *top* spit, a width of about 2 ft 6 in. being the minimum for convenience.

(*b*) Divide the trough by eye or measurement into two long strips. Dig out the front strip of this *second* spit and wheel away the spoil, keeping it separate from the top spit.

(*c*) Fork over the *third* or bottom spit, incorporating manure as necessary.

(*d*) Dig out the back strip of the initial trough and throw it forward to replace the second spit of the forward strip, incorporating manure.

(*e*) Fork over the bottom spit of the second strip.

(*f*) Return to ground level. Take out a new trough of top spit, half the width of the initial trough, and throw it right

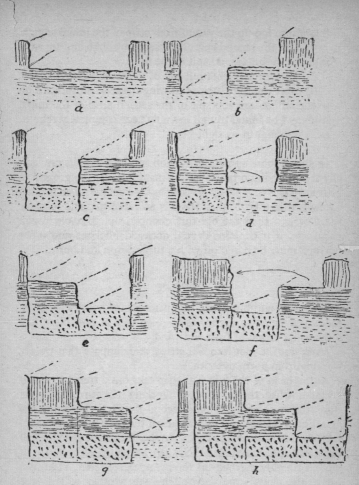

Trenching, the full operation: *a*, initial trench about 2 ft 6 in. wide, the spoil wheeled away; *b*, second spit of front strip taken out and away; *c*, bottom spit of front strip forked over; *d*, second spit of back strip replaces that of front strip; *e*, bottom spit of back strip forked over; *f*, top spit of second trench replaces that of front strip of initial one; *g*, second spit of second trench replaces second spit of initial one; *h*, bottom spit of second trench forked over.

forward to top up the vacant front strip of the initial trough.

(g) Dig the second spit of the second trough and throw it into the vacant second spit of the first.

(h) Fork over the bottom spit of the second trough.

(i) Start the third strip, throwing the top spit forward on to the still vacant top spit of the second strip of the initial trough. The initial trough has now been completely rebuilt, each spit kept in its right place.

In any of these operations the top and second spits are usually the more important ones for manuring. If the ground to be treated was previously grassed, as for example when making a new bed in a lawn, then there is no more valuable food for the new bed than the old turf chopped up. But old rough pasturage, if it contains couch, docks, dandelions and other horrors, must be pared off with a turfing-iron and burnt.

Ridging

This is an autumn or winter operation for heavy clay soils, the object being to expose as large an area as possible to the pulverising action of frost and wind.

Mark out the plot into 3-ft strips, and suppose that we are working from north to south.

At the head of the first 3-ft strip take out a trench one spit deep and wheel the spoil away. Working backwards down the strip, throw the spoil from a second trench forward into the first, but at the left and right edges of the strip turn the spadefuls inwards towards the centre, to the intent that a ridge shall run north and south down each strip, as though ploughed or as though roughly earthed-up for potatoes. (Sketch, page 59.) Leave the clods large and rough—the weather will do the crumbling better than you can.

Manuring

We have seen how to incorporate animal or vegetable organic matter in digging jobs. Rough and unrotted stuff should go into the bottom spits in full trenching or bastard-trenching, but the top spit should have only fully or nearly decomposed stuff, whether rotted animal manure, or compost, leaf-mould, hop-manure, peat, and so on.

Serious and often deadly injury is done to a great many plants if their roots have direct contact with fresh *animal* manures. If dung is applied in the autumn, planting in the spring will be safe for most things, but if planting is to follow soon after manuring, then 2 in. or so of plain and fine soil should intervene between dung and root; normally the bottom of the first spit is deep enough. The objection does not apply to well-rotted dung.

In handling manures, make small dumps in convenient places and feed from these into the trenches, rather than spread the stuff all over the ground; thus it does not get trampled on and compressed. Remember not to apply lime at the same time as animal dung.

Granular or powdery manures or fertilisers, organic or otherwise, go into the top spit. The quick-acting chemicals and fish manures are spread on the surface and 'pricked in' by hoe or other implement into the top inch or two of soil either just before planting or during the season of growth. Slow-acting stuff such as bonemeal can go in at any time, but the most convenient is during autumn digging.

Weeding

For convenience we can class weeds into three degrees of abomination:

Fibrous-rooted weeds that have not yet flowered. Get at these early and often with the hoe when the soil is dry and the sun hot, and leave them on the surface to wither.

Similar weeds that have flowered or seeded. Use the hoe again but collect them up or the seed will ripen and germinate. They can go on the compost heap if you are skilful at that job, but it is safer to burn them.

Tap-rooted weeds such as dandelions, underground creeping horrors, and 'vegetative serpents' such as couch grass and ground elder, and a few bulbous weeds. These brutes laugh at the hoe, as love at the locksmith. Any fragment of them that is left in the ground sprouts afresh, and there are only two ways of extermination—by poison or by burrowing patiently to their uttermost extremities.

Dandelions are effectively disposed of by painting the leaves with a '2, 4-D' hormone weed-killer as used on lawns, being careful not to make the solution stronger than advised by the manufacturer; two doses may be necessary, at a few days' interval. A dab from one of the modern 'touchweeders' will also do the trick, especially in awkward places.

Bindweed, once such a curse to gardeners, is now also very easily disposed of by a hormone solution. Just paint the tips or dip them into a jam-jar of the liquid and the whole plant will die. Don't let leaves so treated touch other plants.

Ground elder may also be tackled with this hormone, but with a good deal less confidence. Two or three dressings in a season are necessary. Where there is a large patch of the beastly stuff you can water on the solution or use sodium chlorate as shown below. The roots are very brittle, snap easily, and any fragment left behind means a new plant. They love worming their way into the roots of your choicest plants, and there is then only one remedy—lift the plant in autumn or spring, shake the earth out of the roots, and sort out the horrid tangle. If this happens to a bush or tree too large to lift, persecute the weed with relentless hoeing, and in time it will die from lack of the energy foods it needs from the air.

Two other methods of weed destruction are available if one is confronted with an impenetrable jungle—the flame-gun and mass poisoning. The flame-gun is not nearly so alarming as it sounds, and will settle the account of all top growth that it touches, but until you have learnt the technique you are likely to make the air lurid with oaths. Good for paths.

The most virulent weed-killer is sodium chlorate, which will kill nearly everything. About 6 oz in 2 gallons of water does 10 sq yd. Other good poisons are Atlacide and Abol Double Strength. Of course, neither fire nor poison distinguishes between weeds and flowers.

On paths and terraces use one of the preparations based on Simazin (e.g., Weedex), but they must not trickle into a flower-bed or soak into the edges of a lawn or down to the roots of precious plants that may run beneath. In such places use a weed-killer in powder form (e.g. Atlacide), and hoe away the corpses when brown, or use a flame-gun.

Watering

All watering of plants must be *gentle* and must be *thorough*. So that it may be gentle, never use hose or can (except very small cans with thin spouts) without a rose, sprinkler or similar fittings. Be especially careful when watering flower-pots not to wash out a hole in the soil.

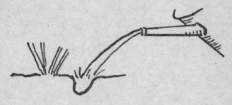

How not to water.

Thoroughness also, when using a hose, can only be achieved by the use of a rain- or mist-forming fitting. Give a steady, gentle and prolonged soaking, instead of playing about by holding the hose in your hand. A surface wetting merely draws the fine rootlets to the surface and causes excessive transpiration. Test for penetration with fingers or a tool, and if dry soil is encountered within 3 in. of the surface then the watering has been insufficient.

In the south and east of England we do not water our gardens nearly enough. In my own garden the hoses come out if there has been ten days without rain—sooner if the weather is hot.

Some plants, such as Hydrangea and Rhododendron, need repeated heavy waterings in dry weather, but Rhododendrons prefer rain-water, if available, to hard tap water. Sweet and garden peas also dislike cold tap water, and if no rain-water is available a large tub may be filled from the tap and left outdoors in the sun for at least twenty-four hours. Rain-water is, of course, preferable for all watering operations when possible.

For watering when transplanting, see the next section but two.

Staking

Staking is necessary for non-rigid plants not of a lowly stature in order to prevent damage by wind and rain. It is rather a bore, and nowadays there is a tendency to stock as far as possible with plants that don't need it.

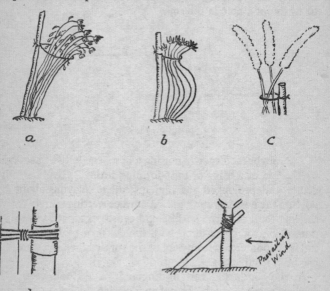

Staking: a and *b*, how not to do it—the Weary Willy and the Hangman's Noose methods; *c*, delphiniums need one cane per flowerstem, not as here; *d*, staking a tree, showing band of sacking, etc., and a simple method of tying to prevent chafing; *e*, another method, appropriate to fruit trees.

Delphiniums, Gaillardias, peas and Sweet Peas, Antirrhinums, and a few other things need staking early, but generally the right time is when a plant has made about three-quarters of its full growth. Staking must also be thorough and tidy; a large clump of Chrysanthemums tied with string to a single stake is a horticultural Belsen.

For general work the easiest, neatest, and least conspicuous stakes are twiggy pea-sticks. Cut them to the required height, and plant them firmly so that they completely surround the plant or plants, with one or two extra in the middle of large clusters. The growing foliage will soon hide the sticks.

Less decorously, one may use bamboo canes instead, several to a plant, with string or raffia tied round at perhaps 15-in. intervals. Large Dahlias and others need something stronger, and square-cut posts are sold for this purpose; Dahlias, however, are often over-staked and usually four 4-ft bamboo canes are enough.

Delphiniums are dealt with in Chapter XI.

Mulching

This is the process of spreading a layer of compost, manure, lawn mowings, leaves, peat, etc. on the surface of the soil. Its usual purpose is to keep roots moist and cool during a dry spell, but in addition it provides nutriment and for roses it checks the upward movement of fungal spores from the soil. It is nature's method of regenerating soil, and Man doesn't do it nearly enough. For this purpose alone almost everything benefits from a thick autumn mulch of leaves, especially shrubs and trees of all sorts, hedges, and the herbaceous border, and the process is one that should replace the often harmful one of autumn digging. Undoubtedly mulching is the thing. But you must mulch only when the soil is moist and warm. Thus leaf, peat, and compost mulches (contrary to what is often said) are best given in autumn. Grass mulches, applied during the mowing months, must be free of seed and occasionally stirred; they get very hot. Don't use grass that has recently been treated with a 'hormone' weed-killer.

On the other hand, mulches of animal manure should be given as the sap begins to rise in spring, or its elements will be washed away by winter rain.

Keep all mulches of animal manure away from actual contact with the stems of plants. Do not mulch Irises.

Planting

Slovenly planting is the cause of many a good young plant growing into a straggly weakling. The operation of starting off a plant really well in its new home is of critical importance to its future.

In general terms the requirements are—a well-worked soil, friable, damp but not sodden; a hole slightly deeper and slightly wider than would appear necessary; an arrangement of the roots in the hole so that they are let well down or spread well out and not crowded, twisted or cockled-up; a fairly firm treading or pressing-down of the soil with hand or foot; and a good watering-in, using rain-water if available.

A few plants have their special requirements, of course, and some, especially trees, shrubs, Carnations, and all the cabbage tribe, need especially firm planting. Roses need not be watered-in. Depth of planting is also often critical. Generally it suits the need barely to cover the crown, but Carnations should be planted very shallow, Phloxes rather deeply, dwarf Roses covered by just about an inch, Peonies not more than 2 in., and so on. All trees and shrubs should be planted to exactly the depth of the old 'soil mark' showing on the stems, and the method I use for ensuring this is to lay a hoe or rigid stick across the open hole, so that when the plant is lowered into the hole the soil mark should be level with the stick and the roots only barely touching the bottom and sides of the hole.

Whenever in doubt about the right tool to use, choose the larger—a trowel rather than a dibber, a spade rather than a trowel.

Plant always in what is called 'open' weather—that is, when

the ground is neither frost-bound nor saturated. The soil should be damp, but not so wet that the boots clog. If, as often happens, planting has to be done in a dry summer spell, soak the ground thoroughly the night before with the hose if the job is a big one, or water the plants in extra thoroughly as you plant. I often put a little water into each hole with a thin-spouted can before popping in the plant, and the effect is excellent. Of course, if planting a large number of seedlings one can't afford to be so finicky.

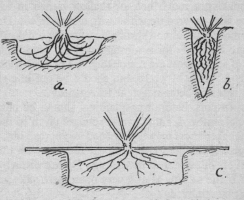

Wrong and Right Planting: a, roots crowded, cockled up and crossing, crown above ground; *b,* ditto, crown too low; *c,* right, showing use of rigid stick to keep correct depth.

The actual process of planting in a normal instance may be thus described:

Assuming the hole to have been correctly made, take the plant in the left hand, lower it into the hole, ensure that there is enough depth for the roots without crowding, cockling, or telescoping, and enough width if the roots are widespreading. Now work in some loose, fine soil with the other hand, or with a trowel or spade, according to size, give the plant a little up-and-down shake so that soil will work in between the roots, top up the hole with soil, and firm the soil with fingers, knuckle or foot. Bushes and trees may need the processes of working-in soil, shaking, and treading more than once before the final

71

topping-up to soil-mark level. For planting small seedlings by dibber, *see* Chapter IV.

Some plants, especially 'flag' Irises and asparagus, need a slight refinement that we call 'saddle planting'. Having made the hole, shape the soil roughly into a saddle, ridge or gentle mound below ground level, and lay the roots astride it.

When plants come from a nursery get them in their homes as soon as possible. If delay is unavoidable, they should be unpacked and 'heeled-in' somewhere convenient. This simply means making a rough hole or shallow trench in which the roots are laid, covered up with earth, and watered. Don't lose the soil mark of trees and shrubs by covering too deeply. The plants are then safe for a substantial time. Those that arrive in time of severe frost are reasonably safe in their packings for probably a couple of weeks, but should be put in a shed and their foliage and roots moistened frequently.

Plants in pots, before transplanting, should be tapped out, the crocks removed, and a gentle squeeze given to the ball of soil so that the roots may be loosened and spread out.

Evergreens should arrive from the nursery with their roots in a ball of soil, wrapped in sacking. Do not disturb the ball of soil. If the sacking is of a very open mesh, like netting, it need not be removed.

CHAPTER VI

BE FRUITFUL AND MULTIPLY

PROPAGATION GENERALLY—PLANTS FROM SEED—
CUTTINGS—ROOT CUTTINGS—LEAF CUTTINGS—LAYERS—
DIVISION

Propagation Generally

VIRTUALLY all plants can be grown from seed. In practice, however, there are often objections to this method of propagation, either because germination is difficult, or because growth is slow, or because the offspring may not resemble its parent. Nature herself employs other methods, as by stolons or suckers, by layers, by the formation of new bulbs, and so on. The tips of blackberries and loganberries, drooping to the earth, will take root and form new plants. The strawberry sends out its 'runners'. The stems of Jasmine, Hydrangea, Clematis, and many other plants, laid on the ground, may take root anywhere along their length. The gardener takes advantage of these propensities of nature, and has invented some other methods himself. By his choice of method he is able to perpetuate a particular strain or to develop new ones.

Thus, moreover, will he save himself many bawbees. To buy the best stock his bank manager will allow in the first place, then to cause it to increase and multiply, is the way of the good gardener. Naturally it is slower than buying the full tally of ready-made plants, but from a small initial stock of the best quality he can fill his garden in a year or two and will very soon, indeed, find himself with plenty over.

The several methods of propagation otherwise than by seed are called 'vegetative' as a useful distinctive term. A prime merit of plants so raised is that to all intents and purposes they are certain to be exactly like their parents, whereas seed, especially of the highly cultivated modern hybrids, may produce something quite different.

Broadly speaking, in modern practice annuals and biennials, including virtually all vegetables, are raised from seed, and other categories of plants are more usually multiplied by one or other of the vegetative means. Thus the typical method of increasing Carnations and Rhododendrons is by layers, shrubs by cuttings or budding, fruits and roses by budding or grafting, many herbaceous perennials by division of roots, while some Begonias will take root merely from a leaf laid flat on the soil. I am not in this book dealing with methods of grafting and budding, which usually require some experience and for which there is only very limited use in small gardens.

Plants from Seed

Quite a wide range of plants, however, can be raised perfectly easily from seed besides annuals and biennials, if one is content to wait a bit. Thus among hard-wooded shrubs Broom seeds very easily; so does Daphne Mezereum, and often with delightful results. Buddleia and Ceanothus, too, are quick and easy. Among herbaceous perennials the opportunity is still wider. Delphinium seed from high-class nurseries such as Blackmore and Langdon of Bath, and Russell Lupin seed from Baker's of Wolverhampton will produce first-class plants often quite comparable with expensive named varieties, though the bag will be a mixed one. Thus if one has the patience to wait a year the perennial border can be filled at very little cost.

The three main methods of raising plants from seed are by sowing by one of the following means:

Outdoors, direct into the plant's permanent quarters (*in situ*); many vegetables and hardy annual flowers are so raised.

Outdoors, but in a seed-bed in a special 'nursery', whence they are moved on into their permanent quarters, or often into an intermediate station, as soon as they are large enough to handle; this is the usual method for the cabbage family, for hardy biennials such as Wallflowers and Sweet William, and for hardy perennials such as Delphinium and Lupin.

'Indoors' in a greenhouse or frame, the seed being sown in boxes, or earthenware pans, or in pots; this is the characteristic method for starting half-hardy plants (*e.g.* Antirrhinum and Stock) and for tender subjects, but hardy plants may also be so started for special purposes.

The beginner should note carefully that only hardy plants can be sown direct outdoors, unless left so late in the season as to be hardly worth the trouble of sowing, but cloches often enable one to steal a march on nature for plants in the borderline of hardiness, such as Zinnias, Schizanthus, and Nicotiana.

It is a broad general rule that plants do best if sown where they are intended to remain, without the wrench of transplanting; and for root crops—carrots, turnips, etc.—this is obligatory. Flowers with tap-roots, e.g. Larkspur, similarly dislike being shifted, and so do some others.

Two golden rules of sowing, whether out or indoors, should be taken to heart early:

Sow sparsely (the parsnip is an exception);
Sow not too deep; large seeds such as broad beans go in 3 in. down, but very fine ones should have no more than a sprinkling of fine soil or sand over them, applied for preference through a sieve; on heavy soils seed is sown even less deeply than on light or thin soils.

SOWING OUTDOORS

Whatever method of sowing is adopted—whether in a nursery bed or *in situ*, and if *in situ* whether in long straight ranks or broadcast—a fine 'seed-bed' must first be prepared. The soil must have been dug at least a few weeks beforehand according to normal methods of cultivation and allowed to settle. Preparation of the seed-bed then consists in reducing the top 2 or 3 in. to a good tilth; the smaller the seed, the finer the tilth.

First, lightly fork over the top few inches only, or hoe deeply. Next, lightly tread down the soil with the feet to crush lumps, moving along the row sideways. Then rake thoroughly to-and-fro, removing stones. Repeat the process of treading and raking as often as may be necessary, according to whether the soil be light or sandy or a heavy clay. The heavier the soil the more the treatment required. The last process is always raking.

This work should be done when there is plenty of moisture below ground but when the surface is sufficiently dry for the hoe to work easily without soil sticking to it. Conditions are generally just right after the east winds of early spring have dried off the surface moisture. 'The beginning of March,' says old Thomas Tusser 'or a little afore is time for a wyfe to make her garden, and to get as many good seeds and herbs as she can, and especially such as be good for the potte.' It is equally a mistake to do the work when the soil is dust-dry right through, and in a dry summer it may be necessary to make a shallow trench with the draw hoe overnight, fill with water and draw the soil back again when the water has drained through.

Having worked up a good tilth, make a 'drill' for reception of the seed. A drill is a tiny trench, which for very fine seed will be no more than $\frac{1}{4}$ in. deep. To make, or 'draw', the drill, set out the garden line, and, keeping one foot on it to hold it taut, draw the hoe along it, canting the hoe so that only a point of it penetrates the soil; a little V-shaped trench results. In my experience the best tool for making the drill is the tri-angular hoe, but the draw hoe is more usual. For very fine seed a pointed stake does well.

For large seeds such as beans and peas normal practice is to make a broad drill the full width of the draw hoe, using the hoe in its natural plane, or to use a spade. In the kitchen garden and the nursery, seed-beds should be neat, orderly and parallel; in the nursery they are usually about 4 in. apart. In clay soils a sprinkling of leaf-mould or peat in the bottom of the drill will help germination.

The seed is now sown along the drill, either by pouring it gently out of the packet, or a pinch at a time with finger and thumb, or by means of a seed-sowing gadget. One seed every inch should normally be enough—larger seeds even more sparsely. The finer seeds may be mixed with sand for easy handling and even distribution.

Sowing "at stations".

The drill in Section.

Drawing a Seed Drill

Seedling, showing first pair of "true" leaves.

One way of using a dibber.

Sowing outdoors and planting out seedlings.

After sowing, cover the seed with the little ridge of spoil from the trench by drawing the back of a rake or edge of a hoe gently over the surface. Very fine seed can be covered by sprinkling fine potting soil or sand from a fine-mesh sieve. A sprinkling of mixed soot and coarse sand on the surface will help deter slugs. Label each row, not forgetting the date.

No further attention should be necessary until after germination, except for a watering with Cheshunt Compound for plants subject to the damping-off disease. In prolonged dry spells a cautious watering through a fine rose may be necessary.

Seed may also be sown by broadcasting—sprinkling more or less at random. This is often done with annuals, but is not a method I care for. It is preferable to sow in irregular drills—serpentine, circular, as you will. Better still, however, not only for annual flowers but also when sowing vegetables *in situ*, is the method of sowing 'at stations'. This means dropping two or three seeds at selected spots, according to the ultimate spacing necessary, and subsequently thinning the seedlings to the most promising one when large enough. This method has all sorts of merits—it is economical, it is quick, it enables seedling weeds to be more easily identified and the hoe plied with greater safety. A good and quick way of sowing flower annuals at stations is to scratch a rough criss-cross pattern, like squared paper, on the soil, and to sow at the intersections of the lines, the lines being at distances apart suitable to the size of the plant—about 9 in. for the general run of medium-sized annuals.

When the seedlings have fully developed their second pair of leaves—i.e. the first pair of true leaves after the cotyledons or seed-leaves—they must be 'thinned out' if they have been sown in their permanent quarters, or 'pricked out' if they have been sown in a preliminary nursery bed. Thinning means reducing them so that those that remain stand at their final distances apart; or they can be reduced first to half-distances and later to full distances. Thus one may reduce carrot seedlings first to 3 in. apart and finally to 6 in. The thinnings can often be used—the baby carrots you would eat, the baby marigold you could transplant elsewhere—but some, such as the parsnip, are useless.

Pricking out simply means lifting the seedlings from this nursery bed (or seed-box)—all of them—and replanting them more widely somewhere else, either into their permanent quarters or into some intermediate quarters. Lift them gently on to a pointed garden label, or similar small implement, with a little soil adhering to their roots, and get them into their next quarters as soon as possible. Do the job when the soil is moist but not sodden.

78

Be most particular to thin and prick out while the nurselings are still quite small; if left crowded together they will become weak and leggy and will never be of strong constitution. The way a plant begins its life is critical to its whole future.

Seedlings that cannot normally go into their final homes for some time, such as biennials (Wallflowers, Canterbury Bell, etc.) and perennials (Delphinium, Columbine, etc.), are pricked out into a nursery bed. This is a vital period for them. Give them a bed generously treated according to their kind, in an open position, not under trees; some will appreciate a degree of shade. In this bed they are planted out at distances suitable to their nature—Wallflowers at about 5 in. apart, Delphiniums at 8 in. or more. A typical course of events is for, say, Wallflowers to be sown in June, pricked out when an inch or so high into a nursery bed, and transplanted into their permanent stations in the autumn.

SOWING INDOORS

For the general run of plants requiring to be started indoors wooden seed-boxes or shallow earthenware seed-pans are used, but sometimes pots instead. The same principles apply to all methods. If home-made boxes are used they should be about $2\frac{1}{2}$ in. deep, and the bottom, if there are no gaps between the boards, should have plenty of holes for drainage. All receptacles must be clean. Old ones should be scrubbed with hot water and soda, or an insecticide, and dried before use. New pots should be soaked for some hours and then dried off.

The receptacles must then be 'crocked'—their drainage holes or slits layered with pieces of broken flower-pot (which are 'crocks'), or stones other than flat ones, to provide controlled drainage. On top of the crocks place a $\frac{1}{2}$-in. layer of half-decayed leaves, or of coarse fibrous soil in particles the size of a small nut, the purpose being to prevent the fine soil above seeping down and clogging the drainage.

The next task is to fill the receptacle with a satisfactory soil for young plants. For this you use the John Innes Seed Compost (a non-proprietary formula), or else the Levington or Croxden soilless composts. Get your J. I. composts from

79

shops of high repute only; the prescription is given in Appendix 3.

Fill the receptacle to within ¼- or ½-in. of the rim. Make the surface quite level by pressing it down rather firmly with a flat pressing-board. Then partially immerse the receptacle in

Seed box, Flower pot and Seed pan, showing methods of drainage, crocking and filling

Pressing Boards, for firming and levelling soil.

Seed box after sowing (sectional view), covered with pane of glass and sheet of brown paper

The glass propped open for ventilation immediately seedlings show.

Sowing seed 'indoors'.

water so that the water seeps up from below and nearly reaches the surface of the soil. Treat with Cheshunt Compound, and drain thoroughly before sowing.

Broadcast the seed thinly on the soil, lightly sprinkle a little compost over it through a fine sieve, cover the receptacle with a sheet of glass and on top of it a sheet of brown paper. Wipe the glass dry every day and reverse it. As soon as the seedlings show their noses, remove the paper, tilt or shift the glass slightly to give more ventilation, and put the receptacle close up to the roof of the greenhouse (*see* page 80). After a few days remove the sheet of glass altogether. From now on see that the soil is kept fairly moist, preferably by immersion as before. If watering is done from overhead, use a fine rose or a spray.

When the youngsters have developed their first pair of true leaves, prick them off into other boxes or pots. If into a box, I like it to be 3 to 4 in. deep, instead of the shallow trays into which most nurseries crowd their seedlings. Use the same compost as before, treated likewise with Cheshunt Compound. Do not crowd the seedlings when pricking off. I like Antirrhinums, if grown this way, to be a good 3 in. apart instead of the usual jungle. Keep them well watered and as close to the light as possible.

Cuttings

It was a fortunate day when someone discovered that by sticking a twig into the ground a new plant would be born.

Not, of course, all plants, but a very great many, from pygmies of the rock garden to big shrubs and trees. Cuttings are a very cheap and often (but not always) an easy method of multiplying. A cutting (by which is usually meant a stem cutting), is simply a limb removed from a living plant at the right time of year, and plunged into suitable soil. The base of the cut stem after insertion forms a callus or healing tissue over the wound and from this roots form.

It is not so easy to generalise about cuttings as it is about seed, since some plants need special treatment, but observance of general principles sees one through. Only perennials can be so multiplied, not annuals (except by experts); though some of those plants which are usually treated as annuals but botanically are really perennial—Antirrhinums, for instance— grow admirably from cuttings if one is so disposed.

81

The dominant considerations when growing from cuttings are:

Selection of the right 'wood' or branch.
Selection of the right spot to cut it.
Provision of a soil in which it will 'strike', or take root.
Provision of a shady site and a moist, close atmosphere.

SELECTION OF THE RIGHT WOOD

Cuttings may be either of 'hard wood' or of 'soft wood'.

A *hard-wood* cutting is a mature or nearly mature shoot preferably of the current year's growth (what one might call a young adult shoot), taken from an established plant in summer or autumn, or sometimes when the plant is quite dormant and leafless. Plants for which the use of this kind of cutting is typical are shrubs, bush-fruits, and roses—though not all of them by any means. The ideal wood is brown, not green and sappy, but the word 'mature' applies rather to texture and substance than to length. Side-shoots rather than 'leaders' are generally best, especially shoots springing from the base. Shoots growing on the shady side of the parent, or from a parent growing in light shade, are better than those in full sun.

A *soft-wood* cutting may be either a young growth from a hard-wooded plant taken while the plant is actively developing in spring (as for Fuchsia), or it may mean a cutting of a soft-wooded plant, such as Viola, 'Geranium', Chrysanthemum, Pentstemon. Here again, on soft-wooded plants the nearly ripened shoots are usually the best; but several, of which Chrysanthemum, Dahlia, Delphinium, and Lupin are characteristic, require very young shoots taken when a few inches high early in the year, preferably cut off below ground level.

In no case are hollow-stemmed shoots any use for cuttings.

THE CUTTING POINT

For our purposes there are three main types of stem cutting:

Nodal—those cut precisely below a node or joint or leaf-junction (examples of a node are the swollen rings of a Carnation or Bamboo);

82

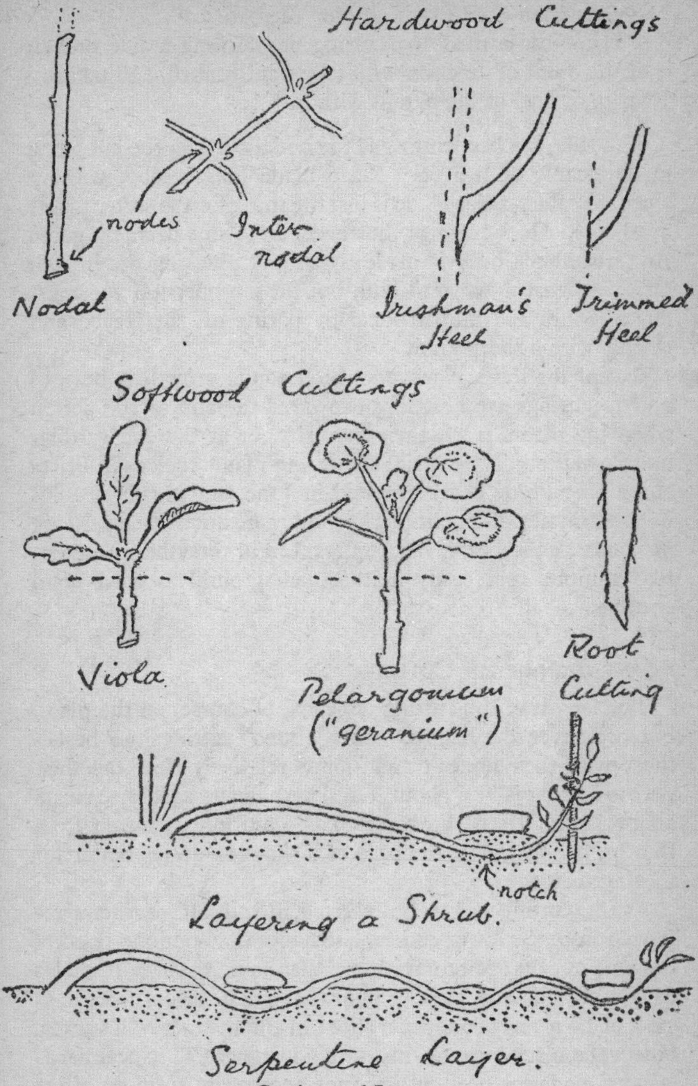

Hardwood Cuttings

Nodal

nodes

Inter-
nodal

Irishman's
Heel

Trimmed
Heel

Softwood Cuttings

Viola

Pelargonium
("geranium")

Root
Cutting

notch

Layering a Shrub.

Serpentine Layer.

Cutting and Layers.

Internodal—used typically for Clematis;

Heel—those made by cutting or plucking a side branch at the point of junction with its parent branch, and taking a strip, or heel of the parent with it.

As a rule, the best cutting is the nodal cutting, the cut being made cleanly with a very sharp blade horizontally, without slope. A safety-razor blade is just the thing for the softer plants or shoots. Heel cuttings, however, are also extremely good. An 'Irishman's heel' is made by simply plucking the branch off by a smart downward pull, but for a proper job you must make it into a 'trimmed' heel by paring off the frayed end cleanly with a sharp knife.

Except for those plants in which young growth is best, as noted, cuttings are best taken towards the end of the period when the plants reach their maturity, or at the end of their first flowering. Thus spring-flowering plants such as Aubrieta and alpine Phlox can be treated in June, and shrub cuttings in late summer. Sometimes the job can be done when pruning in winter; gooseberry, black currant, and forsythia prunings, for example, root easily in the open ground as hard-wood cuttings.

PREPARATION OF THE CUTTING

The length of the cutting depends, of course, on the plant, but, whatever the length, 'short-jointed' cuttings are best— those with their nodes or leaf-joints relatively close together. A rose cutting is best about 9 in. long; an averaged-size shrub about 12 in. If the limb selected is too long, shorten from the tip, not the base; the base of a shoot is always better for rooting than the tip.

As the cutting has to be inserted in soil, all leaves are removed from the lower end for a distance of about one-third of the cutting; do not remove more than is necessary. It is also usual to cut out any 'eyes' or buds that will be below ground, as each of them may send up a shoot in the manner of a sucker, but in the black currant this is an advantage. The ideal hard-wooded nodal or heel cutting (not necessarily so in an internodal cutting) will have about five or six active or dormant buds above ground in the larger plants, and soft-wooded cuttings will have three to five pairs of leaves.

Treat all cuttings, except very easy ones, with one of the root-forming 'hormones', such as Seradix (of which there are three grades) or Murphy's rooting hormone.

SOIL AND ATMOSPHERE

Soft-wood cuttings, taken with their foliage on and the sap running, require a moist, close atmosphere in the shade. If the cutting is allowed to transpire too freely before roots have formed it will die. Sun, wind, and a dry atmosphere cause rapid transpiration.

For normal amateur work all that is needed is a deep box with a close-fitting glass lid, stood in full shade. Grey-leaved plants do not need these close and moist conditions, but do need shade.

Insert the cuttings in pots, in a compost made up of one part medium loam, two parts peat, and one part sharp sand. Insert the cuttings round the edge, and nearly touching it and nearly touching each other. The one time that plants like to be crowded together is when they are cuttings. Plant very firmly, pressing the soil about the stems hard down with the fingers. Intimate contact of the basal wound with the soil is essential. Water thoroughly by immersion of the pots, and after putting them under glass give an occasional syringe of water in hot weather.

If only one potful is needed, push two bent wires into it and pop a polythene bag over them, secured by a rubber band; this is the 'Wisley pot'.

Transplant the cuttings as soon as they have rooted well, either into other pots separately, or into a nursery bed or into permanent quarters.

Hard-wood cuttings are less susceptible to death from excessive transpiration, especially those taken when leafless and dormant. Therefore, if a frame cannot be spared for the long lease they require, they can be inserted in the open ground outdoors, provided the site is a shady one, a bed on the north side of a wall or hedge being best.

Aerate the soil thoroughly by digging and by incorporation of plenty of sharp sand. Make a narrow trench of the depth required by the length of the cutting, sprinkle sand in the bottom of it, put the cuttings in vertically and with their leaves almost touching each other, return the soil, tread down very firmly, and water thoroughly. Such cuttings, inserted in the autumn, may be expected to root the following spring or summer, but top growth often starts first, so do not disturb them too soon.

Root Cuttings

The roots of several herbaceous plants, if cut into small lengths, will grow into new specimens. Examples are Phlox, Gaillardia, Mullein, Anchusa, Oriental Poppy, Romneya, Horse-radish, and Seakale.

Lift the plant, or expose a portion only of its roots, between November and April. Cut up a root into pieces 1–3 in. long (some plants longer). Cut the lower end diagonally and the top square, for identification (Sketch, page 83). Plant vertically 2 or 3 in. apart in a blend of sand and peat and a little loam, square-cut end uppermost, and cover with not more than an inch of sand or sandy soil Thin cuttings, such as Phlox, may be planted horizontally. Plant in deep seed-boxes, pots or a frame; if in boxes or pots, cover with glass as for seed. Water moderately until shoots appear, then more liberally before transplanting into a nursery bed.

Leaf Cuttings

A few plants can be propagated this way, including Camellia, Ramonda, and fibrous-rooted Begonias such as Rex and Gloire de Lorraine. In some the leaf is detached complete with stalk, and the stalk inserted in a compost of moist sand and leaf-mould. In others, as in the Begonias, the veins of the leaf are nicked at several points and the leaf laid flat on the compost, weighted with a pebble or two. A moist, close frame or green-house is necessary.

Layers

A layer is much the same thing as a cutting, except that the shoot is not detached from its parent. Layering is the favourite means of increasing Carnations, and the special method appropriate to them is dealt with in the chapter on that subject.

Many shrubs are also so increased, such as Rhododendron, Winter Jasmine, Hydrangea, and some fruits.

Choose a well-grown young shoot that has not flowered, low down on the shady side of the plant and on its circumference. Make a small slanting cut or a notch in the back on the underside of the shoot, press it down into the soil, making sure that the soil gets well inside the lips of the wound and adding some sharp sand to the soil at that point. Cover that portion of the stem with an inch or two of soil and weight it down with a stone (better than pegging). Stake the growing end of the shoot to induce upright growth. Water. Late summer is the usual time. It is often necessary to build up a small mound or low wall of soil to receive the layer conveniently, and root formation can be assisted by treating the wound with a root hormone as for cuttings. When the layer has rooted well, of which new top growth will be the first indication, sever it from its parent, and move it to its new quarters when convenient.

Division

This is the easiest of all methods of increasing stock. It is applicable to a great many herbaceous plants and to others whose habit is to extend themselves from the centre outwards, forming a dense and often matted 'clump', such as Michaelmas Daisy, Golden Rod, Helenium, etc., or, among shrubs, Hypericum.

Lift the whole clump and drive two garden forks, back to back, through the centre. Levering the forks against each other, gently tease the clump into two, and further sub-divide if necessary. On tough and obstinate roots use a knife. Small plants can be gently pulled apart with the fingers.

The younger shoots round the perimeter of the plant are the best for new stock, and in old clumps the centre should be discarded altogether.

CHAPTER VII

PRUNING

OUTSIDE the ranks of the expert, few garden operations are so misunderstood as pruning. Most of all, apparently, by our local authorities. The mutilation they allow to the trees in our streets and the shrubs in our parks is one of their several forms of vandalism. Another villain, whom I have already indicted, is the jobbing gardener who has had no technical training. One result is that every year our private gardens suffer enormous losses in apple crops alone.

It is notoriously difficult to explain detailed pruning in writing, and practical demonstration by an old hand is by far the best sort of tutorship. However, pruning is not a mystery, nor is it based on unreasoned rules of thumb, and the way begins to open up as soon as it is realised that pruning is based chiefly on intelligent observation of the natural habits and behaviour of a plant. This is the path I hope to point out.

WHY WE PRUNE

The purposes of pruning are to maintain, increase, or prolong the vitality of a plant, or to keep it in bounds, or to direct its energy to a special purpose. Thus, in a young tree, the first task is to build up a sound and well-shaped framework, but when it is well-grown we shall have a different purpose. In the apple we shall seek, as a rule, to induce new fruiting spurs rather than new branches; in a rose we may want a large shrub with many small flowers or we may want it to produce a few large exhibition blooms—and we can prune it for either purpose accordingly. In a hedge we shall want a dense barrier shrouded to the ground.

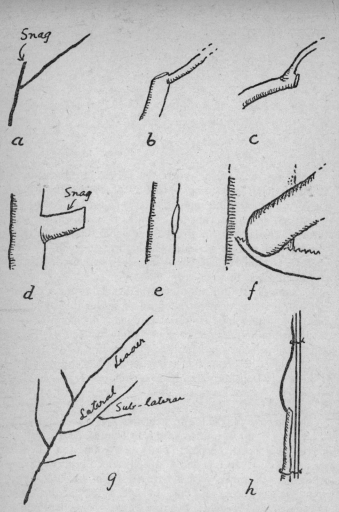

Pruning: a, leave no snag—cut immediately beyond selected shoot (or bud) as in *b* or *c* according to habit of plant; *d* and *e*, wrong and right methods of lopping the branch of a tree; *f*, on any thickish branch, make a slight upward cut with the saw from below first; *g*, illustrates pruning terms; *h*, training in a new or 'replacement' leader by tying a new shoot to a cane.

The most elementary pruning is the 'dead-heading' of border flowers, by which we remove spent blooms in order to induce new ones, and this is a form of pruning that should be constantly going on. No plant should be allowed to go to seed unless it is grown specially for its fruits or berries or unless we specially want to gather seed—provided, of course, that the plant is not so big as to make the task unreasonable. We are also unconsciously pruning when we cut flowers for the house, and the canons of pruning should be observed when we do so. Similarly we are 'pruning' when we disbud roses and chrysanthemums, and when we 'pinch out' the growing tip of a seedling snapdragon or wallflower. However, what we are really concerned with in this chapter are hard-wooded plants—trees, shrubs, roses, fruits, climbers, while hedges of course are a subject to themselves.

This brings us to the really important topic of a plant's habits and behaviour. It is fundamental to note whether a plant blooms or fruits on:

(a) 'new wood', i.e. whether it sends out a new branch or shoot and produces flower on that shoot all in the same season; or

(b) 'old wood', i.e. a branch that grows this year but does not bear flower till next year, or even later.

This is the foundation of most pruning.

Broadly speaking, we may say that trees and shrubs that bloom in the spring or before midsummer do so on old wood developed the previous season, and those that bloom after midsummer do so on new wood. Thus Forsythia blooms on old wood in early spring and its summer energies are devoted to developing the wood for next year. On the other hand, Buddleia (the sorts with purple plumes) blooms in August on new wood that has been developing since the spring of the same year.

Other plants, again, may flower on both old and young wood, such as some of the Clematis. Gooseberries fruit on both one-year-old wood and two-years-old wood.

This follows fairly logically upon what has been said before. In general terms the period for pruning is when the plant has completed one cycle of growth and is about to start another. Thus a raspberry and a rambler rose of the Dorothy Perkins type bloom and fruit on one-year-old wood, so as soon as they have completed their purpose the old canes are cut right down to the ground, to direct maximum vigour into the new wood, which has been shooting up at the same time and on which next year's crop will appear.

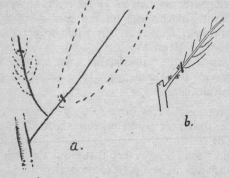

Pruning: a, pruning a spent flowering shoot lightly results in several short new shoots—hard pruning gives two or more long, strong ones (e.g. Forsythia); *b*, illustrates the phrase: 'Prune old flowered wood to three buds of its base' (e.g. Broom).

So in general we may say that trees and shrubs that bloom before midsummer, as Forsythia, the flowering Quinces, winter Jasmine, Kerria, some Ceanothus, are pruned immediately they have finished blooming, in order that all the summer's vigour will be directed into the new growth for next year. Plants at the other end of the time-scale, blooming after midsummer, are pruned in winter dormancy, often at the end of February, as with Buddleia, other Ceanothus, Potentilla, Hypericum.

On plants that bloom on both old and new wood, the gardener encourages whichever he prefers for early or late blooms, or he adopts a middle course, always remembering the principle of encouraging the newer wood.

On bush roses we take advantage of their happy habit of constantly throwing up new wood by pruning out the old as soon as it has done its task. On plants cultivated for their fruits or berries, such as the apple and the Barberry (Berberis), we naturally do not prune after flowering, but leave the task till winter dormancy, if any pruning at all is necessary.

How to Prune

The old axiom of 'spare the knife and spoil the tree' is not always true except as demonstrated by the experienced hand. The beginner should therefore go easy with the knife until he has felt his way. There are a few basic ordinances that must be obeyed, but beyond these it is a mistake to be dogmatic. One man may want to produce a different result from his neighbour, as with roses. General principles are therefore best, and the intelligent man will soon find how to apply them. In the chapters on roses, flowering shrubs, and fruit will be found specific injunctions where they are necessary, and many indeed, as for Brooms and Lavender, amount to emphatic commandments. The most difficult of all common subjects are the apple and the pear.

Taking first the specific precepts which must be observed in every sort of pruning:

First, if in doubt about pruning, don't.

Always and invariably cut out dead, diseased, and feeble, spindly growths.

Cut back into clean, healthy wood that shows no discoloration or scar.

Remove spent flowers and seed-pods, immediately after flowering, except on: Hydrangeas, plants grown for their berries or fruit, and large trees.

Where branches cross each other, keep the one that will most help in making a shapely plant, and cut out the other or part of it; this applies more especially to roses and fruit trees, and one wouldn't be so fussy on a dense bush such as a Barberry.

Use only sharp tools, and make clean, smooth cuts; never

break the branch of a hard-wooded plant (except cobs and filberts).

Cut always just above a new bud (or 'eye') or flush with the junction of another limb; leave no 'snag' or stub. Choose an eye pointing in the direction in which you want the new shoot to grow—usually an eye pointing outwards.

Always make either a sloping or a vertical cut, never a horizontal one on which moisture can lie.

Treat all large cuts—certainly anything more than $\frac{1}{2}$-in. diameter—with a proprietary wound-healer, such as Arbrex.

Normally do not prune evergreen shrubs at all, except for the removal of seed-pods and dead or feeble wood. If the shrub throws an abnormally long shoot, or otherwise gets out of shape, prune late in April, or, if it is then in flower, or bud, immediately afterwards.

Garden trees need no pruning, except for shaping. Birch, walnut, vines, and liquidambar bleed if cut after mid-winter and vines if cut after January 1st.

That is as far as one may dogmatise unequivocally. The more general precepts deal with the awkward problems of which wood should be pruned out? and how hard should it be pruned?

First, build up a shapely form and one suited to the purpose, whether it be a cordon apple, or a Pyracantha hugging the wall, or a rounded bushy Lilac clothed to the ground. Whatever its shape, the plant should be symmetrical and have the quality of grace—not lop-sided, nor tufted, nor gaunt and scrawny. Balance is the thing.

Next, stimulate, year by year, the maximum display of flowers, fruit or berry, by the encouragement of new wood at the expense of the old. In some instances nearly all the old wood is eliminated yearly—or even more often on bush roses. Here again we differentiate somewhat between early- and late-flowering shrubs.

On *early-flowering* shrubs shorten the spent flowering stems as soon as bloom is over to a point where a strong young shoot is sprouting. Forsythia is an example. On F. suspensa you may cut to within 2 in. or so of the base of the spent shoot yearly, but on other Forsythias it is perhaps safer to treat only a proportion of the shoots so drastically each year, and lightly shorten the remainder. Occasionally cut older stems and boughs harder back still, so as to encourage new growth from low down.

On *late-flowering* shrubs remove altogether any old stem not carrying much new growth and lightly shorten others. Most of these need hard treatment, and some should be cut down nearly to the ground, such as David's Buddleia (the big purple-plumed one), and the Ceanothus Gloire de Versailles.

These are good general guides for use when in doubt, but no more. Quite a number of deciduous bushes, in addition to evergreens and trees, need not be pruned at all, as will be seen from Chapter XV.

Old and neglected bushes must quite certainly have drastic treatment, applying the above principles in more severe degree, the main aim being to get rid of old unproductive spindle-shanks.

TERMS USED IN PRUNING

'Eye.' A young bud. Before it waxes fat, is often identifiable as a pin-head with a little curved wrinkle above, rather like an upper eyelid.

'Leader.' A growth by which a stem or branch extends itself along its own axis or line of advance.

'Lateral.' A shoot springing sideways from any main branch.

'Snag.' A superfluous stump resulting from a cut not having been made far enough back.

Others are included in the chapter on fruit.

PRUNING TOOLS AND THEIR USE

Secateurs. Don't buy cheap rubbish. Treat yourself to a Rolcut, a Wilkinson, or a Felco. The action in use is a squeeze; never twist or wrench secateurs.

A pruning knife, of shape according to fancy.

A pruning saw. Various kinds available; avoid the double-edged ones.

A tree-lopper, which is a two-handed pair of extra-strong secateurs; for thick shoots.

A 'long-arm', for severing high-up twigs.

All cuts with knife or secateur must be clean and smooth, without ragged edges. For any task too thick for secateurs the saw must be called in, and the rough surface it leaves pared smooth with the knife.

For branches of large trees a carpenter's handsaw may be necessary. To prevent the under-surface of the limb splitting as the saw is about to come through, first make a short upward cut with the saw from the under-surface, then saw downwards in the same plane (Sketch, page 90).

Rose 'Golden Wings'

Clematis 'W. E. Gladstone'

Lily 'Enchantment'

Lily 'Thunderbolt'

The ground-hugging rose
R. paulii 'Rosea'

Rose 'Sarah van Fleet'

Magnolia grandiflora

Achillea 'Gold Plate'

Red Hot Pokers (*Kniphofia*)

CHAPTER VIII

PATHS AND TERRACES

PATHS can make or mar a garden. They have a strong tendency to dominate the scene, and they have therefore to be considered as objects of adornment as well as of utility. The best policy is to have as few as possible. This rather curt chapter will deal only with their construction, and I am thinking chiefly of paths, but terraces are constructed in the same way.

There is quite a wide choice of materials, from cheap cinders for kitchen garden paths to expensive 'dressed stone' of rectangular pattern. Surroundings and usage, as well as your pocket, will determine your choice. Where traffic is light, nothing is more acceptable than grass, but for heavy usage, especially where wheelbarrows are to travel frequently, something more durable is necessary. One of the most charming treatments across grass, and quite enough for foot traffic only, is by means of 'stepping stones', which are simply slabs of paving, rectangular or 'crazy', embedded in the turf at intervals of one easy pace. The surface of the stones should lie a shade below the turf level, so that a mower can run over them without harm. The treatment is suitable only across broad expanses of grass.

An inexpensive alternative to the use of stone is to cut out some outlines in the turf to a depth of $2\frac{1}{2}$ in., lift the sods, wet the soil below, pour in concrete and level off smoothly.

Foundations. Where slabs of stone or concrete are the order, I have found that it is totally unnecessary to lay down the heavy foundation of hard core so often prescribed by technical gentlemen. Sometimes I merely dump the slabs straight down on the soil (making sure that it is level), but usually I lay them on a bed of builder's soft sand. This seats them comfortably and makes levelling easier. Paths of this sort easily take the weight of man and barrow or a light roller. Solidity is much improved, however, by filling the gaps between stones and bricks with concrete, using a mix of four parts sand to one of cement.

A foundation of hard core is necessary only for: (*a*) gravel, stone chippings, and asphalt; (*b*) heavy traffic (cars); (*c*) soft ground over a high water table. Where such is needed the drill is this:

Remove the fertile top soil and stack it somewhere for future use. Drive in levelling pegs at intervals, and use a spirit-level laid on a rigid board at all stages. Make the bottom of the trench a trifle narrower than the top. Line the sides of the trench with brick, metal sheets, wooden boards well treated with preservative or 2-in. concrete walls—an essential first step.

Now lay a course of 'hard core'—broken brick or clinker— 4 in. deep all along the trench. Provided it runs the right way, this course of hard core, besides its purpose as a foundation, may often serve as a drainage channel, and side drains can be fed into it. For this purpose it is further improved by laying small field drains along the side, especially under gravel paths.

Rectangular Paving. 'Dressed' rectangular paving stones make the handsomest of all paths and terraces, and their formality is softened if the slabs are of different sizes. Old pavement-stones from the streets can often be obtained. Lay them on a bed of sand and joint them in cement, leaving a few gaps for paving plants if you like.

Crazy Paving is the fashion of the generation and is apt sometimes to become not merely crazy, but lunatic. So also is the gardener, when confronted with several tons of stone jigsaw puzzle. But in the right situation it has a charm of its own. Lay them in the same manner as rectangular slabs, the cement jointing being important, leaving gaps for paving plants, which look most attractive in crazy. Set aside all stones with straight edges for the sides of the path, and put the largest stones in the centre at intervals of one stride.

For quantities, reckon one ton of—

'old York' slabs, 2 in. thick, per 8 sq yds;
'quarried York', $1\frac{1}{2}$ in. thick, per 12 sq yds;
broken concrete (non-slip) per 10 sq yds.

I refrain from quoting prices, as they vary in different parts of the country and each year cost more. Broken concrete is the cheapest.

Brick. Weathered red bricks are delightful for the quiet by-ways, being better suited to the narrow track than to the broad sweep. Bed them well in sand as for paving-stones, but lime-mortar may be used in lieu of cement for jointing. The bricks must be hard-baked, and those rejected by the brickworks as over-baked are admirable. They can be laid in a variety of patterns, edgewise or on the flat, and can look awfully well in a mixed design with square paving. A square yard needs 32 bricks of normal size ($9 \times 4\frac{1}{2} \times 3$ in.) if laid flat, 48 if laid on edge.

Gravel is much the best treatment for a broad drive, but requires some skill in the making. For a drive that may have to take the weight of a car, make the foundation a full 8 in. deep.

Spread a good 2 in. of the gravel on the hard core in a moist but not sodden condition. Rake repeatedly to get an even surface without pockets or corrugations, but with a very slight camber—1 in. in 3 ft is enough. Water slightly and roll thoroughly. Rake again to correct inevitable flaws, and continue rolling and raking till you are satisfied. Then treat the surface with a waterproof bituminous dressing, such as Colas, and finish with a sprinkling of fine chippings or pea gravel.

When making good an old gravel path break up the old surface all over to a depth of an inch with a pick, to ensure that the new gravel binds with the old.

Cobbles are very agreeable to the eye, but are not kind to high-heeled shoes. They are best employed for varying a pattern of stone, brick, or concrete slabs, or for the guttering of a path. They have to be bedded in a good 2 in. of concrete. Get the 'hen's egg' size and reckon nearly 2 cwt per square yard.

Asphalt. For utility uses only, such as in the kitchen garden, where it is efficient but ugly. On a sound bed of hard core only 1 in. is necessary. Tamp it down well and give it a distinct camber, or it will be wrecked by the freezing of surface pools.

Concrete in its solid and amorphous form is also an abomination except for severely utility purposes. It can, however, be perfectly acceptable made up in separate blocks with a little skill and artistry to imitate square or crazy paving.

Supposing that the path to be made is 3 ft wide, select a flat piece of ground and lay down a frame of 2-in.-thick timbers, $2\frac{1}{2}$ in. broad, on edge parallel to each other 3 ft apart, and of any convenient length. Fix it rigidly to the ground with pegs. Between the trough so made spread sand to a depth of at least $\frac{1}{2}$ in., levelling with a spirit-level.

Having mixed the concrete, pour it into the trough to a depth of 2 in. Level the surface with a straight-edge board which will fully span the outside frame, first using a sawing motion, then an easy up-and-down dabbing motion.

An hour or two later cut the concrete into slabs of the desired size and shape with a cement trowel, being sure to cut right through to the underlying bed of sand.

Leave the slabs where they are for four or five days to set and harden. When dry, number the slabs with chalk or pencil, and carry them off in the right order to where they are designed to lie.

If rectangular paving is desired, fit narrow strips of timber across the frame before pouring in the mixture

The same method can be adapted for making small slabs in imitation of stone for building pergolas, or other small 'rock' works.

To Mix Concrete. For a solid path in the kitchen garden, garage wash-down, etc., a good general-purposes mix is four parts shingle, two sand and one cement. Insist on fresh cement.

For smooth surfacing and for jointing between stones and bricks, use four of sand to one of cement.

To mix, use a flat, clean surface, spread the sand in a roughly flat heap and lay the cement atop. Thoroughly mix them together with a shovel, till the whole is of an even colour without streaks. Now spread the shingle or chippings, if required, and again mix the whole evenly.

Scrape out a rough hollow in the centre of the heap and pour in a little water through a rose. Mix the whole together with a shovel very thoroughly and intimately, stopping every now and then to add a little more water. Use no more water than is necessary to form a paste of the consistency of a very stiff porridge.

Concrete can be tinted if desired by adding a very small dose of one of the recognised pigments, such as Venetian Red; this is often useful for the jointing between stones or bricks.

Edgings. Paths in the kitchen garden or along the edge of flower-beds need some form of kerb to prevent the soil from constantly spilling over on to the path. Unless box or other dwarf hedging is grown, the kerb can be made from bricks, thick tarred planks, concrete, or imitation stone walling, such as Thakeham or Marshallite. Another very good material, strong and of good appearance, but irregular in size, is old granite sett from city streets, if they can be obtained.

Whatever is used, the surface should be level, not jagged—as one often sees with bricks set slantwise. Bricks really need laying two deep and setting in cement or mortar. Planking should be thick, buried to two-thirds of its breadth and braced with stout pegs. A concrete edging should be 2 in. thick (using the pure sand-and-cement mix mentioned above) and laid to a depth of 3 or 4 in. below ground. It can be laid *in situ* by putting down a light timber 'shuttering' or frame on the spot, kept in place by pegs, and pouring the mix into the trough so made.

Where a border or bed is more than a few inches higher than an adjoining path, the most attractive treatment is to build up a little dry stone wall, but this is not cheap, and imitation stone slabs can be made of concrete instead.

CHAPTER IX

THE SMALL GREENHOUSE AND OTHER GLASSWORKS

GENERAL MANAGEMENT AND USES—WHAT TO GROW—
FRAMES—CLOCHES—SOIL HEATING

General Management and Uses

A 'BIT OF GLASS' is a tremendous asset in any garden and of course for all 'serious' gardening is a necessity. A greenhouse, garden frame, a few cloches, even a glass porch over a doorway enables the range of one's efforts to be extended and cheapened. But it must be recognised at once that without some degree of heating the possibilities are extremely limited. We classify greenhouses into 'hot houses' (which are outside my brief), 'cool' ones, and cold ones. The cool house must be capable of sustaining 40° F in the coldest weather as the barest minimum, and 45° gives a much wider scope. The snag about the entirely unheated house is not only that it admits frost, but also that it admits excessive dampness, particularly fog, at a time of year when damp is most injurious. Thus any form of heating which will keep out frost and damp immediately multiplies the dividends of a greenhouse.

Many people do this quite successfully with special types of oil-heaters which are readily available, and that was how I started myself many years ago. It sufficed to keep alive some things in pots and boxes that would otherwise have succumbed to frost and damp and enabled nurselings to steal a march of a few weeks upon the outside weather. Today I dare say that the ideal thing for the busy amateur without a regular and knowledgeable gardener is electrical heating. Units can be bought for use in the tiniest structure, and a thermostat is a

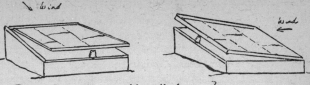

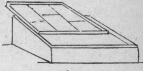

Right Methods of Ventilating Frames

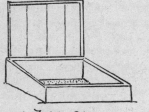

Fully Open

Wrong

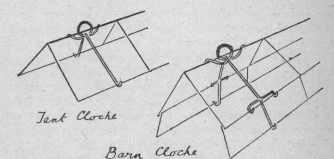

Tent Cloche

Barn Cloche

Frames and Cloches.

further blessing. In a small place the expense is not outrageous and certainly less, I would say, than the cost of seedlings and plants, particularly as it enables you to raise flowers for the dwelling-house at a season when the florist's productions are pretty extravagant. Thus with the introduction of only sufficient heat to constitute a 'cool' house the prospect immediately begins to open up.

The tubular form is usually the most convenient, connected direct to the mains. The loading is about 60 watts per foot, and for a small house a pair suffices if the total loading is about 700 watts. Fit it with a waterproof thermostat of the rod type in the coldest part of the house. Where the tubular form may be difficult to fit, the low-voltage strip-heating system meets the case. Thermostats may safely be set a good 5° below the temperatures culturally advised.

The amount of heat necessary is much influenced by the siting of the greenhouse. For general purposes a span- or ridged-type house (which is the best) should have the ridge running north and south. The lean-to type and the garden frame should if possible be on a wall facing south for general purposes. Old-fashioned wood-frame structures (especially if you can run to hardwood) are really better than the modern metal ones, and the whole thing must shut up tight and close for fumigation and the exclusion of draughts and drips. Avoid sliding doors. Hinged ventilators in the roof are essential, and side ventilation is also desirable. Fix a rain-water tank (with overflow) inside the house, fed from guttering under the eaves.

Inside the structure there can be a narrow border of good loam at ground level, especially for perennials such as climbers. More important is a staging of open wooden slats for general use, and some sort of contrivance close up to the roof for accommodating seed-boxes. One great boon is to fit some exterior roof-blinds for mitigating both the fiercest suns and fiercest frosts; and a wire-netting grill over lean-to structures will break the fall of snow from the roof of the dwelling-house.

Whatever sort of glass structure is used, there are certain basic ordinances to be obeyed, not all of which are susceptible of precise definition.

First and above all is cleanliness. Glass structures are terrible breeding-houses for both insect pests and fungal diseases. The whole structure must be washed down and scrubbed inside at least once a year, and fumigation will be necessary from time to time. Pots and boxes, and the crocks used in them, must also be clean. No dirt or rubbish should be allowed to accumulate and all dead or dying foliage should be removed.

Next is ventilation, and this is very much a question of experience and judgement. Broadly speaking, for the range of subjects with which the non-expert is concerned, the first rule is to ventilate very freely, especially from the ventilators in the roof. A free circulation of fresh air, but without draughts, should always be encouraged. At high noon in summer everything will be open, on cold winter nights everything will be shut, and between those two extremes one cannot prescribe beyond the reminder that the things to be excluded are frost, draughts and excessive winter dampness.

Humidity is a factor closely related to ventilation. In winter the general rule is to keep the atmosphere and the plants on the dry side. The colder the weather the less the watering. Water plants only sufficiently to prevent them from flagging, and turn on the heat when the air becomes raw and moisture-laden. In high summer the rule is the very reverse—sprinkle the floor, walls and staging with water each morning, syringe the foliage, and look over all pots and boxes to ensure that the plants do not lack moisture and so suffer from excessive transpiration. The standard test with clay pots (it does not work so well on plastic ones) is to tap it with knuckle or small wooden mallet, and if the pot rings hollow, water is needed. To overdo greenhouse watering, however, invites mildew, red spider, and thrips.

These elementary rules show that a greenhouse is by no means a thing that can take care of itself. Let us face the fact that it needs a great deal of attention. The house that, say, in autumn needs to have but one light opened before master leaves for the office, may need to have everything fully opened by noon, but shut up again a good hour before sundown to retain warmth. For these emergencies one must call up the feminine reserves or install an all-automatic house, in which the heating, ventilation, watering, and screening are all done as by a fairy wand (and at a fancy price).

In small places another problem is what *not* to grow. There is at first a natural impulse to get in everything the place will hold—a grape vine, tomatoes, seedlings, flowering plants, bulbs, and so on. But with only one house it can't be done. One of the earliest lessons to be learnt is that one must select; for plants vary greatly in their needs, especially in temperature and humidity. A vine, once it has started into leaf, virtually shuts the door to any other lodgers, for its foliage casts all into shade; Begonias, however, will accept these conditions, and in the vine's dormancy early seedlings and bulbs in pots will be welcome visitors. In a small place a vine is not really economical and tomatoes are much more profitable and less trouble. After these, Chrysanthemums will handsomely increase the greenhouse dividends, especially if there is enough heat to keep out the frost. After them in turn—and here a trifle of heat is essential—one can enjoy freesias, cinerarias, azaleas, cyclamen, and so on.

Greenhouses or glazed porches that open off a living-room often challenge the gardener's skill for adorning a naked prospect. Provided that the glass does not perversely face a cold quarter, the gardener can meet this challenge, even without heat, from at least early March to late November with a programme starting with bulbs, going on with those hardy and half-hardy annuals that take kindly to pots, and ending with Chrysanthemums; and he could include one or two near-hardy climbers such as the lively blue Plumbago, and, of course, a climbing Rose or two. An entirely utilitarian programme in an unheated house would be confined to tomatoes in summer, the starting of Dahlia, Begonia and potato tubers, and the germination of hardy and some half-hardy seeds a little earlier than they would outdoors but a little later than with heat.

Earlier chapters have dealt with the raising of seed in boxes and pots. New pots must be soaked in water for several hours and dried off again before use. Always use John Innes Seed Compost, or the Levington or Croxden soil-less ones, for starting seeds. For potting-on the nurselings use the John Innes Potting Compost or, again, the potting grade soil-less ones.

Remember to pot hard-wooded plants, and those of slow growth, very firmly, ramming the soil down with the butt of a trowel, but other plants less firmly. Nurselings in small pots are 'potted-on' into bigger ones when their roots have filled up the first one.

What to Grow

Here is a very short list of plants for the decoration of small greenhouses, cold or warmed. For a rather more comprehensive study for new gardeners, I recommend *The Small Greenhouse*, by H. Witham Fogg, in the Pan series.

ANNUALS

Many of the hardy and half-hardy ones do well. A normal spring sowing gives an early summer display, but many can with great success be sown in August–September to give a show in spring. After germination, prick-on into small pots and then pot-on to larger ones, the 5-in. pot being suitable for the majority.

Pride of place is won by the lovely 'Butterfly Flower', Schizanthus. Its nickname aptly describes its dainty beauty. Get a packet of mixed colours from a first-class seedsman, of a tall or dwarf strain. Sow in August or September, and again in January if you like. No heat needed. Keep them close up to the light while young, and pot on as necessary. Pinch out the tips after first potting, and feed with liquid manure.

Other good and easy annuals (*see* more fully in Part II) are: Clarkia (one of the best), sow in March for June blooming, or in August for May blooming, sowing two or three seeds direct into small pots (not seed-boxes) and moving the best on to 5-in. pots; Godetia, similar treatment; the Cornflower Jubilee Gem; the trumpeting Salpiglossis; Antirrhinum, sow in August or March; the beautiful little annual Delphinium Blue Butterfly; Forget-me-not; Bartonia; Nicotiana; Petunia.

BULBS

Most of the popular bulbs do excellently in pots, particularly Hyacinths, Daffodils, Tulips of all sorts, bulbous Irises, Crocuses, Begonia (in summer keep a rather damp atmosphere,

107

and screen from fiercest sun), the Harlequin-coloured Tigridia and Gladiolus. Many lilies are also easy enough, particularly Lilium regale.

Those who can take the chill off their greenhouses, however, should make **Freesias** their very first pick among bulbs. Their lovely clustered trumpets, so richly scented, can now be had in a range of sparkling colours, and they last wonderfully in a vase as well as in the greenhouse. For a succession of bloom, pot up a few at a time from August to October, putting about six in a 5-in. pot. Just cover the corms. Put them outdoors for two months, perferably in a cold frame, keeping them just moist, and covering them only if frost threatens. Then take them into the greenhouse. A temperature of about 50° suits them.

Other good bulbs for our purposes, given a modicum of warmth, are:

Clivia. Scarlet, lilyform, scented flowers in big clusters, of easy culture, blooming in spring. Plant in March in good soil. Ease off the water in October and start again in February. They like being pot-bound, but can be increased by division.

Lachenalia. Elegant spires of drooping temple bells in yellow or orange, of easy culture. Raise as Freesias. For pots or hanging baskets.

Scarborough-lily. (Valotta purpurea). Showy scarlet trumpets in late summer. Of easy culture; needing very little heat. Pot the bulbs in March, one to a 5-in. pot. Water stingily till growth begins, then fairly freely. Give them sun. After flowering almost stop watering from November to March. Very nice room plants.

CLIMBERS

The greenhouse, if large enough, has a wide choice of handsome climbers, which are best grown in the greenhouse border rather than in pots. Roses come high on the list, four of the best being the grand old fragrant yellow Maréchal Niel, the chaste white Niphetos, the pink Climbing Ophelia and Paul's Scarlet. Where there is enough artificial warmth to maintain a winter minimum of 40°, however, preference even over roses might be claimed for the beautiful Lapageria rosea, which, when trained up between the rafters, enriches the scene with chains of festive red bells. It needs shade and an acid soil. Water it very freely from April to September and syringe daily.

Next I would put Plumbago capensis, which throws out Cambridge-blue flowers in trusses like those of Phlox. Easy and decorative, and all the better for just a little winter warmth. Water and syringe daily throughout summer, and prune in March.

For smaller greenhouses, with the minimum of heat, the following few climbers offer themselves. The first three are very easily raised from seed sown in early spring and are so nearly hardy that, outdoors, they are treated as half-hardy annuals, though in fact perennials.

Eccremocarpus scaber. Sprays of jolly orange tubes from lacy foliage. Grows 10 ft in a season. Survives mild winters outdoors.

Cobaea scandens. Large, wide-mouthed bells that start white, turn mauve and deepen to purple. Sow the seeds on edge. Easily grows 15 ft in a season.

Maurandya. Large trumpets in purple, rose, or white. Not too rampant. Cut back hard in February. The usual one is properly called M. barclaiana.

Hoya. Tightly packed clusters, like pink snowballs, of small, waxen florets, borne on slim and flexible twining stems, amenable to being twisted about anyhow at your will. Looks tender, but isn't.

GENERAL

Astilbe. The feathery plumes of the astilbes are delightful in greenhouse pots (Chapter XI).

Azalea. Pot into 48s or 32s in September in acid soil, peat, and leaf-mould, firmly rammed. Stand in rain-water up to soil level till soaked and rest them in cool shade for ten days. Then house them, raising the heat gradually to 65° or more. Syringe the foliage daily and keep the soil moist. Next May, sink the pots outdoors in shade.

Bleeding Heart (Dicentra spectabilis). This graceful

hardy perennial (*see* Chapter XI) can be lodged in 6-in. pots to flower early. Heat is not essential, but of course brings it out earlier still.

Broom. The pretty little bush, animated for many weeks with golden pea-flowers, usually called Genista fragrans, is of the easiest culture and needs no heat. Grown cold, it blooms in April. From June to September stand it outdoors in the sun and keep it watered. Multiply by cuttings in spring or autumn, and when established pinch out to get bushy growth.

Busy-Lizzie (Impatiens sultanii). Popular, free-blooming plants of the easiest culture where a winter temperature of a good 50° can be maintained. Water liberally in summer, meanly in winter. Full sun. Can be planted outdoors June 1st. Trim back old plants in February and repot. Easily multiplied by spring or summer cuttings in sandy soil in some warmth.

Cineraria. With enough warmth to maintain a winter minimum of 40°, these beautiful daisy-form flowers of many colours are not difficult to raise. There are large-flowered sorts, the small, starry stellatas, and good intermediates. The law and the prophets on Cineraria culture is this: at all stages keep them *cool* and well ventilated, never over-water them, never bury the plant's tiny crown when transplanting. For a spring display, sow *very thinly* in boxes in a frame under a north wall in late July. Prick off into deeper boxes, move on singly into 3-in. pots, and finally into 6-in. pots. Never close the frame entirely except for a day or two after transplanting. Move into the greenhouse early in October. Continue ventilating as freely as weather allows, but from now onwards be very stingy with the water. Kill the leaf-mining maggot with a pin, and spray with derris against greenfly.

For a winter display, seed must be sown indoors in April in a temperature of 55° or more.

Fuchsias of the less hardy sorts are perfectly easy, given just enough warmth to keep out frost. The dwarfer ones are the more suitable, and the pendulous varieties are as charming on the greenhouse bench as they are in hanging baskets.

Heliotrope or 'Cherry Pie'. Definite heat is needed for

propagation, but if plants are bought the adults will be safe during winter with a minimum temperature of 40°. Those that have been planted outdoors (which is done the first week of June) must be brought inside at the end of September, put into the smallest pots that will take their roots, and pruned fairly hard.

Marguerite. In the unheated place Chrysanthemum frutescens is very useful for summer decoration. Will last for some years, growing bigger and bigger. Multiply by cuttings of young non-flowering shoots in spring or late August in a propagating frame.

Pelargonium. Soi-disant 'geranium'. The main types for the non-expert are the Zonal-leaved Pelargoniums (which are those commonly seen in bedding-out schemes), the larger Irenes, the daintier ivy-leaved Pelargonium, which is a trailer or semi-climber, very decorative for tumbling down over the front of a pot, a window-box, or a hanging basket, and the charming miniatures. All have an uncommonly long season of bloom if dead-headed.

In the greenhouse give Pelargoniums the amplest ventilation in spring and summer; in the winter a temperature of 42° is desirable. Those grown outdoors must be brought in by the end of September. Nodal cuttings taken in August strike easily in pots either in greenhouse or frame, allowing them to wilt slightly before insertion. Move them separately into $3\frac{1}{2}$-in. pots in March, and when these are full of root move on into 5-in. pots. Cuttings may also be taken in spring for rooting in the greenhouse. These can be induced to flower in the winter by continually picking off the flower-buds as they appear. Stand them outdoors in a frame from June to September. There are quantities of named varieties to choose from.

Outdoors, the only point to make is that Pelargoniums should have a rather poor, gritty soil and, preferably, full sun.

The superb Regal Pelargoniums, with their flared colours, need rather more skill, but not much more warmth. The main thing is to pinch out the growing shoot at about five leaves and repeat the operation on the four new shoots that result. Also trim back the spent flower heads to a point of new growth.

Water fairly freely and feed with a general fertiliser when in full growth.

Primula. Of the winter-flowering greenhouse types, P. sinensis is the loveliest, malacoides is the easiest; obconica and the golden kewensis are also charming. Malacoides and kewensis need only just enough warmth to expel frost. All are treated as annuals.

A temperature of about 60° is needed for the usual March sowing, but malacoides can be sown in May or June with no trouble. Prick off the seedlings when they have three leaves into pans or trays, then into 2½-in. pots, and finally into 5-in. pots. Plant the crowns very shallow, so that water does not lodge in them. Keep in the greenhouse or frame all summer, but shade them from hot sun. Water moderately in summer and very sparingly in winter. After flowering the plants must be discarded.

The Frame

The greenhouse is by no means essential in a garden, but the frame, or at least the cloche, is. Its uses are manifold—to raise early seed, especially for the kitchen garden, for cuttings, for hardening-off non-hardy plants and for over-wintering them, for growing late and early lettuces, and so on. Indeed, one frame alone is by no means enough except in the smallest places.

Frames with brick or concrete sides are best, but wooden ones are acceptable, and the portable wooden Dutch frame has a special value. For cuttings a shady place is needed, but for general purposes the site should be in full sun, and better still if sheltered from the north by a wall, fence, or hedge. Have it close to the greenhouse if you can. It can be fitted with electric soil-heating cables for special uses, and indeed in every way can be treated as a small greenhouse. Thus by keeping it sprayed inside one can create that close atmosphere needed for soft-wood cuttings. Perfect control of watering, of ventilation, and of shading from hot sun when necessary is given by the frame.

Normally, as in the greenhouse, the fullest ventilation should be given at all times, according to the weather. This is done by lifting (*not* sliding) the lid, either to its fullest extent in fine weather, or propped open a mere inch or two, and of course completely closed on frosty days and nights. Open it always in a direction away from the wind. For really tough winters, Archangel mats or thick sacking should be spread over the top.

Seedlings in pots or boxes should be kept as close up to the light as possible, by propping them on bricks or inverted flower-pots.

By making up a special bed of soil, out-of-season vegetables can be grown in the frame, such as lettuces, carrots, and radishes. Winter violets may also be indulged in, lifting the plants from their outdoor quarters in September, and filling up the frame with soil so that the plants are close up to the light.

Cloches

These are a real treasure to the small gardener. Their crowning uses are in the kitchen garden—to bring on early vegetables, to continue the growth of late ones into autumn, to over-winter lettuces for early spring maturity, to bring on early strawberries, late tomatoes, and haricot beans when summer is over, and so on. They have, of course, similar uses in the flower garden, and, like the frame, are valuable for providing some closeness of atmosphere for cuttings.

The cheapest type of continuous cloche is the 'tent' form, which is adequate for raising seed and for plants such as lettuces when small, but it will soon be found that the larger 'barn' type is wanted. One may reckon that cloches allow you in spring to steal about three weeks' march on nature. They are grand for early lettuces, peas and French beans. Their use is simplicity itself, but a few tips will save buying experience.

In cold weather block up the ends of the 'runs' of cloches with sheets of ordinary glass. Do likewise for even single cloches when used for cuttings.

If the soil is too wet for sowing, put the cloches in position ten days ahead to dry off the surface.

Keep them clean, so that light is not obscured. When not in use, stack them in nests on their ends.

Watering is the obvious problem, since the cloche keeps off rain. The answer is to dig the soil fairly deep, work in plenty of granulated peat into the top spit, and decayed organic matter down below, and to wet the soil thoroughly a day or so before sowing or planting if at all on the dry side. Thereafter, the rain shed by the cloche and percolating through the soil laterally will give enough moisture in a normal season. If not, one can put on the hose for prolonged spells without moving the glass, but in persistent drought it will, of course, be necessary to move them all.

In prolonged warm weather lift a cloche or two here and there for extra ventilation. Discard the cloches when the power of the sun waxes strong in full summer. Glass cloches are far better than plastic ones.

Soil Heating

Inexpensive low-voltage electrical equipments are now available for heating soil either in the greenhouse or outdoors. Their special value to the small gardener is to provide 'bottom heat' in a propagating bench in the greenhouse for bringing on one's own half-hardy seeds, such as Zinnia and tomato, and for rooting soft-wood cuttings. Another valuable use is to warm the soil for tomatoes when grown in a border in the greenhouse, bringing them on nice and early.

These equipments use a negligible amount of current and save warming the whole house. They require a transformer, of course, but no thermostat, for, since the temperature of soil changes so gradually, ordinary hand-switches and occasional observation of the temperature with a thermometer in the soil are sufficient. You may have to switch on overnight only. In a heated house a 100-watt transformer does for a bench of about 24 sq ft, or 15–20 sq ft in an unheated one. Temperatures should be kept from 55° to 60°.

The propagating bench or box is simply a small garden frame, or home-made glazed structure, erected on the greenhouse staging with 6 in. or more of either seed or cuttings compost, according to purpose. Or you may have simply a bed of peat and plunge pots and seed-pans in it. The electric wires are laid in sand or peat at the bottom of the box, and the soil must be kept moist. Ventilate the frame occasionally. For a tomato bed, pre-warm the soil.

PART II: FLOWERS

Now we emerge. From the earth to the fruits thereof. 'The folded leaf is wooed from out the bud', and we arrive in such a jocund company as makes even a modern poet sometimes gay.

I have picked the company with some care. It is not helpful to the initiate seeking positive guidance to offer him a multitude of choices. Worthy plants, and worthy plants alone, are admitted here, few of them difficult in appropriate soils and circumstances. Study the catalogues critically, even sceptically. Avoid the cheap-jack and the 'bargain lot', and cock a suspicious eye at over-effusive blurbs. Facts are what you want. Does it tolerate lime? Will it stand shade? How big does it grow? Is it hardy? And so on.

It is an old saying that the apprentice starts gardening with annuals, journeys on to herbaceous plants, and when he has reached the status of master-gardener turns to flowering trees and shrubs; unless he is lured into those crevices where the pygmy sirens of the rock garden dwell. Don't tread that path. Begin with shrubs and little trees, which are easy and permanent and make a backcloth for whatever else you like to show upon your stage. Lay out an herbaceous or mixed border, rose-beds, a carnation bed (separate, please), and use your annuals for filling, for the 'odd spot', or for little bedding schemes; not all annuals are easy by any means.

Finally, *label your plants durably*, especially shrubs, roses, and clematis; it is vital for the purpose of pruning, which is one of the secrets of successful gardening. For general use I commend the Hartley labels—they are cheap, enduring, adaptable.

In the appendices will be found some classifications of plants to suit various conditions and soils.

117

CHAPTER X

ANNUALS AND BIENNIALS

BEDDING—THE BEST ANNUALS AND BIENNIALS

In this chapter I shall deal with: hardy annuals (h.a.), half-hardy annuals (h.h.a.), and hardy biennials (h.b.), and shall include those gay favourites which, though they are not botanically within those classes, are culturally treated as though they were, such as Antirrhinums and Wallflowers.

Though repetition is a literary sin, I shall for emphasis say again that if you really look for that 'crowded holiday of scent and bloom' that the annual and biennial can give you, you must give them good cultivation just as much as you would to their longer-lived brethren. There are only a few exceptions. The popular notion that you have only to sprinkle a few seeds about the place to get a 'riot of colour' is entirely mistaken. Give them, therefore, ground that is well drained, deeply dug, and reasonably fed with organic foods. Most of them want plenty of sun, and I implore you not to crowd them too closely together. The result of such treatment will be bonny plants full of blossom, instead of the scraggy starvelings so often seen. Among annuals this is especially true of Clarkia, Larkspur, and Chrysanthemums, which when grown in deeply dug and well manured soil will astonish people who have never treated them that way.

Plants that are naturally bushy, such as Wallflower and Antirrhinums, should be pinched out when a few inches high to induce shrubbiness, but those of a different habit, such as Larkspur and Stock, should be left alone. When in doubt, refrain. Most plants in these classes need staking at a very early stage with twiggy sticks. Pick off all dead blossom persistently to encourage further blooming, though some sorts, such as Stocks, make no second effort.

As a rule, annuals and biennials look best in their own beds, but many can also be used to fill up blanks in the border or partnered with spring bulbs, or used as edgings. Foxgloves and Evening Primroses are entirely right among shrubs, and Canterbury Bell takes her place with dignity and grace in the herbaceous border.

'Stopping' or 'pinching' some young plants (e.g. Antirrhinum) makes them sprout more vigorously.

The term 'F₁ Hybrid' will be met in the better catalogues. These are hybrids raised afresh every year by controlled cross-pollination, as they do not themselves produce true-to-type seed. They cost a bit more than other seed but are good.

HARDY ANNUALS

The best results come from sowing direct into the plants' permanent quarters. If beds are occupied at sowing time, many can be raised in seed-boxes, or in a reserve bed, but some do not transplant well, such as Larkspur, annual Poppies, Californian Poppies, annual Chrysanthemums. If sowing in a box, use a John Innes Compost or a modern soil-less one.

For sowing in the open, dig the bed well in advance, allow the soil to settle, and prepare a fine seed-bed by treading and raking. The usual time for sowing is late March, if weather permits, but any time up to the end of April will suit; if delayed longer many will have but a short season of bloom. For the reasons already given in Chapter VI, sowing 'at stations' is better than broadcasting.

The hardiest of the annuals can also be sown in later summer (about mid-August) to over-winter and provide early bloom for next year. Those that will stand this treatment are often called 'winter annuals' as a convenient term.

For those who would like a ready-made selection of hardy annuals, I should say that the pick of them is: Sweet Pea (in a class by itself), Larkspur, Godetia, Love-in-a-Mist, the Rose Mallow, and Clarkia. But there are some excellent ones that are little known, are just as delightful, and that would give a gay diversity to our gardens if more widely grown; of such are the annual Delphinium Blue Butterfly, the Gentian-blue Phacelia campanularia, and Bartonia.

HALF-HARDY ANNUALS

These must generally be raised in gentle heat in March, or they will mature too late: otherwise they must be got as seedlings from a nursery at the end of May, and this is what the beginner is best advised to do. To raise your own, sow in boxes or pans and prick off into other boxes, using the same composts as before. Before being planted in their permanent quarters they must be 'hardened off', which means accustoming them to the colder outdoor conditions by degrees. The process consists in opening up the greenhouse or frame gradually more and more according to the weather, shutting off the heat about the end of March if the season is normal, and finally leaving the plants outdoors altogether for about ten days before planting. Hardening-off should not be hurried, and any risk of frost must be avoided, especially at night. The earliest safe time for planting out half-hardy subjects is the first week of June—'the first week-end after the Derby' was the rule that my old gardener taught me, though I must say that in the South nowadays one takes a week or two's licence and risk. The use of cloches is a great help, and plants can be got out into permanent quarters some three weeks earlier beneath their shelter.

Biennials

These provide some of our bravest flowers and are pretty easy. Sow some time in June, or a bit later in the South, in well-prepared nursery beds. Sow thinly in drills. As soon as the plants are big enough to handle, prick off into good soil in a reserve bed in straight lines at distances appropriate to the size of the mature plant—say 5 in. for Wallflowers, and 9 in. for Canterbury Bells. They will be ready to go into their permanent quarters in early autumn.

Bedding

To bed out means to fill a flower-bed with plants already well advanced in growth, and often actually in flower. Characteristically, such plants are the semi-hard ones that have to live under glass till June. Most famous of the bedders, I suppose, is the Pelargonium (or 'Geranium'), often in dual marriage with the Calceolaria and Lobelia, though they marry even more gladly nowadays with Petunias, Antirrhinums, and Marigolds. Without your own warm greenhouse, you must get Pelargoniums from a nursery, and so you must the beautiful Heliotrope (Cherry Pie) and Verbena. The jocund Begonia, which you will find dealt with in the chapter on bulbs, you can raise yourself as a rule.

Flowers from this chapter that make splendid summer bedding schemes, according to one's taste, are the scarlet Salvia, Antirrhinum, Zinnia, Drummond's Phlox, Nemesia, Ageratum, Petunia, and Stock. All can be bedded out from the seed-boxes into which they were pricked out, but if you can get them grown-on into pots, they will unfurl their banners all the sooner.

There are also spring bedding schemes, which are planted out in autumn. Bulbs usually take first place. There is still nothing more lovely for spring bedding than the old marriage of the pink Tulip Clara Butt with the azure of Forget-me-not.

Wallflowers, Brompton-Stocks, Polyanthus, and Auriculas also make very fine spring bedding.

The Best Annuals and Biennials

The following list of varieties contains a small selection only of the more meritorious. The more difficult sorts, the very fleeting, and the less interesting are omitted. Named varieties are far too numerous to quote in this chapter, especially as nurseries have the annoying habit of calling a variety 'So-and-So's Perfection', or something of the sort. I have assumed that the best-known kinds need no description.

Ageratum (h.h.a.). One of the best pygmy edging or carpeting plants, embellished with toy powder-puffs in varying shades of blue or mauve. Get an F_1 hybrid or a variety such as Blue Mink. Spacing 6 in.

Alyssum maritimum (h.a.). Familiar little cushions, usually white, used for edging or carpeting; the lilac forms are also attractive. Almost hardy and can be raised direct outdoors under cloches in April. Happy in poor soils and tolerate partial shade. The yellow Alyssum is something quite different; *see* A. saxatile, Chapter XII.

Antirrhinum. A perennial, but best treated as h.h.a. The 'intermediate' varieties are the most usually grown, but there are several other types, from dwarfs to giants, with confusing fancy names. They flower best and are hardiest when planted out in a rather lean, stony soil.

The beginner should get a box or two of seedlings from a nursery, plant out 9 in. apart in a sunny bed in the first week of June, stake with twigs at once, and nip off the tips after a week. Antirrhinums are very subject to the rust disease, but this may be prevented by a copper fungicide or by using one of the 'rustless' strains.

The non-beginner who has glass and a little heat can raise Snapdragons from seed sown in January or February, guarding against the damping-off disease, to which they are very liable, with Cheshunt Compound. Early and good results can be got by sowing under glass in October and moving on gradually into small pots, before hardening off, and some may go into 5-in. pots to flower in the greenhouse. If so minded, you can also propagate them easily by heel or nodal cuttings of firm young shoots, stuck in sandy soil in pots in a close frame in late summer.

By persistent dead-heading Antirrhinums can be induced to flower continuously till autumn. They love rocks and brick walls, and will often last for years in old brickwork. Whichever style you like—dwarf, medium, or tall—I would go for one of the F_1 hybrids or the rust-resistant strains if that disease is prevalent in your area. Unfortunately the best new strains are rarely obtainable from local nurseries as growing seedlings.

Aster (h.h.a.). These great summer favourites are not really Asters at all and must not be confused with the large perennial Asters (Michaelmas Daisy). They are very decorative, extremely flowerful, and fine for cutting. Treatment is as for Antirrhinums, but, if raising from seed oneself, do not sow before mid-March; very little warmth is needed. Seedlings are very subject to the damping-off disease. Destroy any plants seen to wilt after being planted out.

One is often confused with the variety of types under fancy group-names in catalogues. I would keep at first to the charming single-flowered Chinese Asters, which are like coloured Marguerites and about 15 in. high, or to the slightly shaggy Southcote Beauties. Ostrich Plume Asters have large feathery heads, and the Mammoths are similar but taller. Comet Asters are large and double without the shagginess, and Californian Giants are larger still.

Bartonia or Mentzelia (h.a.). An easy summer annual with large golden buttercup-like flowers that should be more grown. Very gay. Sow *in situ* and thin to 10 in. Height 15 in.

Calendula. *See* Marigold.

Californian Poppy (Eschscholtzia, pronounced Esholtzia, h.a.). One of the easiest and most colourful, with festive trumpets of orange, gold, red, pink. Likes warm, dry conditions. Height 9 in. Sow *in situ*, and thin to 7 in. Keep spent blooms removed. Does best in poor stony soil. Seeds itself profusely.

Candytuft (Iberis, h.a.). Easy and familiar. Usually white, sometimes pale mauve. The usual form is the dwarf, but you may care for the tall, hyacinthine spires of the varieties of I. coronaria, for which nurserymen have their own pet names. Sow *in situ*, and thin to 8 in. Winter annuals. *See also under* Rock Gardens.

Canterbury Bell (h.b.). Member of the Campanula family and one of our grandest old garden favourites. Very easy to raise. Some have a bell only, others a ring of coloured sepals which give them the name 'cup and saucer'. 3 ft. high in white, pink, blue, or mauve, and very broad and bushy.

Chrysanthemum. The annual forms are very showy and distinctive, characterised by rings or zones of contrasting colours in the petals. They vary in height from 18 in. to 3 ft. Deep and generous soil treatment is essential. Sow *in situ*, and space the big ones at 15 in. at least. Must be staked. A winter annual. For the perennial Chrysanthemums, *see* Chapter XVIII.

Clarkia (h.a.). Deep and generous soil treatment is necessary for the brilliant results obtainable from this lovely annual (C. elegans) with its spires of frilled blossoms in many colours, instead of the poor stunted things usually seen. A first choice that richly rewards good treatment. Sow *in situ* (will not transplant) and thin to 10 in. Succeeds in partial shade. Stake very early. A winter annual and a good pot plant for the greenhouse.

Convolvulus. Some of these are weeds, but C. tricolor has produced some first-rate varieties, of which Royal Ensign is particularly fine in its colours of rich royal-blue and gold. A hardy annual, it is a foot high and one of the best. *See also* Morning Glory.

Cornflower (Centaurea Cyanus, h.a.). The pink and mauve shades are nearly as lovely as the traditional blue. A beautiful dwarf one, among the best of annuals, is Jubilee Gem, which measures a foot. Avoid the very tall sorts. Fine for cutting. Sow *in situ*.

Cosmos, or **Cosmea** (h.h.a.). Graceful marguerite-like

124

flowers in pastel shades and thin ferny foliage. Some go to 3 ft and others are dwarf. Excellent for cutting.

Delphinium. The annual Delphinium named Blue Butterfly, as distinct from Larkspur, is an outstanding annual, producing deep blue flowers in great abundance, and making a compact bushy plant 1 ft high. Excellent also in pots in the cold greenhouse. Though treated as an annual, since it flowers from seed the first year, it is actually perennial, and may be kept to give of its bounty another year.

Dimorphotheca (h.a.). South African daisies, usually in brilliant yellows, that close up at night. Easy, showy, and quick, 9 in. Besides the old D. aurantiaca, there are now some splendid hybrids of which Sutton's Orange Giant (or Goliath) is outstanding. Must have full sun and a light, rather dry soil. Sow *in situ* and thin to 8 in.

Evening Primrose (Œnothera biennis, h.b.). The biennial sort is a 3-ft bush studded with gay blossoms of primrose hue, fleeting but successional, opening late afternoon. Excellent among shrubs, tolerating partial shade as well as full sun. Space at 18 in. in groups of three or more. *See also* next chapter.

Flax (Linum). There are several species of Flax, perennial and otherwise. Of the hardy annuals, one that is quite outstanding is L. grandiflorum rubrum. Its slender, filigree foliage is crowned with brilliant rose-scarlet clusters of satin trumpets, individually fleeting, but following each other in rapid succession in July and August. A foot high, it is as easy as possible. Sow *very sparsely* and thin to 8 in.

Forget-me-not (Myosotis alpestris hybrids, treated as h.b.). This easy old favourite prefers moist places, is lovely in shrubberies, and is a beautiful groundwork for tall tulips; but it exhausts the soil, which must be re-invigorated with organic matter. One or two old plants heeled-in in a moist corner will seed abundantly.

Foxglove (Digitalis, h.b.). The modern hybrids, now in a wide range of colours, have great beauty. Sutton's 'Excelsior' hybrids, which carry their flowers all round the stem and pointing a little upwards, are very distinctive and promising. Especially valuable for growing in shade, even dense shade beneath trees. The nursery bed, too, should be in partial shade. Final spacing 18 in.

Godetia (h.a.). One of the half-dozen best, forming a bushy pyramid enlivened with sparkling porcelain cups in many colours. Succeeds almost anywhere, including shade, if the soil is well dug. Heights vary from 8 in. to 3 ft. Sow *in situ*, and thin to 6 in. for the dwarfs and 1 ft for the tall ones. Good winter annual. Kelvedon Glory is a fine variety.

Kochia scoparia (h.h.a., pronounced Kokia). Graceful and shapely little bushes just like dwarf cypress in appearance, grown essentially for their foliage, which is a tender green in summer and fiery red in autumn. Equally good for the poor man's rock garden (instead of cypress) or for little avenues or other formal, rather prim effects, but not in a border. Can be raised under glass without heat early April. Don't call it 'Burning Bush' which may also mean Dittany.

Larkspur (h.a.). If the Sweet Pea is the queen of annuals, the Larkspur, or annual Delphinium, is certainly the princess royal, but to attain her full 4–5 ft of glory she must have deep and generous soil treatment, like Clarkia. A very top choice. Get the double-flowered form in mixed colours and sow *in situ*, thinning to 1 ft; don't transplant. Excels as a winter annual.

Lavatera. *See* Mallow.

Lobelia (h.h.a.). The ever-popular little edging plant with multitudes of tiny flowers of vivid blue. One of the best places for it is at the feet of standard roses. The showiest is the royal-blue Crystal Palace. Rosamond is claret-red and Sapphire is for window-boxes, slopes, walls, etc. Spacing 5 in.

Love-in-a-Mist (Nigella damascena, h.a.). Of this lovely and easy family, with their blue cockades half-veiled in slender foliage, the variety Miss Jekyll is quite the best. A thing of delicate grace and beautiful form and atmosphere. Sow *in situ* and space to 18 in. A winter annual.

Love-Lies-Bleeding (Amaranthus caudatus, h.a.). This is the Amaranth, or Flower Gentle, so loved of our ancestors. It has long, dropping trails, like catkins, of deep crimson, most effective when dotted among other plants, rather than massed.

It needs sun, and looks well tumbling down a bank. 30 in.

Mallow, or **Rose Mallow** (Lavatera trimestris, h.a.). One of the biggest annuals, making a bushy plant nearly 4 ft high, with blooms like a single Hollyhock. Easily the best varieties are Sunset and the similar Loveliness. Sow *in situ* and thin to 2 ft. An exceptionally good seaside plant, resisting salt, filtering the wind and, in spite of its height, needs no staking.

Marigold. The familiar Pot Marigold (so-called because its dried petals are used to flavour soups and stews) is Calendula officinalis (h.a.). It does well anywhere, including poor soils. Sow the large seeds 5 in. apart and thin to 10 in.; the thinnings will transplant. There are orange and lemon shades, and the variety Radio has attractive quilled petals.

The African Marigold has stiff stems $2\frac{1}{2}$ ft tall, topped with orange or lemon orbs whose brassy splendour shows at its best only when the soil has been well cultivated and in hot, dryish places in full sun; in the right place it can be very fine.

The French Marigold usually has crimson or chocolate showily mingled with its gold. There are many forms, but the dwarfer double-flowered ones are best. Gay, flowerful, and easy.

Both the Frenchman and the African are h.h.a. and are species of Tagetes. New varieties of both are constantly coming out, and they have been much inter-married. The brisk little plant usually sold as Tagetes in the market is T. signata pumila, and in mild districts can be grown as a h.a.

Space the tall foreigners at 1 ft and the smaller ones at 8 in. They are really Mexican, not French or African. Keep all marigolds dead-headed and they will bloom a long time.

Morning Glory (h.h.a.). This name is given to more than one of the twining plants that display brilliantly coloured bugles until the afternoon. The best is Ipomoea rubro-cærulea, especially its variety Heavenly Blue. Another is Convulus major, a short climber to 5 ft in assorted colours. Sow in peat pots in some warmth and plant out complete about June 1st.

Nasturtium (h.a.). Has stolen this name from the watercress, as it was apparently introduced here as 'Indian Cress', its spicy leaves being good in a salad. Legally it is a Tropæolum. It does best in poor soils. Try strains of Gleam and Festival. Sow the big seeds 6 in. apart, 1 ft for the trailers or 'climbers', which are excellent for tumbling down a bank of poor, stony soil. The seeds, gathered young, can be used as a substitute for capers.

Nemesia (h.h.a.). These showy little bedding plants of many colours are not easy to grow well, and the poor specimens often seen are usually the result of their having been left crowded too long in the seed-box. They dislike a check and, after germination, must be moved along quickly, into small pots if necessary, before planting out. They like things moist, cool and peaty at all stages.

Nemophila (h.a.), is a pretty little annual, alive with a multitude of small, azure, white-eyed flowers for many weeks after midsummer. It grows only 6 in. high. Sow *in situ* in a sunny place in any good garden soil. Thin to 5 in. A winter annual. Order N. insignis.

Nicotiana (the Flowering Tobacco, h.h.a.). The 3-ft stems carry a number of blossoms having long, tubular necks and wide-open faces that embalm the evening air with their fragrance. Very decorative and easy and very welcome under a sitting-room window. Lime Green is a delightful variety. Spacing 15 in.

Pansy, or **Heartsease,** is a form of Viola and a perennial, but usually treated as a h.b. Unless the outdoor seed-bed is of very fine soil, start them in seed-boxes in a J. I. Compost about the end of June. When pricked off, the nursery bed should be of fairly rich soil in partial shade, and the same conditions suit their permanent quarters. Must never lack moisture. As with all Violas, keep the dead blooms cut down. Most pansies have large, nearly black splashes in their centres, but others have clean faces, and some have amusing whiskers. The Roggli strain from Roberts, of Faversham, is superb.

Petunia (treat as h.h.a.). This popular flower has erupted into all manner of varieties and colours, small or large, flamboyant or tender, single or monstrously double. Choose at your will from the catalogues. Delay sowing till March and give the same quick-moving treatment as for Nemesias. Excellent for any use, including window-boxes and hanging baskets.

Phacelia (h.a.). A little-known but very desirable 8-in. plant of special value for its brilliant and rare Gentian blue and for its long season of flowering. Sow in full sun *in situ* in mid-April and thin to 8 in. for July blooming. Order P. campanularia. A winter annual.

Phlox. The annual type is P. Drummondii (h.h.a.), 1 ft only, adorned with large trusses of bloom in delicious colours. A pearl among annuals, but it is useless to expect good results without thorough digging and really generous soil treatment and plenty of sun. Move into small pots about the end of April before planting out in June.

Poppy (Papaver). Finest of all is the Iceland Poppy, P. nudicaule, which illumines the border or the vase with jaunty flowers of orange and lemon or of pastel pinks and apricot. A delightful adornment in any garden. Needs full sun, a soil containing plenty of leaf-mould or peat, and plenty of moisture. Best treated as h.b., though really a perennial.

Of the annual Poppies, the two main sorts are the popular Shirley Poppy, 2 ft, and the Opium Poppy, with grey leaves, 3 ft, both in many colours. The former can be had in either single or double forms, and in delicate pastel shades or flaunting reds. The Opium Poppies are very large doubles, either 'Peony-flowered' or 'Carnation-flowered' with fringed edges. For either kind a packet of mixed colours is best. Sow *in situ* (will not transplant well) and thin to 1 ft apart. Keep dead blooms rigorously cut down. Unfortunately their foliage becomes an eyesore as they near the end of their time.

All sorts have very fine seed, which should be merely dusted over.

Salpiglossis (h.h.a.). Graceful plants 2 ft high with trumpets of various colours delicately veined. Good for an unheated greenhouse, but quite suitable also for outdoors if sheltered from wind, well staked, and given plenty of sun. Rather short-lived.

Salvia. The 15-in. plant of vivid pillar-box red, used for summer bedding, is S. splendens (h.h.a.). The seed has to be raised in a temperature of 66°, so those without this facility must buy the plants and put them out the first week of June. If you can raise them yourself, prick them out first into small pots and then into 4-in. ones. They are infinitely at their best when their flamboyance is abated by other colours, especially blue. Space at 1 ft. *See* Chapter XI for the splendid perennial Salvias.

Stock. One of the garden's prime favourites. Of the rather confusing classification with fancy names given in catalogues, first choice for Southern gardens is the popular 'Ten-Week' Stock. Is a h.h.a., but may be raised under glass without heat in mid-April. Guard against damping-off. Plant out 10 in. apart. Do not pinch out the tips, and do not discard the smaller seedlings, which often turn out the best. You must get the Dutch Hansen strain, in which the desired double-flowered ones can be identified in the seedling stage by their noticeably paler foliage.

'East Lothian' Stocks are the ones to have in the North, particularly Scotland, where they prosper with hyacinthine splendour from the end of July onwards. Sow in heat in February, or treat as biennials and sow outdoors in late July.

'Brompton' Stocks are treated as hardy biennials. They bloom in the spring at the same time as Wallflowers, which they certainly equal and perhaps surpass in beauty, charm, and fragrance. Raise them in exactly the same way, but plant out 15 in. apart. In cold and damp districts they may not stand the winter outdoors, but elsewhere they are grand.

'Beauty of Nice' Stocks are for heated greenhouses only. 'Virginia' Stocks are easy 6-in annuals for edgings and crannies. 'Night Scented' are dwarfs of insignificant appearance but glorious perfume, exhaled as evening approaches. Sprinkle them under the sitting-room window, or in a window box, mixed with more showy things.

Sunflower (h.a.). All the Helianthus are 'sun flowers', but the one popularly so called (H. annuus) is the giant with rubicund face nodding over the cottage wall. It needs well-dug soil and full sun to attain full stature. Sow a seed or two every few feet in April and thin to one at each station. If the seeds are wanted for parrots or chickens, cut off the flower-head as soon as the seeds begin to loosen in September and dry it off indoors in a sunny window. *See also under* Helianthus in Chapter XI.

SWEET PEA (h.a.). There are two methods of raising this queen of all the annuals. The first is for ordinary garden

Sweet Peas. When growing for big blooms, remove leafy axillary shoots A and B, but not the young flowering stem C. Take care to distinguish between the two.

decoration, and the other is for getting specially fine blooms on long stems for the vase or for exhibition. For either purpose, note especially—first, that the Sweet Pea demands full sun, and secondly, that it is a gross feeder and needs large quantities of animal or vegetable organic food.

For Garden Decoration. Probably the best method is to grow them in clusters or clumps 3 ft or 4 ft in diameter.

Prepare the site in the autumn; never later than February. Bastard trench, enriching both spits with manure or compost, and adding bonemeal, good soot, and fresh wood-ashes in the

131

top spit. The areas of prepared ground should extend 10 in. or so beyond the sowing stations.

In April work the surface into a good tilth, and sow the seed 1 in. deep and 3 in. apart. If mice are feared, dip the seeds in paraffin and then roll them in red lead. Protect the seedlings against slugs as soon as they appear, and plant bushy pea-sticks, 4 ft high, thickly and deeply.

Pick blooms for the house as soon as you like, go on picking, and always remove spent blooms. If the soil is very dry, give a thorough soaking with rain-water or with tap-water exposed to the sun for at least twenty-four hours; light watering is harmful.

When flowering is all over, cut the plants down to the ground; wet the haulms, chop them up, and add to the compost heap, leaving the nitrogenous roots in the ground.

For Big Blooms. The object is to get long stems bearing many blooms. This is done by gross feeding and confining all growth to one or two stems like a cordon apple, instead of a bushy plant with many laterals. The method needs some enthusiasm in the practitioner, for the initial work is not light, and when the plants are growing away strongly they need daily attention.

Dig the ground three spits deep—the full trenching operation described in Chapter V, the trench being 3 ft wide. Mix manure liberally into the bottom and second spits. In the second and top spits add bonemeal and fresh wood-ashes at a double handful to the yard run, plus mortar rubble and hop manure in heavy soils. Dress the top spit liberally with soot.

The exhibitor gets early results by starting his seeds in October in pots, but otherwise sowing is done *in situ* early in April, after having worked the surface to a good tilth. Sow in two ranks, 15 in. between ranks and 9 in. apart in the ranks. When the seedlings are a few inches high pinch out the tips and then allow only a limited number of shoots to grow—one shoot only for weak growths, maybe three for extra strong ones. After they are well away each shoot has to be provided with a bamboo 7 ft long or more, but, instead of the usual elaborate structure, it is quite sufficient to erect these canes tentwise, in the manner of Scarlet Runner poles; to save them from wind damage, plant stout posts at least a foot deep before sowing at intervals of 10 ft or so, braced to each other at the top with strong wire or lighter poles.

As the plant grows, every side shoot (appearing in the angle between main stem and leaf stalk) is plucked out, and the main stem is secured to its bamboo, the easiest method being by the specially-made Sweet Pea rings. Allow no flower buds to bloom till the shoot is 2 ft high—pluck them out.

Meanwhile keep the surface hoed, including the path inevitably trodden by the ministrant. When the first flower-spike appears feed with liquid manure or soot-water, and repeat fortnightly. About the end of June give a mulch of compost or animal manure.

The plants will soon reach the tops of their canes, and they are then taken right down a few at a time, laid along the ground, and made to start again up a cane at their extremity, so that the plant on No. 1 cane will begin its new career on the eighth or ninth, and those at the end of the first rank are turned round the corner and resume their career in the second rank. This is rather a tricky operation, but the plant's useful life is doubled, and at the end of the season its one main stem may be 15 ft long.

Sweet Sultan. Pretty feathery mops are borne on 18-in. stems from July onwards. An old-time favourite, but China Asters are usually preferred.

Sweet William (h.b.). This fine old favourite is a member of the Carnation and Pink family (*Dianthus*). It therefore likes mortar rubble and any other form of lime. The bi-colour form called 'auricula-eyed' is specially attractive to most people; and there is a dwarf variety. Sweet William stops blooming at an awkward time of year, and something should be grown-on in pots, such as dwarf Dahlias, ready to follow it in July. Space at 10 in.

Sweet Wivelsfield is a pretty hybrid from Sweet William, but of laxer and more dainty form. Good for cutting and very decorative.

Tagetes. *See* under Marigold.

133

Wallflower (Cheiranthus, h.b.). There are two popular sorts—the scented Wallflower in many colours blooming in early spring (C. Cheiri), and the slightly later Siberian Wallflower, which is a glowing orange ball of fire (C. Allionii), immensely vivid and warm. Both easy to raise from a normal June sowing. 'Stop' them when about 4 in. high. The Siberian blooms right on till mid-June, and when it is over presents the same problems of succession as Sweet William. A pretty dwarf in mauve, called Erisymum linifolium, is good for edging and stone work. *See also under* Rock Gardens.

Zinnia (h.h.a.). Either you rave about Zinnias or you consider them stiff and artificial. Certainly they are not worthwhile if poorly grown, and in these islands, to achieve their full splendour—the size of a large Chrysanthemum and 3 ft high—they need a hot summer and generous cultivation. This is another plant that rebels at being checked in youth; don't buy boxed seedlings from a garden shop. Sow in April in a greenhouse with or without heat, and prick them out into pots, or sow direct outdoors in permanent stations under cloches. Space at 15 in., having fed the soil really well organically. Give copious draughts of water during growth. Quantities of new varieties of all sorts and sizes appear nearly every year.

CHAPTER XI

HERBACEOUS AND MIXED BORDERS

The Use and Misuse of Border Plants

THE herbaceous border has long been one of the glories of the British garden, and although in large places there is a tendency to supplant it by flowering shrubs because of the labour involved, it is likely to hold its place in the smaller gardens, in some form or other, for a very long time to come. For the border is relatively inexpensive to stock, especially if the plants are grown from seed, as many of the best can easily be grown if one has the patience to wait a year, using annuals in their place meantime. Those not easily raised from seed, such as Michaelmas Daisies, Phloxes, and Peonies, can generally be multiplied from stem or root cuttings, and others by division, so that from a few initial plants a wealth of stock can soon be built up if desired.

In the small garden herbaceous plants have many uses besides their employment in herbaceous or mixed borders; they may adorn many odd corners, or occupy small beds, and some mingle happily with shrubs. Conversely, there are some *not* at their best in the heterogeneous company of the border, such as Violas and Lilies-of-the-Valley. Others again, being essentially flowers for cutting and not very 'showy' in the border, can with advantage be grown in straight rows in the kitchen garden, such as Pyrethrum and Scabious. But it is with the 'border', not necessarily entirely herbaceous, that I shall be specially concerned in this introduction.

Borders can be of many shapes and sizes—straight or curved, broad or narrow. They can face in any direction, but the south-facing border is the easiest, and the north-facing one requires a special technique in the choice of plants. As a backing for the border, nothing is better than a bank of shrubs, but there is seldom room enough in a small place. Stone or brick walls are excellent, giving shelter for the less hardy things and allowing the employment of wall plants, but of course a border can quite well be out in the open, though shelter from stiff winds is to be desired.

In siting the border, try to have it running directly or obliquely away from the main windows of the house, so that one looks or walks down its length in perspective. A border should not be looked at full in the face, for there are always seasonal gaps.

Borders should never be directly overhung by large trees, but some slanting shade for part of the day will be appreciated by some inhabitants, such as Phlox and Lupin. An all-shade border has similar problems to a north-facing border.

As the plants are to stay in their home for some years, it is common sense to prepare their beds thoroughly. Having made sure of good drainage—the first essential—dig the ground a good two spits deep, incorporating manure or other organic food at all levels and bonemeal in the top one. The work should be done at least several weeks before planting, and for a new border the best course is to dig in autumn and plant in spring. In general, herbaceous plants can be put out any time from November to March if the ground is not frostbound or saturated, but on cold, heavy clays spring is best. Moreover, there are a few plants that should always be planted in spring only, including Scabious, Gaillardia, Pyrethrum, the 'Amellus' group of Asters, and some others mentioned in the notes that follow.

In the after-care of the border, there are some important considerations. First, I do *not* agree with the usual kind of digging-over so often advised for the autumn; it tears up roots and disturbs or damages precious things such as Lilies or other bulbs and Alstrœmerias. A mere hoeing, or very shallow

136

pricking-over, is quite enough. Much more important than digging is to dress the ground all over, in earliest spring, with well-composted vegetable refuse (if free of weed seeds), hop manure, animal manure, or to mulch it with leaves in autumn. Bonemeal is at all times good.

Other after-care measures are the staking of any kinds of plants liable to flop as they attain full height, and the removal of spent blooms. A great many herbaceous plants will go on and on if dead-headed, particularly anything that has the form and shape of a daisy; it is surprising, too, how most Lupins come on repeatedly after the dead-heading.

Unless you have to get at the land for some operation, don't cut down foliage and stems too soon in the autumn—let them die right down till nearly black; then cut them down not too low, so that the stumps may trap wind-driven leaves to provide both a mulch and a frost protection.

About every third or fourth year the border, having become overgrown, will need sorting out. Leave alone the plants that resent disturbance—Peonies, Lilies, and other bulbs if there are any, Alstrœmerias, Delphiniums, Japanese Anemones, etc.; but lift all other herbaceous plants, divide them and re-plant. In big borders a portion can be done annually. If an annual top-dressing has been given, re-manuring will not be necessary.

The use of lime will depend on the condition of the soil and the nature of its inhabitants. The Lupin does not care for much lime, but Gypsophila and Iris do. The general run of herbaceous plants, however, seem fairly indifferent to all but extreme conditions, and on acid soils a dressing every few years may be desirable, varied in strength according to the plant population.

The soil may have been well and truly made ready according to Cocker, but the border may still be a failure if it is not well laid-out. Composition, or design, is the touchstone. It requires, first, a little elementary knowledge of the characteristics of each plant—its height, spread, colour, season of flowering, and foliage—most of which can be got from any good catalogue, but it also requires something less easily taught—an eye.

Variations in height, blends, or contrasts in colour, a bold handling of shapes and forms, a sympathetic grouping of different leaf textures, the counterpoint of light and shade—these are the things that make a border beautiful. I have room for only one or two guiding precepts, but I must emphasise from the first that, just like any other artistic composition, it has got to be worked out with care, indeed loving care, on paper beforehand. There is no other way, and the best paper to use is the large-squared paper of a child's arithmetic book (not graph paper).

Formality is to be avoided like the plague. The hand of man must be in no shape evident. No straight lines, no regimented gradations from the dwarf in front to the giant at the back, no plants dotted singly here and there, save one or two of the more high-pitched colours. Everything must seem as though 'painted o'er with nature's hand, not art's'—and nature sheds her seeds in drifts and clusters. If you possess only three Phloxes, put them all together. While obviously 7-ft plants must not be right in front, nor miniatures right at the back, let a promontory of Helenium or golden Asters thrust out towards the front, and a drift of Pentstemon sweep back towards the centre. Let the clusters be irregular in form—some roughly circular, some elongated, some sweeping away at an angle, and so on.

On colour composition one can in this small compass speak only in general terms. In the small garden there is no room for an all-blue border, an all-red border, and so on, and a communism of colours must be accepted. Plants adjacent to one another should harmonise rather than contrast, with the more vivid colours used just here and there for 'accent' notes, as in music. The red Chalcedonian Lychnis is ideal for such a purpose. The orange and bronze shades are sometimes difficult to fix, and jar discordantly against a delicate blue. Generally speaking, however, the mixed colours of nature do make happy marriages (witness the Fuchsia), and much that is written on this subject is rather arty and affected. No colour scheme, however, is entirely balanced without a few touches of white here and there, and nothing has a greater charm for this pur-

138

pose than the white Campanulas. A few plants of silver-grey foliage—such as 'Cotton Lavender', the silvery Artemesias, Rose Campion (Lychnis coronaria) and the dwarf Yarrows (Achillea) also make melodious variations of the theme.

In small places grace and strength are given to the garden if the herbaceous border is made into a 'mixed' one by inviting into it two other classes—bulbous plants, and the smaller flowering shrubs. Of the former, Lilies add a note of distinction and Dahlias are valuable for filling blanks left by early flowering plants. Of shrubs, there is one lovely little shrub with chaste pale blue florets just like those of a plumbago and with a slender airy habit that I would never do without again. Unfortunately its only name is Ceratostigma Willmottianum. Other small shrubs particularly suitable for a mixed border are Senecio laxifolius, Potentillas, Hypericum patulum Hidcote variety, some Spiræas, floribunda Roses, the dwarfish varieties of Philadelphus, Fuchsia, and the dwarf Helianthemum, which is quite admirable for the front edge.

Another class that keeps excellent company with border flowers are certain of the rock plants for the front edge. Some of the best for this purpose are Aubrieta, dwarf Phlox and dwarf Campanula, Stonecrop, together with various Primulas, Polyanthus, and Primroses.

Depth is a great boon in a border—more important than length. Those who can spare 12 ft or more are fortunate, and anything less than about 8 ft creates problems in composition. For narrow borders or strips there are but two choices—be satisfied with a collection that will give you a full blaze for a short period, or have only a limited number of subjects and cluster them boldly. By way of example, the awkward 3-ft strip is admirably furnished by using only Lupins for early summer, followed by Phlox for mid-season, succeeded by medium Dahlias.

A border about 5 ft wide, if of reasonable length, could comfortably accommodate an arrangement of Lupins, Achillea Gold Plate, purple Salvia, Phlox or Bergamot, Liatris, Michaelmas Daisy, Campanula and a few Delphiniums, together with Pinks, Camomile, Flax, Erigeron, Cranesbill, and Stonecrop at or near the front. And if you are habitually on holiday in August, you can cut out all flowers that bloom at that season.

A Selection of Perennials

The following is a short selection only of the more meritorious and easily-grown perennials. Among them are some unhackneyed plants of great merit that make a border 'something different' and that I specially commend to beginners. These are the 'Ligtu hybrids' of Alstrœmeria, Echinacea, the queenly Romneya, Liatris, the hybrid yellow Aster, Dittany, Heuchera, and the delightful Chrysanthemum rubellum.

Another class is composed of plants which, though perfectly well known in large places, are for some reason rarely seen in small gardens, except the gardens of the experienced and knowledgeable practitioner. Some of these, all perfectly easy, are: the smaller Asters such as the Amellus group, the Achilleas large and small, purple Salvia, the lovely Anemone pulsatilla, Bergamot, Camomile, Mullein (Verbascum), Bleeding Heart, and Lychnis of various sorts.

To all these I call special attention, adding also that this list contains flowers suitable for all sorts of conditions—wet soils and dry soils, sun and shade. The classifications in the appendices may be a help.

Achillea. The Yarrow or Milfoil family provides some tiresome weeds, but also some excellent garden flowers. The finest is A. Eupatorium Gold Plate, an outstanding border plant, vigorous and easy, carrying on its erect 5-ft stems bold and striking golden platters, 7 in. across, which are of great service in giving diversity of form and feature to the border, and which gleam above the foliage for many weeks. Coronation Gold, the handsome, silver-leaved Moonshine and clypeolata, are fine for middle distance planting. Cerise Queen is a gay version for the front of the border but rather invasive. Increase all by division. *See also under* Rock Gardens.

Alstrœmeria, sometimes called Peruvian Lily. The brilliant and rampant orange variety so familiar everywhere

140

(A. aurantiaca) has been displaced by the surpassing Ligtu hybrids, which, with their sparkling pink shades, have a butter-fly brilliance that makes them one of the loveliest things yet introduced. But they require full sun, a deeply dug soil enriched with organic matter and a situation on the dry side. The fleshy roots resent disturbance, and so should not be more than a year old when bought. Plant them vertically, bud end uppermost, 6 in. deep in August or September. Easier still is to grow them from seed. Put three seeds in a 5-in. pot and, when well sprouted, plant out the whole ball of soil without disturbance. Weed carefully by hand only.

Anchusa. Bushy plants (of short life) for the back of the border enamelled with little brilliant blue flowers like Forget-me-nots, 4–5 ft. Valuable for infusing the blue influence in May and June before the Delphiniums, and valuable also for dry soils, being drought-hardy. Opal, Royal Blue and Loddon Royalist are fine varieties.

Anemone. Of this versatile and beautiful family two are of special value. One is the familiar 'Japanese' Anemone (mis-called A. japonica), with slender 3-ft stems and chaste salvers of white, pink or mauve in late summer and autumn, particu-larly striking when planted, fairly closely, in large, bold clusters. It is of special merit for succeeding in the shade, even moderately dense shade, where the white and pale pink forms gracefully lighten up the gloom. A slow starter. *Plant in spring.*

Quite different is our lovely native Pasque Flower, Ane-mone Pulsatilla ('shaking in the wind'). Of low stature, it is adorned in April with silken purple chalices enriched with golden stamens. There are forms in other colours also. Give it sun, but plenty of leaf-mould annually. It is a dweller of the chalky Downs. Some botanists now call it Pulsatilla vulgaris, but most catalogues still show it as an Anemone.

See also Chapters XII and XIII for other Anemones.

Aster. Among the perennial Asters the most important race is the large and splendid class of Michaelmas Daisies, ranging from 6-ft giants to 6-in. pygmies. There is a wealth of choice, and new varieties appear every year with larger and

141

larger blooms, but some of the old guard, such as Beechwood Challenger and Harrington's Pink, still hold their own.

Some of the smaller perennial Asters, though less well known, equal or surpass the big Michaelmas Daisies and are admirable for small gardens. I specially recommend:

A. Frikartii, 3 ft, a joyful profusion of large clear blue, freely branching, from August on; a child of Amellus, and one of the best perennials we have.

The gay 'Amellus' clan, with big, deep-golden discs, about 2 ft high, of great charm and longevity, especially the pink Sonia, the violet King George, and the claret Fra mfeldii. These it is important to plant in spring, not autumn.

The striking yellow Aster hybrid, properly called Solidaster luteus, which is a cross between a Michaelmas Daisy and a Golden Rod. Often listed as A. hybridus luteus, it is thronged with a busy swarm of tiny gold stars in July and August; a great acquisition and seldom seen. 3 ft.

A. Yunnanensis Napsbury, 2 ft, a glowing heliotrope with golden disc that has the distinction of starting as early as June.

All these Asters are increased by division, which should be done about every three years, selecting the outside shoots.

Astilbe. This is a gay family with feathery plumes in brilliant and in pastel colours, 1–3 ft high, often mistaken for Spiræas. Very bonny plants. They prefer a moist and partially shaded position near water, but succeed well elsewhere provided the soil is not a very light one that dries out quickly in hot summers. Give them plenty of peat. Fanal is a dazzling raspberry-red, Etna is scarlet, Koblenz is salmon, and there are many other good ones, including some charming dwarfs. Excellent also in pots in the greenhouse. Easily multiplied from its own seed immediately it is ripe, or by careful division in early spring.

Bergamot (Monarda hybrids). An old-world plant with aromatic leaves and curiously-wrought flowers of bold design and audacious colour. Blooms prodigiously. The dazzling Cambridge Scarlet is the best known, but Croftway Pink is also desirable, and there is now a whole new range in claret, violet, ruby and other shades. A splendid substitute where

Phloxes fail. Needs moist soil. Top-dress each spring with fine soil and bonemeal. Sometimes short-lived.

Bleeding Heart (Dicentra or Dielytra). From graceful, arching wands are suspended strings of pink jewels in the shape of a broken heart. It has an air of wistful elegance, and it likes a rich soil and ample moisture to prolong its rather short display in July. It is also an easy pot-plant for the cold greenhouse. D. spectabile, 18 in., is the one to have. Guard against slugs and quilt it with leaves in winter to protect the tender young shoots.

Camomile (Anthemis). For the border there are some cheerful varieties of this old-world favourite with yellow daisies, esteemed for blooming from midsummer right into autumn and fine for cutting. Perhaps the best variety today is Beauty of Grallagh, but there are other good ones of lesser stature. Multiply by division. *See also under* Rock Gardens.

Campanula. No border is perfectly harmonious without the music of the harebells. They rise in airy steeples hung with bells of cool, clear blue or white, giving lightness and grace to their surroundings. They thrive not only in the sun, but also in dense shade, where the white varieties are particularly welcome. Out of a large family the first pick is the blue C. persicifolia ('peach leaved') Telham Beauty, and second comes the white Fleur de Neige. Other fine ones are C. lactiflora 'Prichard's Variety' and latiloba (or grandis) Highcliffe. All about 3 ft. Increase by division. *See also* the chapter on rock gardens for the Carpathian mountain harebell that is specially good for the front of the border.

Carnation. *See* Chapter XVIII.

Catananche. Abundant flowers very like cornflowers, and much longer-lasting. Wants sun and succeeds in very dry soils. The flowers are semi-'everlasting'. Get cœrulea major, June to September. 2 ft. Very good value. Multiply by seed or by root cuttings $1\frac{1}{2}$–2 in. long.

Catmint (a species of Nepeta). This favourite should have a sunny position and does best in dry, poor soils. Plant in spring, not autumn. Do not cut down dead growth till spring. Six Hills variety is a robust 3-footer, but for general use the ordinary lavender species usually catalogued (wrongly) as N. Mussinii is best, or the richer violacea. Multiply by division in spring.

Christmas Rose (Helleborus niger) and **Lenten Rose** (H. orientalis). The elegant but expensive woodland Hellebores have large white or plum chalices, which in turn enrich the scene from November till April. They revel in chalk. Plant in semi-shade and dress with leaf-mould or peat. They are also excellent pot-plants for the cold greenhouse.

Chrysanthemum. *See* Chapter XVIII.

Columbine (Aquilegia). Few flowers are more charming than these dainty wing-footed ballerinas dancing on slender stems, but their time on the stage is short. Easily grown from seed sown in June, and a packet of 'mixed long-spurred hybrids' will delight anyone. They succeed in partial shade as in sun.

Cranesbill. The true Geranium, as distinct from the summer-bedding Pelargonium that has pinched its name, is a decorative hardy perennial making a leafy, spreading bush, bearing multitudes of dainty chalices in sun or shade and good for woodland also. Remove spent blooms for a continuous show. Best of the lot is G. grandiflorum alpinum, pale blue. Other good ones are the pink endressii, the rose Russell Prichard and armenum (psilostemon), a richly barbaric magenta. Several of the rock-garden Cranesbills, which are probably the most attractive, can also embellish the edge of the border. *See* Chapter XII.

Delphinium. Those who want to see the queen of the border in her full measure of stately beauty must give her better treatment than the common herd. Good drainage, a soil deeply dug and well enriched with organic food, a place in the sun and plenty of elbow room are her due. She prefers a fairly heavy loam, not too acid; very light, sandy soils are unpropitious, otherwise there is no difficulty about her upbringing.

The gorgeous named varieties of the catalogues are expensive, but it is a fact that equally good results can sometimes be got from seed of really good firms, such as Blackmore and Langdon of Bath or Bakers of Albrighton, Wolverhampton.

From such seed I have had 7-ft spikes with massive heads of bloom a yard long and more. The American strain known as Giant Pacifics are also excellent from seed, especially for their pink and white shades. In spring sow 2 in. apart in boxes or pans and put in a cool, shady position. Not in a greenhouse. Transplant when ready into a nursery bed in semi-shade about 9 in. apart. 'Cool, moist, and shady' is the rule until planting into permanent quarters, which is normally in early autumn. Then put them in the sun 2 ft apart. Cut out any flower spikes that form the first year.

Next spring, before the plants are 9 in. high, thin out the young shoots, allowing not more than one or two the first year, three the second and five or six thereafter. Cut cleanly at the base with a sharp knife. This is the secret of long, strong spikes. Then feed well with a liquid fertiliser (I use Maxicrop) and mulch yearly with manure or leaves.

Staking is a serious problem. The gales and heavy rain squalls of June can play havoc with the opulent spires. Plant 4-ft canes firmly when the plants are about 2 ft high. Tie the plants round first when a foot high and a second time just below the flower spike. I and other people like to tie each spike separately (but loosely), to a cane.

When flowering is over cut down each stem just below the bottom of the flower-spike and leave the foliage to die down in the natural way; *don't* encourage a second blooming by cutting them right down on the ground—do that in late autumn. To mask the blank that there will be after blooming, have planted in front of them something that will grow up and flower after them, such as Phlox, Alstrœmeria, Purple Loosestrife or Salvia. In the winter scrape away the soil from around the crown of the plant to a depth of a couple of inches and fill in, and cover the crown itself, with sharp weathered ashes as a protection against slugs, which play the very devil with Delphiniums. *See under* Slugs, page 369.

Once established, don't divide or disturb the plants at all, except for purposes of propagation. You can multiply your favourite colourings by taking cuttings in earliest spring when the young shoots are about 3 in. high. Remove some soil and, with a very sharp knife, cut off these growths as close as possible to the main stool, making sure each has a heel. Take none with hollow stems. Insert them in *very* sandy soil in pots or boxes in a close and shaded frame, taking care to observe all the rules for soft-wood cuttings. In a month they should have roots an inch long; transplant them then into 4-in. pots. Plant them in their permanent stations in May, and you will have some small spikes of bloom in autumn.

Regrettably, I must avoid suggesting named varieties, as new ones quickly replace the old, but old favourites such as Lady Eleanor, Lorna and Wessex deservedly linger. There is a special virtue in the 'short' varieties, not exceeding 4 ft 6 in., of which Blue Tit and Janice are good examples. They are apt for small gardens and usually need no staking.

The Belladonna Delphinium is a less regal kind, growing only to 3 ft, but lasting much longer and costing less. *See also under* Annuals.

Dianthus. *See* Chapter XVIII.

Dittany, or **Fraxinella** (Dictamnus). A fine old-timer, now rare. Aromatic, distinctive, and good, it has 2-ft racemes of mauve-pink (purpureus) or white (alba) in June and July, and will tolerate partial shade. Its peculiarity is that it gives off a volatile gas which will ignite when a match is put just below a bloom on a still evening with no apparent harm to the plant; hence it has been called 'Burning Bush'—but so is Kochia. Dislikes disturbance, but easily raised from seed.

Doronicum ('Leopard's Bane'). Large golden daisies as early as April, of which easily the best is the 3-ft D. plantagineum excelsum, also known as Harper Crewe. A fine plant, of excellent constitution and the easiest culture, which I like to call 'spring sunflowers'. Increase by division.

Echinacea. Includes one or two splendid and arresting varieties sometimes catalogued under Rudbeckia. The King is a fine 4-ft variety like a small crimson sunflower. Robert Bloom, gay in crimson and bronze, is only 2 ft. August and September. Increase by division.

Erigeron. Another ideal 2-ft plant for the small (or big) border, resembling a large-flowered Michaelmas Daisy of low stature, and having a long season of bloom throughout summer. There are several new ones, but I prefer the old. Wupperthal, Quakeress, Merstham Glory, Unity and mesa-grande are all good. Division.

Quite different from these is the engaging dwarf called E. mucronatus. It has little pink-tinted daisies with finely-chiselled foliage and is delightful in the crannies of steps and pavements, flowering from June to September. It is not 100 per cent hardy, but readily revives. Spreads madly by seed. Not suitable for borders.

Evening Primrose (Œnothera). The perennial sorts, too little seen, are mostly 18-in. plants spangled with red buds opening to bold golden cups from June till August. The best is O. missouriensis, low, spreading, with very large, pale-primrose flowers. In contrast to the biennial sorts, they need full sun.

Gaillardia. Those who want good results from these fiery splendours, especially for cutting, must observe three rules—give them a soil generously enriched with manure, compost, etc.; keep them staked from an early stage with bushy pea-sticks; cut spent blooms down to the base of the stalk. Fine varieties are The King and Wirral Flame. Plant in spring, not autumn. Increase by seed, division or winter root-cuttings.

Geranium. *See under* Cranesbill in this chapter *and under* Pelargonium.

Geum. Not as good as the rather similar Potentilla, but, for those who want it, the best (but not commonest) are Fire Opal, 18 in., and the shorter orange Borisii, both excellent flowers for the front of the border.

Gypsophila. Beautiful for its border effects as for its cutting value. It relishes lime, whether in mortar rubble or other form. The best is still Bristol Fairy; Rosy Veil and Pink Star are good too. Plant in clusters of three, and dig the ground deep, for their tap-roots go far. Increase is difficult, but can be made by taking sturdy basal shoots with a heel in July, inserting them in sandy soil under close, moist conditions.

Helenium. Provided you have no prejudice against bronzy shades, Helenium will give great satisfaction for its showiness, ease of culture, and long season of bloom. It has yellow, bronze, or mahogany daisy-form flowers, grows to 3 ft high, and should be planted in clusters of three or more 18 in. apart and in full sun. Very flowerful and good. Mœrheim Beauty, Butterpat, Bruno, and Wyndley are fine sorts. Increase by division.

Helianthus. This is the Sunflower family. They require not only the full beam of the sun, but also good drainage and well-enriched soil. The genial monster of the cottage garden, which is usually what is meant by 'sunflower', is an annual (*see* Chapter X). Others incline to be lanky and coarse or terribly invasive, but Capenoch Star and Loddon Gold, 5 ft, behave well, though they need staking. Avoid Miss Mellish. Protect the crowns in winter with a few inches of weathered ashes. Division.

Heuchera. These have graceful sprays of dainty brilliance, rather like London Pride, in brilliant reds and pinks, and are delightful for the front of the border and for cutting in June and July. Scintillation and Red Spangles will do you well.

Heucherella Bridget Bloom is a pretty pink hybrid of 18 in. Division.

Hollyhock (Althæa). This fine old fellow is best treated as a biennial, and is easy to raise from seed sown in June. It also seeds generously, and always looks best in the odd corners and crannies that it selects for itself.

Hosta. Much prized by flower-arrangers for their big, ribbed, and beautifully tailored leaves, the hostas also have elegant, lilyform flowers, often scented. Usually they are planted in partial shade. A first picking would include H. crispula, with leaves broadly margined white, H. fortunei albo-picta, with young leaves of primrose (good in sun), and H. sieboldiana (or glauca), with large, crinkled, blue-green leaves.

Iris. See Chapter XVIII.

Kaffir-lily. (Schizostylis; pronounced Skyz-). Pretty flowers of gladiolus form, specially welcome for blooming in the drear days of late autumn; need a warm spot in the shelter of a sunny wall. Plant 3 in. deep in April. Water well in summer. The pink Mrs Hegarty blooms in November and

Viscountess Byng (which should be cloched) in December.

Liatris. The monstrous name of L. pycnostachya ('densely clustered') obscures one of the most useful but little known characters of the border stage. It flourishes 3-ft truncheons densely wreathed with rosy-purple tassels, needs no staking, and blooms all July and August. An acquisition and good for cutting. Another fine liatris is called Kobold. Liatris needs sun, a well-drained and deeply-dug soil, and a good share of rain. Increase by offsets from its corm-like base, or by seed as soon as it ripens.

Lily-of-the-Valley (Convallaria majalis). Not suitable for the mixed border and should be planted in partial shade. It is essential that the soil be deeply and richly cultivated, its particular requirement being leaf-mould, with which also it should be mulched every March. Plant the 'crowns' 6 in. apart in autumn, covered with one inch of fine soil. When overcrowded lift and divide. Also easily grown in pots.

Loosestrife, Purple (Lythrum Salicaria). The Purple Loosestrife is a gay and easy plant with tall steeples thronged with small blooms. It prefers a moist situation with some shade, but also does well elsewhere. Very reliable, and good for cutting. The carmine variety The Beacon and the roseate Lady Sackville are excellent. Division.

Lupin. The modern strain of Russell Lupins, with their astonishing range of colours in nearly every hue of the spectrum, has displaced most others. The named varieties, which come out anew every year, are expensive, but first-class results come easily from seed, which may be got from Bakers of Albrighton, Wolverhampton. Those one may not like when they bloom can be discarded. Sow in June in a nursery bed in partial shade. As the Lupin has long, fleshy tap-roots, deep digging is necessary in the permanent bed, and a soil fairly free of lime is best. Give them *no manure* whatever, but plenty of bonemeal. They succeed in situations of partial shade as in full sun. One's favourites can be multiplied by taking cuttings of firm shoots in the same way as advised for delphiniums.

For convenience, the Tree Lupin (Lupinus arboreus) may also be mentioned here. This is an excellent bushy evergreen,

5 ft high, densely covered with scented yellow blooms in June. Good at the seaside, easy from seed sown in pots, but short-lived.

Lychnis. From this large and versatile family I shall pick two only, both of which give individuality to a border scheme.

L. chalcedonica is a bold, erect grenadier, 3 ft tall, terminating in an orb of scarlet. One of the few things best dotted about singly or in small clusters, when they look like guardsmen in the park. No other plant is so good for this purpose. Try it in front of a tall Achillea. Excellent in wet soils.

A fine little fellow with a long name is L. viscaria splendens plena. Rather like a stock, 15 in. high. It flowers from June right till September and grows anywhere. Don't get put off with anything that omits the appellation 'splendens plena', or you may get something like Ragged Robin (which is also a Lychnis).

Michaelmas Daisy. *See* Aster.

Monarda. *See* Bergamot.

Monkshood (Aconitum). Bushy plants with the form and habit of Delphinium, but less showy; their blossoms are hooded like a monk's cowl. One of the best shade plants. The best is the blue-and-white A. napellus bicolor; most others rather sombre.

Mullein, or **Aaron's Rod** (Verbascum). A grand old family with some progeny that are quite first-class, and easily within the dozen best for border work. They have the habit of the Hollyhock, but most are not more than 4 ft, and bloom throughout June and July. The following are the best: Cotswold Queen, bronze and pink; Cotswold Beauty, amber; Pink Domino; and Vernale, a handsome 6-footer in lemon-yellow, slightly later. Increase by root cuttings or raise from seed. V. Broussa is a curiosity thickly coated in down like cotton-wool, but it is not perennial.

Pansy. *See* Chapter X.

Pentstemon. The popular hybrids of this good border plant display carillons of long, tubular bells that are borne for long periods on erect stems. They are fairly hardy and are very satisfying in full sun and light soils, but they need to be raised afresh every year or two, for they quickly exhaust themselves by exuberance of flowering. You can buy named varieties if you like, but they are easy to raise from seed—in a packet of mixed colours—sown about July under glass and pricked off into boxes in a cold frame. You can also sow in February. In either case, plant out in April. Those that take your fancy can be multiplied by heel or nodal cuttings of young, basal, un-flowered shoots taken in August and planted in a close frame. Of the named varieties, the most reliably hardy are Schon-holzeri and Garnet.

Peony. Another lovely, but expensive, family whose beauty is all too fleeting. They pay us a three-weeks visit in May or June and are gone. They will flourish in sun or shade, some in dense shade, but need deep digging with plenty of organic food, including bonemeal. O.K. in lime. It is essential to plant them with their crowns not more than 2 in. below the surface, or they may fail to flower. Plant firmly. Once in the ground they should be left undisturbed. Top-dress each early spring, but on no account allow animal manure or chemical fertiliser to touch the crown. The mixed border is not really the place for them, but if put there they should be at middle distance behind some later-blooming plant.

There is a host of very lovely varieties, many scented, and for a start you are recommended to Lady Alexander Duff (white with crimson markings), Mme Jules Elie (silver-pink), and Sarah Bernhardt (pink).

The 'Tree Peonies', which are shrubs, are scarcely begin-ner's plants, unless it be the 7-ft, yellow P. lutea ludlowii.

Phlox. The border sort is P. decussata (or paniculata), with big trusses of bloom in a handsome range of colours from July onwards. To do well they need a rich soil with plenty of moisture, and they enjoy a little shade. It is, moreover, very important to plant them rather deeply, burying the crown an inch or so. Feed and mulch well early in May. In soils where Phlox is attacked with eelworm, use Bergamot instead. There are a hundred varieties to choose from; Norah Leigh, the cream-leaved one popular with arrangers, is a plant of very uncertain behaviour.

151

Phlox is increased by root cuttings in winter, or by firm young stem cuttings in April. *See also under* Annuals *and* Rock Gardens.

Pinks. *See* Chapter XVIII. In contrast to Carnations, many are useful and valuable in the border.

Polygonum. In a family that contains several weeds and rampant growers, there is one to be welcomed for a shady corner—the bell-flowered P. campanulatum. From a full, rounded bush, it throws up clustered trusses of little bells branching from wiry stems 3 ft high in summer. See also Chapter XII.

Poppy. The Oriental poppy (Papaver orientale) flowers in barbaric splendour in late spring, but is a grizzly mess afterwards. The Iceland poppy (Chapter X) far excels it.

Potentilla. The variety Gibson's Scarlet is a really fine front-of-the-border plant—much better than the more usual Geum—with crowds of brilliant red cups on 1-ft stems all through the summer. It needs full sun and succeeds even in the driest soil. Increase by division. *See also under* Trees and Shrubs.

Primula. A large and versatile tribe is the genus Primula. It includes the Primrose, the Cowslip, the Auricula, the hybrid Polyanthus, and innumerable other hybrids, besides many species that are known simply as Primula So-and-so. Some come from waterside haunts, others dwell in the mountains or the woods. A great many are for the expert only, especially the genuine species. None, easy or difficult, are really plants for the formal border, but they are admirable for small beds, odd places, among shrubs or skirting a path. For those purposes the easiest are those beloved by gardeners for so many centuries—the Polyanthus, the coloured Primroses and Keats's vestal flower, the chaste Auricula. They have wide variations of colour, and leading nurseries cherish their own 'strains'. The hybrids of P. Juliana, such as Wanda, are deservedly popular in their shades of claret, ruby, and rose.

Give all these sorts a soil that does not dry out, and behead them when they finish flowering. Increase by division in July. They are also easy, but not true nor quick, from seed, sown preferably under glass about March in cool and shady conditions.

Almost as easy as these popular hybrids, if the soil is moist, is the species denticulata, which, on an erect stem, holds aloft an orb of lilac. In a waterside garden, or very moist soil, if you are not a complete novice, you must certainly grow also the beautiful 'candelabra' Primulas, such as japonica and pulverulenta whose stems are ringed with tier upon tier of floral circlets. *See also* Chapters IX and XII.

Pyrethrum. These florist's favourites, like coloured marguerites, are one of the most desirable of cut flowers, but a bit 'thin' and short-lived for the herbaceous border. I grow them in the kitchen garden in straight lines for cutting only. They need generous soil treatment and don't do their best till well established. Eileen May Robinson, Kelway's Glory, and Queen Mary are very good varieties.

Red-hot Poker (Kniphofia, usually pronounced Niphofe-ia). These flaming red or yellow torches need sun and really good drainage but a rich, moisture-holding soil. Plenty of summer rain is welcome, but winter damp fatal. They are splendid seaside plants, resisting salt spray and high wind with equanimity. The six-footers take up too much room for small gardens, but there are some excellent hybrids of short stature, of which none is better than Galpinii. Of the taller ones, pick Royal Sovereign. All need careful placing to abate their flamboyance, and one of the best homes for the autumn varieties is among Michaelmas Daisies, with which they make a splendid marriage of form and colour. Plant in spring, not autumn.

Romneya. The 'Californian Tree Poppy' is a splendid, queenly plant, half-shrub, half-herbaceous. It makes a bush of 6-ft stature bearing very large, immaculate, silky white 'poppies' adorned with a boss of golden anthers from July to September. A thing of great beauty that is hardy enough in all but the coldest counties. It multiplies itself generously by underground runners, and thrives even on poor soils, given ample sun and a fairly dry situation. The sort usually quoted is R. Coulteri, but tricocalyx is virtually the same. The secret of success is to cut the plant right down almost to the ground either in early spring or in late autumn. Increase by winter root cuttings $2\frac{1}{2}$ in. long.

Rudbeckia. 'Goldsturm' (R. fulgida sullivantii), a pretty, daisyform dwarf of 15 in, with black disc and golden rays, is better than the usual tall and rangy sorts.

Salvia. The Sages provide us with one or two of our most splendid border plants, and are one of the first essentials in any herbaceous scheme, though curiously neglected in smaller gardens. First choice is Salvia superba, a grand 3-ft bush that throws up sheaves of erect stems, needing no staking and crowded with small, dark-blue flowers with purple-red bracts, which give colour for months and blend happily with the grey-green foliage. Another splendid one is hæmatodes, luxuriant with lavender spikes; short-lived and grown from seed. For the scarlet bedding Salvia, *see* Chapter X.

Scabious. Like Pyrethrum, Scabious is essentially a flower for cutting rather than for the border. It is sparse in bloom, but successive. A creature of chalk soils, it is an ardent lime-lover. Plant in spring, not autumn. The outstanding variety is Clive Greaves, but Miss Wilmott is a lovely white. Increase by division, or grow from seed.

Sea Holly (Eryngium species). Distinctive and very attractive plants with bristly teazle heads and spiny foliage, esteemed for their all-over metallic sheen and for the diversity of form they give to a border. For a start, take alpinum, oliverianum, and variifolium, the last steely blue all over. Avoid rich feeding.

'Shasta Daisy'. *See under* Chrysanthemums, Chapter XVIII.

Sidalcea. Sometimes called Greek Mallow, this is another first-class border plant, easy and well-behaved. It has slender stems, thickly bedizened with pink or red blossoms like miniature mallows or hollyhocks. It usually has to be well staked. Very nice ones are William Smith, the dwarf Puck, and Mrs Aldersen.

Solidaster. Included under Aster.

Spiræa. A large family that includes many shrubs. The herbaceous sorts are first-class border plants. Like Astilbe, with which it is often confused, the majority prefer a moist situation, but will do well enough elsewhere, provided the soil is not one that dries out in summer; so give them some peat. Venusta magnifica is a fine fellow with waving plumes of deep pink 6 ft high, and Aruncus, the 'Goat's-Beard', is a similar one in cream. By contrast, palmata is a crimson two-footer of foaming splendour, and filipendula, for *dry* places, is like a gracefully drooping feather; both of these, by their form and habit, give a light and dainty air to a border when placed near the front. Increase by division. I have stuck to the older, familiar names. Most of them are now supposed to be called Filipendulas, but the goat's-beard is Aruncus sylvester. For the shrubby Spiræas, *see* Chapter XV.

Statice (pronounced *stat*-issy). Also called Sea Lavender because one species grows close to the sea's edge. A fine border plant, its large and gay panicles borne on rigid 15-in. stems in late summer. If cut just before full bloom and hung up under cover upside-down for a week or two, some kinds will last indoors (without water) all the winter. The lavender S. latifolia Blue Cloud is the usual. No staking. Full sun. Plant in spring. Should now be called Limonium.

Stonecrop (Sedum). Most of these we grow in the rock garden, but S. spectabile, to be seen in most gardens, is a fine, showy and easy one for the border, with large pink platters, very welcome in September and October, and fleshy, pale-green leaves. 15 in. Autumn Joy is a great splendour in crimson. Rarer and more distinguished is a slightly taller one called maximum atropurpureum, whose foliage is the colour of dark mahogany, with flowers of a bronzed cream; it makes a striking and unusual note in a mixed border, especially when stationed next to a grey-leaved plant, but it needs a place in warm sun. See also next chapter.

Trollius, or **Globe Flower.** Giant orange or lemon 'buttercups' of great merit, flowering in May and after, repeating the performance in July. They prefer moist soils. Most are about 2 ft. The variety Orange Globe is splendid. Increase by division.

Veronica or **Speedwell.** A very versatile family which includes also shrubs and rock plants. Of the herbaceous breed,

155

the typical habit is a short, tightly-packed spike of blue. I like the 18-in., rose-pink Barcarolle, the 30-in. royal-blue longifolia subsessilis, and Minuet, a pretty pink-and-silver, 15 in. Increase by division.

Viola. In this lovely family are both the Violet and the Pansy (*see* Chapter X). What are, in the garden, specifically termed 'violas' are compact and tufted little plants of a neater habit than pansies and more perennial, often with a little yellow eye. Besides the named varieties, leading seedsmen have their own special strains, some of pure colour, others with rays like cats' whiskers.

Violas like a rather moist soil or partial shade, and in dry weather need lots of water. They are overpowered in the herbaceous border, and are better by themselves or at the feet of standard roses or companioned by other creatures of modest stature. Easily raised from seed in June and pricked off into a cool and fairly shady seed-bed. Or they can be increased by cuttings. Select strong plants in August, cut them back to within 3 in. of the ground with shears or scissors, and top-dress with a mixture of leaf-mould and sand. Strong new shoots will then come from the base. Pluck these out with a few small rootlets, and prick them out in a frame or a shady seed-bed under cloches and water well.

Of varieties, the old favourite Maggie Mott is still one of the best. Pickering Blue and W. H. Woodgate are beautiful, and Jackanapes is a jovial little chap that always seems to be laughing. Barbara and Irish Molly are also bonny wenches. *See also under* Rock Gardens.

Viscaria. Shown under Lychnis.

Second Eleven

To conclude, here are some good second choices, for which I have not been able to afford much room.

Baptisia australis. A good substitute for lupins where the soil is limy. Strong, 4-ft plants with blue pea-flowers. Not for wet places.

Coreopsis (or Calliopsis). Of the several species of this

popular yellow daisy-form plant, I suggest verticillata, a dainty plant with fine foliage, 18 in. The much advertised variety Badengold is apt to bloom disappointingly in good soils.

Day Lily (Hemerocallis). Those who like this useful old stager should try some of the new colours instead of the familiar yellow or bronze. Especially good for moist situations.

Dierama pulcherrimum. 'Angel's Fishing Rods', 4 ft long, that swing to the lightest wind, bearing pendant blossoms in August. Sun or partial shade. Get pulcherrima or pendula. Often erroneously called Sparaxis.

Fox-tail Lily (Eremurus). Elegant ladies of hyacinthine appearance and 6 ft stature or more. Expensive and not a beginner's plant.

If tempted, start with the Shelford or Highdown hybrids. Handle the queer, brittle roots very carefully, plant on a slight mound, just covered. Beware slugs.

Golden Rod (Solidago). Popular and awfully easy, but too apt to become a weed. Golden Falls and Golden Gate are better sorts and the dwarfs are good.

Linum narbonnense. Among the perennial flaxes, Six Hills and the enchanting Heavenly Blue are pretty plants near the front of the border.

Meadow Rue (Thalictrum). The best of these, T. dipterocarpum Hewitt's Double, is a beautiful 5-ft plant with clouds of mauve thistledown, but it is not easy or cheap. A moist, peaty soil is needed.

Physostegia virginiana (or Dracocephalum). In spite of its name, the variety Vivid is an admirable and easy autumn plant for the front of the border. Small roseate flowers on rigid stems.

Poterium obtusum. Tufts just like pink bottle-brushes from mounds of bushy foliate in late summer. Good.

Pulmonaria (Lungwort). Familiar little 8-in. bushes that have both blue and pink flowers in clusters in early spring. The usual one is P. saccharata. Easy.

Solomon's Seal (Polygonatum multiflorum). Arching 3-ft stems and ivory, tubular flowers in early summer in the habit of Bleeding Heart; valuable for thriving in deep shade under trees.

Valerian (Centranthus). This common wild flower makes an excellent border plant, especially the newer deep-red forms of C. ruber. Very good for dry, stony places and beloved by Sir Winston Churchill.

CHAPTER XII

ROCK GARDENS AND STONEWORKS

THE LURE AND THE HAZARD—THE ROCK GARDEN PROPER—DRY WALLS—MORAINE AND SCREE—WHAT TO PLANT—SECOND CHOICES—PATHS AND PAVING—PLANTS FOR WALLS—FOR BORDERS

The Lure and the Hazard

I HAVE already warned you about rock gardening. If you allow this particular siren to ensnare you, you are likely to be her slave for life. But it is a benevolent captivity, and if your friends think you have got life a little out of focus through rhapsodising over some pygmy darling of one-inch stature, you may console yourself that you have a deeper vision.

Few branches of gardening reach a higher degree of specialisation, and the beginner must naturally start on simple lines, but they should be the right ones. A rock garden which is well conceived, well built, and well stocked with carefully chosen plants will be a joy for many years; wrongly done, it will be an eyesore, a source of constant trouble, and the jest of those who know. You are warned that to do the job thus is not cheap, though the first cost is the last except for occasional replacement of plants. Good stone is heavy and expensive, and a ton does not go far (nor do the plants at first sight!). You could, of course, start with a wee garden of a few square yards and add to it yearly, but my first advice, however large or small your intentions, is that, if you are not prepared to do the job properly, don't do it at all. Nothing is more dismal to contemplate than the lumps of clinkered bricks or broken concrete that masquerade as 'rockeries'. Clinkers, moreover, are notorious harbours for the pirate snail. A rock *garden*, properly conceived, should represent a natural outcrop or other formation of rock, seemingly unmolested by the hand of man, though more *soigné* than nature in the rough. If one's chequebook permits nothing better than those clinkered burrs, dip them in a cement wash tinted to the colour of stone—it makes the world of difference.

Fortunately, however, there are several ways of employing rocks, and growing flowers among them, which do not constitute true rock gardens, and we can enjoy many of the lovely creations of cliff- and mountain-side in settings which do not profess to simulate natural scenery and are frankly the artificial work of man. In particular there is the so-called 'dry wall', which can be employed in many forms. It can be a retaining wall supporting a terrace or a formal sunk garden or the edge of a raised flower-bed; or it may be a stone facing to an awkward bank, planted with Brooms and other plants that thrive in a dry, hot environment; or it may be just a wall for its own sake and purpose employed instead of a hedge or fence. There is also the more restricted medium of the pavement, into the crannies of which we may insinuate prostrate plants that suffer being trodden on. All these are intended to simulate nature's encroachment and man's neglect. Again, there are little edgings of flat stone that are employed for neatness here and there, ornamental steps, and so on. Moreover, several rock plants can, of course, be most effectively used on the edge of a mixed border.

The Rock Garden Proper

In our true rock garden any fault in concealing the hand of man and in simulating an extract from nature is a measure of artistic failure. It is difficult to prescribe in print just what this implies except in general terms, for a little art may adapt the most unlikely place convincingly—even within the unpromising wooden palings of a suburban villa. Taste and judgement must be our guides, but a few general suggestions may be given. Obviously the middle of a lawn is an unnatural

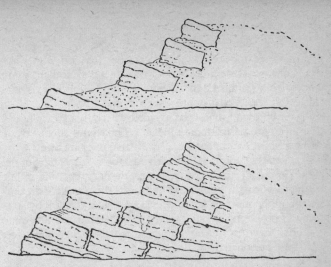

Top: Sectional view of a simple, naturalistic rock garden suitable for a small place; drainage not shown. *Bottom:* Profile of another simple scheme.

place in which to suffer rocks to erupt, and on any flat site there is always a danger of incongruity. But the *end* of a lawn —yes, with the grass gradually merging into a low and scattered outcrop. The shape and design of the rock formation must be informal, irregular, and loose, but not an unplanned jumble. The outline may be compounded of bays or jutting promontories. Its size, and its height in particular, should be in proportion to the garden as a whole. Advantage should be taken of any unevenness of ground there may be, and a naturally sloping bank or depression is a great opportunity for a naturalistic design. Unless something specialised is intended, the rock garden should be in full sun for the greater part of the day, and not under trees, but if part of it can have a north aspect, with a little shade from its own rocks, a greater range of plants can be introduced.

One method I have found successful in achieving congruity within these general principles is to separate the rock garden from the rest by means of a dry wall.

161

Types of Rock

The rock should be all of the same type and of a porous nature. Sandstone and limestone are best; a hard, impermeable stone such as granite is not sympathetic. Excellent stone comes from Cumberland, Westmorland, Derbyshire, Yorkshire, and the West Country, such as the attractive Cheddar stone. Limestone should be avoided where it is specially desired to grow lime-hating plants. The stones should be of varying sizes, and in small places flattish ones are best. What is particularly important is that the striations or graining of the stone should all run one way, as they do in nature, and in like manner, when the stones are built into the new garden, they should all lie more or less in the same plane, stratum by stratum. If proposing to build the rock garden oneself, it is quite essential to go to the nursery or stone merchant's and select the stone personally.

Building the Rock Garden

The first essential is good drainage. This above all. What is most wanted is protection from damp, not frost. If natural drainage does not exist, dig out about 18 in. of soil (preserving the top spit), lay in a bed of broken brick or clinkers, and dig a channel to a soakaway or to some other outlet if there is one. On top of this drainage lay a mat of close-set turves upside-down.

In any case, remove the top spit from the selected site and keep it on one side. Using this top spit as base (if it is good enough), prepare a soil mixture of two parts of this loam with two parts of leaf-mould or granulated peat and one part of sharp sand; for lime-loving plants incorporate with it liberal handfuls of small limestone chippings or of mortar rubble, but of sandstone for lime-haters. Soil for rock plants should contain plenty of grit and not be too rich; but, while draining off excessive rain, should be capable of retaining sufficient moisture through the agency of the peat or mould.

Assuming the rock garden to be a raised one, work from the bottom upwards over the whole expanse, placing the rocks layer by layer. The function of the rock is to provide the plants with a *cool root-run*. In general, about one-third or so of each rock should be buried. The rock should *emerge* from the soil, not appear to have been dumped on top of it, and there should be an impression that a mass of solid rock lies hidden below surface. Tilt all the pieces slightly backwards and their noses just a little upwards, but always preserve the graining parallel, for one rock standing erect or otherwise out of plane will spoil the whole picture. Nor should the pieces slope generally to the front, or both rain and soil will be washed away. Don't put a big rock on top of a small one.

Bed the rock in firmly, ramming the earth well down with a pick helve or something of the sort. There must be no chance of the soil being washed out by rain. *Fill every cranny and crevice*, and make sure that there are some vertical crevices for plants that like that sort of home. The pockets of soil between rocks should vary in size from a few square inches to broad 3-ft expanses.

If it is intended to grow lime-hating plants, such as dwarf Rhododendrons or the lovely Lithospermum, then either the whole of the soil mixture may be made from lime-free constituents or selected pockets may be so filled, but in such a plan avoid limestone rocks, and have your lime-haters in peat-beds, on the top storey of the garden. Lime-loving plants on the other hand, such as Pinks, Stonecrops, Gypsophila, and House Leeks, should have big handfuls of small limestone chips or old mortar rubble mixed into their pockets; chippings, or fine, clear gravel in lieu, should also be thickly strewn on top of the soil right up the collar of each plant.

PLANTING

Good nurseries send out most of their rock-garden stock in pots, and therefore they can be planted at any time of the year when the weather is suitable. Those not sold in pots are usually best planted in early spring unless that is their flowering time. First-class nurseries will not send their stuff except at the right time. Normal planting rules apply—well spread-out roots, firm planting, ample watering-in, especially of shrubs.

Think out the planting plan carefully with due regard to the ultimate spread of the plants (often considerable), their habit, the colour scheme and season of blooming. Try to ensure that there is colour in the rock garden from early spring to late autumn, while for winter the Mountain Heather (Erica carnea) will do you proud.

Plants that have to go into crevices between rocks, whether horizontal or vertical, should be planted while the rock garden is being built, but few of us are clever enough to plan so exactly.

Dry Walls and Banks

A dry wall is one which is made without cement or mortar. For this purpose one orders 'walling stone', of which there are several good sorts, such as York or Somerset walling, the cream tints being effective for several uses. All should be fairly flat, and they should not be too dissimilar in size. Bricks, especially dark, matured ones, can quite well be mixed with them informally.

In building the wall, a layer of prepared soil should be laid between each course of stones. The stones must be properly 'bonded'—those of one course overlapping the junction of two stones in the course below it.

When building a wall proper, as distinct from the retaining face of a terrace, a raised herbaceous border or the sides of a flight of steps, build it with two faces, and fill the space between the two faces—about a foot—with rammed earth of the same blend as for the rock garden. Finish, if you like, with a narrow ribbon bed at the top of the wall, except in wet and cold districts, where the wall should be topped with coping-stone, to prevent the lower courses being shattered by frost after heavy rains. Unless the wall is a very low one, give a slight backward tilt—or 'batter' as architects call it—to each course of stones, so that the top is a little narrower than the base. If much more than about 2 ft high, put in extra-long stones as 'ties' at intervals of about 8 ft horizontally and 18 in. vertically; insert them, of course, edgewise, like a book into a bookcase. Such a wall should also have a strong foundation of fairly large stones just below ground level.

Both sides of the wall (if two-sided), and the top, can be studded with plants, but if the wall runs east and west then the

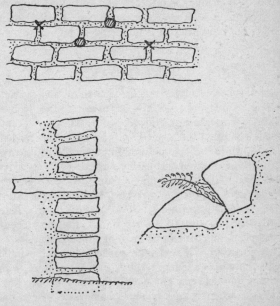

Top: Front view of a dry wall; the circles show the right places to stow plants and the crosses wrong ones. *Below (left):* Sectional view of a dry wall, showing slight backward slope and tie-stone. *Below (right):* Wrong way to house a plant; roots trapped in a stone prison.

north face should receive shade-tolerating sorts, and all should be plants which tolerate a good deal of dryness. Put in the plants as you build the wall, preferably at the bottom of a junction between two stones. At the bottom of the wall put the least choice, such as aubrieta and polygonum, at the top the daintier ones and those most capable of standing drought, such as dwarf Brooms, Stonecrop, Potentilla and Thyme.

Moraine and Scree

These are specially stony conditions prepared for plants from high mountains. A scree is a raised bed with more stone and grit than soil, having very sharp drainage. A moraine has a controlled water supply underground (usually a pipe drilled with a few small holes) and a scree has not. These refinements are best deferred until one is no longer an apprentice.

What to Plant

I am purposely keeping this list very short, and restricted to the simple things. It is a mistake to advise the beginner to attempt any *recherché* or difficult plants. He who becomes an enthusiast is often dissatisfied with his first rock garden and pulls it down to build something more ambitious, incorporating a moraine or scree and perhaps a little running water and pools as well. Then is the time for the specialist's plants—for Daphne rupestris, for the wayward Androsace, for Anemone alpina, the Asiatic primulas and so on. Meantime, better to gain experience with the easier things first, and even here there is plenty of scope for something unhackneyed.

The purist says that a rock garden should be inhabited only by those plants that grow among rocks in nature. I am not preaching purism, but one should be wary about recruiting outside the accepted rock tribes. Again, taste, discretion, and the length of one's purse must rule. Obviously only small plants should be chosen, and if expense is at first an obstacle one can in the first year or two fill up with small annuals from seed. Phacelia campanularia, so like a gentian, is very appropriate. Others acceptable are the pretty little Leptosiphon, the Pimpernel (Anagallis), annual Candytuft, Kochia (which looks exactly like a dwarf cypress), Forget-me-not (very like a true rock-garden plant), Alyssum, and that pleasing little nuisance Limnanthes Douglasii. Other suitable ones are Auriculas, dwarf Ageratum, Portulaca (for mild districts and dry sites), Mesembryanthemum (likewise) and dwarf snapdragons.

Apart from this rather unorthodox company, there are, broadly speaking, three groups of plant for the rock garden— prostrate shrubs and dwarf conifers, bulbs of miniature size, and the general run of soft-wooded plants, some evergreen and some deciduous. Many of the little bulbs, endearing and tempting though they are, are generally expensive for the display they give, and can be omitted till another year's budget. But the mountain Anemones are inexpensive and far too lovely to omit, and other small inexpensive bulbs can go in, such as the dwarf Alliums, Chionodoxa, Snowdrops, and Scillas.

I am afraid that in this chapter it is inevitable that in many instances I should use longish botanical names again, if you are to be certain of getting the right things—and many haven't got any other names.

Next shrubs—without being too particular as to what is botanically a true shrub. The following is a short selection of the best and easiest, further details being given in the chapter on shrubs:

Helianthemum. Easy and good; beginner's first choice.

Conifers. Two or three should be included for their 'atmosphere'. Start with the toy sentinel Juniper (J. communis compressa) and the golden Chamæcyparis lawsoniana Minima Aurea. These must be neighboured by something prostrate or creeping, or their effect will be spoilt. Plant them about mid-way up the rocks, not on top.

Brooms. The prostrate Kew Broom (Cytisus kewensis), spangled with pale gold, and the prolific Ardoinii of deeper hue; put these drought-resisting plants high up, to fall in cascades.

Daphne Cneorum and other dwarf Daphnes.

Ericas in great variety, especially the pygmies and those that glorify the winter (Chapter XVIII).

Euryops acraeus (or evansii). A beautiful shrublet, brightly silvered, with yellow daisies for a short period in summer. Full sun and gritty, quick-draining soil.

Hypericum. Dwarf rock varieties of the favourite Rose of Sharon with her cheerful golden bowls. Not all are good, but others make ideal toy shrubs. I recommend H. Coris, like a 6-in. Heather clothed in gold, the 9-in. olympicum and the prostrate reptans.

Lilac. The dwarf form, true lilac in colour and fragrance, is something quite new to most people. There is a bother about its name, but you must ask either for Syringa microphylla or for S. palibiniana. For the larger rock garden.

Rhododendron. Three excellent ones are the mauve impeditum, the dark-red Carmen, and the rosy-mauve keleticum.

Roses. For those who like the very dwarf, the most appropriate for the rock garden is Rosa Roulettii, a perfect miniature of elfin charm, 6 in. high and pink. Others you could have are Oakington Ruby and Peon, but they will reach 15 in.

We come now to the soft-wooded plants, and for the apprentice's assistance I shall group these into first and second choices; and it may be a help if I say at the outset that if I were asked to pick a First Eleven for him this would be it:

Anemone blanda atrocoerulea (alternative, the Apennine anemone).

Campanula—a great many all on a par, but I would choose the lovely C. pusilla Miranda.

Phlox subulata, variety Vivid.

Aubrieta—variety according to one's colour fancy.

Thyme—the red prostrate Thymus serpyllum coccineum. Any dwarf Pink.

Potentilla tonguei.

Geranium (Cranesbill)—the rose-pink dwarf G. sanguineum lancastriense.

Saxifrage—one could easily pick an eleven from this large and versatile breed alone; let us choose the pretty pink hybrid Cranbourne.

Auricula hybrids.

Sedum cauticolum, for autumn.

I have said that we would keep to the fairly easy things, but it will be noted that in the following lists I have included Gentians and Lithospermum, which not everyone would call easy. However, the apprentice often succeeds with them where the master gardener fails, and they are so very lovely that it would be a pity not to try; but do treat them conscientiously.

Most of these plants will flower for very long periods, or make a second blooming, if the spent flowers are removed; those that make close and dense growth may be trimmed back with shears, such as Aubrieta, Candytuft, Soapwort, Viola,

"Here lies poor Fido"

Top: The wrong sort of 'rockery'—the 'Dog's Grave' type.
Bottom: Two methods of finishing off the top of a dry wall.

Cranesbill, and the mossy Saxifrages, etc. The figures included below are the normal height and spread in inches.

Æthionema is a toy shrub like a celestial candytuft with roseate crowns, and the variety Warley Rose is one of the best of rock plants. Excels in a dry wall. Give it full sun and a gritty loam. Not for severe climates.

Anemone. A first choice. Specially suitable for a partially shaded site are the Apennine anemone (A. appenina) and A. blanda atrocoerulea. *See* chapter on bulbs.

Arenaria. Two easy ones. Montana is a very pretty, ground-hugging plant covered with gleaming white moons at midsummer, 4 × 20. Balearica is a minute creeper that closely hugs the ground, shining with a myriad tiny white stars. 1 × 30. Both easy from seed.

Aubrieta. Everyone knows these. Perhaps the perfect plant for Everyman's rock garden, but much overdone; they really need a background of grey stone. Raise them from seed (very easy) or buy a named variety of the colour you like. 4 × 20.

Campanula. The prostrate rock harebells, crowded with their jaunty little bells in mauve, blue, or white, rising from a close green carpet, are quite essential in all gardens. The best to start with are the following species, all of which have several varieties with fancy names. Avoid C. Poscharskyana, a ruthless invader.

The demure pusilla (or cochlearifolia), which wanders here and there in an engaging and harmless manner; especially the silver-blue variety Miranda or Miss Willmott.

C. muralis (now C. Portenschlagiana), very rampant, but good for a dry wall.

C. garganica. Radiating stems with blue, starry flowers over kidney-shaped leaves in June–August. 4 in. Sun or part-shade. A favourite variety is W. H. Paine.

Hybrids of the very large-flowered Carpathian harebell C. carpatica, especially the cool sparkling white Everest; cut it back hard and it will bloom again. Excellent for a dry wall, for crevices, for steps, and for the front of the herbaceous border.

All these harebells will tolerate some shade, but prefer sun, and they are the mainstay of the garden in the summer months with prolonged and brilliant displays. Increase by division. Avoid the difficult ones, such as Allionii.

Cranesbill (true Geranium). Before reaching this stage of the book, the reader will, I hope, know what a Geranium really is. The race provides some sparkling rock plants, spilling over with dense and delicate foliage and crowded with vivid coloured cups for long periods in summer. One of the best and easiest. First choice is G. sanguineum lancastriense, a warm rose-pink Cranesbill from the Isle of Walney in Lancashire, flowering all summer if the spent blooms are removed. Another fine one is the Dalmatian Cranesbill, G. dalmaticum, with low hummocks and *vin rosé* cups. There is also a saucy crimson fellow with black eye called subcaulescens splendens (or cinereum); insist on the full name, or you will get something inferior. 4×30. Increase all by division in spring.

Gentian. The queen of the rock garden, with her sensational fanfares of true blue trumpets, shares with the Madonna Lily and with Daphne Cneorum a secret not yet discovered by the horticulturist—why it will grow like a weed in one garden, as the Chinese sort does in Scotland, while next door, with all the care in the world, it never blooms at all. Three points are to be noted—first, that Gentians need a rather richer soil than most rock plants, so incorporate some old cow manure or well-rotted compost; secondly, that dry conditions are inimical, so, while being well-drained, the soil must be able to retain moisture; and thirdly, that some Gentians like or tolerate lime, while to others it is poison.

I suggest that the beginner might start with Gentiana septemfida, not quite the very choicest but very good indeed and fairly easy (8 in. late summer). Of the more famous sorts, the Gentianella (G. acaulis) and the Star Gentian (G. verna) both like lime, are a vivid deep blue, like the sun, and flower in the spring. The Gentianella is notoriously wayward and coy in the south and east. The Star Gentian grows wild in some counties, but turns shy when brought into the cultivated gardens. It seems to demand a moist, gritty, peaty, or leaf-mouldy soil in full sun, with frequent water. The best variety is Angulosa.

Opposed to these in every way is a cluster of gems that are lighter blue, flower in the autumn, and hate lime. The best and probably most wooable are G. sino-ornata, and its two offspring, the Macauley and Stevenage Gentians. Feed these on lime-free loam, granulated peat, and sharp sand in equal parts.

171

Top-dress after flowering. They should be grown in shade or partial shade, and do well facing north.

Geranium. *See* Cranesbill.

Gypsophila. The prostrate and trailing forms are easy and delightful for the rock garden, especially in dry situations and in a dry wall. They relish lime. I specially like G. cerastioides, Cooper's variety (quite large white flowers, crimson-veined (3 × 18) and Fratensis.

House Leek (Sempervivum). Great favourite of odd charm and special usefulness for bare rock ledges, crevices of dry walls, and roofs. Needs practically no depth of soil but best started on a 1-in. spread of fairly rich soil. Must not get water-logged. Readily increased by removal of baby offsets once they have rooted. Start with any variety of the 'cobweb' House Leeks (S. arachnoideum).

Iris. In addition to specialists' sorts, those suitable for the rock garden are histrioides Major and reticulata. *See* Chapter XVIII.

Lithospermum. The prostrate species is a pearl of the rock garden. The little flowers are a vivid gentian-blue, and indeed resemble pygmy Gentians, crowding the ground over a square yard. But it hates lime, and requires a peat-and-loam soil with maximum sun, and good drainage. Grace Ward is of rare loveliness, but Heavenly Blue is nearly as good. Lithospermum is another jewel that may cheat the expert and reward the novice. 6 × 24. May–June. Increase by cuttings in sand in summer.

Narcissus. *See* Chapter XIII.

Omphalodes. Very like Forget-me-not. The species cappadocica is excellent and easy for shady spots, flowering in early summer and again in autumn. 8 × 15. O. verna is Blue-eyed Mary, a lovely creature that flourishes anywhere, but is very sprawling and invasive; April–May. Don't attempt O. lucilliæ, which is a specialist's treasure.

Phlox. The prostrate species are quite indispensable. The most popular are the named varieties of P. subulata, which are dense, matted plants, with small, moss-like leaves, and smothered in late spring and early summer with lovely little

Phlox blooms in red, pink, mauve, or white. Have a mixed bag, but give first choice to the subulata variety Vivid, brilliantly, pink and compact in habit. Sprite is very similar. The varieties of P. Douglasii are also justly popular. Two other phloxes that are quite invaluable for their use in shady places are P. adsurgens and the variety of P. stolonifera called Blue Ridge—most charming. 4 × 30. Cuttings in early summer or division.

Pinks. The rock-garden species and varieties are among the most enchanting of the great Dianthus family, and for our purposes I make no apology at all for calling all these little chaps Pinks, quite simply. Give them the same general treatment as recommended in Chapter XVIII—full sun, plenty of limestone chips or old mortar rubble, and (most important of all) a pocket of soil where they will have really good drainage. Many prosper exceedingly on a dry wall. Trim them back after first flowering, and many will go on all summer. Plant in September. Here are a few of the best and easiest for a start.

(*a*) The Cheddar Pink (D. cæsius), glowing rose-pink, good anywhere in the sun, including crevices and dry walls, one of the dozen best rock plants, having every virtue; but go to a reliable nursery and get a good form or variety, such as the Icombe variety or D.c. majus. It lives longest in rather poor, stony soil.

(*b*) The Maiden Pink (D. deltoides), a first-class trailing sort with ruby flowers, grand also for the dry wall; again insist on a good variety, such as E. A. Bowles.

(*c*) Of the hybrids (which I dare say will most catch the beginner's fancy) first choices are: Inchmery; Mars; Little Jock and his hybrids; Ernest Ballard; La Bourbrille; and the Allwoodii alpinus. For details of these refer to Chapter XVIII.

Polygonum. Provides us with some tiresome 'knot-weeds'; but two good ones for us, serving as low, dense, wide-spreading ground-cover, are P. affine Donald Lowndes, handsome in bronze and pink, 9 in., and the old, shorter vaccinifolium, good for covering dry walls and banks.

Potentilla. A most obliging genus, hallmarked by its strawberry-like leaves. Its most desirable member is P. nitida, gleaming in silver and pink, but it is no beginner's plant, needing a gritty, sharply drained soil and a hot summer. Two easy ones are P. tonguei, a fine trailing or tumbling plant starred with orange discs, and P. verna, which spreads neatly in tight, ground-hugging, green-gold mats.

Primula. This great and wonderful family, of extraordinary diversity, includes many gems that are true rock plants and many others that may be admitted. However, care should be taken to avoid those that are of difficult culture, those that belong to the greenhouse, and those that dwell in the riverside and marsh, such as Japonica and Florindæ (unless of course your garden gives these conditions). Most Primulas, however, do demand ample moisture, with cool and partly shaded positions. As a mere introduction to this large subject I suggest a start with:

(*a*) The Auriculas, most economically got by ordering a batch of mixed seedlings, but being careful to avoid the difficult 'Show Auriculas'. Auriculas need a deep, cool root-run in light soil with plenty of leaf-mould. Easy from seed.

(*b*) The popular dwarf named Wanda in wine red, and other varieties of P. Juliana, which are really small coloured Primroses.

(*c*) Any hybrid Primrose of low stature, but not the robust Polyanthus.

(*d*) The drumstick primula, P. denticulata.

Most other primulas need not the typical rock-garden conditions but moist, cool beds. Start here with the charming little P. rosea Delight and with the easier of the Calendelabrum primulas, such as Japonica and the Bartley strain.

Saxifrage. Another enormous and widely diverse family, with innumerable hybrids. Many are difficult. All must have a moisture-retaining content in the soil, but drainage must be good. The easiest are London Pride and the mossy sorts. The main groups or sections for us are:

(*a*) 'Silver' or encrusted Saxifrages. Showy plumes or sprays of blossom from 2 in. to 3 ft spring from rosettes of richly silvered leaves which betray their love of lime. Summer flowering. Need full sun and gritty, stony soil, and look well in vertical crevices and dry walls. Varieties of S. aizoon, cochlearis, and cotyledon are all good, and Tumbling Waters is by way of a sensation with its foaming white 2-ft waterfall. Kathleen Pinsent is another delight.

(*b*) 'Cushion' or Kabschia Saxifrages. The neat and compact cushions of tiny foliage are animated with multitudes of lovely Dresden-china miniatures. Early spring flowering. Extra gritty soil, fast drainage, and a little shade. Suggested first choices are Elizabathæ, L. G. Godseff, and Jenkinsæ.

(*c*) 'Mossy' Saxifrages. Soft, moss-like foliage, fast-growing, flowering April to June. Kindergarten plants for *shady* places. Get a mixed bag in red, pink, and white. Most are about 4 in. Trim back sharply after flowering. Scraps transplant easily.

Soapwart (Saponaria). The trailing S. ocymoides grows anywhere and spreads rapidly with a multitude of pretty little pink flowers through June and July; a good beginner's sort. 4 × 30. Easy from seed.

Stonecrop (Sedum). We have reviewed these fleshy-leaved plants in the previous chapter. For rocky places of all sorts we can have:

(*a*) S. cauticolum, beautiful semi-trailing plant from Japan, purplish foliage, dense crimson flowers, spreading and enriching September and October.

(*b*) S. spathulifolium, especially the variety Cappa Blanca, prostrate, spreading, brilliant gold flowers on decorative 3-in. stems; grand for dry walls, steps, and the chinks of pavements.

Thyme (Thymus). To omit the creeping wild Thyme, T. serpyllum, from any garden, is almost unthinkable. Tightly hugging the ground, it makes a dense mat in brilliant colours— coccineus (red), Annie Hall (flesh pink), Pink Chintz, and others—and the thing to do is to have six or more in different colours. For the rock garden, the dry wall, the pavement; it likes being trodden on, when it gives out its aromatic fragrance. 2×24. Also very charming is the toy shrublet T. citriodorus Silver Queen, which has variegated leaves, 9 in. high. Plant all Thymes in sunny positions in soil on the dry side.

Veronica (Speedwell). The rock-garden species of this very versatile family are mostly dense trailers or prostrate shrubs. No soil fads. Easy, colourful and hardy are V. prostrata (or rupestris), ground-hugging and spreading widely, and the delightful shrublet Carl Teschner, violet, 9 in., now classed as a Hebe.

Viola. Many of the larger hybrids and the woodland sorts look out of place in the rock garden, but gracilis is a very pretty, dense, mat-like creature in violet, yellow, or white varieties, but its life is often short.

Some Second Choices

Achillea. The dwarf breeds of the big border Yarrow are effective and flowerful. Some are weed-like, but very good ones are the sulphur King Edward VII and argentea, silver-leaved and white-flowered.

Alyssum saxatile. Familiar lusty plant of golden splendour often seen associated with Aubrieta. Showy but not choice and too rumbustious for small rock gardens. The lemon-yellow citrinum and the small, double, long-lasting flore pleno are better. Prune it hard, or it wears out very quickly.

Arabis albida. Kindergarten rock plant, with profuse white blossom and greyish leaves, that grows anywhere, but gets out of hand. Get the double kind (flore pleno) or the new pink-tinted sort. April and May. Increase by division.

Aster alpinus. Miniature Michaelmas Daisies, 6 in. high. Several varieties, e.g. Beechwood. Early summer.

Candytuft (Iberis). The perennial forms are bonny plants, much ill-used. Give them full sun and a poor, stony soil, and trim them hard after flowering. Besides their rock uses, they make fine pygmy hedges. The perennial sort is I. sempervirens, of which Snowflake is 10 in., spreading widely, and Little Gem is 6 in.

Chrysogonum virginianum. Showy 8-in. plant, blazoned for months with deep gold stars. Easy in any soil.

Dryas octopetala. A flat evergreen carpet with foliage like tiny oak leaves, spangled with flowers like white Anemones in June. Full sun. Delightful in a pavement. Is the mountain Avens.

Erinus alpinus. Endearing, tiny-flowered plant that spreads and clings to rock surfaces like a vest to the body. Good for dry walls, too. Best-known is the carmine Dr Hanele, 3 in.

Frankenia thymifolia. Prostrate spreader with minute leaves and the prettiest little lilac stars. Nice for pavements.

Haberlea and the closely related *Ramonda.* Choice plants particularly valuable for the special task of filling vertical crevices on the shady side of the garden. Plant so that the leaves are nearly in the vertical plane, to shed off the rain, but put plenty of moisture-holding peat or leaf-mould at the roots when planting. Both throw up 6-in. clusters of charming flowers of unusual form. Get H. rhodopensis and R. pyrenaica (or Myconi).

Thrift (Armeria). Most people know this hardy maritime cliff-dweller with tufts of grass-like leaves, flowered with many pink globes. The crimson variety Vindictive is most recommended. 9 in. Early summer.

Wallflower (Cheiranthus). For the rock garden the one to have is the hybrid Harper Crewe, a bush densely robed in gold; April–June. This is the old Scotch Double Wallflower. 12 × 15. Increase by plucking off the young side-shoots for cuttings in summer.

Rock Garden Paths and Pavings

Small walks, paths, or other places liable to be trodden on in and about the rockery often present a problem. If grass is used, the mower cannot get at them. But there are happier solutions than grass. One is to plant these places with Camomile (Anthemis nobilis), and the other is to plant with low creeping things. The creeping Thymes, in different colours 8 in. apart, are the stand-by for this. Add to them the Frankenia mentioned above, Mentha Requienii for use in shade; a resistant little plant called Cotula squalida, with tiny fern-like leaves closely hugging the earth; and the prostrate New Zealand Burr, Acæna microphylla. A carpet of this sort is both picturesque and economical—and the poorest soil will suit.

The same plants can be used in paving-stones, together with such plants as Dryas octopetala, Toadflax (Linaria), dwarf Thrift, Veronica prostrata, etc., for the places less trodden upon. Dwarf pinks also excel in pavements. One of the most engaging, especially for steps, is the little daisy Erigeron mucronatus, referred to in Chapter XI.

Plants for Dry Walls

Æthionema Warley Rose (not in severe districts).
Alyssum saxatile (large walls only).
Arenaria balearica (shady side).
Aubrietas.
Dwarf Brooms—Cytisus and Genista species.
Campanulas, especially muralis (or Portenschlagiana).
Cheddar Pink, Maiden Pink, Inchmery, La Bourbrille and other hybrid Pinks.
Perennial Candytuft.
Erigeron mucronatus (Chapter XI).
Gypsophila cerastioides and repens.
Helianthemums.
House Leeks.
Lithospermum (if no lime).
Phlox subulata varieties.
Polygonum vaccinifolium.
Potentilla Tonguei.
Soapwort.
Saxifrages (mossy varieties on the shady side).
Stonecrops.
Thymus serpyllum.
Veronica prostrata.

For Herbaceous and Mixed Borders

The following rock plants are adaptable and effective for front edges and for small beds:

Aubrieta, dwarf Aster, Candytuft, Campanula, Cranesbill, Helianthemum, Phlox, Pinks, some Primula, some Saxifrage such as London Pride, Thrift, Veronica, Viola, Wallflower Harper Crew.

CHAPTER XIII

BULBS AND THEIR KIND

BULBS IN GENERAL—BULBS INDOORS—A SELECTION
OF BULBOUS PLANTS

Bulbs in General

BULBS, corms, tubers, and rhizomes are all forms of swelling
which different plants have evolved as devices for storing
energy during their periods of dormancy, as electricity is stored
in a battery. A quality of freshness and virginality dwells in
them. They are easy to handle and to plant. If they come from
a good nursery they are almost certain of success in their first
year, but success in subsequent years depends on good cultivation.

This easy first success deludes many people into thinking
that bulbs can take care of themselves in any sort of conditions;
whereas the success of the plant this year is the result mainly
of the good treatment it was given last year, and if it does not
go on being well treated it will deteriorate.

In evolving their storage devices the bulbous families have
exploited different parts or members. In the bulb proper, as
in the Narcissus or Daffodil (and in the onion), the battery is a
swelling of the leaf bases, which form a sheath round the
embryo flower within, perfect and complete in all its parts.
The corm, on the other hand, as in the Crocus and Gladiolus,
is a swelling of the stem. A rhizome is also a stem swelling, the
most familiar example being the 'Flag' Iris. The tuber may be
a swollen underground branch, as in the potato, or a swollen
root as in the Dahlia and the popular breeds of Anemone.

Except for many of the small bulbs, and all Lilies other than Madonna, a habitation open and sunny is best.

As ever, good drainage is the first care; yet the top soil must be of a loam that will retain a certain amount of moisture. Anything in the nature of free water in the sub-soil on the one hand, or of complete drying out on the other, may well be fatal.

Organic matter—compost, leaf-mould, hop manure, peat—provides these conditions. *But on no account use animal manures for bulbs* unless old and well rotted. In Cornwall and elsewhere seaweed is used. Bonemeal is always excellent, and heavy soils may be lightened with sand. Most bulbs are tolerant of lime, but to certain Lilies it is damaging.

Unimaginative planting can quite spoil the natural charm of the bulbous families. Hyacinths, Tulips, and Begonias indeed look their bravest when dressed in ranks like regiments of light-opera soldiers. But the care-free beauty of all others abhors rigidity. Daffodils in straight lines are as ill-suited as ballet dancers in battle-dress. Informal drifts and clusters are their best formations. There is no better dodge for getting the right effect than the old one of taking a handful of stones, of size according to the bulb, tossing them down casually, and planting where they fall.

A special problem of planting is that, once the beauty of their blossom has passed away, too many bulbs become dowdy and unkempt in their foliage. Therefore, make a special point of planting these sorts—Narcissus, Tulip, Muscari, Hyacinth, Gladiolus, etc.—where their sere and drooping foliage is not an eyesore, e.g. in the middle or back (not the front) of an herbaceous border, where the early ones will enliven the naked earth before its other occupants are fully awake, but where they will be covered by the oncoming foliage of those others when they sink to rest; or among shrubs, where the smaller breeds in particular look well; or naturalised in grass; or in beds by themselves, where, if need be, they can be lifted and removed after flowering.

These, of course, are generalisations. You wouldn't plant

tulips among shrubs, and rarely in grass. Nor is all bulb foliage disagreeable—Anemones, for example, go excellently in the front edge of a sunny border. Taste and discretion must be the guides. But there is one place where virtually all bulbous plants are absolutely barred—the formal rose bed. Not only will the bulb be completely out of its element, but also it will do the roses no good, and the dying foliage on the bare beds will be an eyesore. I would allow only the miniature Irises of winter.

Sorts that go well among shrubs, especially deciduous shrubs, are Snowdrops, Muscari, Crocus, Fritillary, Scilla, Chionodoxa, the woodland Anemones, Cyclamen, Winter Aconite, and, with discretion, Narcissus. They adorn the bare feet of the shrubs very charmingly in spring, and their foliage in decay is less objectionable.

Many of the small ones also go well in the rock garden, and there are some specially bred pygmies of elfin beauty and charm for this purpose.

NATURALISING

Those best for naturalising are Narcissus, Snowdrop, Crocus, Fritillary, and Chionodoxa, but the smaller flowers should, of course, not be in tall and rampant grasses. The mower should on no account go over places where these bulbs lie till their foliage has died right down, so plant them in clusters or drifts convenient for manœuvring the machine, preferably near the corners or edges of the lawn in small gardens.

Planting can be done with a special tool for naturalising; alternatively, lift a few slices of turf with a turfing-iron or spade, fold them back, dig and loosen the soil beneath, plant in the ordinary way, and replace the turf.

PLANTING

Take care always to plant bulbs at their correct depths. In the cultural notes that follow, 'plant 3 in. deep' means that there must be 3 in. of soil above the top of a bulb. In very light soil plant a bit deeper, in heavy soils not quite so deep. For most Lilies a spade must be used, but generally a trowel is the best tool. Never use a dibber, except for planting a lot of very small bulbs; then use a blunt dibber, not a sharp one. There must be no air pocket beneath the bulb. In heavy soils seat the bulb on $\frac{1}{2}$ in. of sharp sand.

The time for planting the great majority of bulbs is September–October. Start early. Daffodils are best put to bed in August, and Snowdrops and autumn Crocuses as early as July. Don't plant Tulips, nor the turban Ranunculi, however, before the end of October. Another group is planted in March–April, chiefly Gladioli and the hybrid Anemones.

AFTER-CARE

When the flowers wither, nip off all seed-pods. Never, if avoidable, cut or damage the foliage. Leave it to die and wither completely.

One of the menaces to bulbs is the enthusiastic autumn digger. I have said elsewhere that, once a bed is properly prepared and planted out, it should not be dug over—only hoed—until it becomes overcrowded. Avoid planting bulbs where you may have to dig.

LIFTING

With few exceptions, bulbs are best left in the ground once planted, until they multiply sufficiently to need dividing and replanting. The chief exceptions are Begonia, Gladiolus, Tulip, Ranunculus, Dahlia, but others can be lifted if necessary to make room for bedding plants, though this should never be done to Lilies, Amaryllis, Crinum, or Cyclamen. If avoidable, do not lift till the foliage has died right down or is touched by frost. Then dry the bulbs, etc., clean off the earth, separate, grade, and store in a place that is cool, dry, and airy, but frost-proof.

Although lifting is best done after complete withering of the foliage, it may nevertheless be done earlier to make room. In such an event, lift carefully and complete with roots and a ball of soil, and 'heel in' the plant in a reserve quarter in a trench deep enough to cover the bulb, water, and leave till the foliage has died; then treat as in the previous paragraph. This frequently has to be done to Tulips, whose formal nature generally requires them to be put in a bed of their own, to be followed by a summer bedding-out of Begonias, Antirrhinums, etc.

PROPAGATION

Many bulbous plants can be raised from seed without great difficulty but usually it is a long business. For the general run of the more popular bulbs and corms proper—Daffodil, Crocus, Gladiolus—one's stock is more easily multiplied by detaching the young bodies that form at the base or side of the parent and planting them out separately, the smaller ones in a seed-bed. Hyacinths unfortunately are a subject for the expert only. Tubers are treated differently.

Many of the most endearing little ones, however, happily multiply themselves in the most natural manner if left to run to seed, forming ever-widening colonies. Among them are such jewels as: Anemone blanda, the hardy toy Cyclamens, Chionodoxa, Scillas, Snowdrops, and Muscari.

Bulbs Indoors

A limited range of bulbous flowers can be grown indoors to enliven the grim days of January and February, by growing them either in pots in a normal compost or else in prepared fibre in undrained bowls. Only a few can be successfully reared in fibre, and when ordering it is as well to specify if bulbs are wanted for this special purpose. Hyacinths excel in this mode of life, and so do some Narcissi. Several Tulips, Crocuses, and Snowdrops also are good. Less usual and of rare charm are the dwarf Irises, histrioides Major and reticulata, which do particularly well in fibre or in a mixture of peat and sand in the rectangular 'pans' used by nurserymen. Many more grow bravely in ordinary soil in flower-pots, reared in unheated greenhouses or frames.

September is the right time to do all such planting. The methods of cultivation are much the same whether by pot or bowl. Use pots large enough to take at least three Hyacinths or five Tulips. Bowls must be non-porous, and circular ones are better than fancy shapes. Pack the bulbs as closely together in the receptacles as you like, provided they do not actually touch one another. There is no need at all to bury the bulb, all it needs being a firm seating, and it is therefore quite enough to insert it to only half its depth. Leave sufficient space between the level of the soil and the rim of the pot to permit watering. For bowls, the fibre should be thoroughly moist but not sodden, so that when squeezed in the hand moisture is not pressed out. If the fibre does not arrive in this condition from the shop or nursery, tie it up in sacking or similar porous material and suspend it with a weight in a cistern of water for at least a day.

Hyacinths planted in a bowl of fibre, with charcoal at bottom.

The bulbs having been planted, they must now go into darkness for several weeks. The method of putting them in a dark cupboard or cellar should be adopted only by those who have no garden. They are much better outdoors. My own experience is that the best method is to bury them in sand, peat, or weathered ashes to a depth of a good 6 in. in a shady position, preferably under a north wall, and forget about them altogether, for six weeks at least. Then unearth and inspect, taking care not to damage any young shoots. Those that are well through by 1 in. or more can be taken out, and others put to bed for a further short spell.

Whether the outdoor or the cupboard method is adopted, the bowls must next go into a place of semi-shade, but still quite cold, and then gradually move up into full light. From then on give them utmost light and careful watering, seeing that the soil or fibre is nicely moist but never sodden. You can give them heat presently if you like for early results, but it should only be very gentle. Never hurry them; light is more important than heat. Bowls, of course, are normally brought into the dwelling-house, where they should go right into a good light window until they are in blossom. Keep them well away from any gas-fire or lamp, and out of any room with violently fluctuating day and night temperatures. The bulbs that are in pots can also be brought into the house, provided they are stood in a receptacle to take water from the drainage hole; or they can go into a greenhouse, conservatory, frame, or glass porch as long as one likes. In the little conservatories attached to many small houses there is no better method of providing early spring cheer. The taller sorts will need staking as the flower-heads develop, and for heavy-headed hyacinths in bowls of fibre thinly split canes with sharp points, or rigid wires, should be thrust firmly into each bulb itself.

Bulbs grown in this artificial manner get pretty exhausted and are quite unfit for similar use again, but if, after drying off, they are planted among shrubs or in odd corners, they will provide a little quite cheerful bloom in subsequent years.

In addition to the varieties of Narcissus and Tulips mentioned in the notes below, and to nearly all Hyacinths, the following bulbs do well in bowls, adding variety and charm to the indoor scene:

The Dutch Irises, Wedgewood and Imperator. Iris reticulata. The Alliums moly and neapolitanum. The Crocuses Whitewell Purple, Striped Beauty, and Queen of the Blues. Puschkinia libanotica. Muscari. Chionodoxa.

A Selection of Bulbous Plants

In the following list I have chosen those on which most people would like some guidance, together with a few of the less hackneyed things that are specially recommended. A few of the things I specially suggest, as 'something different' are: Allium, the 'plumed hyacinth', species Crocuses and Tulips instead of the usual hybrids, Belladonna Lily, Crinum, and especially the lovely rock and woodland types of Anemone. Nor omit on any account one or more species of Lily.

The general advice which has been given for soil preparation, planting, lifting, etc., will not be repeated save in special instances.

Allium. Though these are garlics, many varieties are virtually odourless and are of striking beauty, their rigid stems crowned with splendid orbs in many colours during May and June. Very suitable to the herbaceous border, to which they lend a note of distinction. Quite easy and inexpensive. Plant 3 in. deep in autumn and leave undisturbed till overcrowded, then lift and divide. Some good ones for a start are: Azureum, sky-blue, 2 ft; the delightful dwarf Ostrowkianum and Karataviense, both pink, 6 in.

Anemone. In this sumptuous race there are many breeds. The most widely grown, sold in the shops by the million, are the flaunting hybrids of A. coronaria called St Brigid and Caen Anemones. They are rarely well grown. They need full sun, a well-dug soil, well-drained but moisture-holding, and liberally supplied with leaf-mould or peat, with bonemeal, and with sand if the soil is heavy. They like lime. Plant for preference in March, alternatively October, though others times of year will also suit if soil and weather allow. Plant little more than an inch deep, ensuring that the little scar left by the old leaf-stalks is uppermost; if in doubt, plant on edge. In light, warm soils they may be left alone, but in others it is best to lift and dry them off, when the foliage fades. Easily grown from seed sown very thinly in June in a sunny position and light soil $\frac{1}{4}$ in. deep, leaving them to flower in the seed-bed the first year.

Very like them, but better still, are the hybrids of the Peacock Anemone called St Bavo. They have a crisp and brilliant beauty, and are just as easy, but a warm, sunny place is specially important. Grow these rather than the coronarias.

The lesser-known species Anemones, however, have a chaste and porcelain beauty much more desirable than the holiday riotousness of the St Brigids and their kind. They are exquisite. Plant in September or October 2 in. deep. They may usually be left in the ground and some, such as blanda, rapidly colonise by seed. Some (such as alpina and hepatica) are apt to be difficult, but specially commended for ease and beauty are:

Blanda atrocœrulea (late winter) with daisy-form rays of fragile and virginal blue—for sun or half shade in gritty, gravelly soil where water drains away well. Does well among the roots of shrubs and small trees.

Nemorosa, especially its variety Robinsoniana, whose silver-blue rays are adorned with golden anthers; a haunter of the woodland, requiring shade.

See also Chapters XI and XII.

Begonia. In the forefront of tuberous plants, begonias are not hardy, and the more sophisticated ones, such as Rex and Gloire de Lorraine, need heated houses. Of the popular outdoor sorts, the very large and sumptuous named varieties are plants priced for the enthusiast, but those unnamed and sold by colour are excellent. So are the 'multiflora' begonias, which are smaller but more riotous in flower and entirely suited to Everyman. The so-called 'B. pendula' is for hanging baskets and window-boxes.

Start the tuberous sorts in early March in some warmth (the kitchen will do if allowed) in seed-boxes in a blend of loam, sand, and leaf-mould or peat. Plant hollow side upwards, the tuber just covered. Keep moist. When rooted, pot into 4-in. pots and, when necessary, into 6-in. ones. Harden-off in May and plant out about June 1st.

After the first autumn frost dig them up with a ball of soil and pack them in boxes in a cool but frost-free place. Leave the foliage and stem to wither naturally, then store the tubers in clean, nearly dry sand.

B. semperflorens is the gay little chap, only a few inches high, that makes a magical bedding display for months in red, pink, or white, with leathery leaves, often themselves coloured. Impervious to all weather, except frost. This is a fibrous-rooted begonia, not tuberous, so you must start afresh next year. The dust-fine seed needs heat, but nursery-grown plants can be put out about June 1st.

Belladonna Lily (Amaryllis Belladonna). Those who live in the South and have a really warm south wall should have a go at this enchanting flower. It opens its fanfares of fragrant pink trumpets in September, borne in clusters at the head of a 2-ft stem, which shoots up from the bare earth after the foliage has died down (to reappear in winter). It must have a very warm, very sandy soil mixed with plenty of leaf-mould, and its foliage must be copiously watered in summer. Plant in June–July, 3 in. deep in the south-west, 5 in. deep elsewhere, and blanket it with leaves in winter.

Chionodoxa. One of the jewels of the bulb world, for which the translation 'Glory of the Snow' is too high-sounding. In earliest spring it throws up blue starry flowers 4 in. high, looking their best in clusters or drifts near shrubs or hedges, in the rock garden, or short grass. Plant 3 in. deep in autumn and leave undisturbed. The prettiest is probably the white-eyed C. Lucilæ; also successful in bowls and in pots.

Crinum. Very beautiful, pink-and-white, swan-necked trumpets like Lilies 3 ft high in summer. Treat like Belladonna Lilies though they are hardier and more reliable. Powellii is much the best. Plant so that the shoulder of the long bulb is 7 in. down.

Crocosmia. *See* Montbretia.

Crocus. Plant the corms of the popular garden hybrids 3 in. deep in early autumn in drifts and clusters, not as edgings. They naturalise beautifully in grass, and are attractive among trees and shrubs. Once planted, leave them alone until thick enough to need dividing.

Much more dainty and desirable than these big hybrids, to my mind, are the smaller species Crocuses, and their variations, which flower not only in spring but also delight the heart in late autumn and the depths of winter. They must, however, have sunny positions and good drainage in a privileged bed, not in grass, and they are delightful in rock gardens. Some of the best are:

189

For autumn—speciosus, which forms drifts like pools of deep blue water; the fragant lævigatus, with feathered lilac petals; and the bi-coloured pulchellus and zonatus.

For midwinter—the purple imperati and the little yellow ancyrensis.

For late winter—chrysanthus, especially the delightful varieties Snowbunting, in white, gold, and purple, E. A. Bowles, in gold and bronze, and the unique Blue Pearl.

For spring—the easy Tomasinianus, a charming silvery lavender.

The autumn and winter sorts should be planted in July, the spring ones in September. *See also* Meadow Saffron, unfortunately styled 'autumn crocus' in popular usage. Much more like a real Crocus, and an autumn one at that, is the golden **Sternbergia lutea**, said to be the biblical 'lily of the field' that did neither toil nor spin. It looks exactly like a Crocus, and is the colour of a buttercup, with the same enamelled sheen. It needs a hot, gritty, fast-drainage slope in baking sun. The leaves come after the flowers have died.

Cyclamen. The big, showy sorts that one gives and receives at Christmas are Persian Cyclamens and subjects for the greenhouse. The hardy outdoor pygmies are altogether more lovely, having an exquisite, elfin beauty all their own. They are among the few things that really succeed under trees, and they can indeed be planted in the root-crannies near the bole. The loveliest and best are neapolitanum (autumn), europæum (August), and coum (midwinter). There are others, too, for other seasons. Plant them only ½ in. deep and leave them severely alone, but mulch them with leaf-mould each winter. They associate miraculously with the daintier of the 'species' Anemone. Europæum wants complete shade, the others partial. These little Cyclamen are not cheap, but they are easy, are likely to outlive you and me and spread quickly into ever-widening colonies through the helpful agency of the ant.

Daffodil. *See* Narcissus.

Dahlia. One of those flowers you either rave about or can't stand. There are quite a lot of Dahliaphobes, but the Dahlia has many virtues, for, although not hardy, it is easy to grow, virtually free of disease, prolific with its blooms if spent ones are persistently picked off, and it provides lasting cut flowers.

Dahlias are officially classified in numerous groups. Average gardeners not concerned with exhibition will probably be satisfied to know just the chief types.

Decoratives have a large number of broad overlapping petals, very solid and sometimes of huge size.

Cactus Dahlias have rolled or quilled petals.

Collerettes, an outer ring of large petals and an inner ruff of small ones, showing the disc.

Anemone-flowered. Pin-cushion effect, the disc hidden.

Peony-flowered. Doubles, showing the disc.

Pompoms are precisely spherical and formalised.

Ball. Larger style of Pompom, less formal.

Dwarf Bedding of various sorts. *Single-flowered* explain themselves.

When received from the nursery, Dahlias are 'ex-pots'. Except in the mildest frost-free districts, they must not be planted out till the first week of June. The position should be in full sun, and the ground should be deeply dug and well enriched, for Dahlias are gross feeders. They enjoy bonemeal. The tall ones should be 3 ft apart, ranging down to 15 in. for the dwarf bedders. All but the dwarfs must be well and firmly staked *before* planting, but stout 4-ft canes, four to a plant, are quite enough. If large blooms are wanted, disbudding must be practised. Take precautions against earwigs and greenfly.

When the foliage is blackened by early frosts lift the tubers at once, cut the stalks down to within a few inches of the base, drain the water out of the hollow stems, dry, and store the tubers in a frost-proof place. Dry peat is a good storage material.

Next spring there are the following choices of method of treatment of the old tubers: (*a*) Having a little heat, start the tubers into growth in February in boxes of soil in greenhouse or frame, take the new shoots as nodal cuttings and insert them in pots of sandy soil. (*b*) With unheated glass, start them in April, and before planting out in June divide the cluster of tubers with a sharp knife, ensuring at least one shoot per tuber. (c) With no glass, plant the whole cluster outdoors early May with at least 3 in. of soil over it, and protect young shoots before June with cloches or with flower-pots at night. In mild counties you can leave them in the ground all winter—contrary to all teaching!

Dahlias are easily raised from seed in the manner of half-hardy annuals, but only the dwarf bedders are really suitable.

When ordering, tell your nurseryman whether or not you have glass, so that he can send them at the best time.

To select varieties is difficult. New ones appear in quantity every year, and the darling of today is cast aside tomorrow, but I daresay that such established favourites as Doris Day, Gerrie Hoeck, Glorie van Heemstede and Klankstad Kerkrade will hold their own for a few more years.

Erythronium. The nickname 'Dog's Tooth Violet' refers only to the shape of the bulb. These endearing little flowers are like pygmy, wide-mouthed lilies, 5–9 in. high, with diapered foliage, flowering March and April in many colours. But they need these conditions—partial shade, and a cool, moisture-holding soil with peat or leaf-mould. The dens-canis varieties are the cheapest and easiest. Plant 3 in. deep in September.

Freesia. *See* Chapter IX.

Fritillary (Fritillaria). There are two very different types (both shy at first). One is the big Crown Imperial (F. imperialis), with a peculiar cluster of red or yellow bells hanging from a tuft of leaves that terminates the erect 3-ft. spire. Those who like them should plant them 5 in. deep in clusters of three or more.

Totally different and more dainty is the Snake's Head Fritillary (F. Meleagris). Its deep-mouthed bell, hung from a thread-like 10-in. stem, looks down demurely to its feet. The typical bloom is speckled like a snake's head, but the white varieties are also charming. For damp beds or woodland or naturalising in shady grass. Plant 3 in. deep in early autumn and leave alone.

Gladiolus. Our main interest is in the large and showy hybrids that bloom in late summer, though the smaller butterfly and primulinus varieties also have charm. All must have full sun. A rich soil is not necessary, but gives more splendid results.

To my mind the Gladiolus is essentially a flower to cut for the house, and not for the adornment of the pleasure garden, for when the blooms are over, the 'sword flowers' look like a shattered army. For house decoration, therefore, plant the corms in rows in the kitchen garden 4 in. deep and 6 in. apart, any time from March till May. Thus grown, lines of string or wire stretched between occasional stakes will be sufficient for their support, but in the pleasure garden each spike must have a separate cane.

When cutting, try to take the flower-stem only and *no leaves*.

The Gladiolus not being fully hardy, the corms must, except in the mildest districts, be lifted in the autumn for storage. The expert tells us to do this six weeks after flowering is over. Cut the stem off an inch above the new corm, dry and clean the corms, break off the old shrunken one underneath and store in a cool but frost-free place, after dusting with a mixture of DDT and flowers of sulphur. For the usual reason I must leave you to pick varieties from a standard catalogue.

Gladioli are attacked by aphis and by the minute, sucking thrip, which shows itself in a silver or brown streaking or patching. Use a systemic insecticide or spray with gamma-BHC.

Grape Hyacinth. *See* Muscari.

Hyacinth. Besides being the finest of bowl plants, the Hyacinth is very beautiful indeed outdoors, but nowadays its price discourages its use in large numbers. Plant 5 in. deep and 6 in. apart in a sunny and well-drained site in October, with a pinch of sand under each bulb. Formal regimental planting suits them best. They are likely to need staking. Remove the spent flower-heads but leave the bulbs in the ground. Perhaps the most beautiful, for indoors or out, are: Winston Churchill, Princess Elizabeth (pale pink), Ostara (rich deep blue), Queen of the Blues, Lady Derby (lovely flesh-pink, my own favourite), Jan Bos (best red). If you want very early Hyacinths indoors you must get the specially doctored 'prepared Christmas Hyacinth', available in a few varieties, or the loose 'Roman Hyacinth'.

Iris. *See* Chapter XVIII.

Ixia. Pretty stars in brilliant colours in June, 15 in. high, good for cutting. Plant 3 in. deep in October in a warm, sunny position, enveloping the bulb in sand. Do not lift in autumn, but protect against frost with a thick coverlet of leaves.

Lily (Lilium). The Lily is a difficult subject to write about in small compass, for one man's experience is not the same as another's. Moreover, the needs of one species differ widely from those of another, but we may note at the outset these fundamentals:

(*a*) All lilies insist on good drainage, anything like water-logging in the sub-soil being fatal.
(*b*) They dislike gross manures, but rejoice in leaf-mould.
(*c*) All, except the Madonna Lily, need basal shade.
(*d*) Some like or tolerate lime, but to others it is poison.

On no account buy Lilies from a shop, nor as a 'cheap line'; but only from reputable growers. Lilies are rarely if ever dormant, should be out of the ground the minimum possible time, and must not be allowed to dry up. Plant them immediately they arrive, or, if this is impossible, store them in damp peat. Never accept any bulbs that are lacking their basal roots.

Cultivation. Very sandy soils and very heavy clays are usually unpropitious, but most lilies are well suited by any good medium soil in good heart, provided the drainage is beyond doubt. Do not use newly manured beds, but (except for Madonna) soil really well treated according to Part 1 can be used in the second or third year, digging in plenty of leaf-mould, deep down. In heavy soils add plenty of sharp sand also. For positive lime lovers, such as Henryi and Madonna, work in some mortar rubble or broken chalk. Plant the bulbs 8 in. or more apart.

Except for Madonna, plant where the roots and lower stems will be in shade, but the heads in sun or partial sun.

Among low shrubs or in semi-woodland are ideal situations. Spread the roots out well on a little saddle of soil (as shown for Irises on page 280) at the bottom of the hole. Encase each bulb in sharp sand.

Depth of planting is *critically important*. It is vital to know that some lilies root only from the base of the bulb, but that others root also from the stem above the bulb; the latter, therefore, need deeper planting than the former. The best practice for the stem-rooters is to plant about 6 in. deep and to add a thick mulch of leaves, 3 in. deep or more, on the surface; this mulch may be removed in February and a fresh one spread on.

Planting depths for lilies.

Once planted, do not disturb the bulbs until they become overcrowded. Label their positions, so that they are undamaged by digging or hoeing. When lifting becomes necessary, do so when the foliage has completely died down, and replant with the least possible delay.

Lilies can often do without staking, but I find it safest to support the taller sorts, particularly in windy places, or they will loll forward. I use light canes, but plant them well away from the new shoots when they sprout in spring. Stunted shoots may be caused by slugs attacking the underground stems.

Propagation. Several methods, fairly easy but slow. One method is to divide the bulbs and their babies when digging up.

Another is to remove any number of the scales of the bulb, plant them right way up in pots or boxes in a mixture of leaf-soil (or peat) and sand, with the tips just showing. In a greenhouse or warm frame bulblets form in about six weeks. Transplant when established.

Species and Varieties. Omitting the more expensive enchantments, I select the following few as perhaps the easiest and most beautiful. The phrase 'Turk's cap' is here used to describe a Lily with petals completely reflexed, as in the Tiger Lily, in contrast to the trumpet-shaped sorts.

Madonna Lily (L. candidum). A fine old lady, albeit temperamental. She will often take kindly to the cottage plot, but spurn the lord's demesne. Madonna is specially fond of lime, and a plain, stony diet suits her best. Unlike other lilies, she demands a position in full sun from head to foot. *Be most particular* to plant her only 1 in. deep on light soils, and only barely covered on heavy ones. Madonna is base-rooting, and has a cluster of sumptuous white trumpets borne at the summit of a 4-ft stem. Plant in July or as soon as possible after.

L. regale. Perhaps the easiest and certainly one of the most beautiful. 4 ft high with a large cluster of white trumpets. Ample shade for roots most important. Lime-tolerant. Stem-rooting. Depth 5 in. plus mulch. Easily grown from seed—leave the pods till quite ripe, dry the seeds, sow at the end of March in light sandy and peaty beds in shallow drills, 2 in. deep and apart; or in deep pots or boxes the previous autumn. Will bloom the second year.

Royal Gold is a fine yellow version of regale.

Henryi. Very easy. Densely crowded with orange Turk's caps. Stem-rooting. Notably lime-loving. 7 ft.

Hollandicum (umbellatum). Very easy. Wide-open cups, looking upwards. 2½ ft. Stem-rooting, lime-tolerant.

Martagon. Pyramids of Turk's caps looking down. Base-rooting, lime-tolerant. The white variety is the best, others often muddy.

Thunderbolt. Superlative clusters of wide-open trumpets in apricot. Stem-rooting, lime-tolerant. 5 ft.

Limelight. Lovely, cool, shining lemon. Stem-rooting. 4 ft.

Mid-Century Hybrids. This is a 'strain', with many colour variants. First-class beginner's plants. Grow anywhere that daffodils will. The favourite named variety is the flame-coloured Enchantment. Stem-rooting. Seems lime-tolerant. Average 3 ft.

Olympic Hybrids. Another popular and easy 'strain'. White, yellow, or pink-tinted trumpets. Stem-rooting. 4 ft.

Green Dragon. Large white trumpets, flushed chartreuse on the exterior. 3½ ft. Black Dragon is flushed deep maroon, 6 ft. Stem-rooters.

Plenty more are available, many fit only for skilled or fortunate gardeners. Those who have an acid soil, deep in old leaf-mould, and very well drained should go for the varieties of the sumptuous L. auratum and L. speciosum or the hybrid Imperial strain in crimson or gold. Not cheap.

There is much disease among lilies. Dust the bulbs before planting with Botrilex. Apply a systemic insecticide when in growth, against greenfly. Watch for small, brownish, watery markings on the leaves, which then turn brown and drop. This is botrytis; spray with a copper fungicide, such as Orthocide.

Meadow Saffron (Colchicum). Misleadingly called 'Autumn Crocus'. Not a Crocus at all, and the autumn-flowering true Crocuses are much more attractive. Meadow Saffron has large coarse leaves, and its best place is under trees, planted 2 in. deep in August and left alone.

Montbretia. Colourful gladiolus-like flowers blooming July–September, which we are now expected to call Crocosmias. The fashionable species is C. masonorum, which, producing long, bending sprays of blazing orange in summer, seems quite hardy. Plant the corms preferably in March, 4 in. deep. I still have a strong affection for the old, less hardy His Majesty, scarlet and gold, 4 ft.

Muscari. The lovely toy 'grape hyacinth' is available in several colours, of which Heavenly Blue is perhaps best, though the lighter-hued Cantab is also delightful. Plant 2–3 in.

deep in autumn in any good soil in the sun and leave undisturbed. They multiply readily and spread. Easy and charming, but the foliage is untidy. Excellent for bowls in fibre.

Less well known is the rather taller 'plumed hyacinth' (M. plumosum for short), embellished with a plume of blue feathers; very decorative and distinctive.

Narcissus (Daffodil). Daffodil is simply the English vernacular for narcissus, whether the trumpet be long or short. Daffs have been segregated by the RHS into several pigeon-holes, according to their floral forms. Ignoring the various subdivisions, these are:

Division i. Large trumpets.
Division ii. Large cups or short trumpets.
Division iii. Small cups.
Division iv. Doubles—horrible abortions.
Division v. Triandrus or 'Angel's Tears'. Clusters of small, nodding flowers, for porous, gritty soil.
Division vi. Cyclamineus. Delightful, pensive flowers with swept-back perianths. For damp soil.
Division vii. Jonquils.
Division viii. Tazetta. Having multi-flowered stems.
Division ix. Poeticus. Flat flowers with small, bright-eyed central disc.

Culture. Plant in August or earliest September if possible, but later plantings will do. Cover the bulb with soil $1\frac{1}{2}$ times as deep as the length of the bulb. Place them where their dying foliage will be concealed in summer—the middle or back of a mixed border (not the edge), the shrub garden or naturalised in grass. Leave them undisturbed until overcrowding requires them to be lifted and divided, which is done in July.

When they get overcrowded, with a lot of flowerless foliage, dig them up, divide them, and replant each bulb separately at the right spacing.

Varieties. Among the less expensive sorts, the following are excellent standard varieties that I recommend:

198

Division i. Among the yellows—Golden Harvest, Dawson City, Garron, Rembrandt (early), and Binkie. Among the lovely all-white daffodils—Mount Hood and Beersheba.

There is now an exquisite range with pink or apricot trumpets, but at present the only one of modest price is Mrs R. O. Backhouse, which I greatly enjoy, but you may not.

Division ii. Havelock, Fortune, John Evelyn, Carlton, Scarlet Elegance, Carabineer, Daisy Schaffer, and Kilworth.

Division iii. La Riante and Firetail.

Actæa is a splendid and vigorous Poeticus; and Geranium inaptly names one of the best Tazettas.

Miniatures. Some of the easiest and most endearing are: Minor, most reliable of the tiny trumpet daffodils; 'Angel's Tears' (N. triandrus albus), 7 in.; the cyclamen-flowered daffodil (N. cyclamineus) with swept-back perianth, 6 in., and the 'hoop-petticoat daffodil' (N. bulbocodium), 6 in., like a little bugle with virtually no perianth. Some charming hybrid miniature trumpets are Little Beauty and Little Gem.

Absolutely top-class hybrids have come from the parental influence of cyclamineus, especially February Gold and March Sunshine (1 ft) and Bartley (or Peeping Tom) 15 in. These would always be uppermost in my thoughts when making a selection.

I hope that, before very long, we shall see some of the newer, very beautiful daffodils coming down into the popular price range, such as Kingscourt, Cantatrice, Salmon Trout, and Trousseau. Look out for them.

Puschkinia. Pretty wan blue stars are thickly clustered on a 6-in. spire in April. Easy and good in sun and a light soil, and successful in bowls. Order P. scilloides and plant 3 in. deep in September.

Ranunculus. The tuberous forms of the garden buttercup, 9 in. high, glowing in a splendid galaxy of colours in May and June, are splendid for cutting. They need heaps of sun and a well-drained soil with ample leaf-mould or peat. Plant claw downwards, 2 in. deep, the 'Turban' types in November, and the French and Persian types in March. Lift and store in July, being sure they are dry.

Scilla. This includes the bluebell (of England) and the little blue Siberian squill, an enchanting midget. The variety to get is Spring Beauty. Plant it in autumn among bushes or in borders 2 in. deep and leave it alone. It spreads rapidly until the earth looks as though it had been sprinkled with sapphires.

Snowdrop (Galanthus). The world provides many lovely Snowdrops, but you cannot do better than stick to the common British one, G. nivalis, or one of its variants. Naturalise it in short grass, or drop it among bushes and trees. Plant very early—July or August—3 in. deep. Leave it alone to increase naturally. It transplants best when in bloom. Other fine ones, large-flowered, and fitted best for special places, are Elwesii and plicatum. All these are of sound constitution and easy culture, but the autumn Snowdrops should be left to the expert. If you want Snowdrops in autumn, then plant the equally charming **Snowflake** (Leucojum), of which there are also several kinds, very like a real Snowdrop but larger. L. autumnale is an exquisite 5-in. plant with pale pink bells, and there are charming ones for other seasons, such as æstivum, which is called the 'summer Snowflake' or Loddon-lily and is tipped green, and of which Gravetye is a good form, but is too tall at 2 ft. It prospers in deep shade. For spring there is the 9-in. vernum which succeeds in the poorest soils.

Tulip. *General Culture.* Choose a site in full sun and very well drained. Plant the first week of November (never earlier than late October), 4 in. deep. The best effect usually is from formal, geometrical patterns.

Tulips may be attacked by the 'fire' disease, shown by a scorching of the leaf edges. To discourage it, lift and store the bulbs every year after the foliage has died down (or heel in earlier with a ball of soil if the ground is needed), and do not plant Tulips in the same bed year after year. Should the disease appear, no Tulips must be grown for at least four years.

Species and Varieties. All sorts of forms of the Tulip have been evolved in centuries of hybridisation, but none is more beautiful than some of the original wild species. They eclipse the popular hybrids in brilliance and in colour and grace of form, but not all are easy. Of these wildlings (which often have several variations) these are recommended:—

The Water-lily Tulip (T. Kauffmanniana), a tulip of lovely form and glittering colour combinations, with many variations on the theme of primrose-carmine-cream, about 7 in. high. Excellent and early in bowls. Now has several varieties which are not cheap.

Batalinii. A 6-in. charmer in primrose.

Tarda. Starry gold-and-white miniature.

Fosteriana. Enormous bloom of dazzling oriental scarlet on a 15-in. stem; Mme Lefeber is a fine form.

Eichleri, another scarlet dazzler, 10 in.

Popular Hybrids. These fall into several classes. There is no point in singling out varieties, and one cannot do better than order a mixed bag of '100 bulbs in 10 varieties'. The following are the main classes:

Early Singles: Bloom with the daffodils in April in a wonderful range of colours on short stems, usually about 1 ft.

Early Doubles: Solid peony-like blooms in lovely colours, very long-lasting; short stems. Excellent for bowls or pots.

Parrots: Fantastic in design with fretted edges and splendid colourings.

Darwins: The well-known tall Tulips of May with ramrod stems and flowers of severe and formal elegance.

Cottage Tulips and Lily-flowered Tulips: Relatively less known, these are far more desirable than the Darwins, having a more graceful form and lighter carriage. Flower in May.

Viridiflora hybrids: Stunning concoctions of green and other colours, as in Artist.

Greigii hybrids: Dazzlers with striped leaves.

Many, but not all, Tulips are suitable for growing indoors in pots or bowls. A few suggestions are: Ibis, Prince of Austria, Van der Neer, Fred Moore (tall), Couleur Cardinal, Sunburst (all Earlies), and the Doubles. The Duc van Thols and their hybrids, the Mendels, are specially good for forcing as early as January. Among Darwins (for pots, not bowls) good ones are Franz Hals, Farncombe Sanders, Princess Elizabeth, City of Haarlem, Queen of Bartigons, Golden Harvest.

Winter Aconite (Eranthis hyemalis). Only an inch or two high, is like a buttercup with a green ruff round its neck. January and February. Plant in shrublands 2 in. deep in early autumn and leave alone. Shy at first. Tubergenii is considered by some people as superior to hyemalis.

CHAPTER XIV

ROSES

FIRST WORDS—SHAPES AND FORMS—BREEDS OF ROSES—
CULTIVATION—PLANTING—AFTER-CARE—PRUNING—
THE ROSE'S ENEMIES—PROPAGATION—LAY-OUT AND
DISPLAY—VARIETIES TO CHOOSE

First Words

I HAVE no doubt that in any Gallup poll of garden favourites
the 'Queen of flowers all' would easily head the list. Like
Cleopatra, 'age cannot wither, nor custom stale, her infinite
variety'. It is not surprising, therefore, that for hundreds of
years eager hybridists, both amateur and professional, have
been busy breeding new forms, encouraging special virtues
and eliminating inherited weaknesses, but occasionally sacri-
ficing something, as, for example, luxuriance of foliage.

The main efforts of more recent hybridists have been directed to giving us the highly decorative roses now so popular—
large, full of glowing colours, with buds of shapely elegance,
reflexed petals, and often highly fragrant. They are commonly
grown in beds in the forms of 'dwarf bushes' and little standard
trees, and for our convenience I propose to group these together as 'bedding roses'. The rose, however, shows her
variety not only in form and colour but also in habit and purpose, and we must begin by being clear about these things.

The Shapes and Forms of Roses

Bush or **Dwarf** roses are the form commonly seen everywhere in formal beds. They are bushes in name only, for their
foliage is very sparse, and they are not to be confused with

'shrub' roses, which in the language of the fancy means something else.

Standards have little erect tree-stems about 4 ft high budded at the top with the same variety of rose as the dwarfs. They look delightful on either side of a path as a little avenue. There are also half-standards. A *Weeping Standard* is budded with the flexible 'rambler' rose types drooping to the ground.

Ramblers are roses which, like Dorothy Perkins and other Wichuriana varieties, produce long flexible canes; they are best used to clothe pergola, arch, or trellis, but not walls. Most have one short and very vivid season of bloom and are then over.

Climbers are commonly confused with ramblers, but there are sharp differences. Climbers are either long-caned 'sports' that have sprung from the dwarf bedding types of rose (e.g. Climbing Mme Butterfly), or else they are developments from the wild species of rose or are crosses with the rambler types. These grow as a rule less rampantly and less flexibly than the ramblers, but are larger in flower and some of them bloom intermittently throughout the summer. They are also less liable to mildew. The climbing sports have exactly the same flowers as their dwarf parents. Neither of these classes are really 'climbers', having no apparatus for clinging except their thorns. They look best on walls, pergolas, or isolated pillars, rather than on arches or trellis; many are called 'pillar' roses and show their full glory best that way. Unfortunately some nurseries mix the climbers and ramblers together in their catalogues.

Shrubs. This term includes (a) the wild species (see next page) and (b) several exciting modern hybrids, some of which bloom 'perpetually' all summer; they grow very large and, like the species, are not suited to formal rose beds.

The Breeds of Roses

A rough idea of the classification of roses by breeding is a practical necessity. The parentage of many, however, is so complicated that often even experts disagree. One grower will call a rose an H.T. and another will call it something else. All we need do as practical gardeners is to group them together for purposes of treatment and use.

First there are the familiar large-flowered **dwarf bedders**. The great majority are called 'hybrid teas' (H.T.), but a few 'hybrid perpetuals' (H.P.) are still with us. These all have the same use, and for gardening purposes differ only in their vigour and thus in spacing and pruning.

Floribundas are characterised by densely clustered heads of blossom. For our purposes there are two groups. One is the low, dwarf bedding form formerly called polyantha roses, with massed trusses of little pom-poms. The second is an exciting series which are the result of a happy marriage between polyanthas and H.T.s and now called 'floribundas'. Their development has been striking. They are very showy and ideal bedding plants. Many have large blossoms like the H.T.s, but few have scent so far. We shall see many more of these large-flowered floribundas, for they make splendid garden roses.

Wichuriana Roses and their hybrids. These have given us the greater number of our extra-vigorous popular ramblers, such as Dorothy Perkins.

Other types of climber, mostly hybrids, have been referred to in the previous section.

Species. A term loosely applied to the true species, or wild roses, and their hybrids. They are easy of culture, need little pruning, and often flourish on poor soils. They vary greatly in style, habit, and size. Many bloom for a short season only, and others may be too big for small places. Some, however, such as the Rugosa roses, have a very long season and are ideal for any garden.

Rose Stocks. This is a convenient place to say that all hybrids are normally propagated by budding the cultivated 'scion' on to a root 'stock'. The quality of this root stock is of the greatest importance to the buyer. His safeguard is to go only to a rose *grower* with a good reputation. One may always be satisfied if assured that the stock is Rosa canina, the wild dog-rose generally referred to as 'brier'. Rugosa is another good stock, especially for standards, recognisable by its thickly prickled stem, and there are other reliable ones.

Cultivation

Because the rose is one of our most willing and gallant triers, and will do well in so many soils, some ancient misconceptions still linger.

For example, it was for long a prevalent notion that roses demanded clay and that they needed lime. Neither idea is true. Certainly they will put up a good show under these conditions, but what they really like best is a medium loam a trifle on the acid side—one that is well drained, well aerated, and easily worked, but which will retain moisture and not dry out quickly in hot spells, as sandy soils do. What they will not stand is waterlogging or very acid peats. As for lime, they like best a pH reading of about 6.5. Lime should therefore be given only if there are indications of strong acidity or sourness, or if there is a *physical* need to crumble down a stubborn and sticky clay.

For all that, roses are so tolerant that most of them will indeed succeed on limy soils, even up to pH 8. Some of the species even thrive in chalk if fortified with quantities of organic matter and thickly mulched every year.

Situation is almost as important as soil. Except for the sorts grown on walls, roses hate being shut in. They are fresh-air fiends, and demand an open situation where the air and the breezes can circulate freely. They also demand sun, and must on no account whatever be directly under trees, but they do not dislike slanting or oblique shade at midday, especially those of the yellow and orange shades.

If possible, do not plant roses where other roses have long grown. Soils become 'rose-sick'. If unavoidable, import some fresh top soil from elsewhere in the garden or from outside.

Prepare the soil well before planting—a month ahead if possible. Bastard trench it. Invigorate both spits with organic matter, especially for standards, which have to go in a little deeper than bushes. Use old turves, roughly chopped up and turned upside-down. In the top spit compost is excellent, so is hop manure in heavy soils. Then let the bed settle.

If animal manure is used, it must be kept fairly well down, and 2 in. of fine soil should come on top of it, for it is deadly to allow the roots of roses to come in actual contact with animal manure.

Just before planting prepare a special planting mixture made up of fine, crumbly soil, peat, and bonemeal, with a little sand added if the soil is heavy. You can make a quantity in a barrow or mix the materials in each planting hole.

Planting

October–November is the best time, but any time up to March will do provided the soil is neither frost-nipped nor saturated.

When the plants arrive, they may, if absolutely necessary, be safely left in their packing for up to a fortnight, but it is better to get them out, and if you are not quite ready to plant, heel them in a shallow trench, cover the roots loosely with soil, and water. When actually about to plant, bring out only one or two plants at a time if there should be a cold, drying wind. Should the roots be very dry, make a mud puddle, rather stiff, and swill the roots in it.

Look over the roots. Cut out any coarse growth in the nature of a tap-root, and trim back damaged roots with secateurs. Preserve the thin, fibrous roots. Prepare a hole about 15 in. in diameter and about half that in depth, according to the need of each plant. Spread a 2-in. layer of the planting mixture in the bottom. Put in the plant, roots properly disposed. Cover with another 2 in. of the mixture and tread down firmly. Top up with the original soil. Observe the general instructions on planting in the appropriate section of Chapter V, *making sure that the crowns of bush roses are covered by not more than* 1 in. and the roots of standards some 3 or 4 in.

Standards and half-standards need firm staking. Plant the stake, 1 ft deep, before planting the rose. Tie stake and rose-stem together, at the top and lower down, with a piece of felt, sacking, or other soft material between stake and stem to prevent chafing. (Sketch *d*, page 68.) Climbers and ramblers also need tying to some form of support.

Planting distances are:

Bushes: for H.T.s and floribundas a good average is 18 in., but some need more.
Standards: 3 ft.
Climbers and Ramblers: an absolute minimum of 7 ft.
Species and Shrubs: according to ultimate spread.

After-care

Pruning and spraying are the most important measures in the after-care of the rose, and these will be dealt with separately.

Roses should not be coddled. In the colder districts of North and Midlands, if the weather is very severe, it may be necessary to draw up a few inches of earth over the crowns of dwarfs and to tie bracken or straw round the heads and unions of standards; but generally such treatment is to be avoided.

It is customary to ordain that the beds should be hoed constantly. I do not agree. The roots of roses grow very near the surface, and the only necessary or desirable hoeing is to keep down weeds, or possibly to create a surface 'dust mulch' in prolonged dry spells on heavy clays liable to crack. Hoeing should always be very shallow. Any deep disturbance with fork or spade is to be avoided, for it tears the roots and twists their extremities up to the surface. Do *not* dig over rose-beds in the autumn or spring

Subsequently give them a dressing of bonemeal every autumn, lightly hoed in; and in earliest spring, *not* autumn or winter, give them a top-dress of animal manure or peat or compost. Be careful not to let manure touch the crown or stem of the plant. Summer mulches of lawn mowings are often recommended, but they have perils. More important is to give them a tonic early in July. I use Maxicrop or Eclipse.

The H.T.s and the few H.P. roses will need disbudding as

Anemone blanda

Anemone Pulsatilla (Pulsatilla vulgaris)

Dicentra spectabilis

Campanula pusilla 'Miss Willmott'

Alstroemeria Ligtu hybrid

Liatris pycnostachia

An Astilbe

Echinacea 'The King'

A row of young trees of the columnar cherry 'Amanogawa'

Lilium testaceum

Leucojum vernum

A spray of *Rosa Moyesii*

Hybiscus syriacus   A young Witch Hazel

Buddleia alternifolia trained as a standard

A perfect example of how to clip a hedge of *Lonicera nitida*

A hedge of *Berberis stenophylla* in flower

they develop. At the end of each shoot, several flower-buds will generally appear, often in a loose cluster. Reduce them to one central bud by pinching out the others the moment they appear, otherwise the display will be indifferent. Buds appearing lower down the stem may be left. Do no disbudding on other types of rose: floribundas, species, ramblers or climbers. *See* the illustration of disbudding Chrysanthemums, Chapter XVIII.

Finally, keep the beds clean of all prunings and dropped leaves which may carry fungal diseases. Burn them.

Pruning

Chapter VII dealt with pruning generally, and the application of those principles to roses is not difficult, the main question being the degree of severity to apply to different sorts. One may attempt to lay down precise and dogmatic rules, especially for exhibitors, but the general run of people need some simple general rules at first, and here again 'group treatment' is an answer.

The problem is immensely simplified by an understanding of the natural habits of the rose. In a state of nature the rose is constantly throwing up new growth. Into these new shoots it gradually directs its sap, and the older growths become starved out. What the pruner does, therefore, is to hasten the rejection of the old wood before it becomes useless and to encourage the plant's instinct for producing ever fresh young shoots; especially does he encourage those from the base of the plant, though in some types new growth does not come readily from the base but sprouts from some point high or low on the main stem.

That is the sum and substance of pruning in principle, and intelligent observation will point the way. The important things to know are: Does the particular rose bloom on new shoots of this year's growth, or on old wood grown in a previous year? Does it bloom on main stems or on laterals? What is its degree of vigour?

For example, Dorothy Perkins, the familiar Wichuriana

209

rambler, flowers on 'wood' or shoots that grew last year, but Climbing Ophelia flowers on laterals and sub-laterals as well as sending up occasional new wood. And, among the bedders, Hugh Dickson's tremendous vigour means light pruning, while the gentler Shot Silk may be cut back hard. Thus, while it is important to keep roses durably labelled, observation of habit and vigour will be sufficient guide if identities are lost.

Bearing this in mind, and the general principles of Chapter VII, we can write down certain guiding precepts, some general and some particular.

GENERAL PRECEPTS

For all roses, of whatever nature—

Prune harder in the first year than in subsequent years. Prune spring-planted trees harder than autumn-planted;

SUCKERS

(Rose or anything else.) On the left—wrong; cut at ground level, the sucker breaks again, more strongly. On the right—plucked out (not *cut*) at the point of origin.

standards harder than bushes; weak varieties and thin shoots harder than vigorous varieties and strong shoots.

Root out all suckers at their point of origin. A sucker is a shoot from the root stock appearing below the point of union— from below ground in a bush, but in a standard either from below ground or from the main stem. It is recognisable by the foliage being quite different from that of the cultivated scion. If coming from below ground, scrape away the soil, find the point of origin and smartly pluck it out; don't *cut*. Be careful of recognition in ramblers and climbers which also sprout from the ground legitimately; and bear in mind that any growth from the ground in a 'species' rose may be true to type and

210

should not be cut out, the Scotch Rose, which suckers freely, being an example.

For all bedding types (H.T.s and H.P.s, Floribundas, etc., whether dwarfs or standards): Except on very sprawling types, cut always down to an outward-pointing eye, and keep the centre of the plant open, seeking to build up a cup-shaped structure; for Floribundas this is of less importance. When two shoots cross, cut one back below the point of crossing.

When midsummer blooming is over, cut back to some strong outward eye for the next display. Observe pruning rules when cutting for the house.

Weeping standards are pruned as ramblers.

Time for pruning: A much debated matter. The old rule was the last week of March in the South for bedding types, ten days later in the North. Most people, however, have come round to the view that you follow the rule for any deciduous shrub: prune in winter dormancy. This sounds sense. I start after Christmas and reckon to finish by February. Do not, of course, prune during a hard frost and if your young buds are frizzled up after pruning you must cut back again.

Ramblers: soon after flowering is over.

Climbers: Thin after flowering, and prune in winter.

Particular Precepts

This concerns the *degree* of pruning for different types. Dogmatism here is out of place, but the following notes will be a good guide for general garden display.

Bedding Types (*other than floribunda*): In the first winter or spring cut down to a bud about 3 in. from the ground, lower still on weak shoots. In subsequent years prune to about five eyes on strong basal shoots; and to three or less on weaker basal shoots, on strong laterals, and on plants of very dwarf growth. On H.P.s and some very vigorous H.T.s prune less severely, e.g. Peace, Perfecta, President Hoover, Prima Ballerina.

Bush Floribundas: First season, cut down to about 5 in. from the ground. In after years, for normal usages, shorten the best stems by about a half, and remove the remainder.

211

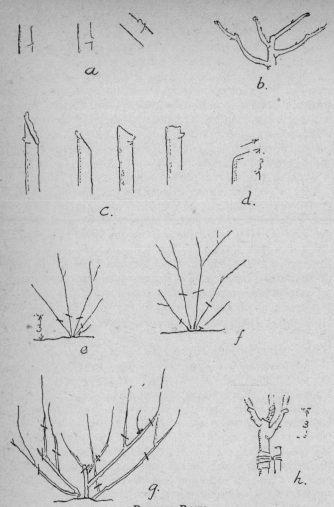

PRUNING ROSES

a, Typical rose 'eyes'; *b*, prune to an outward-pointing bud; *c*, wrong
pruning—jagged, below the eye, wrong way, too flat; *d*, just right;
e to *g*, pruning a weak-growing rose, one of moderate vigour and a
vigorous one; *h*, hard-pruning of a first-year standard.

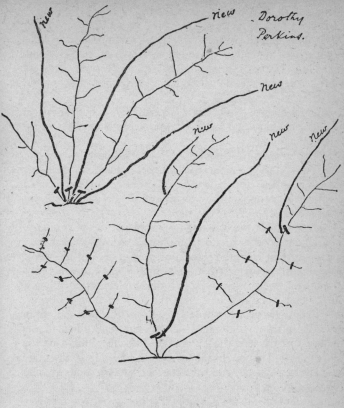

Dorothy Perkins.

Top: Pruning a rambler of Dorothy Perkins' family; cut all old flowered canes to the ground in autumn (unless no new canes). *Middle:* On other ramblers and climbers generally, prune according to the vigour of new wood; on old wood that is retained, shorten laterals. *Bottom:* A dwarf bush rose correctly planted.

213

Alternatively, you can get a brilliant mass effect with the pom-pom types by cutting right down to within 3 or 4 in. of the ground annually. Conversely, the floribundas can by light pruning be built into charming low hedges, though some wood must always be removed each year. Varieties of great vigour, such as Queen Elizabeth, are pruned much more lightly.

Species Roses. No pruning, other than occasional removal of exhausted old wood, or such trimming as is needed to keep a good shape.

Ramblers and Climbers. Here classifications are not clear-cut and the boundaries of breeding indistinct. Habit of growth must therefore be our guide, and the following formula is intended to simplify the problem on the basis of intelligent observation.

Cut out old-flowered wood in proportion to the degree to which new wood is produced. Thus (a) for every new cane springing right from the ground or near it, cut out the whole of an old cane, provided that the plant as a whole does not thus become too poorly furnished; if, for example, there is only one old cane and one new one, treat the old one as in (c) below. (b) When new growth sprouts not from the base but from somewhere on an old cane, cut the old cane down to the strongest of the new shoots, and cut back the laterals on the remaining old wood by about two-thirds. (c) If there are no new canes at all, cut back the old laterals as above, and slightly shorten the tip.

Easiest of all is the Dorothy Perkins group of *ramblers*, characterised by their *lax, flexible canes* (cf. Climbers, p. 204). These behave exactly like raspberries and loganberries. Long new canes sprout from the base every year, and they flower the following year. Therefore, we cut *all* the old canes down to the ground every year after flowering.

By the same token, you amputate Dorothy's family in the year of planting to 15 in. of the ground (or to within five buds of the crown on weeping standards), expecting *no bloom the first summer*. This is a cardinal injunction and you mustn't funk it. On other groups, especially the climbing sports, you

214

need not cut back in the year of planting, bar any weak or damaged shoots.

One or two special cases remain to be dealt with:

Gloire de Dijon (Climbing Tea) is dealt with for practical purposes as a climbing H.T. sport.

Mermaid, queen of all tall roses—do not prune at all the first spring, and very little afterwards, except for the re-removal of decadent old wood.

The Rose's Enemies

In Part IV I have dealt with the gardener's enemies in general, and only a little amplification is necessary here. Normally the rose is an easy plant to keep in good health, provided action is taken early.

Let us briefly catalogue the insect pests first. Commonest is the greenfly that in its myriads sucks the sap from young shoots, and the spittle-bug that likewise sucks away under the shelter of his slimy foam. The slugworm delicately chisels out the skeleton of a leaf, the sawfly grub rolls up the leaf like a paper-spill and the leaf-cutting bee scollops out neat half-moons on the edges of the blade. The caterpillars of the tortrix moths burrow into the heart of a young bud, and the rose chafer consumes the blossom itself.

All of these, except the adult chafer, can be dealt with by insecticides. A big advance has been made in the 'systemic' insecticides (e.g. Abol X and Murphy's), which are absorbed in the sap of the plant and kill insects eating leaves and stems. They are viable for quite a long time and, personally, I have found one spraying in May quite enough. Otherwise, use an insecticide, preferrably derris or pyrethrum, which are excellent but need frequent application.

Under good cultivation fungus diseases are normally even fewer. Mildew appears as grey powdering of the foliage; 'black spot' is shown by black or purple-brown patches; 'rust' is a rusty speckling; and 'leaf scorch' starts as small yellow patches, later turning brown and dropping out, giving the leaf the appearance of having been peppered by shot.

The commonest of these are black spot and mildew. The former, very conspicuous and ugly, can be a killer but does not invade the larger towns, in which the foliage is protected by the sulphur in the atmosphere. The usual remedy is captan, but maneb and zineb may be better. Mildews are widespread and troublesome everywhere except open and windswept places. Karathane is the usual corrective. Murphy, PBI and others sell combined sprays for both ailments. For rust, so deadly in the West Country, Dithane (from PBI) is advised. In all these things study the labels on the bottles or packets.

A systemic fungicide is promised us very soon, and if it is a success will be a godsend. Meantime, we must spray with the above concoctions frequently; rain washes them off. Start spraying in early May and repeat every fortnight till late September.

Some fungicides and insecticides can be mixed together for a two-in-one job. Follow the manufacturer's directions. A combined spray of this sort, used early and frequently, is often all that is needed.

Propagation of Roses

The propagation of roses by budding and grafting is great fun and not particularly difficult, but the easiest way for amateurs to increase their own supplies (of certain sorts) is by cuttings. Experience and opinion on this subject varies a good deal, but it is generally agreed that ramblers are easy and that the H.T.s with any yellow in them are not.

Early autumn is the time. Take 'trimmed heel' cuttings (*see* Chapter VI) from firm, ripe wood of the current season's growth, or nodal cuttings from low down on the same wood. If longer than about 10 in. cut them down to that length or less, shortening from the top of the shoot, not the base. Cut out all eyes on the lower half, and treat the cuttings with a rooting hormone. Insert to nearly half their depth in well dug, sandy soil in the shade of a north wall or fence, not directly under trees. Tread very firmly and water well if the ground is at all dry. Protect from north and east winds. By the following autumn the young plants will be ready to go into their permanent stations.

You are not likely to get 100 per cent 'strikes' from your cuttings, especially in heavy clays, so take more than you need. Roses grown this way have the advantage that there is no 'brier' to throw up suckers, and any growth from below ground can be left alone, or transplanted.

Lay-out and Display

It is an axiom of the purists that roses should never lie in the same bed as other flowers. This may be too severe a morality in the confines of a small garden, but any bed-mates you give them must be chosen with care. Nothing rumbustious. Ideal companions are violas and lobelias, and a fringe of pinks round the margins of the bed is also charming.

As compared with the shrub species, the bedding roses are creatures of the drawing-room. They demand formal beds, rather prim, and they demand especially a carpet of green grass round about them, having so little green themselves. The lawn is the perfect setting for the rose. Let the situation always be open—not shut in by walls, trees or high hedges. But a low decorative hedge, or a little dry wall dotted over with rock plants, are happy methods of enclosing a quiet rose garden where there is room to shut it off from the rest of the world.

Varieties to Choose

From the enormous Who's Who of roses there are at least three or four dozen that merit the term 'outstanding', and it is difficult enough to make up one's own mind which twelve roses one most likes personally. All one can do to advise the beginner is to give a brief guide to the best sorts and let him choose for himself. One cannot peer into the future beyond a year or two, so what I have done in the following lists is to pick a few that seem likely to hold their own for the next

217

few years, omitting varieties better left to the exhibitor, those that behave badly in rain, those that are particularly subject to disease, and any that have other faults. You must get their descriptions from the better catalogues.

Avoid all new roses until they have been tested in commerce and do not swallow all the guff about 'each new-hatched, un-fledged' darling.

H.T.s. Most of the following have scent.

Wendy Cussons (every virtue)	King's Ransome (best yellow)
Super Star (tall and slim)	Pink Favourite
Piccadilly (best bi-colour)	Mme Louis Laperrière
Silver Lining	Ena Harkness
Stella	Mischief
Prima Ballerina (great vigour, erect)	Rose Gaujard (vigorous)
	My Choice
Ernest H. Morse	Peace (great vigour)

The old pale-pink Ophelia, Mme Butterfly, and Lady Sylvia, small but beautifully formed, still engage many hearts and still take a lot of beating. I can't recommend any white H.T. All have cultural faults, but Virgo is so far the best.

Floribundas. A fast-expanding class, getting more and more of the H.T. element in them, sometimes to the detriment of their continuity of bloom.

Allgold	Dickson's Flame
Paprika	Lili Marlene
Pink Parfait	Anna Wheatcroft
Orange Sensation	Red Favourite (never stops)
Dearest	
Elizabeth of Glamis	Nathalie Nypels (never stops)
Evelyn Fison	

I exclude Queen Elizabeth and Iceberg, because, on account of their great vigour, I count them as shrub roses.

Dwarf (Pom-pom) Polyanthas. The Fairy, Paul Crampel, Cameo, Coral Cluster, Ellen Poulsen (scented).

Climbers. First the climbing sports. Nearly all are excellent, but they give little bloom after their June display. I suggest: Climbing Etoile de Hollande, Cl. Mme Butterfly, Cl. Mme E. Heriot, Cl. Mrs Sam McGredy, Cl. Shot Silk.

Of other first-class climbers: Allen Chandler (the most continuously in bloom), Chaplin's Pink Climber, Mermaid (a pre-eminent rose for walls and pergolas), Lemon Pillar, Gloire de Dijon (grand century-old fragrant rose, good on a north wall), Paul's Scarlet Climber, Mme Alfred Carrière (the best white, fragrant, another good one for north walls), Leverkusen (not too rampant). Danse du Feu and Nymenberg are the best 'perpetual' sorts.

Ramblers. For pergola, arch, or trellis, but preferably not for walls: Albertine (scented, the best), American Pillar, Thelma, Crimson Conquest (scented), The New Dawn, Emily Grey, François Juranville (scented), Crimson Shower for late effect, Dorothy Perkins.

Pillar Roses or short climbers. Golden Showers, Aloha, Zephirine Drouhin (bad for mildew). All these flower 'perpetually'.

Weeping Standards. Any of the Dorothy Perkins family (not American Pillar), plus François Juranville and Leontine Gervais.

Species and their Hybrids. Those I specially recommend are:

'Canary Bird' (*R. xanthina spontanea*). Gleaming yellow, single flowers, quite large, on a dense mound of fine foliage, 7 ft high.

R. ecae. Long sprays of small yellow flowers on a slim and elegant plant that sways with the wind.

R. moyesii. A rose of lyric beauty. Its colour is that of a dusky, antique red, and it bears a crop of handsome bottle-shaped hips in autumn. It will grow to 10 ft, has naked legs and so should go at the back of a border. 'Nevada', said to be a Moyesii hybrid, is one of the loveliest white roses in creation.

Hybrid Musk Roses, from R. moschata. Wonderful roses for any garden. Very vigorous, strongly perfumed, very prolific. Cut the flower clusters back to a strong eye for succession of bloom. Prune out old growth occasionally. Good hedgers. Penelope, Cornelia, and Prosperity are fine varieties,

219

of charming form and habit. Totally different are the newer German hybrids in strong colours, making large bushes, Bonn and Wilhelm are both reds, and Wilhelm will grow to 8 ft.

Rugosa Roses. These splendid roses are densely bushy, with thick, dark-green foliage to the ground. 6 ft × 6 ft. Three fine varieties are the purple Roseraie de l'Haÿ, Frau Dagmar Hastrup, and Blanc Double de Coubert.

Scotch or Burnet Brier (R. spinosissima). Very sturdy, vigorous, spiny, suckering freely. Strong, impregnable 5 ft hedges. The variety Stanwell Perpetual is particularly good, fragrant and ever-blooming. The modern hybrids Frühlingsgold and Frühlingsmorgen are tall, very beautiful, flowering in spring only.

Bourbon Roses. Of an old-world drawing-room loveliness, richly scented. Mme Pierre Oger is an ever-blooming shell-pink, erect in habit. Louise Odier is akin.

China Roses. Cécile Brunner is an enchanting miniature, like a toy Ophelia, and Perle d'Or is similar in apricot. Both have climbing sports.

Other Shrub Roses. Try to find room also for at least these three beautiful and distinctive moderns: Golden Wings, 5 × 5 ft, with a constant succession of single, yellow flowers; Sarah van Fleet, 6 × 5 ft, very thorny, with lovely roses of soft pink; and Erfurt, yellow and pink, 5 × 4 ft.

Note. Readers who would like to pursue the matter further may care to read my *Roses for Small Gardens*.

CHAPTER XV

FLOWERING SHRUBS AND SMALL TREES

INTRODUCTORY—A CHOICE OF TREES AND SHRUBS

Introductory

TREES and shrubs are dominant elements, and their shapes, textures, and manners immensely influence the general atmosphere and character of a garden. There are tall slim trees, plump round ones, light and airy ones, those with dark green leaves, others with silvery or purple leaves, and so on. Outline and skyline and architectural effect are critical factors, and variety and contrast must therefore be sought in making one's selections of trees and shrubs, whether they are to be used as backgrounds or screens, or planted as conspicuous 'specimens'.

But I would particularly draw attention to the immense usefulness in the small garden of that form of tree known as 'fastigiate'—that is to say, slim, erect, columnar, in the fashion of the Lombardy Poplar. They take the minimum ground space and do not overhang and enshadow the soil. There are several of these among small trees, and one can often get a fastigiate form of a tree normally known only as a standard or as a bush—for example, the Hawthorn, the fastigiate form of which (Cratægus monogyna stricta) is not only charming but also of practical merit, forming a screen many feet high. It is especially useful for poor soils.

Another picturesque one is the Koelreuteria in its columnar form, slim and elegant, which you can see at Kew. But above all there is the fastigiate flowering cherry which is called Amanogawa which becomes a fluttering pillar draped with pale pink flowers. There are also fastigiate crab-apples, and some choice small conifers are available in the same form, such as Fletcher's graceful form of Cypress.

Another very desirable form of small tree for providing variety of form and outline is the 'weeping' shape. Here again there are several, including weeping cherries, a weeping almond, a nice weeping crab-apple (Malus purpurea pendula), all looking like great umbrellas mantled in pink or white and splendidly decorative. Another fine one is the Cotoneaster

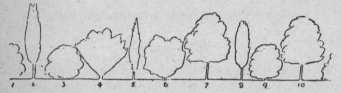

The idea of architectural skyline in a screen of small trees and shrubs, 110 ft long. To get the skyline effect, cover the lower part of the drawing. If space allows, small and medium shrubs can be planted in front of the screen to cover tree-trunks and gaps. The planting here is: 1, Lilac; 2, Cherry Amanogawa; 3, Lilac; 4, Cherry Ukon; 5, Koelreuteria; 6, Cornus mas; 7, Maple griseum; 8, Columnar Hawthorn; 9, Lilac; 10, Crab-apple Eleyi or Lemoinei. Trees shown at nearly full-grown heights.

hybridus pendulus, its drooping wands festooned in berries. Of no floral value, but of decorative form, are the little weeping birch and the Camperdown elm, beloved of children. There is also a pendulous Holly, called Perry's Weeping.

Other forms to consider when making a plan are trees or shrubs grown specially for their beauty of foliage, such as the exquisite little Japanese Maples for slightly shady places, the copper or purple forms of crab-apple and others, the very solid forms of the Barberries, and, of course, there should always be a proportion of evergreens.

All these considerations imply that, when thinking of a planting of trees and shrubs, planning is essential. Plot it out on squared paper, according to the *ultimate* height and spread of the plants, and plotting out the skyline as well. Catalogues of the best nurseries, such as those issued by Jackman's and by Notcutt, enable you to do so.

If your catalogue does not give the spread as well as height, you may for general purposes take the spread as being three-quarters of the height, but of course there are exceptions. Do not at any cost crowd the plants, and if your plan shows great gaps of 10 ft or more, as it will do, you can for the first two or three years fill up with herbaceous plants, bulbs or annuals and biennials. The choicer trees and shrubs are best planted in selected and separate positions as 'specimens', on a lawn or elsewhere.

A problem that is felt by many people who live in houses very close together is that of forming some screen from neighbours' overlooking windows or to mask off some unsightly prospect. If speed be the prime object, the things to have are Leyland's cypress or Thuja plicata or Jackman's Green Hedger, which are dense, fast-growing conifers.

Planting follows normal rules, as described in Chapter V. Generally, the best time is about early November. But, if the weather is open and the soil not sodden, any time up till March will do. In cold areas and at the seaside evergreens should wait until the middle of April.

Pruning is dealt with in general terms in Chapter VII, and more specifically where necessary in the cultural notes on each plant. Remember especially not to prune trees, evergreens or berried shrubs, except as stated in Chapter VII, and to prune deciduous bushes according to their season of flowering. Note those that should not be pruned at all except for the removal of dead or feeble wood.

A Choice of Trees and Shrubs

1. SMALL TREES. 2. FLOWERING SHRUBS, MOSTLY DECIDUOUS. 3. WINTER-FLOWERING SHRUBS. 4. SHRUBS FOR LIME-FREE SOILS. 5. EVERGREENS. 6. DWARF AND CARPETING SHRUBS. 7. SECOND ELEVEN. 8. CONIFERS.

In this chapter I shall not give an alphabetical lists of plants, but will deal with them in groups, as this is a greater help to the reader in making selections.

223

1. SMALL TREES

None of these necessarily demands any pruning except the removal of dead, weakly, or misplaced shoots.

First comes that wonderful group which comprises the ornamental fruit trees—flowering cherries, almonds, and so on, all belonging to the genus **Prunus.** They are among the loveliest things in the world, their mantles of massed pink or white blossom, displayed sometimes in the darkest days of winter, being nature's nearly most perfect work. All are of easy culture, given a sunny, uncrowded position, good drainage, a reasonably rich soil, and a thick mulch of leaves every autumn. Their glory is enhanced when they stand with their feet among daffodils. They are obtainable in the forms of standard, half-standard, or forking close to the ground in the manner of a bush, and it will be a long time before they take up all the space I quote for them. Do any pruning that may be essential in late May, *not* winter, and treat all pruning cuts with Abrex, Medo, or white lead paint.

First the cherries, of which I have already mentioned the columnar Amanogawa. Of other forms, first among all cherries in popular favour comes Kanzan, a thing of enchantment with its dark cyclamen-pink luxuriance and its noble form, and deservedly the sovereign choice; it is also sometimes called Hisakura or Sekiyama. Then there are the glorious, queenly-white Tai-Haku and the unique, less-known Ukon, crowded with its almost untrue green-gold treasures. All will reach 25 ft. In quite small gardens Okame is ideal.

Smaller still, and more of a bush, is the Fuji Cherry (Prunus incisa), a perfect small-garden tree in flesh-pink that may reach 9 ft. In the weeping forms there are P. yedoensis pendula, a particularly lovely little tree, Cheal's Weeping Cherry (P. serrulata rosea), and the smaller 'rosebud cherry' (P. subhirtella pendula). And for winter there is that great treasure P. subhirtella autumnalis rosea, whose pink stars challenge the darkest days; insist on rosea. 20 ft.

Of other small Prunus species, the following are all uncommonly good and very desirable:

Prunus triloba multiplex. Ideal as an elegant little standard, its slender wands wreathed with pink rosettes. Each year after flowering prune it right back to a strong new shoot near the crown. 7 ft. Beware suckers.

Flowering Plum, P. cerasifera Blireiana. A splendour of cyclamen-pink among bronze foliage and a prime choice. 15 ft.

Flowering Peach, P. persica Clara Meyer, with pink rosettes. Spray in autumn and late winter against the nasty peach-leaf curl; likewise on almonds.

Flowering Almond, P. communis (or Amygdalis). Pollardii is a fine hybrid.

Flowering Apricot, P. Mume, 8 ft.

Next among the flowering ornamental fruits are the **Crab-Apples** (Pyrus Malus), sometimes mistaken for Prunus. I pick first the superb 25-ft Lemoinei, resplendent with crimson flowers and purpled foliage. Eleyi is also splendid. Less ebullient, and of gracious habit is the charming floribunda in palest pink. Another fine one is John Downie, splendid for its handsome and edible fruits.

Magnolias are among the most tempting of flowering trees and are quite easy in most districts if protected from the east. They are rather a specialist subject and are expensive and slow and some of them take many years to flower. My own favourite among the smaller ones is Lennei. Its chalice-flowers in April are wine-red without and white within; 18 ft. M. Sieboldii, pure white and dizzily scented, is lovely and hardy, but needs acid, woodsy soil; about 15 × 20 ft. Smallest of all is the 'Star Magnolia', M. stellata. Only about 10 ft high, and rather more across, and crowded with small white flowers in spring, which I personally find rather ragged. There is a pretty pink form, Rosea. Some Magnolias are altogether too big for small places, and I have seen all the front windows of a little villa completely obscured by a large Magnolia. But if the house is big enough M. grandiflora, planted close to the wall (though quite hardy), is a splendid architectural adornment, enriched with big, fragrant white goblets in late summer with handsome, evergreen foliage. Get the varieties Exmouth or Goliath.

Laburnums, Tennyson's 'dropping-walls of fire', have two or three fine varieties, as well as inferior ones. One is the handsome L. Vossi, 25 ft high, and the other is the smaller Scotch L. alpinum, a lovely little tree (20 ft), especially if you can get the golden-leafed form. A curiosity is L. Adamii, partly yellow, partly purple. The secret of Laburnums is to pick off the seed-pods when flowering is over—a boring job, but worth the trouble, for seeding exhausts the plant's energies. Voss's Laburnum, however, usually discards its pods naturally.

Koelreuteria paniculata I have already mentioned. Mantled in golden blossom in late summer, it is normally a broad, bushy tree (as at Hampton Court), but Hilliers have the unusual fastigiate form. Very decorative, but rather slow and not yet cheap. The normal form is too big.

The **Hawthorn** (Cratægus) I have already mentioned also. Besides the unusual fastigiate form, it is handsome also as a standard. Easy and excellent for small gardens. Probably the most striking of all is Paul's Double Scarlet Thorn, a tree of vivid splendour. Another good one is the Cockspur Thorn (Cratægus Crus-Galli), which has very large berries and whose foliage turns a vivid scarlet in autumn.

For any garden that can accommodate a tree 30 ft high and 20 ft in breadth a first-rate tenant is **Catalpa bignonioides.** Extra-good in town gardens, it is fast-growing, has large, handsome leaves, and in July bears trusses of blossom like those of the horse chestnut. The golden-leaved aurea is a little dwarfer and very handsome.

Two choice little trees are provided by the **Dogwood** family (Cornus). One, often called the Cornelian Cherry, is C. Mas, whose naked boughs are encrusted with pale gold in the chill of February, followed later by large reddish berries. The silver-leafed form Variegata is specially desirable, being only 12 ft high. The other is the Chinese C. Kousa, which in May is thronged with brilliant ivory bracts beautifully chiselled. 20 ft. A very beautiful creation, but its success on limy soils is doubtful.

The berried **Rowan** or Mountain Ash (Sorbus Aucuparia), is a familiar favourite that does well anywhere. For small places one of the very best is the elegant little Chinese species Vilmorinii, with ferny foliage and roseate berries. Often more of a shrub than a tree, it reaches 15 ft and needs a rather moist soil.

The exquisite Japanese **Maples** (Acer), though not flowering trees, have a rare elegance of form and habit. There are purple-, green- and silvery-hued varieties. My favourite, with its delicately sculptured, almost fern-like foliage, answering to every breath of wind, is A. palmatum dissectum, especially the deep purple form atropurpureum. Each tree has its own individuality; you generally see them only about 7 ft high, but some are low, gnarled, spreading bushes. Pick your own choice in the nursery, and give them a position with a little shade and protected from east winds. Expensive.

Another attractive one, but quite different, is A. griseum, a short, stocky Maple less than 20 ft high, with deeply-cut, sinuous leaves that turn brilliant red and with a very handsome stem like polished mahogany. Yet another is japonicum aureum, golden in summer and crimson in autumn, perhaps 15 ft high. Quite different from all these is the popular A. Negundo and its variegated forms, a much larger tree, too often badly mutilated. Plant all these Maples where they will make a colour contrast with other trees and shrubs.

For the 'Strawberry Tree' *see under* Evergreens, and for the Spindle Tree *see under* Euonymus in the next section.

2. FLOWERING SHRUBS—Mostly Deciduous

Reasons of space oblige me to be highly selective and to omit many attractive things that the reader will no doubt welcome later on. I can do little more than introduce the subject. Don't forget the shrub types of **Rose,** dealt with in the chapter on that genus.

Although the plants in this section are classed as 'shrubs', there are several which can be raised as little standard trees, and as such are of great charm and elegance. Examples are Forsythia intermedia spectabilis, Buddleia alternifolia,

Viburnum Carlesii, Cytisus præcox and Cotoneasters. The leading nurseries that specialise in trees and shrubs can always provide a few of these handsome little standards. Now for a few shrub selections.

The **Barberry** (Berberis) is a large, handsome, and generous family. They give us flower in spring and berry in autumn. There are both evergreen and deciduous varieties, several make splendid hedges, and they normally need no pruning. They need a good, loamy soil that does not dry out too quickly, and in severe districts some of the evergreens are not fully hardy. My first choice is for the evergreen and hardy stenophylla, which is adorned with gracefully arching cascades of deep gold that make a glittering display in May—a thing of strong, masculine beauty, maybe 9 ft high, born near Sheffield and succeeding equally in clay or sand or chalk. Stenophylla also has some fine semi-dwarf varieties ideal for small gardens, including the golden gracilis, the ruddy coccinea and the pink corallina—all about 4 ft. Almost as good as stenophylla is Darwin's Barberry (B. Darwinii), a noble 8-ft bush, glossy dark-green, ablaze with orange flowers in April.

The deciduous Barberries are generally hardier but of less interest; Wilsonæ and Thunbergii are two of the best. There are also some very good dwarf and prostrate Barberries, particularly B. thunbergii Atropurpurea Nana, 2 ft. high and a bit wider, very dense and very good indeed.

Grouped with the Barberry but now officially classed as a separate genus is the **Mahonia,** or holly-leaved Barberry. It has large leaves and handsome golden sprays, and is valuable for doing well in shade. The best is M. japonica, which has long, luxuriant primrose tassels, strongly scented, often confused with the not-so-good, unscented Bealei. A great success in full shade, as elsewhere, and welcome for its winter flowers. To 6 ft. The dwarfer B. aquifolium is a good ground-cover beneath trees, where it will form a dense thicket.

Buddleia to most people means the large bush that throws out long purple plumes in August and is good in town gardens. This is David's Buddleia, B. Davidii, or variabilis. The right treatment is to cut it fearlessly down every February, even to within a foot of the ground, when it will throw up finer wands; otherwise it deteriorates. A much better one is the smaller, grey-leaved, lavender-flowered fallowiana Loch Inch, of 5 ft.

Even more desirable is the Chinese B. alternifolia. It is adorned with slender arching wands thronged with soft mauve lilac-seeming florets in midsummer, and as a small standard tree (reaching about 12 ft) it is a delightful decoration in any garden and is one I much commend. It prefers a rather dry situation. Cut out a proportion of the old flowered wood immediately after blooming, otherwise it becomes very untidy especially when grown as a bush. If you want it as a standard, grow it from seed (very easy). and keep it to a single stem until it reaches 5–6 ft.

The Buddleia with drooping clusters of round orange flowers is globosa; cut it back lightly after flowering. Propagate all sorts by cuttings of firm young shoots in October; or seed sown under glass in early spring will flower in autumn.

The **Ceanothus** is one of our very finest large blue shrubs, profusely garnished with little tuffets in various hues. Some are evergreen, these being very good for dry soils, some flower before midsummer and others after. Few if any are completely hardy in the coldest counties, and they are therefore usually grown on a south wall, for which purpose they are beyond praise. Selection is awfully difficult. Of the early varieties the loveliest is rigidus, dark blue dusted with gold, dwarfish, but it is for mild counties only; elsewhere use dentatus. Of the late sorts, Autumnal Blue or Burkwoodii. My own favourite is Delight. For colder places, thyrsiflorus is the hardiest, but it is ultra-vigorous. All these are evergreen and delightful furniture for a wall. Prune the early-flowering sorts after flowering, the late ones in April.

Deciduous Ceanothus are hardier and make lovely open-ground bushes in mild districts, the best being Gloire de Versailles in powder-blue, and the rich, deep Topaz. Cut these back *very hard* in April. Ceanothus grows quite easily and quickly from seed.

Another lovely blue shrub, ideal for small gardens in all but the severer districts, labours under the burdensome name

229

Ceratostigma Willmottianum. Rarely exceeding 3 ft, it rejoices the late summer and autumn with trusses of vivid azure flowers like those of the Plumbago, and it is an ideal shrub for mixing in the herbaceous border. Give it full sun and cut it down almost to the ground every April.

There is small doubt, however, about the hardiness of the **Cotoneaster,** a fine family of berried shrubs too often represented in small gardens only by the commonplace variety horizontalis. The Cotoneaster rejoices in a great variety of forms, some evergreen and some deciduous. Something very distinctive, for example, is C. hybridus pendulus, grown as a weeping standard, which, with its long trails of red berries drooping to the ground, is one of the most decorative sights of the autumn. Other good ones, either as bushes or as standards of normal habit, are the evergreen Franchetii, 8 ft, with grey-green pendulous foliage, and the splendid, fast-growing Watereri, 20 ft high and wide, whose berries are borne in large clusters. Its parent frigidus is too large for small places, I think. Simonsii makes a particularly fine hedge, and Wardii (so called) is good for training on a wall. There are also dwarf and prostrate varieties for the rock garden and elsewhere such as microphyllus cochleatus, which hugs and moulds itself attractively to the ground, good for rough banks and the like.

Nothing is more gay, colourful, and easy to cultivate than the **Brooms** (Cytisus), which mostly flower in May and June. They will flourish not only in normal conditions, but also in dry, parched and poor soils. A sloping bank that dries out quickly is an apt place for them; they go well also in a mixed or herbaceous border, and the dwarf or prostrate ones are first-rate on the upper slopes of a rock garden. In most gardens, unhappily, Brooms are allowed to get top-heavy, lop-sided, and bare at the base, through improper pruning. The *vital* thing is to cut back the flowered branch to within one inch or two of its point of origin immediately flowering is over. Like Lavender, Broom does not grow new shoots from old wood, and a bush neglected can't be cured. See sketch *b*, page 92.

Named varieties of cytisus are very colourful, but short-lived; one of the nicest is the sulphur Praecox, April-flowering.

A fine fellow is Battandieri, the pineapple broom, 12 ft; this does produce new basal shoots. Best on a warm wall.

Genistas are also Brooms. Pick of them all is Lydia, loveliest when tumbling over a terrace. All Brooms resent root disturbance. They seed very easily, but sowing should be in pots.

In contrast to the Brooms, the fragrant and delectable **Daphne** should never be pruned at all. Some members of this lovely family are difficult, but no garden should be without the favourite old D. Mezereum, so easy of culture and so inspiring in the grim days of February with her wreathed wands of perfumed mauve. In a good loamy soil she grows up to 4 ft. Let some seed ripen and fall—they are easy and good. Of the other, evergreen species, the most wooable are Tangutica and Retusa, with lustrous foliage and scented, rose-purple flowers, growing slowly to 3 ft. D. Cneorum Eximia is enchanting in rocks but fickle. All daphnes need sun, a rich, humusy soil, limy or acid, and sharp drainage.

The **Weigela,** still sometimes called the Diervilla, has some species and varieties that are excellent and easy small-garden bushes with their petals of pink or red trumpets in June. Tidy, shapely, easy to grow, generally reaching about 7 ft, they are greatly improved if the spent flowering branches or laterals are cut back nearly to their point of origin. Do not touch the young shoots. Give them good, well-heartened soil, retentive of moisture. The two best are the deep-rose Styriaca and the bright red hybrid Bristol Ruby, both about 7 ft and both first-class plants for all gardens, but the dark-red Eva Rathke has some merits in small places, growing only 4–5 ft. Rather more vigorous is W. florida variegata, which has nice cream-edged leaves and flowers of fresh pink.

One very versatile family is the **Euonymus.** It does well on chalky soils and produces trees, bushes, hedges and a creeper. The most useful are:

The 'spindle tree' (E. europæa), a handy little deciduous tree for the smallish garden, 15 ft × 15 ft, turning to brilliant colours in the autumn, and carrying a crop of pretty, quaintly shaped, dependent 'berries' in pink or red. Easy from seed.

E. japonica is a tough utility evergreen valuable for resisting salt-laden winds at the sea; usually looking pretty dowdy.

The creeping Euonymus, which is evergreen, is a valuable acquisition for several uses. It will carpet the ground beneath a tree or in an awkward place in the open, it can be trained as an edging, or it will climb up a wall for 15 ft or so. This last is a most valuable use, in which it acts as Ivy. Its name is E. fortunei (radicans); I would get one of the forms with silvered foliage, especially gracilis. The dainty little minima is fine for covering a tree-stump.

Forsythia must be one of the first choices in every garden. Its golden bells, strung along flexible wands, are one of the glories of the early spring, and it will succeed in shade almost as well as in sun, and in town as well as in country. For general uses the best is intermedia spectabilis, going 10 ft or more—a glorious bush. Lynwood is also very fine, with extra large flowers, and Primulina is a very soft yellow. For training on a trellis or wall the drooping variety, suspensa, is better— excellent for garnishing a north wall in deep shade. Prune Forsythias by cutting the spent flowering branches *hard* to a strong young shoot at their bases, treating one-third or a half of the bush like this each year. Multiply by cuttings of well-ripened young growth in autumn outdoors.

Only a few **Fuchsias** are hardy, but in those mild parts of the southwest and west and in Ireland they are among the chief joys of the countryside. The most reliable kinds are varieties of F. magellanica. One is called Riccartonii, a splendid 7-ft plant in purple and scarlet, and another is gracilis— smaller, more elegant, with graceful, drooping wands. Riccartonii in particular makes a fine hedge. Both bloom for three months from July onwards. Good named sorts are Mme Cornelissen, Princess Dollar, Uncle Charlie, Mrs Popple, and Tom Thumb. Give them sun, plant deeply about June 1st and water freely. In autumn cover them with 6 in. of ashes, gravel, etc. In spring disinter them and cut them to the ground.

Of the relatively few shrubs that bloom in late summer, the Syrian **Hibiscus** (Hibiscus syriacus) is one of the best. Totally different from the flamboyant creatures of high-temperature romance, they have blooms very like those of the Hollyhock, borne on stiff, erect stems reaching to 9 ft. Often dormant and leafless in the first year, they will reward patience. The outstanding variety is Blue Bird, a very fine plant. Give them full sun, and no pruning.

Hydrangeas must be differentiated, for our simple purposes, into three main groups. One is the breed with sumptuous, semi-spherical trusses of bloom in August and September, so widely grown in pots and embellishing hotel lounges. These are one of the branches of H. macrophylla and are usually known as the Hortensias. Some of the best of them are Maréchal Foch, Ami Pasquier, Westfalen, Générale Vicomtesse de Vibraye, and the dwarf Vulcain.

Another group, less opulent, more refined, are often called Lacecaps, having a circlet of brilliant sterile florets besieging a bevy of more demure females. Blue Wave is first choice of these and Lanarth White is a charming dwarf. H. villosa is valuable for doing well on chalk.

The blue tints so often admired in all these Hydrangeas may sometimes occur naturally or may be obtained by using a blueing compound. However, you can't blue them on a soil containing much lime, nor, apparently, in an acid soil if it is of peat. What seems best is a lime-free turf-loam. Even then not all varieties will succeed. But if you have the right soil all the varieties I have mentioned should blue magnificently, especially Vibraye, and if you haven't, they will still be very fine indeed in their reds and deep pinks.

Our third group of Hydrangeas comprises the hardier forms. The hardiest is H. paniculata grandiflora, a connoisseur's and showman's piece with enormous conical trusses of cream turning to pale pink (cut back to about five buds on each branch in March).

The mop-heads and the lace-caps need copious draughts of water, with mulchings of leaves or lawn mowings. They enjoy a west aspect and a little noonday shade, and are first-rate on north walls also. They are best unpruned, except for getting rid of dead or spindly shoots. For increase, cuttings root with ease. For blueing, the amateur is best advised to use a proprietary blueing powder, which has to be applied every week from the moment the buds begin to show in spring.

The **Hypericum,** or St John's Wort, is known to most people as providing the useful evergreen dwarf 'Rose of Sharon' (H. calycinum) with its golden salvers and gold boss of stamens, so valuable for flourishing under trees. It does even better, however, in the sun, and is a grand little plant for making a ribbon border or carpeting an awkward bank. Greatly improved by being trimmed back *hard* with shears early March, and easily multiplied by division. Good for towns. Less known is the excellent larger bush, H. patulum Hidcote, which produces the same golden flowers on rounded bushes some 4 ft high in great abundance from July onwards, is of the easiest culture and very showy. An Everyman's bush. Cut the old flowered branches fairly hard back in March.

Lilac is deservedly one of everybody's flowers. Its right botanical name is Syringa, and the white, perfumed bush often so miscalled is not a Syringa at all. Given a good, loamy soil, acid or limy, and an open position in the sun, Lilac is of the easiest culture, but too often it is allowed to grow into a dowdy, straggly bush with naked legs. Newly planted stock should be cut back boldly to make them bushy, for new growth comes from the tips of the shoots only. Cut out all weak and straggly growth, and always remove dead seed-pods as soon as flowering is over. A dressing of sulphate of potash may be hoed in during June. Ask the nurseryman if the plants are 'on their own roots' or grafted on other stock; if grafted, look out for suckers and wrench them out at once.

A few of the finest Lilacs are: Katherine Havemeyer, lavender-mauve; Masséna, Souvenir de Louis Spath and Charles Joly, all variations on the theme of purple; and Mme Lemoine, double white. Young hybrid plants are not always true to colour at first. A lovely and unusual little species for small spaces is the white Persian Lilac, Syringa persica alba. The Preston hybrids, such as Bellicent and Elinor, are splendid but rather large. *See* Chapter XII for the dwarf Lilac.

Lilacs are hearty eaters. Feed them well accordingly.

Potentillas are most useful little shrubs anywhere in the garden, decorated continuously all summer with flowers like those of the strawberry, usually in gold. They need full sun, but a soil not too dry. Most are varieties of P. fruticosa. All are good, but you won't do better than the 3-ft, large-flowered Elizabeth, or, for a shortie, the delightful Beesii, in gold-on-silver. In Tangerine there is a red tint. All make delightful low hedges. No pruning necessary. Easy from seed or cuttings. See Index for other Potentillas.

Another easy one, the **Philadelphus,** so often erroneously called 'Syringa', is one of our best midsummer bushes, clothed in a glittering white mantle of spicy fragrance, but not very glamorous after flowering. If you want to call it by a fancy name call it Mock Orange, but don't call it Syringa, which is Lilac. Given sun, Philadelphus succeeds in almost any soil. Some varieties are too big for small gardens, and those I most recommend are the dainty microphyllus and the hybrid Manteau d'Hermine, both under 4 ft. Of the many larger ones, perhaps Belle Etoile is loveliest. Cut flowered shoots hard back to strong new shoots after flowering.

There are few greater glories of the winter and early spring than the Japanese flowering **Quince,** oddly known in general speech as 'japonica', regardless of species. These Quinces make wonderful bushes aflame with colour, usually in red, but also in pink and in white. Their fruits make good quince jelly. All do well in sun or shade and the best-known species is often grown on a chill north wall; this old favourite, formerly Cydonia japonica, is now *Chænomeles speciosa* (or *lagenaria*). 8 ft. There are several fine varieties, such as Boule de Feu and Moerloosei.

Less known, but equally splendid, are the dwarfer Quinces, particularly the one hitherto known as Cydonia Maulei, 3 ft high, but spreading widely, and ablaze for two months in late spring with brilliant brick-red. Its new name is *Chænomeles japonica* and its chosen variety is Alpina. Simonii is blood-red, smaller, slower, a dashing and vivid creation.

Wall-grown quinces should be spurred back like apples, by pinching out the tips of laterals late June and August. Even quite experienced people get mixed up in these names, and it is really best still to use both the old and the new when ordering.

A very variable genus is the **Spiræa,** a name that is still valid for some of our finest flowering shrubs. One sees rather too much of Anthony Waterer, that drab thing with flat trusses of dull carmine. Far lovelier are the white spiræas. The tiny stars of Thunbergii enliven March, then comes Arguta, the bridal wreath, aptly festooned, and in May the big Vanhouttei delights us. For damp soils, Menziesii triumphans is most useful with bold, upright plumes of deep rose in July. Cut the old flowered branches back *hard* to new young growth, summer varieties in March, early varieties immediately after flowering.

Another large and versatile family that includes both summer- and winter-flowering varieties, evergreens and deciduous, is the **Viburnum.** The gem of them all in my opinion is one which has the unique and striking habit of branching horizontally in tiers, and these tiers are smothered as with heavy snow in May. It is V. tomentosum Mariesii, and it is a wonderful picture isolated as a specimen plant, or first-class for hiding an untidy fence. 9 ft × 12 ft. Lanarth is similar.

Characteristic of other Viburnums is their habit of throwing out handfuls of China-white bloom like snowballs, often sweetly scented and pink-tinted. Bodnantense, replacing the old fragrans, embalms the air in mid-winter and in spring come the 9-ft Burkwoodii and the 5-ft Juddii (a much finer shrub ultimately than Carlesii). All these are fragrant. The popular Laurustinus (V. tinus) also blooms in winter, is densely evergreen, good in towns, and a fine plant much misused and mutilated.

The 'Guelder Rose' is V. opulus, with white heads in June followed by red berries, 10 ft, and an improvement on it is the 'Snowball tree', which is opulus sterile. Choicer than either of these, and good for towns, is the 'Japanese Snowball', which is V. tomentosum plicatum, 8 ft. No pruning for Viburnum. I quote the names in general use.

3. Winter-flowering Shrubs

Among shrubs and small trees there is quite an array that braves the frosts and some of these I have already mentioned in the previous sections—the winter-flowering cherry and other sorts of Prunus, Daphne Mezereum, the Cornelian Cherry (Cornus Mas), the Mahonias, and some of the Viburnums. Others, having borne flower in the spring or summer, will gladden the winter with bright berries, such as Holly, Barberry, Pyracantha, and Cotoneaster, while Garrya flutters her golden-green tassels in the wind. Some of the best—Jasmine and Honeysuckle—are climbers or wall plants, and will be dealt with in that chapter.

In addition, there is one shrub that stands out as a winter decoration. It is the **Witch Hazel,** a thing of piquant and captivating charm. You must ask for Hamamelis mollis, which is the best. From Christmas till well into February it bears on its naked branches ingenious little twisted frills of spun gold—a merry bush that should be the haunt of elves. But you must allow for it some 10 ft or more of breadth and as much height. Its sprays are marvellous in a vase. It does best, perhaps, in a soil with little lime content.

Almost as attractive is **'Winter Sweet',** the fragrant Chimonanthus fragrans, but it takes some years to do itself justice, and is therefore fitter for larger places.

In addition wonderful winter displays are provided by some of the Ericas, and these are dealt with in Chapter XVIII.

4. Shrubs for Lime-free Soils

Most of the trees and shrubs mentioned in the previous sections of this chapter will succeed perfectly well on acid soils, but there are several important shrubs that will prosper in no other. Probably the best soil for most of these is a lime-free loam; failing that, a mixture of loam with ample peat or leaf-mould. After planting, and every autumn, they should be mulched with fallen leaves, preferably forest leaves, several inches deep, or with hops, or with green bracken in June. Such treatment provides for two characteristics of this group. First,

237

such a soil will retain the moisture which is essential for their roots in summer (and if the summer is very dry they will need copious watering). Secondly, the mulchings satisfy the surface-rooting habits of these plants. For this reason, moreover, the beds once planted must on no account be churned with spade or fork, nor, if possible, should they even be hoed, for the mulch itself will keep down the weeds.

A further characteristic is that, with a few exceptions, all these plants prefer, but do not always insist upon, some degree of shade. The ideal is the 'high' shade, or dappled shade, of thin woodland. Plant firmly, using plenty of peat. No pruning, except careful removal of spent flowers.

First and above all, the **Rhododendron.** Some will succeed in full sun, chiefly those one calls the 'hardy hybrids'. Be careful to plant very shallow. The only pruning normally necessary is to snap off spent flowers and seed-pods after blooming; this is important and should be done carefully to avoid damaging the new growth that is starting for next year. In dry spells they need copious watering, preferably with rain-water. There are varieties in almost every colour except true blue, and in every size from prostrate rock-garden pygmies to great bushes 15 ft high and more. Many of the glorious hybrids with 'fancy' varietal names are expensive and too big for small places, and Azaleas (which may be deciduous or evergreen) are generally to be preferred. As there are over 2500 Rhododendrons listed, it is pretty tricky to give selections, and the best plan is to consult a good nurseryman, specifying colours and heights preferred. Three very good starters for small gardens are Blue Tit, Blue Diamond, and the red Elizabeth; and Carmen is splendid as a dwarf. For medium height, three of the best are Bow Bells, Doncaster, and Britannia. For those who do want suggestions for the best larger varieties, the following is a primary guide: Pink Pearl and its offspring (e.g., Professor Hugo de Vries and Souvenir de Dr Entz), Scandinavia, Purple Splendour, Susan, David, Orbiculare, May Day, Betty Wormald, Fabia, Sappho, Goldsworth Orange, Bagshot Ruby, and the widely grown Cynthia. *See also under* Rock Gardens.

Rhodos associate very beautifully with Lilies, with the smaller bulbs in contrasting colours, and with such dwarf plants as Forget-me-not and Aubrieta. They go well also with Heathers, most of which like the same soil conditions. Propagate by layers in spring or autumn.

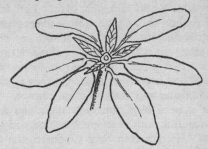

When removing dead blooms of Rhododendron, be careful not to damage the new buds (shown slightly exaggerated) growing immediately below the old.

A branch of the Rhododendron clan is the **Azalea,** equally showy, generally smaller, often perfumed, often more tolerant of dry conditions. Many are deciduous. I recommend a start with the evergreen Kurume or Japanese near-dwarf varieties, which are among the most perfect little flowering shrubs produced for the small garden. First choices are: Hino-Mayo, a sumptuous pink; Amœnum, wine-purple; Hino-Degiri, crimson; Benigiri, scarlet, and the dazzling Hatsujiri.

The deciduous azaleas grow larger in a wide range of superb colours. The ones to go for are the brilliant race known as the Knap Hill hybrids and the wonderful Exbury azaleas, hardy, vigorous, and splendid. As these finish the Ghent hybrids, or 'honeysuckle Azaleas', come on. They have small, tubular flowers, often sweetly scented, have a graceful habit, are amazingly flowerful, and extra hardy. The inexpensive wilding 'Azalea pontica' (*Rhododendron luteum*) is one of the best of the lot and makes a fine hedge. The Azaleas you buy in a pot in the winter are not hardy and can be grown outdoors only in favoured places.

Closely similar to the rhodo is the **Kalmia** but it has

239

bunches of dainty pink cups instead of the rhodo's big throats. The usual one is K. latifolia, but for small places the much smaller polifolia or glauca, about 30 in., is better. Very flowerful and attractive. Plant in sun, *not* shade as often advised.

A lovely little shrub-like tree for gardeners with patience is the **Eucryphia.** Rarely exceeding 15 ft × 12 ft, it is crowded in July and August with chaste white salvers sparkling with golden stamens and its foliage falls in a blaze of autumnal glory. The safest bet is 'Nymansay', a clone of the hybrid E. Nymansensis. It is broadly columnar in shape, will tolerate lime and chalk and is evergreen. E. glutinosa is more beautiful, but a lime-hater and wants a warm climate.

The same general conditions will allow you to grow the exquisite **Camellia,** with its serene blossoms and glossy evergreen foliage. Hardier than once supposed, the Camellia is nevertheless best protected from the east, so that it shall not be chided by rude winds or by the sudden impact of early morning sun on frost-covered blossoms and buds, but an open south aspect is equally undesirable, as most camellias want partial shade and cool roots. Good and generous feedings and mulching, as suggested in the introduction to this section, are essential, with liberal watering in dry springs and summers, especially in July, when the buds form.

Probably the best of all varieties is the hybrid Donation, a glorious pink Camellia that will flourish in full sun as well as in shade. Otherwise the beginner is best advised to start with the japonica varieties. The most reliable include Adolphe Audusson, Elegans, Lady Vansittart, and Gloire de Nantes. All these japonicas flourish in shade, even on a north wall, where Nagasaki is particularly good. Western counties may grow the big Reticulata varieties, such as Captain Rawes.

The **Pieris** is another superlative genus, with rich foliage and sprays like lily-of-the-valley. The finest are the Wakehurst and Forest Flame forms of P. formosa forrestii; shade essential. Sun-hardy ones are Taiwanensis, a great mound of green, and the small Floribunda Grandiflora.

Pernettyas make dense, evergreen thickets with marvellous autumn berries. Get one male to five females.

5. EVERGREENS

Of whatever size, every garden should contain a proportion of evergreens, both as a solace to the eye in the skeletal bleakness of winter and because the handsome deep foliage that many of them carry provides a backdrop and a foil for the coloured drama of summer. Except Lavender and Rosemary, normally none needs any pruning.

Evergreen forms of some varieties have been mentioned in the second section of this chapter, such as those of the Barberry, Hypericum, Ceanothus, Daphne, and Viburnum, and nearly all those in the section on lime-free soils are also evergreen; so, of course, are conifers. Others again, such as Pyracantha, are in the small garden more conveniently grown on walls, and are therefore dealt with in the chapter on climbers.

The most handsome of all evergreens, when properly grown, is the **Holly.** Besides its use as a hedge, it can be grown as a tree or a bush, and in small gardens the bush form is best, when it should be clothed to the ground. Many people like the variegated forms, with golden edgings and so on, but to most epicures the dark green is the most handsome. The important thing about holly is to ensure that the chosen variety is bi-sexual or that males and females are associated; thus Golden King (female!) is pollinated by Silver Queen (male!). So will you have berries.

Challenging it closely is the glittering **Elaeagnus pungens** Aureo-variegata (or maculata). This handsome shrub is densely clothed with leaves heavily splashed with daffodil, its golden beauty most appreciated in winter. It will reach 10 ft high and wide, prospers in sun or shade, in chalk or loam. What more could one ask? Flowers? No. If any dark-green shoots appear and do not turn yellow, cut them out at the point of origin.

The **Escallonia** is another handsome fellow, with small, glossy leaves, and sprays of pink or red bells. Not entirely hardy everywhere, but particularly valuable at the seaside, the gloss of its leaves resisting spray and wind. Also fine inland where the climate is not severe. Plenty of good varieties:

241

e.g., for small gardens the pink Donard Brilliance; for seaside hedges, Macrantha or Crimson Spire.

Evergreen *trees* for the small garden are rare, and therefore there is particular value in the handsome **Arbutus**. Sometimes called the 'Strawberry Tree', it carries, at one and the same time in autumn and early winter, clusters of pretty white or pink flowers like lily-of-the-valley and of small red fruits vaguely resembling the strawberry. Prefers a peaty soil, but does well almost anywhere. Forks low down like a shrub, and makes about 20 ft × 15 ft. You ask for A. Unedo. Slow.

In mild districts a small shrub of great value in the little garden is the **Cistus**. Don't call it the 'rock rose' or 'sun rose', because in some catalogues and books both those names are also given to the Helianthemum. The Cistus makes a wonderful show in June with colourful blossoms that have the delicate texture of tissue paper. It thrives on dry, poor soils and wants no feeding or pruning, but must have all the sun it can get. Outstanding in popular favour (but not mine) is the little 3-ft hybrid Silver Pink. Of special value are the low, wide-spreading sorts; lusitanicus decumbens is the handsomest and corbariensis the most hardy. Among taller species, the 7-ft cyprius and laurifolius are fine and pretty hardy.

Hebe is the name that should now be used for the shrubby plants formerly included in the genus Veronica (now reserved for the herbaceous species). Hebes are small, evergreen shrubs, hardy only for the seaside and other mild districts. I suggest Midsummer Beauty and Autumn Glory, shrubs about 3 ft high with lavender or violet spikes. No pruning.

Very different from all these are the **Lavender** and the **Rosemary,** both too well known to need description. What is not so well known is that these delightful old-world plants are made or marred by their pruning. The vital thing is, immediately after flowering is over, to cut the young growth which has come on during the current season hard back with shears. New shoots will not break from wood more than a year old, and if this treatment is not given, especially to young plants, the result will be a top-heavy blob on a naked leg. For the same reason it is useless to try to correct previous neglect by cutting right back into old wood. The only remedy is new plants.

Of varieties of Lavender I most recommend the dwarfs. Two of the best are the splendid deep-purple Hidcote variety, 15 in. high, and the softer French nana compacta. The rather larger Twickle Purple has long spikes spraying out fanwise for 2 ft or so. For sachets, etc., Lavender should be cut just before the flowers are fully open and hung up heads-down in bundles in a cool, shady, airy place. All make splendid dwarf hedges. Propagate by firm cuttings in late September.

The usual variety for Rosemary is officinalis, but the less hardy angustifolius Corsican Blue looks very promising for mild climates.

6. DWARF AND CARPETING SHRUBS

For convenience of garden arrangement and planning I have put these separately. They are suitable not only for the front of the shrub garden, but also for the herbaceous border and many for the rock garden.

Probably the most useful of all is the **Helianthemum.** Like the Cistus, it is nicknamed in popular parlance either 'sun rose' or 'rock rose', so when ordering the only safe name to use is its legal one. The Helianthemum is far hardier than the Cistus, is only a few inches high, but spreads very broadly and rapidly, and is thronged for several weeks from late May onwards with a crowd of delicate flowers the size of a florin in red, pink, yellow, or white. Very easy, but it must have full sun and a dry soil, and will indeed flourish on parched, ill-nourished banks. After flowering, trim it hard back with shears to keep it compact and flowerful. You may buy named varieties, but they come very easily from seed, and a packet will give you dozens, though the colours will not be predictable. Use them anywhere, including the rockery and the dry wall. Propagation by cuttings in July is as easy as possible; take maturing young growth with or without a heel.

The 'cotton lavender', **Santolina,** is another easy and good dwarf shrub, whose silver foliage in the front of the herbaceous border is of special value as a foil to the prevailing colours.

243

Evergreen, 18 in., with small golden globes in July. Needs sun, but does well on poor soils. The most popular one has been known for long as incana, but now you ought to use the horrible mouthful S. chamæcyparissus; there is a good green form called viridis. For good results trim back the previous season's growth pretty hard in March. Both these make excellent little dwarf hedges planted a foot apart, but an even dwarfer and more picturesque effect is got with the Lilliputian S. incana nana, which makes a charming 9-in. edging, highly 'frosted'.

Senecio laxifolius is another silver-grey shrub and one of the very best, low-growing and spreading widely. Cut it hard back each April to keep it compact and it becomes one of the dozen best shrubs, bearing golden daisies. Very easy from summer cuttings.

The popular **Cotoneaster** horizontalis, with its red berries in winter, tough and hardy, has already been mentioned for its usefulness in concealing unsightly spots or broken ground, with its horizontal and spreading habit; C. microphyllus cochleatus (page 230) is usually to be preferred. No pruning. Easy from seed, but not true.

Then there are 'carpeting' plants for covering rough places or growing under trees. The Rose of Sharon is one of the most useful of these, and in lime-free soils the Partridge Berry, Gaultheria procumbens, takes its place.

The **Periwinkle** (Vinca) is a useful trailing plant, with pretty blue flowers, for the like purpose. V. minor is better than V. major and Bowles's variety is better still.

More beautiful than any of these, however, are the dwarf forms of larger shrubs, such as Rhododendron, Daphne, Broom, Barberry, Potentilla, and the dwarf conifers, together with the semi-dwarf forms of Philadelphia, Quince, and Deutzia mentioned elsewhere in this chapter or in the chapter on rock gardens.

7. SECOND ELEVEN

Reasons of space and a desire not to confuse the beginner with an embarrassment of choice have induced me to restrict the above selections. Here, however, are a few very brief notes on some others:

Caryopteris clandonensis. A pretty powder-blue shrub for the same uses and season as Ceratostigma.

Choisya ternata. Very beautiful evergreen, with fragrant orange-blossom flowers. 6 ft. Milder districts only, and there a prime choice.

Deutzia (pron. 'Doitzia'). The usual D. scabra is a tall shrub densely covered with white blossom at high summer, too apt to become leggy and scrawny. The dwarfer hybrids rosea carminea and elegantissima, however, are charming small bushes, the first in soft pink to 4 ft, the other rose-purple to 5 ft. You must cut back the spent shoots hard after flowering.

Flowering Currant (Ribes sanguineum). Easy in any conditions, including shade and town gardens. The best is the blood-red King Edward VII. March–April.

Garrya elliptica. Evergreen with long, golden-green catkins in winter. Needs protection of a south wall. 8 ft. Specify male plants.

Halimium. Low, spreading, grey-green shrubs, almost quite hardy, enamelled with many buttercup-form flowers. The usual one is H. lasianthum, maroon-eyed. Very nice. 2 ft × 4 ft.

Indigofera Gerardiana. Another pretty blue bush, with pea-blooms, for the same uses as Ceratostigma. Cut to the ground each April. 4 ft.

Kerria. Easy and very common shrub. Sparse foliage, yellow blooms. Most people prefer the double variety. Sun or shade. Cut old flowered stems hard back to new shoots in June.

Rhus. This includes the familiar 'stag's horn sumach' (R. typhina), a bold-foliage shrub with fiery autumn hues; and the 'smoke plant' (R. cotinus), with dense feathery masses, purple or tawny, and brilliant autumn hues, now called Cotinus coggygria.

Kolkwitzia amabilis. A beautiful, arching shrub clustered with small pink bells in June. 7 ft.

8. CONIFERS

A sprinkling of conifers is important in garden design, but only a few are really suitable in small places. They rarely succeed in towns and are unsuitable for mixing in a shrub border. The statuesque columnar shapes are particularly good, and those with golden, silver-blue, or other tints are most picturesque. There are also many dwarf and pygmy conifers which lend character to the rock garden, or add a finishing touch of formality to terraces or steps. Forgive the unavoidably long names.

Lawson's Cypress (*Chamæcyparis Lawsoniana*, with the Ch pronounced as K) provides some of our best garden forms, and of them I choose first Columnaris (or Columnaris glauca). Slim, erect, tall, tapering, with blue foliage, it is the ideal small 'specimen' tree. Of similar habit, but much shorter, are Fletcheri (say 15 ft) and Elwoodii, 9 ft.

The ordinary form of Lawson's cypress that you see everywhere, growing to about 30 ft or more, easy, reliable, fast-growing, and cheap, is also an excellent tree if planted with discretion; but Leyland's Cypress (Cupressocyparis leylandii) is better and valuable as a shelter-screen.

Other picked ones are:

C. L. Stewartii or *Lanei* for a golden one.

C. pisifera plumosa. A handsome, broadly conical tree, 25 ft × 12 ft, with fine feathery foliage; again there is a slower, golden variety, aurea.

Cupressus arizonica 'Conica'. Like the slim Italian cypresses, soaring to 35 ft.

Juniperus communis 'Hibernica', the slender Irish Juniper. Makes a dense pillar 10 ft high by only 2 ft. When aged, needs to be tied round.

Taxus is the Yew, and the most suitable forms for small places are the columnar Irish Yews, T. baccata fastigiata, and its golden form aurea. Both grow in time to 16 ft or more.

Thuja, the Arbor-vitæ. Used mostly for making quick screens. The best for this is T. plicata, glossy-green and fast. Zebrina has a golden tint, but is slower. Moist soil.

Among the many really dwarf conifers for the rock garden it is difficult to make recommendations. It is essential really to visit the nursery and pick those of a shape and habit you like best in consultation with the nurseryman. There are little columnar ones, and globular sorts and others prostrate and spreading. Of the erect, conical sorts, I offer:

Chamæcyparis lawsoniana minima aurea. Greeny-gold. Fine.
C. pisifera plumosa Rogersii. Golden and feathery.
C.p. Boulevard. Steely-blue. Part shade.
Thuja occidentalis Rheingold. Gingery-gold.
Juniperus communis compressa. Tiny Noah's Ark tree.

The gold ones want full sun. Boulevard and Rheingold will reach 6 ft in time.

The very opposite effect is obtained with Juniperus communis prostrata. This grows only 12 in. high, but will spread 5 ft over the ground and mould itself to its shape. So also will the larger Sabine Juniper, J. sabina tamariscifolia; dense and shapely, it will measure about 3 ft × 8 ft. Both of those, apart from their natural grace, can also be employed as utility plants to cover an awkward spot.

Another good form for contrast is the 'obtuse' or rounded form, as in the delightful form of Lawson's Cypress called obtusa nana, of which there are several variations. The miniature Scotch Fir, Pinus sylvestris pumila, is another gem for rocks. And, besides the Cypress and the Juniper, there are some excellent toy Spruces, Yews, and Thujas.

When planting conifers, water the soil and foliage copiously. In dry spells wet foliage and roots daily until established.

Shrubs from Seed. Many trees and shrubs, especially if not hybrids or named varieties, can be raised from seed quite easily and often quite quickly. Examples are: Buddleia alternifolia and B. davidii, Ceanothus, Brooms, Helianthemum, Santolina, Daphne mezereum, Laburnum, Hypericum, Philadelphus.

CHAPTER XVI

CLIMBING AND WALL PLANTS

To grow a creeper over a house is something of an insult to an architect. Unfortunately not many of our houses have been designed by architects, and even so it is a regrettable fact that too many are improved by being hidden. How many of our dwellings owe their only claim to grace or mellowness to the soft shroud of the Virginia Creeper!

But even if our house has beauty enough to stand before the world naked and unashamed, there is generally something else that is better hidden—an old fence, an out-house, a tree-stump. And if still there is nothing of the sort, then we should deliberately create an excuse—pergola, arch, or trellis—for giving admittance to some of the loveliest plants in the catalogue.

The general word 'climber' is ambiguous, and we can divide the field roughly into three. There are the clingers, such as Ivy, Virginia Creeper and the climbing Hydrangea, which cling to their host as it were with claws; these need merely to be planted at the foot of a wall, and away they go by themselves. Then there are the twiners and ramblers, such as Clematis and Honeysuckle, which need some visible means of support in the shape of a trellis, arch, or a host-shrub. Finally there is a wide range of bushes which are adaptable to being planted against a wall, and will, either naturally or by inducement, grow up and along the wall or fence or whatnot; this last class includes some of our very finest wall plants, such as the Rose, Ceanothus, flowering Quince, and Pyracantha. Not counted among these is a yet further range of plants which, by reason of some tenderness in their constitution, benefit from the

248

protection which a wall provides against wind and frost, but which remain at their normal stature.

Thus, in choosing 'climbers' for particular places and tasks, we have to consider both habit and vigour. The clingers require a large wall-face of brick or stone not too much broken up by windows. The twiners are generally of lesser vigour, and, being provided with a suitable host, are appropriately draped over doorways or arches or trellis screens. A third, and most important, factor is aspect. While almost anything will grow on a south-facing wall or fence, those that will grow well on a north wall are limited, and are of particular value, for a north wall has too often a colourless and gloomy visage. The following choice of the better flowering and berried climbers and wall plants for various aspects may be of help.

South wall. Almost anything except plants that hate full sun, e.g. Camellias, Clematis unless the roots are shaded, and Honeysuckle unless the ground is damp. The best wall for Campsis, Passion-flower, and Ceanothus.

West wall: An ideal wall, good especially for Clematis, Honeysuckle and Camellia.

North wall: Provided the wall is not overhung by trees, the following will all do well, though usually better still on other walls: Morello Cherry, Pyracantha, Cotoneaster, climbing Hydrangea, Clematis, winter Jasmine, Forsythia, Camellia, and some Roses.

East wall: as for the north wall, except Camellias and Clematis.

Some wall plants will prosper in any aspect, however, such as the flowering: Quince, Celastrus, Pyracantha, winter Jasmine, and Forsythia. Before going on to consider the merits and use of individual plants, there are one or two special points I would like to make.

The 'footings' of a brick, stone, or concrete wall are usually very dry and littered with builders' rubble; therefore set your plant in the ground a good 12 in. away. Prepare the site with the same cultural care as you would for an open-ground bush.

Wooden-pale fencings are seldom objects of beauty, but they make excellent stations for the third class of plant I have mentioned. Make full use of fences, and plant them with Pyracantha, Quince, Jasmine, fruit of various kinds, and so on. Their stature can be raised, if desired, by topping the fence with trellis-work.

Whatever artificial host you provide for the twiners, make sure that it is strong, permanent, sufficient in extent, and sightly; a Honeysuckle or Clematis that is flopping all over the place in a tangled mass, held up to a nail by a piece of string, is not a thing of beauty. If against a wall, such support can be provided either by a strong wooden trellis, or by wires held away from the wall by galvanised 'wall-eyes' driven into the wall or by one of the new square-mesh wires, which are excellent and easy to fix.

Before deciding on any climbers or creepers, consider the use of fruit trees as discussed in Chapter XX. They are both economical of space and decorative—on a south wall the pear or nectarine, on a north one the Morello cherry and the fan-trained redcurrant, on fences the berried fruits on canes or as cordons. For arches and arbours there are the hardy vines, which have every delight.

Now for the clinging plants, of which there are only a few. The **Ivy** (Hedera) offers us some handsome sorts, particularly those with variegated leaves, and they will thrive in shade. For an awkward corner under the deep shade of trees, for covering old tree-stumps, or for carpeting rough ground, Ivy is excellent. The most impressive is the large-leaved, grey-and-white Canary Ivy (H. canariensis), and for a gold-leaved one there is Persian Ivy in its yellow form (H. colchica Dentato-variegata). Many others have small leaves, charmingly tinted.

As a covering for large walls the **Virginia Creeper** is not easy to surpass. There is a great bother about names. The right one is the apt Parthenocissus ('virgin ivy'), but catalogues still cling to such old names as Ampelopsis and Vitis. The finest is the true Virginian, the five-lobed P. quinquefolia, gloriously coloured in autumn and as magnificent when climbing a decadent tree as when clothing a house.

Far less stereotyped, and worthy of much wider use, are two

handsome flowering creepers. One is a **Campsis**, a race famous in hot climates for its wonderful golden trumpets. The one for us is C. radicans, hardy in most parts of Britain given a warm south wall, with 3-in. orange trumpets in late summer and large pinnate leaves, highly decorative but deciduous. It needs a hearty loam and will climb 20 ft. The secret with it, as with Wisteria, is to prune back the young laterals in winter, as on a vine, to two eyes. *See* the sketch in the passage on grapes. In some catalogues called Tecoma or Bignonia. Needs a warm August to flower well; cool nights make the buds drop.

The other is the climbing **Hydrangea**, H. petiolaris, which in its native Japan climbs to the tops of trees. Quite hardy, it has bold, handsome leaves and large flat corymbs of white blossom, arranged similarly to the lace-cap shrubs. Deciduous, turning pale gold in autumn. Any aspect, but less good on the north than elsewhere. Rather similar to it is another useful one cumbrously named Schizophragma hydrangeoides, its sole outer floret like a fluttering handkerchief.

We turn now from these few clingers to those plants that mount by means of twining tendrils, leaf-stalks, or stems.

Vitis is the vine, and it gives us a few fine foliage climbers in addition to those dedicated to Bacchus. Grandmaster of them all is V. coignetiae, which has enormous vigour (it will climb a tall tree) and very large, handsome leaves that in autumn flame with tints of ruby and cornelian. A top choice for expansive walls and for outbuildings. There are splendid colours also in some of the varieties of the grape-vine (V. vinifera). Thus Purpurea has handsome purple leaves, and Brandt has leaves that become ensanguined in autumn with crimson and orange. They are excellent for quick screens on trellises or for embracing an arbour.

Noblest of all climbers, however, is the **Wisteria**, with its sumptuous trusses of cascading lilac blossoms. Its tremendous vigour is rather too much for the very small house. It will prosper in any reasonable soil and on any wall except the north one, but likes the south best. Easily trained where you want it to go—straight up the house with branches between each storey; or kept low along a balcony, terrace, or fence, and marvellous on a pergola. Can also be grown with great effect in the open garden as a standard tree or bush trained umbrella-wise, or as you will. The usual and best variety is W. sinensis. After training it as you want, summer-prune the young shoots or laterals at the end of June to within about five leaves of their point of origin, and in winter cut back again to about three buds. Neglected old Wisteria may need to have a few older shoots judiciously cut out in winter. You can cut back as hard as you like.

Queen to the Wisteria is the **Clematis**, and she is so important a lady that I have given her a section to herself in Chapter XVIII. **Roses,** which do not come comfortably within any of these classifications, are dealt with in Chapter XIV.

Another popular twiner is the **Honeysuckle** or Woodbine (Lonicera). The usual ones are the Early Dutch and Late Dutch, which are quite nice, but a better one for general use is L. americana. This has scented, purple-and-rose flowers and is nearly evergreen. For utilitarian purposes—to cover an outhouse or form a quick, dense screen—there is the ever-green, fast-growing L. japonica, in one of two forms: Halleana, with biscuit flowers, or Aureo-variegata, with leaves dappled yellow. Far more splendid visually, but lacking scent, are Tellmanniana and Tragophylla, sumptuous plants with opulent clusters of golden trumpets.

All honeysuckles, especially the better sorts, should have their roots in *moist shade*. They excel on trellises, screens, climbing up trees, and on sunless walls.

Many people think that the **Passion Flower** (Passiflora) is tender, but it comfortably rides most English winters in the milder counties if given the shelter of a south wall. Its intricate, exotic blooms, exquisitely chiselled, are so attractive that space should certainly be found for it if possible. Its passport to success is a poor, stony, gravelly soil or a severely restricted root area. Order P. cœrulæa and give it a small-mesh wire grid as host. Early in March cut back secondary growth to within two or three buds of their base.

For an east (or warmer) wall, for a shed, or as a tree climber, a most decorative twiner is the **Celastrus,** a group of vigorous shrubs with brilliant leaves and berries in the autumn and winter, easy to grow in any soil. Use C. articulatus (syn. orbiculatus), whose berries and seed-vessels (too much loved of birds) provide a glowing orange-and-lemon display. Quite hardy, and all too little known, the Celastrus is very vigorous and will climb 30 ft.

Another useful one worthy of wider use is **Solanum crispum,** animated with dainty mauve flowers like those of the potato, and blooming all summer; excellent for an arch or trellis, on which it makes a dense screen, in the milder counties. Not on a wall. The white S. jasminoides is delicate.

A twiner of quite a different order is **Polygonum** baldschuanicum, a very rampant and express-speed climber common in early autumn, with its smother of big feathery bunches of ivory flowers. Very effective and attractive when properly used. Reserve it for utility tasks such as covering up unsightly sheds. Grows anywhere. Cut it back as hard as you wish in spring.

Here we leave the real climbers and meet the **Jasmine** (Jasminum), which has no climbing mechanism and, if for a wall, must be tied up to it. No British garden is complete without the Winter Jasmine, whose golden bells on green stems bring cheer when little else of colour enlivens the dark days. Plant it where you can see it at close quarters from a living-room window, and order J. nudiflorum. It flourishes even on a north wall, and its only failing is in scent. After flowering cut back the flowered shoots to two or three buds.

The summer Jasmine (J. officinale), however, is full of the loveliest perfume and its flowers are white and it wants a S. or W. aspect. Don't prune except for any necessary thinning out after flowering. Jasmine needs training out and tying up carefully for good effect. It is increased with great ease by simply weighting a shoot down to the surface of the ground, when it will take root as a layer. Still greater splendours are J. primulinum and polyanthum, but they are fit for the warm, western counties only.

We come now to those plants which naturally are open-ground shrubs, but which, by being planted close to a wall, can be induced to assume an ascending habit. They provide some of our very finest wall plants. Descriptions of most of them have been given in Chapter XV. First choices for a small place would be:

Ceanothus. Use almost any of the evergreen species or varieties. S. or W. aspect. Up to 20 ft high and 15 ft wide. Autumnal Blue and Delight are strongly tipped.

Flowering Quince (Chænomeles or Cydonia), especially the varieties of Chænomeles speciosa. Any aspect, including partial shade. Outstanding.

Pyracantha. This is a handsome race of berried and thorny shrubs which I have left to this chapter because in small gardens it is employed essentially as a wall plant, in which rôle it is a splendid actor. Entirely hardy, it will flourish even on a bitter north wall. The best species for small walls are P. rogersiana and P. watereri.

Cotoneaster horizontalis. For the sort of job mentioned in Section 6 of Chapter XV on any wall.

Euonymus (Section 2 of Chapter XV). The species fortunei is a fine evergreen for a small space, simulating Ivy. Any aspect. No pruning.

Not quite of the same classification, but most effective against a wall, is the lovely pendulous Forsythia suspensa. N. or any other aspect. Wall, fence, or trellis.

For the first three pruning is important, not only for the usual reasons but also to train them in the way in which they should go, and to make them hug the wall instead of growing outwards as rounded shrubs. Laterals should be led along horizontally in the manner of an espalier or fan-trained fruit tree. Those that flower before midsummer on wood grown the previous summer should have the outward-growing wood cut back to two or three buds of their base after flowering. Pyracantha should have its laterals shortened in this manner in summer, and again in March, to produce 'fruiting spurs', like apples.

Many other shrubs look fine on walls, without materially

254

changing their rounded or bushy habit. On a lime-free soil Camellias are an exquisite adornment, but remember that many are liable to sunstroke on south or east walls. For larger houses Magnolia grandiflora is sumptuous. On really warm, sunny walls you may enjoy several beautiful shrubs on the borderline of hardiness, such as the Coronilla, the various Abutilons, the Myrtles, Abelia Schumanii, and the choice little Hebe hulkeana. Many others more tender still are at the command of those who live in the favoured West.

CHAPTER XVII

HEDGES AND EDGES

WHAT TO PLANT—LIST OF HEDGING PLANTS—RENOVATING
OLD HEDGES

In this chapter we shall consider briefly the various sorts of
plant barriers and screens that may be needed in the small
garden—thick hedges between one part of the garden and
another (such as the masking-off of the vegetable garden or
the enclosure of a rose-garden), together with dwarf screens to
flank a drive or footpath and low edgings for various purposes.

Unless one specifically wants a decorative open type of
screen, as might be provided by certain sorts of roses, the first
essentials of a hedge are that it should be thick, dense, as tall as
you want it, and clothed right down to the ground with foliage.

> As thick as is a castle wall,
> That who that list without to stand or go,
> Though he would all day pryen to and fro,
> He should not see if there were any wight
> Within or no.

Even in Chaucer's day they thought so. A straggly, moth-
eaten hedge with shameless naked legs is an abomination in
men's eyes and a failure in its twin tasks of acting both as a
mask and a barrier. To enable it to do its job properly and to
look comely into the bargain, we must bring it up properly
from its earliest days, for to cure an adult hedge that has gone
wrong is as difficult as to reform an old lag.

The formula for its early training is: sound preparation of
the ground (this above all), proper spacing of the plants and
strict pruning (in most cases) so that the youngsters will throw

out strong side branches immediately above the level of the soil.

Hedge cultivation differs from that of other plantings chiefly in the fact that the plants are set very closely together. It follows that the preparation of the ground must be particularly thorough. This should be done several weeks before planting, which may be carried out at any time between October and March provided the weather is mild and 'open', autumn being the best except on cold, heavy soils; in cold areas leave evergreens until mid-April. The trench should be at least 3 ft wide for a double hedge, 2 ft for a single one. The soil should be broken up a full 2 ft down, it must be well-drained and it must be generously fed with some sort or organic manure—dung, compost, hops, old turves, etc.—and well dressed with bonemeal. This bottom feeding, besides improving the hedge, will encourage its roots to go deep down, and will thus allow other crops to be grown much nearer to the hedge than is otherwise possible.

The proper spacing of hedge-plants is important. A single row is usually quite sufficient, and in any double row the plants are staggered as in sowing peas, thus: ∴ ∴ ∴ ∴ Spacing is influenced by which side you back in the speed v. cost contest. Close spacing (within limits) will generally provide a barrier more quickly but means more plants. When a hedge is planted close to a fence, it should be at least 18 in. away from it.

Plant according to the rules applying to any other tree or shrub. If the situation is a windy one, or if the plants are of large size or very bushy, they must be firmly staked until the roots have taken good hold. If the weather is on the dry side, water thoroughly. Evergreens may be expected to lose some foliage after transplanting without any need for alarm, but if the leaves shrivel and *stay* on the plant something is amiss; in such an event cut the plants back fairly sharply, water them often and give shade if possible.

PRUNING

Bushy growth must be encouraged from the start, but the methods and degree of pruning will depend on the subject. The general rule to remember is that in the first year or two *frequent* pruning is even more important than hard pruning, and that the fast-growing species, such as Privet, Lonicera and Lawson's Cypress, need harder and more frequent cuttings than the slow ones, such as Yew and Holly. Broad-leaved plants, such as Laurel, should never be clipped with the shears; trim them with secateurs.

Hedges of flowering plants require slightly different treatment, and here one should follow what has been said in Chapter XV of flowering shrubs when used in their normal setting—that is to say, according to their habit of flowering.

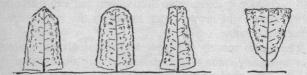

Hedges in cross-section. Three good shapes—and a bad one.

In all cases the ultimate shape of the hedge should be borne in mind from the beginning; and here there is one governing rule—that all tall hedges should be narrower at the top than at the bottom. Moreover, except for strong trees such as Holly and Yew, they should not be cut square at the top, specially in districts liable to heavy snow; the top should instead be either rounded or else in the form of a pointed ridge, the latter being particularly necessary for anything of weak or lax wood. This, of course, need not apply to dwarf hedges or to open screens of roses, etc.

AFTER-CARE

The hedge having been established, the chief need is obviously clipping or pruning according to the nature of the plant. People without a really straight eye haven't a hope of maintaining a hedge that needs close-clipping and should employ an experienced professional. In any case, the beginner should not make his first attempt without using a garden line and a few lathes as guides. The standard time for clipping non-flowering evergreens is about 1st August.

It is too often forgotten that established hedges need food as much as other plants, perhaps more so. Therefore give a generous top-dressing of manure or leaf-mould or a feed of a fertiliser every few years, and a feed of bonemeal as often as you like.

What to Plant

How little imagination is shown in the hedge-planting of our smaller gardens! The list below, short though it is, shows what a wide choice there is. I would make a special plea, particularly as internal hedges, for certain of the flowering and berried shrubs that lend themselves to this treatment. A floral hedge in full bloom is a picture not to be forgotten. Unfortunately few nurseries offer these as hedge-plants at low prices, but one can usually get a special quotation for a quantity.

BOUNDARY HEDGES

In many situations floral hedges can be used with beautiful effect for boundary hedges also, but more often boundaries demand something solid and uncompromising.

Yew and Holly are undoubtedly the best. Properly grown, they make a solid wall many feet high, through which only a mouse can infiltrate. But unless one's purse can stretch to the price of full-grown plants they have the objection in these impatient days of being very slow—about ten years is the time that small Holly and Yew plants take to make a full-grown hedge, and if you can afford to wait it is well worth doing so. The same is true of Box, seldom seen now as a tall hedge.

I think that my very first choice for a hedge, after Yew and Holly, would be one of the evergreen pyracanthas, with a strong leaning towards Rogersiana. It is dense, reasonably fast, and will give us both blossom in spring and berry in autumn. Darwin's Barberry (Berberis Darwinii) and B. stenophylla are also fine. The latter, with its arching cascades of gold, glittering and fragrant, is a model of picturesque and informal grace, but in town or suburban gardens abutting on to a pavement Darwin's species is more suitable. Barberries are slow, however, and these two may ultimately spread 8 ft. wide.

Similar in character to Pyracanthas are the Cotoneasters. They are very suitable for small gardens, taking up little lateral space, and enlivened by their loads of red berries late in the year and often all winter; the Cotoneaster is not, however, fully evergreen. Escallonias, so decorative with their glossy foliage and red, pink or white flowers, are excellent for the seaside in the west and south, resistant to salt and wind.

Another handsome and similar pair are the Beech, either green or copper, and the Hornbeam. The Beech delights in chalky lands or other lime conditions, and on cold, heavy soils the Hornbeam is to be preferred. Their handsome russet-brown leaves, clinging all winter, make them as good as evergreens. Two of the best and cheapest.

Of the conifers, probably the best choices are Leyland's Cypress, Jackman's Green Hedger (a variety of Lawson's Cypress), and Thuja plicata, subject to soil and climate.

It is the fashion among some people to disdain the Privet as 'suburban' or bourgeois, and no doubt it is overdone. The real pity is that it is too often badly grown or wrongly trimmed. But the truth is that for the small garden there is nothing which so well fills the bill for speed, cheapness, ease of handling, evergreenness, and adaptability to nearly all conditions, including partial shade. When really well cultivated, clothed to the ground, and with rounded crown, or ridged like a roof, it is very satisfying. Privet, however, demands to be really well-tailored by frequent clipping, and thus looks best in spruce, rather formalised surroundings. The biggest objection to Privet is that it is a hungry brute, and nothing will grow satisfactorily close to it.

Then there are hedges for special soils and situations—

flowering ones at that. Thus for mild climates there are bountiful Fuchsias; for tough, wind-bitten places the double-flowered Gorse or Broom in flaming colours; and for heathlike or lime-free soils there are tall Ericas.

At the seaside, with its violent, salt-laden winter gales, special selections must be made, but fortunately there are several good candidates.

INTERNAL HEDGES

Here we have an even wider choice, and many purposes to serve. For all these purposes the larger sorts of hedging used for boundary barriers are perfectly suitable if desired, according to the scale of the garden. But there is here a special opportunity for gay floral hedges, and the need may be for a 6-ft hedge or for only a dwarf one.

For high screens, open rather than dense, we have a handsome choice between Forsythia's showers of golden bells in early spring, the crimson or pink ones of the evergreen Escallonias, and the scarlet or pink blossoms of the flowering Quince. Not only for internal hedges, but also as boundaries between small properties, especially between front gardens, provided impenetrable privacy is not insisted upon, these floral hedges are a delight and a fine background for anything grown within. For dwarf hedges there are some charming things to choose from—the dwarf Philadelphus, with their sparkling white blossom and spicy fragrance, all too little known as hedges; the charming Spiraea thunbergii, crowded with white stars in early spring; Lavender; and several Potentillas in yellow or cream. For flanking drives, nothing is better than a hedge of Roses or of Rhododendrons, according to soil and circumstances.

For low edgings there is a wide choice, though I can suggest only a very few. There is a special value in some of the dwarf shrubs, such as the silver-crested, pygmy variety of 'Cotton Lavender' (Santolina incana nana), or the shapely little Thyme called Thymus nitidus. For edgings in difficult shady places, even the dense shade under trees, there is a happy solution in the Rose of Sharon (Hypericum calycinum). Even the humble

Candytufts, in their perennial forms, make thick-set miniature hedges, close-clipped like privet after flowering: 1 ft high in Snowflake, 6 in. in Little Gem.

List of Hedging Plants

The figures given at the end of each note are—first, the height which may be expected in about five years under conditions of normally good cultivation; and secondly, the recommended spacing in inches for a reasonably close hedge.

Abbreviations: F = Floral hedge. B = Berried hedge. E = Evergreen. AF = After flowering, cut back the spent shoot nearly to its point of origin, unless otherwise expressed. Note the difference between 'pruning' and 'clipping' or 'trimming'. For descriptions of the flowering sorts, *see* Chapter XV.

Barberry (F & B). Choose Stenophylla or Darwinii for a tall hedge, Verruculosa for a 4 ft. Prune AF, but responds to close clipping if overgrown. E. 5–3 ft, according to variety; 22 in.

Beech. Shear side-shoots hardish in early August (some gardeners prefer February), but leave the leading shoots until the desired height is reached. 4 ft 6 in.; 21 in.

Box. Slow, dense, succeeds in part shade and in chalk. Clip May and August. E. 3 ft; 18 in. For dwarf box, 1ft.

Cotoneaster (F & B). Choose Simonsii, Lacteus (evergreen, strong) or Franchetii. Treat as Pyracantha. 5 ft; 18 in., 24 in., and 18 in respectively.

Cypress. For quick work use Leyland's Cypress or Green Hedger (from Jackman). Can be clipped with shears, at midsummer. 7 ft; 30 in. Avoid Macrocarpa except as a temporary job.

Erica (F). Appropriate where heathers flourish. Use E. arborea alpina, 5 ft; 18 in. Or E. mediterranea, 4 ft; 15 in.; trim lightly AF. Others are good, too, and the small ones are grand for edgings. *See* Chapter XVIII.

Escallonia (F). Choose the tough Macrantha or Crimson Spire for the seaside. Trim AF. E. 4 ft 6 in.; 18 in.

Forsythia (F). Prune hard AF. 5 ft; 2 ft. Use spectabilis for a tall hedge, ovata for a low one.

Fuchsia. Magellanica Riccartonii (F). For W. and S.-W. counties. Fine by the sea. Trim end of February. 4 ft; 2 ft.

Gorse (F). Glorious in any exposed place, but not appropriate for towns. Must be pot-grown. Get the double variety Ulex europæus flore pleno. E. 4 ft 6 in.; 24 in.

Holly. Clip May and end of August. E. 3 ft; 18 in.

Holm Oak or Evergreen Oak. Must be pot-grown. Clip August. E. 4 ft; 18 in. A toughie for the seashore.

Hornbeam. Clip as for Beech. 4 ft 6 in.; 21 in.

Laurel. A loosely used term covering several species. For small gardens the Portuguese Laurel (Prunus lusitanica) makes an excellent, dense small-leaved hedge. E. 5 ft; 3 ft. The large-leaved P. laurocerasus and the Aucuba should be pruned with secateurs about 1st August.

Lavender (F). The dwarf ones, for 18-in. hedges, are the best. Prune hard AF. E. Space 1 ft.

Lonicera. The shrubby honeysuckle. The best one now is L. nitida fertilis. Neat and compact when properly treated, otherwise ragged. Clip very closely June and August. 5 ft; 15 in.

Myrobalan (F). The ordinary 'cherry plum' (Prunus cerasifera), one of the cheapest, planted in single or double rows at 24 in., can make an excellent hedge if really well treated; its purple-leaved variety Pissardii is very fine indeed, but expensive. 4 ft 6 in. Clip June.

Privet. Green privet is better than the golden and very much cheaper. E. 3 ft 6 in.; 15 in.

Prunus cistena (F). A lively dwarf with crimson foliage. Clip AF; keep it down to 2½ ft. Useless in sandy soil.

Pyracantha (F & B). Use Rogersiana, Angustifolia, or Atalantioides. Resistant to fierce winds and frost. Flourish in a N. aspect or in shade. May be close-clipped in spring, or lightly pruned to display flower and berry. 4 ft 6 in.; 18 in.

Quickthorn. Dense, fast, cheap. More suitable for country districts; clips well if properly looked after. Cut to

6 in. of the ground first year. 5 ft; 18 in. Is Crataegus monogyna.

Rose (F). The choice is wide, according to purpose: the Scotch Brier (R. spinosissima) and its hybrids; the hybrid musks (first class); the floribunda roses, such as Frensham, Iceberg, Dainty Maid, and Queen Elizabeth, for hedges flanking a drive or path. *See* Chapter XIV.

Sea Buckthorn (Hippophae). Tough wind-filter for the actual seashore. 10 ft; 4 ft. Prune hard.

Spiræa (F). S. thunbergii makes a charming floral hedge. 4 ft; 18 in. Prune AF.

Tamarisk (F). Another toughie for the sea. Pretty, too. Feathery pink plumes in May. Hardiest are T. anglica and T. gallica. Cut back by two-thirds AF. 10 ft; 4 ft.

Thuja. A conifer; decorative and good in warmer counties, but needs good soil. Use T. plicata (or Lobii). Trim sides May and August but leave leading shoot till desired height is reached. E. 5 ft; 36 in. Not for dry or limy soils.

Veronica Traversii (F). For seaside and milder places. Grow informally with secateur pruning AF to display bloom. 4 ft; 20 in. The dainty cupressoides is also good, and something quite unusual.

Yew. Finest of all. Trim May and August. E. 3 ft; 21 in. Leave leading shoots till desired height is reached.

Renovating Old Hedges

The renovation of shabby old hedges that have become bare-legged, straggly and of moth-eaten appearance often, but not always, demands the ruthless use of knife and saw.

The following will serve as a general guide for the surgical operations which should be carried out on deciduous types during late dormancy—say late February, when the sap is about to stir. On evergreens March is usually considered the best time.

Cut down very hard, to about 3 ft 6 in. of the ground in bad cases: Beech, Hornbeam, Privet, Yew, Holly, Lonicera.

Cut laterals and sub-laterals hard with secateurs after

flowering: Quinces, Cotoneaster, Prunus varieties. Treat late-blooming floral sorts the same way late February.

Cut Fuchsia down to 1 ft of the ground.

Thuja and Cypresses—a judicious and firm removal of top and side growth with secateurs, bearing in mind that new growth does not break from old wood. With Cupressus macrocarpa there is nothing to do for a bad old hedge but to scrap it and plant another—preferably something else.

Lavender, Broom, and Rosemary will not sprout from old wood, and there is no cure but to replace with new plants.

After the amputations, hoe in some bonemeal, mulch thoroughly with an organic manure and replace old trees that are too far gone.

CHAPTER XVIII

SOME SPECIALITIES

CARNATIONS AND PINKS—CLEMATIS—CHRYSANTHEMUMS—
IRISES—THE HEATHER FAMILY

IN this chapter I deal specially with a few favourites which for one reason or another are not conveniently dealt with elsewhere. Note that all, except the Heathers, are more or less lime-lovers.

Carnations and Pinks

The great and lovely Dianthus family includes Carnations, Pinks, Sweet William and many plants that have no fancy or popular names, but are simply Dianthus so-and-so. The last-named include many ravishing rock-garden Pinks. The branches of this ancient family with its poetic memories of 'Coronations', 'Sops-in-wine', and 'Gilly-flowers', cross-breed readily, and there are many hybrids. There are also annual Carnations and Pinks, while Sweet William and the jaunty Indian and Japanese Pinks, so called, are biennials. In this chapter I shall deal with the perennial Carnations and Pinks that can be grown outdoors in the mixed border or in a border by themselves.

A characteristic of the Dianthus family generally is that they appreciate lime. Of the several forms available, limestone rock is the best, being natural to them, and the late Montague All-wood said that the best treatment is to use the limestone as a dust on light soils and as chippings on other soils, applied as a top-dressing. A mild acidity, however, is no bar.

Other things that this family likes are good drainage, the

266

full beam of the sun, bonemeal, potash and plenty of grit. They hate: wet and undrained sites, acid peats, leaf-mould, very stiff clay, and fresh animal manures. Also, better not give them the usual chemical fertilisers.

BORDER CARNATIONS

By this term is meant hardy Carnations that can be grown outdoors instead of in a heated greenhouse. Be careful about this when ordering plants, for I have known the mistake to be made. The term does *not*, however, mean that the outdoor Carnation should be grown in the *herbaceous* border. Only pressure of space justifies one growing them in a mixed border, for undoubtedly they look best in a bed of their own and made to their own requirements. These requirements can be set out quite simply.

As they demand good drainage, give them if possible a slightly raised bed in full sun. Incorporate into the soil, when digging, plenty of old turfy loam and plenty of fresh wood ashes and burnt earth from the bonfire. Add a little bonemeal. Top-dress with limestone chippings or dust—in default, crushed chalk, old mortar rubble, or ordinary hydrated lime.

Set the young plants out at least 12 in. apart. Plant very firmly indeed, and plant shallow, not burying the ball of soil in which they are rooted nor drawing any soil up to the stem. These two injunctions are absolutely cardinal.

As they come on, some thinning of the buds is necessary, even if not growing for exhibition. Pinch out the small buds clustering just below the main terminal bud on each shoot. Of buds arising from lower down the stem, a few may be retained at your pleasure according to the strength of the plant. 'Stopping', or pinching out the main stem, should not be done with border varieties. During the growing season feeds of soot-water are good. Some neat staking is essential.

Propagation is by 'layering'—a fairly simple process. It is done from mid-July to early August, using non-flowering shoots. With a very sharp knife or razor-blade make a slit longitudinally up the middle of the stem from the underside, starting just below a node and passing through and beyond the

267

node—a cut of half an inch or so in all. Having reduced the soil to a fine tilth, remove all leaves from that portion of the stem which will be underground, and lay the stem down in the soil with the wound gaping and the tongue of the cut projecting downwards. Press in very gently, cover with half an inch of soil, and keep in position with a hooked peg, a special layering pin, or a stone. *See* sketch. Some sand at the point of layering helps. Water. Layers should root in seven to ten days if kept moist, and will be ready for severance from the parent plant in six weeks, but if the weather has been hot and dry, leave them longer; there is no hurry.

Layering a Carnation.

After severance from the parent, the layering may be left in the bed where it is if there is room, or it may be lifted and transplanted; October is best, but spring will do.

Varieties of border Carnation are numberless, new ones constantly replacing the old, so there is no point in making suggestions. Leave the choice to a good nurseryman, stating the colour you like, but insist that all should have these qualities—a stiff, erect stem, a strong calyx that will not be burst by heavy blossom, and a long flowering period. Personally, I also insist on scent, except for the yellow varieties.

Good named varieties of Carnation are expensive, but it is not difficult to grow from seed if you will be satisfied with a mixed bag. You can then increase the ones you like best by layering. Sow in a John Innes Compost in March or April, and prick out early into prepared beds having plenty of sharp sand and limestone or fine mortar rubble. They should be

268

bushy plants by September or October, ready for permanent quarters.

Cottage Carnations may be described as small border Carnations. Hardy, early, gay, and floriferous; no disbudding. **Picotees** are Carnations with a piping of colour round the edge of the petal.

PINKS

These smaller members of the Dianthus family are of great diversity, from tiny five-petalled alpines to lusty hybrids very like small Carnations. Nearly all are of great charm, and all but a few are of easy culture, a characteristic being an exceptionally long season of bloom if spent flowers are removed. They have not the formality of Carnations, and can be freely used almost anywhere in the garden, given a sunny position, including the herbaceous or mixed border, while many of the smaller breeds are enchanting in the rock garden or the dry wall (*see* Chapter XII).

Of the many wild species, the most important to us are the Cheddar Pink (D. cæsius) and the Maiden Pink (D. deltoides), dealt with in the rock-gardening chapter, but for general uses we rely more on the wonderful range of hybrids, of which I give a small selection. I hope the reign of Mrs Sinkins will soon be over. Though she has delighted several generations, she is a slovenly creature who always bursts her calyx, and there are many better ones.

Quite outstanding for general garden use are the Allwoodii and the Lancing Pinks. They have a truly astonishing range of both colourings and forms, may bloom the whole summer through, and need no attention beyond dead-heading. I like them best in a mixed bag and in large sweeps. Unfortunately they are expensive, but they are easily raised from seed or obtained as seedling plants. Usually need light staking. About 10 in. high. Doris is a famous one.

Here are brief descriptions of a few other first choices for general use:

Inchmery. Tender pink. Every virtue. For any and every use. Propagate by either layers or cuttings.

Little Jock and his hybrids. 4 in. high. Pink with dark eye. Grand for any use.

Mars. 5 in., crimson, perfect temperament. For rockery and edgings. Layers or cuttings.

Whiteladies. 12 in. Like a pure white carnation. Far superior to Mrs Sinkins.

La Bourbrille. A neat, vigorous, good-tempered pink dwarf. For rockery, dry wall, or pavement.

Dad's Favourite. 1 ft. Double white with chocolate markings.

Sweet Wivelsfield. 12 in. *See* Chapter X.

The pretty annual pinks (Baby Doll, Bravo, etc.) are easily raised from seed, the 'Japanese' D. Heddewigii being treated as a half-hardy.

PROPAGATION

Pinks are generally increased by cuttings, but, as seen above, many can be layered. Cuttings must be from non-flowering shoots. In autumn take them with a 'heel' (Chapter VI), or in spring cut with a razor-blade immediately below a node. Trim off the lower leaves in the usual way, baring two or three nodes.

Propagation by seed is easy for all these popular pinks. Use a compost of equal parts fibrous loam, leaf-mould, sharp sand, or other gritty stuff, such as crushed flower-pots, with an extra helping of the last in the top $\frac{1}{4}$ in.

Clematis

If Wisteria is the king of climbers, Clematis is certainly the queen. Yet she has no petals, for her beauty resides in the brilliance of her sepals and in the boss of stamens that they enfold. Wonderful in her range of colour, highly flowerful, modest in stature, adaptable to many uses, Clematis is an ideal plant for the small garden, as for the large. But she does demand a little special treatment, neglect of which makes her appear a mere chorus-girl instead of the star she is. Clematis in her due season should be clothed with blossom almost from

270

foot to crown, but too often she is a long, naked, spindle-shanked creature brandishing a tangled mop.

In nature the Clematis grows in semi-woodland in lime-bearing soils, often above chalk, scrambling over bushes and up into the branches of small trees. The bushes provide shade at ground level and an annual mulch of leaves over the roots. Let us apply these factors to her cultivated state.

SOIL

A rich soil of light, loamy texture is to be aimed at. Dig two spits down and a good yard square for each plant. Work in organic matter—compost, leaf-mould, old manure, or turves—together with bonemeal. On heavy clays add ample sand and old mortar rubble. Chalky or limy soils are not essential, but I would always add chalk or mortar rubble if the soil is very acid.

PLANTING

October is best, but, the young plants being in pots, any time from September to May will do if weather and soil are right. Make a wide hole in the prepared site deep enough to plant the root crown 2 in. *below* the surface. Knock the plant out of the pot, squeeze the ball of soil gently to loosen the roots, spread the roots out well, work in some leaf-mould and fine sifted soil and make firm.

The young stems are extremely fragile and brittle. Handle carefully and do not remove the cane to which they are tied. After planting protect the stems securely with a cage of twiggy sticks against damage by the hoe, the cat, and other enemies. Encircle the stem also with sharp cinders against the slug. The causes of failure in first-year Clematis are the slug, fractured stems and a fungoid 'wilt', which may be inhibited by the sprays used against black spot on roses.

THE SITE

All Clematis insist that their roots shall be shaded and cool, but their flowers in sunshine, or at least in full light, un-obstructed from overhead. This is an order. The shade of a small bush—i.e. one on the south side of the Clematis—is the usual thing. But other forms of shade will do, such as a wall or fence; indeed, certain Clematis—to wit, the Jackman, viticella and montana types—will thrive nearly as well on a completely sunless north wall as elsewhere, provided it is not overhung by trees.

The Host

Besides the bush-host—something of the size of a large Holly or Laurustinus, etc.—impressive effects come from giving the Clematis the run of another climbing plant, such as an outdoor vine trained over an arch, or a wall plant, such as the Pyracantha, Cotoneaster, Ceanothus, Forsythia, Wistaria, etc. But remember always to give shade for the feet of the Clematis if the host itself does not provide it.

Whatever host-tree is chosen, think carefully what pruning problems—either of the host or of the Clematis itself—are likely to arise. If the Clematis is of a breed that can be cut down to 3 ft each year, then the rose makes a marvellous host. A pergola of climbing roses and Clematis is quite sensational. So also is a hedge of roses with Clematis wandering over it in its native manner.

Artificial hosts are more difficult. It is a great nuisance trying to train a Clematis over an arch or porch or something of the sort. Constant tying has to be done, and the thing looks miserable when bunched together tied to a nail. On a wall or fence a wide and high grid may be made, either of wire netting or of the plastic-covered chain-link.

Pruning and After-care

Thousands of Clematis are ruined by wrong pruning or no pruning. The methods vary according to the type of Clematis, so the detail is left till the next section, but for non-specialist purposes the thing is quite simple, provided you keep your plants really well labelled. Meanwhile the following few pruning rules apply to all Clematis:

Cut all *new* plants right down to within 9 in. of the ground —and no shirking.

Cut just above a node or joint, where twin buds appear.
Cut out all dead, damaged and weakly shoots.

In May of each year pinch out the tips of all new shoots to encourage branching.

Apart from pruning, the important things are to water liberally and to feed generously with mulches of manure, leaves, tea-leaves, or with a proprietary fertiliser. When using artificial hosts, some training-out of the new shoots is necessary as they grow, to prevent their becoming a tangled mass.

VARIETIES

Clematis are classified into a number of 'groups'. For our purposes the significant differences are in their seasons of flowering and accordingly in the methods of pruning. But we need not make heavy weather of it, and I shall simplify to the uttermost. If you are sufficiently interested you can get the finest results by studying the needs of each type and variety in a larger work.

In my book *Climbing Plants for Walls and Gardens* I have gone into this and other matters in some detail, but the practical gardener not interested in the finer points will do well to disregard at first the old classifications—viticella, lanuginosa, etc. The simplest of all plans is to stick to the later-flowering species and varieties, which you prune simply by cutting them down thigh-high *every February*. These include many splendours—Jackmanii Superba, Hagley Hybrid, Perle d'Azur, Gipsy Queen, Comtesse de Bouchard, Ernest Markham (optionally), and the delightful yellow species Tangutica (the Chinese lantern clematis) and Orientalis (the lemon-peel clematis).

By sticking to these varieties, you avoid all pruning headaches, but you miss some others that are not only very beautiful but which also elegantly adorn the garden from May to September. The first of these are the spring-flowering species and their varieties. They include: Montana and its pink varieties Elizabeth and Rubens, which will grow 30 ft or more, Chrysocoma, reaching 20 ft, Macropetala (the delightful ballet-skirt clematis), Alpina in its several varieties, and the half-tender evergreen Armandii (for warm places only).

These flower on shoots that have developed during the previous summer, and so you prune *immediately after flowering* (say end of May). This also is easy enough if you have taken the trouble initially to train out the shoots to form a basic framework. All you do then is to shear back all the flowered shoots crisply near to the main framework. Armandii is best left alone, and Macropetala will come to little harm if you merely cut off the seed heads.

A third group consists of the midsummer hybrids, which often flower again in early autumn. These can become tangled up in the most awful 'bird's nests', especially if you follow some people's advice to 'leave them alone'. Again, if you start by fanning them well out, you may follow the rule of 'light pruning', cutting back each shoot to some pair of strong buds. This you do *in February*. This group includes such great favourites as Lasurstern, Nelly Moser, Ville de Lyon, William Kennett, and Marie Boisselot.

Propagation. Cut down a strong shoot, shorten it to about 5 ft and make layerings, just as with Carnations. Two or three serpentine layers may be made from one shoot, but the best comes from a node near the tip.

Chrysanthemums

Apart from the annual sorts, dealt with in Chapter X, there are a good many breeds, and hybrids, of Chrysanthemum. Several can be grown outdoors, but those that bloom late in the year must be protected from hard frosts. What is important for the beginner is not to order greenhouse sorts if he intends them for the border. I shall deal with outdoor sorts first.

OUTDOOR TYPES

The herbaceous or mixed border is the right and happy place for them. The position should be in full sun. They like a bit of lime in the soil, which should be well drained and well dug. Dig in old turves, old manure and some bonemeal and mortar rubble if you want good results. Avoid fresh manure. The following are the types that are commonly grown outdoors.

'Early Flowering' Chrysanthemum. This term means the popular large-bloomed sort, double or single, growing 4 ft high or more, differing from greenhouse types only in their season of blooming, which is August and September.

If the plants are received from the nursery before planting time, move them into 4-in. pots in a John Innes potting mixture, or else plant them 5 in. apart in boxes a good 4 in. deep. Water well at first, then sparingly till the weather warms up. Keep them at first under some form of glass in full light, then harden off before planting in early May, a good 18 in. apart. Plant very firmly.

Chrysanths are surface-rooting, so give them plenty of water in dry spells, and give them also occasional feeds of a liquid manure. Particular attention must be given to the processes of stopping and disbudding. Very few varieties other than the singles are satisfactory if allowed to grow at will—they merely become lanky and top-heavy, with a mass of insignificant blooms. A compact and bushy shape is to be aimed at, with some decent-sized blooms, even if not of exhibition size. A simplified method is given later in the paragraph on stopping and disbudding.

In November, after the stems have been cut down to within a few inches of the ground, orthodox treatment is to lift the plants, and replant them, closely packed in soil, under a frame or in the greenhouse for the winter; in mild places, however, they survive perfectly well outside until the time comes for taking cuttings for next season. The practice of allowing them to grow into large clumps does not give best results; they deteriorate. See the later paragraph on propagation.

As in so many other fanciers' flowers, a choice of varieties today is liable to be out of date in a year or two. The British Chrysanthemum Society or a good specialist nursery will help you, but enquire about size, habit, 'stopping', etc.

Chrysanthemum maximum. This is the Shasta Daisy, King Edward Daisy, etc. Large, bold white 'daisies' from

July onwards. Hard as nails, treat it as an herbaceous perennial, lifting only to divide every few years. Plant in autumn or spring. No stopping or disbudding. Probably the best varieties are Everest, large, bold and pure, and Ben Lomond, with double, fringed flowers.

C. rubellum. Delightful, fragrant, single, daisy-form blooms in great profusion, about 2 ft high. Unhackneyed, and much more attractive than the Koreans or Windsors. No stopping or disbudding. Early September onwards. Sometimes shy the first year. Clara Curtis is a radiant soft pink, and Jessie Cooper a bold brick-red; they go well together. Very strongly recommended.

Koreans. Hardy, stocky, easy and trouble-free. Prodigal of bloom but colours not good, to my mind. Pinch out when 2 or 3 in. high. No staking or disbudding. Leave undisturbed except in severe districts. There are also several dwarfs, very flowerful little chaps for the edge of the border. The outstanding varieties are Denise and Janté Wells, with their profusion of little golden rosettes, so much prized not only for edgings but also for autumn window-boxes in towns.

INDOOR TYPES

In favoured districts October chrysanths can be grown outdoors, but normally anything that flowers from then onwards needs to be grown in a greenhouse. Commonly classified as 'mid-season' and 'lates', they include many decorative forms—incurved, reflexed, single and the striking Japanese mopheaded creations. For ordinary amateur purposes no heat is necessary unless and until frost or autumn fog actually penetrates inside the greenhouse.

The following is the course of treatment:

On receipt from the nursery, plant in 3-in. or 4-in. pots, using the John Innes potting mixture and planting very firmly with a rammer. As the roots fill the pots, move on into larger pots, coarsening the compost by adding more loam, preferably in the form of old turfy stuff or 'top spit'. Their final homes are 9-in. pots, using the John Innes No. 3 Potting Compost or some equivalent. Keep the plants in full light and ventilate the greenhouse very freely. Water in moderation till the weather warms up.

Towards the end of May, the plants being then in their final pots, stand them outdoors, on ashes, stone or planks to prevent the entry of worms. Give them an open position in full sun, but protected from high winds. Keep the soil moist (the leaves will throw off much rain) and the foliage syringed in dry spells. As the roots begin to fill the pots, give weekly drinks of a special chrysanth fertiliser (e.g. Bentley's) or a good general one, using weak doses at first.

In the last week of September bring the plants back into the greenhouse again, giving plenty of light and plenty of room between plants. Dust early with green sulphur against mildew, and fumigate the house against aphis. Ventilate very freely. Fix muslin below the top ventilators to minimise the entry of fog and damp. Close the lights at night when frost begins to threaten. Water the plants only when the soil seems to be drying up. Gradually raise the temperature to 50°, but don't attempt to force.

After the plants have finished blooming cut them to within a few inches of the soil. Do not interfere with the young growth springing up from the base, which will be wanted for cuttings.

STOPPING AND DISBUDDING

The secret of growing successful chrysanths, as distinct from shaggy and untidy growths of small blooms, lies in stopping or pinching and disbudding, which are separate processes. Stopping or pinching means nipping out the main stems in

Chrysanthemums: A prepared cutting—Stopping—Disbudding.

their early upward growth, and disbudding means the removal of excess flower-buds.

Apart from a specialised thing like the cascade chrysanth, these processes are applied only to the large-flowered *double* sorts, i.e. the sorts grown in the greenhouse and the 'Early Flowering' varieties grown outside in the border. If you want to grow fine blooms consult James Smith's book in this series (*Chrysanthemums for Small Gardens*), but otherwise the following simple rule will serve well.

'Stop' the young shoots when about 5 in. high (earlyish in April).

On indoor varieties, in mid-June, stop also the branches that result from the first pinching.

As flower-buds develop, remove all those clustering round the major bud at the tip of each main stem, and remove also the buds appearing in the leaf-axils.

These processes will produce one good-sized bloom at the top of each stem. You can modify the process as you like— e.g. quite decorative cluster effects result from removing the lower axillary buds only. Don't disturb or stop the *single* varieties, but thin out any weak shoots.

PROPAGATION

Ordinary division, or splitting up of old clumps, will suit for the Shasta Daisy, C. rubellum, the Koreans, and dwarfs. The large-flowered sorts, outdoor and in, should be cultivated yearly from fresh cuttings for best results.

When flowering is over, cut the stems down to within a few inches of the soil, to encourage new basal growth. In un-heated houses take cuttings in March. Shoots growing out of the old stems are of less value than the basal shoots springing from below ground. Cut these basal shoots just below soil level, trim them back with a sharp knife to a point immediately below a node or joint, remove the lower leaves, dip the cuttings in a nicotine insecticide, and insert them $\frac{3}{4}$ in. deep in boxes (better than pots) in a sandy compost. A close, damp atmo-sphere is not necessary provided they are watered fairly freely. When the cuttings have rooted, move them singly into small pots in a potting compost.

In selecting shoots for cutting, avoid both the lanky ones and the plump sappy ones; take firm, short-jointed specimens about 3 in. high.

Outdoor varieties may be propagated by taking shoots from the old 'stools' with roots attached in March, and potting them up.

Irises

This ancient and lordly race holds such sway in the hearts of gardeners that it has its own Society and its specialist nurseries. Irises of some sort bloom throughout the year, some with their feet bathed in water, others exulting in hot, dry soils. Almost all are beautiful, but many are too difficult for us unless we have just the right conditions and a good deal of expertise.

For our purposes we can divide the garden Irises simply into four sorts—the slender bulbous Irises, the splendid sun-loving Bearded Flags of martial carriage, the beardless Waterside Flags, and the little Irises of winter. Nobody really knows why Flags are so called, but I like to think that it is because the Fleur-de-Lys, which is the yellow waterside Iris, was the flag of old France.

Bearded Flags. These are the stately creations, often 4 ft high, which grow in every garden and which originate in that great race of so-called German Irises, since one of the ancestors in its mixed breeding was I. germanica. Their 'beards' are the hair-like growths on the drooping falls of the blossom. They are essentially lovers of the sun. Their special characteristic is that their rigid leaves rise from a thick, fleshy rhizome which is often mistaken by the apprentice for a bulb or root, but which is in fact a stem. Since it is a stem, it should not be buried, but should be planted flat (and firmly) on the surface and only barely covered with soil, its roots lying astride a little saddle or mound of soil roughly formed below ground with fingers or trowel. Deep or loose planting of this rhizome is the cause of many failures. The rhizome should face south.

Flags are undoubtedly best grown in a border of their own, where, with their sword-like leaves, they suggest a squadron of bannered cavalry. What to do with the bed when flowering is over is sometimes a problem, for they are soon over, and nothing must be allowed to hinder the rhizomes from getting the sun-baking that they need. Thus they are very much separatists.

The bearded Flags will grow well in any good soil, but they prefer it on the light side and are great lime-lovers. If lime is not already sufficiently present, add mortar rubble or broken chalk, though not all the pundits agree on this. If the soil is very light, thicken it up with well-rotted compost or leaves; if very heavy, lighten it with coarse sand and mortar rubble.

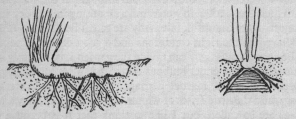

Planting Flag Irises. On the right, end-on view showing roots astride a saddle.

On all soils add bonemeal before planting, and again every February. In no case give animal manure. A slightly raised bed suits them particularly well.

The best time to plant is early in July, but autumn or early spring will do. After planting cut the leaves down to 9 in.; cut them down also on established plants at the end of August, not quite so hard. Remove seed-pods after flowering. Established beds should be broken up and divided every three years or so. Cut up the rhizomes into pieces about 2 in. long with ample root attached, and discard old and decaying portions. Do this in July.

For the usual reason I avoid giving varieties, though I should never forsake dear Jane Phillips in her pale blue gown, quite a veteran now.

280

There are also some endearing little dwarf bearded irises. Two of the best are I. pumila, a plump little cherub squatting almost on the ground, and I. chamæiris, a little taller. Each has varieties in divers colours.

The new race of 'intermediates' may well be the answer to the gardener's prayer. Hybrids between the giants and the dwarfs, they flower freely from April to June.

Waterside Flags. Apart from the heraldic Flower-de-luce, we need notice only three of this group, differing mainly in the degree of their appetites for water. The first is the stunning I. kæmpferi, a goddess too exacting for most of us, for she likes her toes in acid soil that is wet in summer but dry in winter. The second is I. lævigata, a beautiful water iris in many colour forms, which grows with its rhizome just submerged, but is content with any very moist soil. Third is the common Siberian iris, I. sibirica, which prospers in any soil that does not dry out. It has many varieties in shades of blue but too small flowers for too much foliage.

The Gladdon (I. fœtidissima) is valued by arrangers for its sealing-wax seed. Moist soil in shade.

Bulbous Irises. The best known are those which are popularly called Dutch, Spanish and English irises. Inexpensive, of easy culture and good for cutting, they have slender stems and petals that are more strap-like and less solid than the Flags. They are in bloom from early June to mid-July, following each other. Plant in September, 3 in. deep, in any good soil. Leave them in the ground until overcrowded, then, after the foliage has died, lift, dry, divide and replant.

The English are the largest, with colours mostly in blue shades; they prefer to be near water. The sweet-scented Spanish I think the daintiest and most artistic, lovely varieties being Hercules, Mouche d'Or and King of the Blues. Of the Dutch, I think Wedgewood the most attractive. It is lovely, too, in pots or bowls.

Winter Irises. The little Irises that 'warm the cold bosom of the hoary year' have a brave Cinderella charm. The largest, but still of only 1-ft stature, is an Algerian of exquisite beauty in blue and gold, always known as I. stylosa until the learned ones re-christened it unguicularis. It blooms in succession all winter and should be picked for the house just as the buds show colour, when it will gladden the room for many a day. It has a rhizome and is best planted at the end of September. Flourishing only in austere living, it needs a light, dry, sun-parched, poor, stony, limy soil with a course of broken bricks or gravel 8 in. below for sharp drainage. If necessary, make a bed of this nature, built up. Take special and intensive measures against slugs, for whose piracy it is a favourite prey. Cut down the foliage early in June so that the sun can ripen it—heaps of sun and stones are its needs.

Then there are two lovely little bulbous ones. Best known is the violet-scented reticulata—the small

> Blue-netted iris, like a cry
> Startling the sloth of February

in Miss Sackville-West's words. I like it best in Cambridge blue. But more beautiful is the less well-known histrioides major, a glowing ultramarine, a 3-in. darling that enchants the beholder for six weeks in January and February. Easy in good soil in full sun and excellent in bowls. Avoid the disappointing yellow Danfordiæ.

The Heather Family

The flowers of the heath—Heather, Ling and their associates—make delightful and trouble-free gardens. Indeed, they are perhaps the least troublesome of all plants, for, once well established, they carpet the ground and make life a poor lookout for weeds. They are perennial, mostly hardy, evergreen, bloom for astonishingly long periods, and need no attention beyond a light clipping once a year to induce new growth and an occasional top-dressing of peat or leaf-mould. There are varieties for every month in the year, those that bloom in winter being especially welcome. With only a few exceptions, all are of low growth. Many make splendid hedges or edgings.

The majority of the 'hardy heaths', as the catalogues call them, will not, however, tolerate a soil impregnated with lime.

Be watchful about this. On the other hand, the few that succeed regardless of the lime content are among the best of their family; none, however, will succeed with *chalk* too near the surface.

Heath plants need a sunny, open situation. A peaty soil is no doubt best, but any light soil which is not too rich but which has peat or leaf-mould in the top spit gives good results, provided the lime factor is borne in mind. Plant from October to March, according to flowering season. Work some peat into each root pocket, plant deeply, and press down very firmly. Stake the taller 'tree' heaths.

The easiest method of propagation is by rooted layers of the lower branches that result from deep planting; but cuttings are easy enough.

Although nearly all the flowers of the heath prosper in rather light soils, some do well in other conditions also. On this occasion, therefore, soil conditions being important, I am classifying them in a manner to show which breeds are the most suitable for different types of soil. Only the most reliable are included.

For clay soils, with or without lime (but no chalk).

The Mountain Heath, Erica carnea. A splendid 10-in. dwarf and perhaps the best of all for general use, flowering from Christmas to Easter. The gems are Vivelli, King George, Queen Mary, Springwood Pink, and Springwood White.

The hybrid E. darleyensis, especially its fine dwarf form George Rendall, a deep pink, 12 in. high, in bloom all winter.

The pink E. mediterranea, spring-flowering, 4 ft high, and excellent for a hedge. Its dwarfer and more sparkling offspring Brightness, 2 ft, is delightful.

E. stricta (or terminalis), 6 ft high, pink, June.

For a medium loam, lime-free.

The Cornish Heath, E. vagans, flowers from July to September, and is a 12-in. species, with excellent varieties in Lyonnesse, Mrs D. F. Maxwell and St Keverne. Not for the colder counties.

The 'Tree' Heath, E. arborea, from the roots of which 'briar', or bruyère, pipes are made, must be pot-grown. The best variety is alpina, of a modest 7-ft stature. Stake it in windy places, and tie it round with cord against snow. Makes a splendid hedge.

The Irish or St Daboec's Heath (Daboecia cantabrica); a bushy 2-ft plant with mauve bloom from June to September. Succeeds in partial shade. If hurt by frost, cut it to the ground.

For a light loam, lime-free.

First choice is the 'Scotch Heather', which in England is Ling—Calluna vulgaris. H. E. Beale, Peter Sparkes and the dwarfer J. H. Hamilton are three of the best. July onwards.

The hybrid Dawn, deep pink, dwarf, good.

For hot, sandy soils, lime-free.

The June Bell Heather, E. cinerea, flowering from June to August. The outstanding varieties are coccinea, C. D. Eason, and the unusual lilacina; all about 10 in. Not easy.

For damp situations, lime-free.

The Dorset Heath, Erica ciliaris. Very hardy, flowering from July to October. One of the best is the pink Mrs C. H. Gill, 15 in.

Pygmies.

Two nice little toys for the rock garden are Calluna vulgaris Foxii nana and Humpty Dumpty. They make dense green hummocks, with little flower. Sister Anne is semi-prostrate and makes a thick mat, with lilac flowers.

Although I may, perhaps, have made all these heathers sound rather easy, it has to be admitted that not all of them really settle down happily in average small garden conditions, as compared with the freer spaces. The easiest, given the right soil conditions, are the Ericas carnea, mediterranea, darleyensis, vagans, arborea; unhappiest of the lot is cinerea.

Among the Callunas are many with most beautiful golden or

copper foliage, delightful all the year. They include Sunset, Golden Feather, Gold Haze, and Robert Chapman. Among similar ericas, E. carnea aurea is one of my great favourites. They must have all-day, unobstructed sun.

A few plants associate well with heathers, especially dwarf conifers, the Pernettya, the Rhododendron and the dwarf Barberries. In limy soils the heathers go awfully well with the smaller Brooms (Cytisus and Genista), which provide the yellow touch that most heathers lack.

CHAPTER XIX

THE LAWN

FOR generations it has been an accepted fact that the lawn is the foundation and the special characteristic of the British garden. Nowhere else will you find our shaven swards of molten–emerald, smooth and *soigné*, tight and springy as a pile carpet. It is the perfect setting and foil for the enamelled colours of border, bed and shrub-garden. Indeed, some two-thirds of the whole garden should be grass, you will hear it said.

But in our hurried life of today there are difficulties. Per square yard of ground, the lawn, if it is to be only reasonably good and reasonably well-groomed, occupies more man-hours than any other part of the garden. Our fathers, and many enthusiasts still today, would go over every square yard, marked out by garden line, eradicating by hand those weeds not amenable to mass destruction. It is worth it, of course. But if economy of labour is a really major consideration, then have the maximum amount of ground under flowers, vegetables or fruit, as the French and others do, with only paths between, or have a part of it paved.

The best conditions for a really good grass lawn are: good drainage, a rich top spit, a fairly acid soil and a situation not too overhung with trees. As a rule one wants also a level surface but, unless for games, this is by no means essential. A slight slope, or very gentle undulations, can be very attractive, provided the mower is able to do its job. After levelling, the ground is prepared either for sowing grass seed or for laying turves. Seeding is the slower but the cheaper and easier method, and on the whole the better.

On no account buy cheap seed—you will regret it. Avoid mixtures containing the rye grasses unless you only want a rough job. Go to a good firm and state as exactly as you can your own circumstances and requirements. There are grasses to meet all sorts of needs—mixtures for shade or half-shade, for the hard uses of the tennis-court or the softer uses of bowls, for hot, dry, sandy soils, for damp places and for smoky towns. You cannot, however, expect any grass to succeed under the dense gloom of a conifer or a big hungry beech.

The best time to sow is the third week of August, but in the southern counties any time up till a month later will do. If the soil is too sodden or if there has been a prolonged dry spell, let it wait, and it may even have to wait till the end of March, which is the second best period for sowing.

If the ground has previously been well cultivated, dig one spit down only, but on new ground or in old neglected gardens where there may be a hard pan of soil below, break up the second spit with the fork—in other words, bastard trench it. Dress the top spit well with whatever organic matter you can spare or afford, but use bonemeal only in moderation. Since grass does best on rather acid soils, lime should rarely be necessary, nor should basic slag be used; moreover, lime encourages worms.

Do the preliminary digging if possible in the spring, and leave the ground fallow for several months in order that the weeds dormant in the soil may germinate and be hoed away or dug up during the summer. If circumstances prevent this course, then at least do the digging a good month before sowing, so that the ground may settle. Then complete the levelling with exactitude. A week before sowing apply a dressing of a lawn fertiliser, and work the whole area into a seed-bed of fine tilth by treading, or rolling and raking.

Sow, of course, when the surface is dry. The problem is to spread the seed evenly, and on large areas it is necessary to mark it out in strips or squares, and weigh out the seed proportionately. Use the broadcasting method, and sow half the seed working up and down the length of the area, and the other half broadwise. The normal rate is $1\frac{1}{2}$ oz per square yard if the seed is good and the condition right. Sowing completed, rake the ground lightly in one direction and then cross-rake, to cover the seed partially. Seed that has not been treated with bird repellent needs a defensive network of black thread.

When the young grass is a good 2 in. high, give it a light rolling to firm the roots and next day a light mowing with the blades set high. Actually scything is best, if in these days of progress you can find an exponent of that dying art.

FROM TURF

A one-spit digging is normally enough, but feed the top spit as for seeding, level off carefully and allow the ground to settle. You will hear much about 'sea-washed' or Cumberland turf, but this is not always the best. What one really wants is a good turf from the same kind of soil as one's own. Good lawn turf is now scarce; too much is coarse meadow grass. Turves may be laid at any season if the weather is not frosty or too dry.

Having raked the surface of the soil to a tilth, fit the turves in to one another, not too tightly, bonding them so that the ends of those in one row overlap those in the previous row. Start at one corner so that as you go along you are treading not on the bare earth but on the sods you have just laid, though you should actually use a plank to stand on. Extract any noticeable weed root and branch. Fill any gaps between the sods with peat or fine soil, and correct any unevenness of surface by adding or taking away a little soil from underneath. Beat each turf down with a turf-rammer, which is a flat heavy board, about 1 ft square with a suitable handle. Water copiously if the job is done in dry weather.

After a week, give a light rolling, and mow with the blades set high.

AFTER-CARE

The major canons of lawn maintenance are: occasional good top-dressings with organic matter, frequent raking, frequent spiking and minimum rolling. In rather more detail the main requirements are as follows:

Mowing. Don't cut the grass too short. But cut frequently —twice a week or even three times when the grass is growing fast. Little and often is the rule of mowing. Change the direction of your mowing 'lanes' occasionally. Cut less frequently in long dry spells; if obliged to cut in drought, leave the hood off; likewise for the last cut of the year. Stop mowing when frosts begin, but in mild winter spells further occasional mowings may be beneficial.

Rolling. Once or twice in early spring is usually quite enough, the purpose being to consolidate turf that has been loosened by frost and snow—nothing else. Roll when the lawn is fairly *dry*. The roller should be of about 2 cwt. Don't try to correct bumps in the ground by rolling, but level up little hollows with top-dressings of soil, or lift the turf and correct the levels from below.

Worms. Crush and disperse worm-casts when dry with besom, brush or rake before rolling or mowing. If worms become a serious nuisance, dress the lawn with a modern, non-messy wormkiller in spring or autumn.

Watering. If any has to be done, it must be copious, and a sprinkler of some sort is essential; a mere wetting of the surface in very dry weather may do more harm than good.

Raking and Brushing. Aeration of the soil and clearance of half-decayed matter are of great benefit. Any sweepings with besom or dragbrush, piercings with garden fork or spiked roller, or scarifying with spring-toothed rake are good, especially in autumn, and especially before applying any kind of top-dressing. Rake before the first mowing in spring also, and rake in different directions. In autumn sweep up fallen leaves.

Weeds. Hand-weeding is very virtuous, and for dandelions and other tap-rooted brutes may be necessary, but most amateurs will have time only for mass murder. There are two main methods. The first is with 'lawn sand', which is a preparation of sulphate of ammonia, sulphate of iron and sharp, lime-free sand. It kills about a dozen kinds of lawn weed, is a fertiliser as well and discourages worms. Use between April and September, preferably in spring. Apply only when the

289

lawn is dry, but when rain is likely in a few days—conditions generally provided in April. The dosage is according to maker's instructions, usually about 5 oz per square yard.

The lawn will turn a nasty colour, but soon afterwards will come on more brightly than ever. Lawn sand is particularly good for alkaline soils, which it tends to make acid, but is harmful on soils already over-acid and 'sour'. For a tennis court you want 1 cwt.

A more modern method, having a slightly different result, is to use one of the new 'hormone' weed-killers, such as the 2,4-D formula, or the similar MCPA. These attack the internal structure of the weed and are very effective, destroying a wide variety of weeds, but needing two or three dressings to kill others. They have no fertilising value, but are contained in many weed-and-feed proprietaries. Apply on a still day (when rain is in the offing) and be awfully careful not to let the stuff drift on to adjacent flower beds. Don't use it on new lawns for at least a year. Don't put the mowings of recently treated grass on the compost heap or on beds.

Moss, otherwise than in damp, shady places, may be restrained by 'mercurised lawn sand' or by watering with a solution of permanganate of potash at $\frac{1}{2}$ oz to the gallon. But there must also be measures to increase the soil fertility.

Feeding. Grass needs potash and phosphates in autumn, nitrogen in spring. There are several proprietary lawn fertilisers, but, equally important, is to top dress in late autumn, every year or two, with peat or leaf-mould $\frac{1}{2}$ in. deep, or fine, sifted soil.

Nowadays most people use a dual-purpose weed-and-feed preparation, but it is much better to apply dressings of fertiliser and weed-killer separately, using the fertiliser first. Take note that the hormone weed-killers act as grass depressants if used too often.

Most fertilisers are very expensive, but Maxicrop is cheap and very good. Seasonal needs can also be met by $\frac{1}{2}$ oz sulphate of ammonia per square yard in spring and 1 oz of sulphate of potash in autumn.

Small patches of dying grass suggest the depredations of the leather-jacket. A 5 per cent DDT dust, at 1 oz per square yard, should deal with it. For ants, *see* Chapter XXIII.

Fungal disease may show itself in larger brown patches, roughly circular. Dig out the diseased turf and re-sow or re-sod. Pinkish gelatinous growth and grey-brown overlapping lichens show need for a light dressing of lime. When attempts to cure fungal diseases fail, cut out a small slice of turf 3 in. deep and send it to one of the best grass-seed firms or other authority for their advice.

CHAPTER XX

FRUIT

Definitions (additional to those in Chapter VII):

Tree fruits. Those which, in their natural habit, make thick-limbed trees—apples, pears, plums, cherries, etc.; the term is used irrespective of the tree's shape—whether standard, bush, cordon, etc.

Stone fruits. Those that have hard kernels—cherry, plum, peach, etc.—all species of the genus *Prunus*.

Bush fruits. Gooseberries, red currants, black currants.

Cane fruits. Blackberries, raspberries and their hybrids.

To pinch. To prune with the finger-nails.

Secondary. A little shoot that sprouts as the result of summer pruning or pinching.

Wood or Growth bud. A bud that will later grow into a branch; it is pointed and lies close to the parent branch.

Fruit bud. A plumper, rounder bud that will bear blossom and, later, fruit.

I'M afraid there is no doubt that fruit gets terribly neglected in most private gardens. Enormous crops are lost every year. The main reason is that people are vague about pruning and spraying. And yet, except on the apple and the pear, these are simple tasks.

If there is room, and in even a quarter of an acre of usable space there is, fruit is best grown apart. Alternatively, greater use should be made of walls and fences. Pears and certain cherries and other *Prunus* species do awfully well on house walls. The red currant makes a splendid fan, even on a north wall, and looks highly decorative. It is also quite delightful as a little standard tree, like a rose, and as such, ornamented with drooping red jewels, takes a worthy place in any flower border.

The gooseberry can be easily trained as a cordon or espalier on a fence. Blackberries and logans can earn a dividend on a shady fence.

Whatever the circumstances, don't dot your fruits about the kitchen garden in a random manner; if they have to be put there, plant them in straight lines in a section to themselves and face the fact that, once they are well grown, very few things will grow successfully beneath them. Problems of space are made easier by using cordons and other 'artificial' forms, and by employing special stocks for apples and pears that keep the tree very dwarf. Moreover, the tree fruits, especially cherries, are in themselves ornamental, and can serve both beauty and economy in the flower garden instead of occupying vegetable space. A bush or standard apple never looks better than in a cottage garden surrounded by annual flowers.

The general requirements stated in the following sections on soil, planting, etc., will not be repeated in the notes on the individual fruits unless need arises.

SITUATION AND SOIL

Contrary to popular belief, the hilltop or upper hillside is a better situation for fruit than the valley. The worst enemy of fruit is late frost after the blossom has formed, and although the hilltop may be swept by wind, it is the valley that holds the frost. In frosty bottoms the less hardy fruits, if attempted, should be trained on a wall. Shelter from the east wind is always desirable, as the pollinating insects funk it in very early spring.

Tree fruits should be planted in full sun, though the Morello cherry is famous as a north-waller. The currants and berries will stand quite a lot of shade, but will fruit earlier in the sun.

The soil that most fruits like is a medium loam, not too rich. They adapt themselves to most conditions, but thin, sandy loams of a pale hue and cheesy, unworked clays are unpropitious. All (bar the strawberry, which is in a class apart) like lime, especially the *Prunus* species, which will thrive in chalky soils, though solid chalk less than 3 ft from the surface creates difficulties. The really important thing is good drainage, though not the excessive drainage of solid gravel and sand. The general prescription for soil treatment is this:

Dig at least two spits deep. Except for bush and cane fruits, use no animal manure unless the soil is very poor: but incorporate plenty of chopped-up turves, bonemeal and wood ashes, and some mortar rubble. Increase the mortar rubble for cane-fruits and grapes. Beds for tree fruits on walls should not be less than 3 ft wide and 6 ft long.

After the first year or two the main foods are potash (very important) and nitrogen. Give top-dressings of a manure and, separately, of sulphate of potash at 1 oz per square yard, or use a balanced proprietary fruit fertiliser.

PLANTING

This is best done for nearly all fruits round about November 1st. Follow the general principles of Chapter V, but with special emphasis on two ordinances—plant very firmly and plant shallow. All fruits, especially the canes, carry their roots near the surface and much spread out. On average soils bury the upper roots of tree fruits only about 4 in., currants and canes only 2 in. Plant to the soil mark, and be most careful on tree fruits not to bury the point where stock and scion were united, identifiable as a marked swelling a little above ground level. The larger trees and bushes are a two-man job. Remember to stake the larger ones firmly, inserting between tree and stake a pad of some soft material to prevent chafing of the bark. Trees to be trained on walls should be planted a good 9 in. or more out from the footings.

Planting distances naturally vary, and will be given under each fruit. I implore you not to plant them too close together.

Having planted, never put a spade or fork into the ground anywhere near the roots, which may extend well beyond the branches. Cultivate by shallow hoeing—on cane fruits a mere skimming of the surface.

SHAPING

Space forbids any extensive description of how to train the various shapes of fruit tree, and the reader is referred to

Howard Crane's *Fruit for Small Gardens* in this series. The artificial forms—cordon, espalier and fan—are to be highly commended for small gardens. They are *the* thing. Although apples and pears are the most usual models for these forms, the gooseberry and red currant are equally amenable. The gooseberry as a cordon or as an espalier, and the red currant as a

Standard

Pyramid

Bush

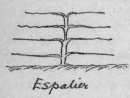

Espalier

U- or Double Cordon

Fan.

Fruit tree shapes.

296

cordon, fan or standard are very economical of space, are easy to look after and produce fruit of exhibition quality. The large, spreading fruit tree is quite out of place nowadays in small gardens.

The training of artificial forms is not difficult, but takes time. Therefore it is best to get them ready trained from a good nursery, but the process of further training will have to go on until the allotted space is filled. Fans of tree fruits need a really large wall. Espaliers and cordons don't need a wall, but an oblique cordon of apple or pear—the best job for those fruits—will go 20 ft long if you like.

The business of shaping a natural form—standards and bushes—and the semi-natural form of a pyramid consists in principle of annually doubling the number of branches and in forming the desired shape. On apples, pears and red currants seek to build up a cup- or goblet-shaped framework, open in the centre. This does not apply, however, to black currants or cane fruits, whose habit is quite different.

Do not allow any fruit to form on any plant from a nursery the first year (except strawberries). Pick off the blossom.

PRUNING

Pruning is the touchstone of successful fruit-growing, yet, as I have said, there is normally no difficulty about it except on the apple and the pear. Study the general principles in Chapter VII before the particular directions under each fruit. The injunctions to cut out diseased and weakly twigs, and a branch that crosses another one, and so on, apply to everything. Note especially the fruits that bear on one-year-old branches and those that bear on older wood. This helps enormously in the approach to any pruning job; for, on all those breeds that fruit only or mainly on shoots grown last year, we want a constant supply of new wood, eliminating the old. Admirable examples of contrast between methods are the black and the red currant, so unlike in all but their names. Sweet and sour cherries provide a similar contrast. The cane fruits are easy. So, as a rule, are the stone fruits, for, once the tree has been built up, you normally don't prune at all, unless it is grown on a wall; what has to be done on them should be done as much as possible in summer, to minimise the danger of disease.

Bear in mind that the effect of pruning is to make the tree sprout afresh; so when the tree is young we prune hard in order to conjure up new branches, but when it is established, we normally prune more lightly in order to induce fruit. If a tree bears a poor crop in any season (other causes, such as lack of

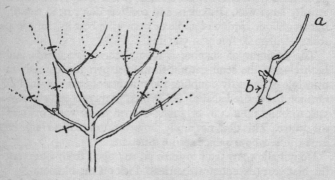

Left: Pruning a young tree for shape; dotted lines show new branches to be expected from cuts as shown. *Right:* Apple and Pear: when summer pruning of shoot *a* results in formation of a fruit bud on its parent shoot *b*, prune to the fruit bud

pollination, being allowed for), prune it lightly in the following winter; and in general terms remember the first rule of pruning —when in doubt, don't. As on the rose, lusty varieties, such as Bramley Seedling, are pruned more lightly than others. Newly-planted young tree fruits, such as apples and pears, fresh from the nursery, need not be pruned at all their first winter.

In fruit-growing there are several special methods of growth control. One is *summer pruning*. Though often a matter of high controversy, it certainly has to be practised on all the artificial forms, and is desirable also on those apples and pears that form close 'spurs'. Summer pruning consists in somewhat shortening the new shoots (not any old ones, *nor any leaders*), as they begin to ripen under the summer sun, as a first stage towards the harder pruning of winter, the notion being that the stoppage of wood growth will stimulate the formation of fruit-buds at the base of the shoot. Summer pruning results naturally in the sprouting of 'secondary' or sub-lateral shoots, just below the cut or pinch, and these themselves are usually pinched back to one leaf. Summer pruning is a bit of a shock to a tree, so should be done a little at a time.

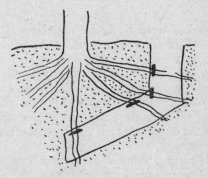

Root-pruning. First year's effort: cut the thick roots only and keep the fibrous ones.

I have mentioned 'spurs'. Some apples bear their fruits at the tips of their branches, but many tree and bush fruits form their crops at definite intervals along the branches. On the apple this fruiting point begins as a little straight branchlet just like the shank of a spur, tipped with a plump fruit-bud in place of a rowel. These gradually multiply and form a gnarled and knobbly cluster. Many fruits spur naturally and others can be so induced. It is a habit that the gardener likes, but on old trees the cluster or compound spur may become excessive and require partial amputation.

Another special type of growth control is root-pruning. This is a brute, but often has to be done on old unproductive trees, and periodically on wall-trained fruit when the wall is not a big one. You dig a narrow trench 2 ft deep half-way round the tree about 4 ft from the bole, severing the thick

299

roots but preserving the fibrous ones, and you complete the circle (or half circle on a wall tree) the next year.

Another method of checking growth and encouraging fruit is ring-barking, but this is a task only for the very experienced. Growth of large, vigorous trees can also be restricted by growing grass, mowing occasionally with the hood off and leaving the mowing as a feed for the tree.

SPRAYING

The second of the busy amateur's bugbears. His problems are, first of all to know what is the right thing to do, and secondly to find time to do it. But again the apple and the pear are the only real problems. Other fruits generally get by with the one common wash of tar-oil in winter, and a special complaint can be dealt with as it appears. But the man who does not spray his apples at least three times cannot expect a sound crop without a lot of luck; the professional often sprays ten times in a season.

The chief purpose of routine spraying of fruits is preventive action. The programme begins at any time after winter pruning, early January being the best, with a 'winter wash' for *all tree and bush* fruits, usually of tar-oil; the purpose is to destroy aphis eggs and parasitic growth. (Mortegg is one good brand.)

Then, for apples and pears and some others, come sprayings of lime-sulphur or an equivalent. This is chiefly against scab, so rife in private gardens. Scab goes hand-in-hand with canker, and—

> Crack follows crack, to laws elastic just,
> And the frail fabric shivers into dust

as Erasmus Darwin observed about 1790. The apple and the pear need at least two or three dressings in spring. About the same time rapacious insects have to be dealt with, such as sawfly, codlin moth, raspberry beetles, caterpillars of all sorts. Use no sprays when blossoms are actually open and don't use lime-sulphur after the blossom has opened on sorts, especially apples, that are 'sulphur-shy'.

In September grease-bands are tied round the trunks of all

tree fruits to trap the wingless females of winter moths as they climb to deposit their eggs. (Stictite is the brand I have generally used.)

The paragraphs on spraying for each variety mention as a rule only the routine sprays and some special treatments. They are summaries only, and Part IV should be studied for descriptions of each ailment and its antidote.

Birds are nowadays one of the grower's worst enemies. The only solution is netting. All small bush fruits and cordons should be caged, but larger trees are pretty hopeless.

LABELLING

It should be evident from these notes that it is vital, especially on apples and pears, to keep the plants durably labelled.

Selections and Cultural Notes
APPLE (Pyrus Malus)

The reader will already have gathered that the familiar apple, to grow *well* with sound and abundant fruit, is really a difficult subject. Not only is it liable to all sorts of ills, but varieties differ enormously from one another in their habits and their needs. Some fruit on spurs and others from the tips of branches, and so have to be pruned differently. Some are 'sulphur-shy', and thus need special spraying treatment. Many, such as Cox, are self-sterile and need a mate to pollinate them, a mate that must bloom at the same time. Others, again, succeed in one kind of soil, or in one county, but not in another.

However, the apple is pretty hardy. Moreover, many of the popular varieties (but by no means all) adapt themselves readily to being grown in one of the artificial forms, except the fan, that are such a blessing in small places. Grow cordons whenever you can, supporting them by a stout, enduring wire framework a good 6 ft high, and tying them to 10-ft bamboos fixed to the wire framework at the desired angle. Espaliers also must have support until fully built up. Vigorous varieties such as Bramley Seedling are not suited to these constricted shapes.

The root stock upon which apples have been grafted or budded is of paramount importance. One of the results of trials conducted by the East Malling Research Station over many years shows that certain stocks produce dwarf trees with great success. These 'Paradise' stocks are designated Malling,

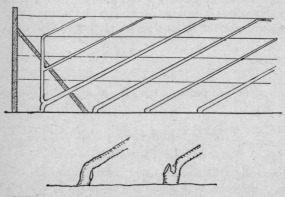

Top: Oblique cordon apples or pears (somewhat formalised). *Below:* When training new young oblique cordons, bend them over on the same side as the union of scion and stock, or there may be a broken romance.

or simply M, followed by a number. Thus M IX is a particularly dwarfing stock, also bringing apples into bearing exceptionally early. M VII and M II are also very good for many purposes. Single cordons on M IX can be planted as closely together as 2 ft, and the dwarf pyramid is another economical form these stocks provide. Certain varieties do better on one stock than on another, and the quality of the soil also affects choice of stock. The subject is technical, and the buyer should always consult his nurseryman.

Few apples, if any, being wholly self-fertile, it is unprofitable to plant only one variety of apple. Whether the mate is a cooker or dessert variety doesn't matter.

Planting distances are: Standards, 30 ft; bushes 15 ft;

302

bushes on dwarfing stock, 8 ft; cordons, 2 ft, with 6 ft between rows; espaliers, 10 ft; dwarf pyramids, 4 ft, with 6 ft between rows. All subject to variety and stock.

Be careful to pick apples at the right time. The early ones, such as Beauty of Bath, should be consumed as soon as ripe, for they will not keep. Others should be picked before they are ripe, and allowed to mature in store. The test for fitness to pick is whether the apple parts readily from the bough on being merely lifted up in the hand, or with only a just perceptible twist; but all should be gathered in by about mid-October. Handle them gently, especially James Grieve, to avoid bruising.

Store in a place that is cool, rather on the damp side, dark or partially so, ventilated, and having a temperature varying as little as possible. A well-ventilated and slightly damp cellar is ideal, a north-facing shed is good, a dry attic bad. Wrapping is desirable, but not essential for most varieties. Newspaper is quite satisfactory. Not tissue paper. Do not store any diseased, damaged, or bruised fruit, nor any stalkless ones.

PRUNING

Apples fruit on wood that is two years old or more.

Once the framework of the young tree has been built up, there are various courses open, according to the fruiting habit of the variety—whether spur-bearing or tip-bearing. It is really best to avoid tip-bearers, unless in the bush form on very dwarf stock (e.g. Bramley Seedling on M IX). The best bet is the close-spurring variety grown as an oblique cordon—least space, least chance of going wrong in pruning, and easiest to get at.

Differences in variety and in stock, however, are by no means the only guide to correct pruning. Even with the same variety, what is right in my garden may be wrong in yours. All sorts of influences, including the soil, are at work. The apple in her infinite variety allows no dogmatism, and there can be no hard-and-fast rules. General principles, intelligent observation, trial and error must be our guides. On no account ever allow the hired hand to commit the crime of the 'annual hair-

Fruit bud

Growth bud

Spur

Fruit buds

Growth buds

Tip-bearer

Old spur cluster
requiring
thinning

Summer pruning

Apple and Pear—buds, spurs, summer pruning.

cut' which is all too common. However, with these reservations, the following will, I hope, be a useful general guide.

Natural Forms (bush and standard). Prune according to vigour and spurring habit. Thus:

(*a*) Those that bear fruit on short spurs: shorten laterals back to three buds in December, and shorten leaders by a half. E.g. Cox's Orange Pippin.

(*b*) Those that bear on long spurs: shorten laterals to five buds and leaders by a half. E.g. Lane's Prince Albert.

(*c*) Tip-bearers: thin out overcrowded and crossing laterals, especially in the centre of the tree, and lightly tip back strong laterals. E.g. Worcester Pearmain.

On bushes and standards aim to keep an outline roughly cup-shaped. Learn to recognise early the difference between a fruit-bud and a growth bud.

If in doubt, or the variety is not known, try pruning different parts of the tree by each method, and observe results.

Artificial Forms. Summer-prune back to five strong leaves about 1st August, and in December cut further back to three buds—a little less severely on long spurrers.

Old neglected trees, bristling at the tip of each branch with tufts like witches' brooms, may need drastic doctoring. Whole branches may have to be amputated and root-pruning performed. Leave the witches' brooms alone for a year, or tip them lightly, in the hope that fruit will form.

Good cultivation and pruning may actually result in overcropping. Fruit may be borne in such abundance that the tree's vitality is too heavily taxed. Then you must harden your heart, and, at whatever cost to your feelings, thin-out the fruit. One cooking apple per six inches of branch, or a cluster of two for desserts, are the utmost limits. Thin when the fruitlets are the size of a walnut, eliminating first the 'king' fruit in the centre of a cluster. Allow for the 'June drop' when apples naturally cast off many of their young. A few varieties, moreover, such as Laxton's Superb and Miller's Seedling, are prone to 'biennial cropping', bearing heavily one year and resting the next.

Tar-oil wash in winter. Lime-sulphur spray at 1 pint to 5 gallons of water when the blossom-bud first shows pink but before it opens ('pink bud', about 1st May). Repeat when nearly all the blossom has fallen (about 20th May) at $\frac{1}{4}$ pint to 3 gallons. On sulphur-shy sorts use Orthocide.

Bud stages on apple and pear, important for spraying—Mouse Ear, Green Cluster, Pink Bud (White Bud on pear).

Also: at petal-fall spray against sawfly, etc., with BHC. In mid-June, DDT (1 lb of wettable powder to 10 gallons of water) against codlin moth. In July tie sacking bands against codlin moth, and in September grease-bands.

The imported fire-blight disease, carried by bees, is now savaging apples (and some related plants). Blossoms are blackened, leaves withered, stems discoloured. Very dangerous. No cure. Cut out affected branches entire; maybe whole tree. Laxton's Superb is specially prone.

Varieties to Choose

Get rid of the idea that Cox's Orange Pippin, noble fruit though it is, is the only apple. There are at least two others virtually as good. Cox is not easy to grow unless the conditions are just right, is a failure in most parts of the North and Midlands, and is very disease-prone.

Apples are creatures of strong local patriotism. The best apple for Somerset may be one that the Yorkshireman has never heard of. So the first step to wisdom is to get local advice from the county horticultural adviser or other authority. Out of some 500 varieties, I have chosen a mere handful of those most widely grown. All have a high excellence of flavour.

There are plenty of other good ones, and among my omissions are three that are normally included in every list for some reason—Beauty of Bath, which has few virtues other than its exceptional earliness, and Laxton's Superb and Blenheim Orange, which are certainly grand fruits to eat, but which in small places present problems of pruning, cropping and spraying.

For what it is worth, my own first choice in normal circumstances would be:

Dessert—Orleans Reinette, Cox, James Grieve, Ribston Pippin.

Cooking—Bramley, Arthur Turner, Crawley Beauty, Lane's Prince Albert.

Several apples are equally good for dessert or cooking, including Charles Ross, Rival (a good one), Blenheim Orange, Wagener. Economically, desserts are the things to grow rather than cookers. Reasonable cookers can be readily got in the shops; good desserts are rare indeed.

Forgive the hieroglyphics. In the column showing season of use, I hope the mere initials of the months will be clear. The column 'Special Forms' shows whether a variety (normally) is suitable for one of the artificial shapes; here E = espalier, C = Cordon, and P = pyramid. Alternatively, the best natural form and most suitable East Malling stock are suggested, and here B = bush and St. = standard.

The column 'Fruiting Habit' shows whether a variety is a tip-bearer or forms short or long spurs either naturally or by inducement.

Other abbreviations: SS = self-sterile and NK = non-keeper.

DESSERT

Variety	Use	Pick	Fruiting Habit	Special Forms	Remarks
Charles Ross	S–N	mid Oct.	Sh. Sp.	P; or B on M 9 or 2	SS., Sul-shy, NK, Scab-resistant, good on chalk.
Christmas Pearmain	D–J	Oct.	Sh. Sp.	C.P.	Neat and small.
Claygate Pearmain	D–F	mid Oct.	Sh. Sp.	No; B on M 7 or 2	SS. Grand flavour.
Cornish Gillyflower	D–F	Oct.	Tip	No; B on M 9 or 2	SS. Mild districts only. Wonderful flavour.
Cox's Orange Pippin	N–J	mid Oct.	Sh. Sp.	C.P.E.	SS. Mild districts and good soils only. Very disease-prone. World-famous flavour. Prune hard and give extra potash.
Egremont Russet	O–N	end Sep.	Sh. Sp.	C.P.E.	Scab-resistant. One of best.
Ellison's Orange	S–O	end Sep.	Sh. Sp.	C.	Biennial-prone. Spicy flavour; some love it, others don't. Extra good Midlands and North.
James Grieve	S–O	Sep.	Sh. Sp.	C.P.E.	NK. Very fine. No manure. Mate for Cox.
King's Acre Pippin	D–F	mid Oct.	Long Sp.	E.	Fine flavour. Stores well.
Lady Sudeley	A–S	as ripe	Long Sp.	C.E.	Early and good. NK. Prune lightly.
Laxton's Fortune	O–N	Sep.	Sh. Sp.	C.P.	Lovely flavour. Good.
Orleans Reinette	D–F	mid Oct.	Sh. Sp.	C.E.	Superb flavour. No flaws.
Ribston Pippin	N–J	mid Oct.	Sh. Sp.	C.E.	SS. Mild districts. Grand flavour. Prune hard.
Worcester Pearmain	S–O	as ripe	Tip	No; B on M 7 or 2	Scab-prone. Fine flavour. Hardy any-where. Prune lightly.

Variety	Use	Pick	Fruiting Habit	Special Forms	Remarks
Annie Elizabeth	D–May	mid Oct.	Long Sp.	C.E.	Midlands favourite. Slow. Scab-prone. Must be wrapped in store.
Arthur Turner	Jul.–S	Sep.	Sh. Sp.	C.E.	Very early and good.
Bramley Seedling	N–Ap.	mid Oct.	Tip	No; St. on M 16 or B on M 9	Best of all. Succeeds anywhere, but grows very big.
Crawley Beauty	D–Ap.	mid Oct.	Sh. Sp.	E.	SS. Needs late-blooming pollinator. Extra frost-hardy, quite first-class.
Early Victoria	Jul.–A	as ripe	Long Sp.	C.P.E.	NK. Very hardy. Early and frothy.
Edward VII	Jan.–Ap.	Oct.	Sh. Sp.	C.P.E.	Scab-resistant. Fine. Very hardy.
Lane's Prince Albert	N–Ap.	Oct.	Long Sp.	C.	One of best and hardiest. Sul-shy.
Newton Wonder	N–Ap.	mid Oct.	Tip and Long Sp.	No; B on M 7	Very hardy, grand cropper. Stores well, but grows very big. Prune lightly. Sul-shy.
Royal Jubilee	O–D	mid Oct.	Long Sp.	E.	SS. Very hardy.
Wellington	D–Mch.	mid Oct.	Long Sp.	E.	Disease-prone. Hardy, stores well, extra good for baking.

APRICOT (Prunus Armeniaca)

In benign districts, free of frost pockets, apricots can be grown in the open as far north as Ayrshire, given a south-facing wall. Grow them as fans. They are self-fertile, so a lone tree can be grown, but, as the blossoms come out earlier than the average bee, hand-pollination with a camel-hair brush or something of the sort is usually necessary. Cultivate in all respects as for a fan-trained peach.

VARIETIES

Moor Park and New Large Early.

BLACKBERRY (Rubus fruticosus)

Easy and delightful, but enormously improved if well fed. Dig in plenty of well-rotted organic matter, top-dress with bonemeal, and don't forget the potash.

Plant in autumn or winter at least 8 ft apart, on a fence, wires, pillars, etc., to which the canes must be tied. They will succeed in shade but prefer sun. After planting cut the canes right down to within a foot of the ground.

Blackberries fruit on one-year canes. After fruiting is over, cut the old canes right to the ground. As the new ones

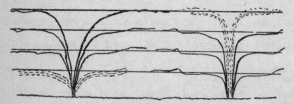

Two methods of training blackberries and loganberries to prevent a murderous entanglement; new shoots in dotted lines.

shoot up each year tie them in away from the old, so that the two don't get entangled, otherwise there will be the dickens of a mess. Handle the new shoots with care, as they are brittle— as well as prickly. Use gloves. After the old canes have been cut out, rearrange the new ones.

Multiply stock either by digging up suckers from around the base of the plant, or allow the tips of some shoots to droop to the ground and weight them down with a stone. The tip will take root. In February sever it from its parent and transplant where required.

VARIETIES

Parsley-leaved Blackberry; John Innes. There are also various hybrids—boysenberry, youngberry, etc.—but none are as good as the blackberry.

BLACK CURRANT (Ribes nigrum)

Another easy one. In severe districts protect from east wind to help pollination. Plant 5 ft apart; and cut all shoots down to 4 in. of the ground after planting.

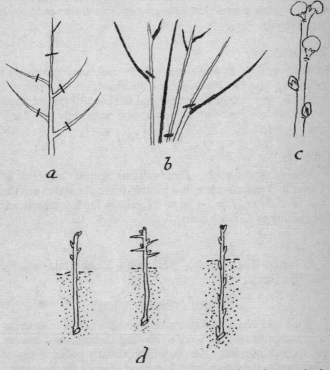

a, Branch of an established red currant; prune new laterals to two buds and shorten leader one-half; treat each branch the same. *b*, Part of black currant bush. Preserve the new wood (black). Cut the old fruited shoots either to the ground or to a strong new shoot. *c*, 'Big bud' on a black currant. *d*, Bush-fruit cuttings—red currant, gooseberry, black currant (lower buds not removed).

The black currant carries its fruit mainly on young branches grown last season. Just as on a climbing rose, some new shoots spring from the ground, others from half-way up an old shoot. Therefore, as soon as fruiting is over, prune the old fruited shoots back to a point where a *strong* new one has sprouted, and cut other old shoots down to the ground according to the number of new ones that have sprung from there; cut out all weak shoots.

PROPAGATION

Take cuttings in mid-autumn from new wood grown that summer. Use the lower part of the shoot, cut just below a node, shorten it from the upper end to about 10 in. and plant firmly *without removing any buds*, and with only two buds above ground.

SPRAYS

Winter tar-oil wash. Lime-sulphur against 'big bud' at $\frac{1}{2}$ pint to 3 gallons water as a routine when the leaves are the size of a shilling: or 1 pint to $2\frac{1}{2}$ gallons for a severe attack (scorching of foliage results).

VARIETIES

Boskoop Giant (early), Seabrook's Black (mid-season), Baldwin (late).

CHERRY (Prunus Avium)

With only one or two exceptions, cherries are all self-sterile. The exceptions are the 'sour' or cooking cherries, most notably the famous Morello. Morello will apparently pollinate any of the sweet or dessert cherries, but sweet cherries certainly must never be planted in one variety alone. The subject is involved and the nurseryman should be consulted, but whatever you choose the birds are likely to get the lot. You are warned.

The sweet cherries do best as standards, in which form they are very decorative but take up a lot of space. Several, however, do take kindly to being grown as fans on a large wall where they can be netted against birds. Morello is famous for its enormous merit of flourishing on a north wall.

As on other stone fruits, do no more pruning than is essential. The unavoidable pruning of wall fans should be done as much as possible in summer. Sweet cherries fruit on wood two years old and more, like the apple, and they spur readily. The Morello, however, bears on one-year-old branches. So—

Sweet Cherries. As standards and bushes, normally no pruning. On walls—when laterals have made six leaves in summer, pinch back to three or four, and pinch out resultant secondaries. Should an old branch become worn out, train in a young one to replace it.

Sour Cherries. Old wood must be replaced after fruiting. Prune as for fan-trained peaches. Do not pick Morello cherries with their stalks; cut the stalks with scissors.

SPRAYS

Tar-oil wash in winter. Lime-sulphur just before buds open against fungal disease. Derris, etc., against observed pests. Watch for silver leaf. Apply greasebands in September.

VARIETIES

Desserts: Early Rivers is the queen, but very large. Next, I would today have Merton Bigarreau and Noir de Guben. Between them all three will be pollinated.

CURRANTS. *See under* Black Currant and Red Currant.
DAMSON. *See under* Plum.

FIG (Ficus Carica)

Figs are not to be recommended for small gardens, but for those who have any already the following notes on pruning should correct the usual errors.

Figs fruit mainly on young branches grown last year—in

fact the fruit begins to form the same year as the branch grows, and over-winters. After leaf-fall cut some of the old fruited wood right out and train in the strongest new shoots as annual replacements. In early summer pinch back to six leaves new side-shoots that are not wanted for replacement or for extension of the older shoots.

Root-pruning is equally important. Figs ought to be planted in concrete or brick pits about 3 ft deep and 4 ft square. If this has not been done, root-prune occasionally in October. Never give any manure.

If you want to plant a Fig, use Brown Turkey as a fan on a warm wall.

GOOSEBERRY (Ribes grossularia)

The gooseberry fruits mainly on two-year-old branches and partly on those one-year-old. Otherwise it behaves very much like an apple. It forms little spurs fairly readily and submits willingly to being trained in any of the artificial forms. The cordon—single, double, or triple—is *the* way to grow them, stopping them when 6 ft high or less. Quite inexpensive.

Gooseberries do well in partial shade, but prefer sun. Like other bush fruits, they need a soil rich in animal or vegetable manure. Plant bushes and espaliers 5 ft apart, single cordons 1 ft, doubles 2 ft, and triples 3 ft.

Pruning

On artificial forms summer-prune laterals, but not leaders, after five leaves have developed; winter-prune them to 2 in., and shorten each year's new leader growth by a half till full height is reached.

For the usual bush shape there is a choice of methods—

For fine fruit, treat each branch as a cordon, reducing leaders by a half in winter.

For general purposes, adopt this method: In winter thin out overcrowded and overlapping new shoots, especially in the centre. Of those retained, shorten strong ones by a half and others by a mere inch. Shorten leaders according

314

to habit—on erect varieties reduce by a half to an outward-pointing eye, on drooping varieties cut at the top of the arch to an upward eye.

PROPAGATION

After leaf-fall take shoots of the current season's growth. Shorten if necessary (from the tip end) to about 12 in. Remove all buds except three or four at the top. Plant very firmly about 8 in. deep. At the end of the first season lift and replant 12 in. apart. Ready for permanent quarters at the end of the second year, when shaping will be necessary.

SPRAYS

Tar-oil wash in winter. Flowers of sulphur at first sign of mildew; or lime-sulphur spray at 1 pint to 5 gallons before blossoms open if disease known to be prevalent. Derris against various caterpillars after flowering or when attacked.

VARIETIES

Gooseberries have strong local associations, especially in the North. Do enquire accordingly, but Langley Gage, Lancer, Lancashire Lad, and Careless are all good. Don't pick too soon; wait for them to sweeten.

GRAPE (Vitis vinifera)

This must be dealt with rather tersely, on the assumption that the reader has already had a year or two's general experience.

SOIL

Dig three spits and mix in old turves in abundance, mortar rubble or small broken chalk, broken or coarse bonemeal, and wood ashes. No manure unless the soil is very poor indeed. If drainage is suspect, excavate the soil and lay in a 6-in. course of brick rubble covered with upside-down turves.

To save a season, it is best to get 'fruiting vines'—those which are ready to fruit next season if you were foolish enough to allow it. When planting, disentangle the roots and fan them out well, working in fine sifted soil.

OUTDOORS

In genial districts, on a warm sunny wall, a few varieties can be grown successfully. For the average amateur, probably the most reliable dessert grape, and certainly the most usual, is Royal Muscadine. The flavour is excellent.

The culture of grapes for Bacchanalian purposes is outside my brief and to a large extent outside my knowledge, but anyone interested might consider writing to the Viticultural Research Institute, Oxted, Surrey.

TRAINING

For fruit, grow as a cordon or as a 'toasting fork'. For a cordon, cut the fruiting vine down to about 4 ft the winter of planting, and it will probably reach the desired height the following summer. Stop it there. Perhaps a better practice is to allow only 3 ft of growth a year (doing the cutting-back in winter). Meanwhile summer-prune laterals at 12 in., and later winter-prune to two buds. For the gridiron style, cut rather lower and train out two laterals right and left for possibly 6 ft. Prune each as a cordon. Then allow laterals to form on these at about 3-ft intervals and train them upwards, pruning each as a cordon.

PRUNING

Induce spurs about every 15 in., rubbing out any buds that sprout between the spurs. Pinch new shoots from the spurs at two leaves beyond the bunches of blossom, and pinch secondaries at one leaf. If no blossom appears on a shoot, pinch at 2 ft. *After leaf-fall* cut back all laterals, whether fruited or not, to two buds, and next year allow only one of these buds to grow. Allow no fruit till the second season and then very little. Except for summer pinching, *never* cut vines after January 1st, or they bleed. If bleeding occurs treat with a styptic pencil or char with a red-hot iron.

As the fruit swells it must be thinned. Using the proper

316

pointed scissors, snip off the berries *inside* the bunch while quite tiny—more severely towards the tip than at the shoulders. Do not touch the grapes by hand, but manœuvre them with a stick.

INDOORS

The old Black Hamburg and Buckland Sweetwater are best for an unheated or only slightly heated house, but where there is ample warmth Muscat of Alexandria is perhaps choicest.

The greenhouse must be properly equipped with wires beneath the glass. Plant the vine in a bed outside the house, leading it through a hole at ground level in the wall; heaven should then do the watering.

Plant indoor vines in March. Train and prune as for outdoors. Don't permit a dense mass of leafage. If only one vine

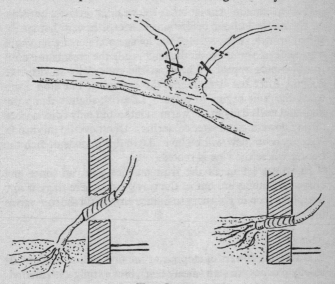

THE GRAPE

Top: Winter-prune to two buds (dotted lines); if both buds sprout next spring, trim back to one (thick lines). *Bottom:* Greenhouse vine with roots outside; two methods of planting—note different soil levels.

317

is grown, train as a gridiron, making the initial amputation at such a height that, when the two laterals grow out, they will be above the level of the greenhouse's brickwork.

WINTER TREATMENT

At pruning time, or not later than 1st January, untie all the rods and let them droop down, suspended by strings, till they sprout in the spring, then re-hoist. This encourages the formation of new growth evenly along the rods. On old vines remove the loose bark by rubbing with the hand (not a knife) when the rods are bare in winter, and, as a corrective to mealy bug, paint the rods with Gishurst Compound, working it into the crannies with a stiff brush.

HUMIDITY

Give maximum ventilation as the weather dictates, but shut up the house an hour before sunset except in very hot spells. When growth starts, syringe the foliage occasionally on warm days with rain-water from the tank inside the greenhouse until the blossoms appear. Then tap the rods daily to disperse pollen. After ten days renew the syringing, but stop again when the fruit begins to colour. Likewise slightly damp the floor and walls daily in the warm months, but only twice a week during flowering and after colouring. Don't overdo this inside wetting, or mildew will be invited. In dry periods drench the border where the vine is rooted.

In winter let in all the frost and ice you can (once any chrysanthemums are out of the way), but, where there is any heat, turn it on in February to induce growth till the sun warms up.

SPRAYS

Dust with flowers of sulphur at the first sign of mildew. If woolly patches are seen (mealy bug), brush stiffly with methylated spirit.

Greengage. *See under* **Plum.**

LOGANBERRY

Believed to be a cross between a blackberry and a raspberry. Cultivate as for the blackberry.

Multiply stock by tip-rooting in summer. Transplant carefully, as the roots, like the young canes, are brittle.

NECTARINE

Is a variation on the theme of peach, and its cultivation is exactly the same. Smaller in size and smooth-skinned, it has the general appearance of a plum. Perhaps the most exquisite of all fruit. Slightly less hardy than the peach, it should be fan-trained on a warm wall.

VARIETIES

Early Rivers and Lord Napier, both maturing in August, are possibly the pick for all-round qualities.

PEACH (Prunus persica)

In all but the more austere parts of the country peaches can safely be grown out in the open, as bushes or standards, like apples, provided they are not in frost pockets. In less-favoured districts they must be fan-trained on a warm wall and protected with muslin at blossom time.

It pays to buy a three-year-old tree on which the preliminary training has been done at the nursery; no pruning is then needed except to shorten old, exhausted branches in order to encourage new ones. The less pruning the better; when needed, do it in May. Fruit is borne on wood of the previous season's growth. Allow for a spread of 15 ft.

Peaches like a rather dry soil. Treat it as advised in pages 294–5, though nowadays there is less insistence on lime. Peaches are self-fertile.

As a fan. The process of building up the framework of the fan may go on for some years according to the size of the wall, but fruit-forming can be allowed concurrently. If your new plant is a three-year-old, a few 'fruiting shoots' can be allowed to grow that year for cropping next year. Part of the frame-building consists, of course, in the longitudinal extension of the main ribs as far as they will go.

The 'fruiting shoots' grow out of the main limbs. It is in the handling of these that people go wrong, yet the thing is not difficult. What happens is this:

The shoot will produce not only fruit but also some new growth-shoots or branches. You will want a new growth shoot to replace the existing one next year, and you will want it from the base of the old. This is called the replacement shoot. So, just after the blossom has fallen, cut out all new

Pruning wall-trained peach. *a*, 'Fruiting shoot', thinned to two fruits and stopped beyond the last; *b*, sap-drawing shoot pinched at four leaves; *c*, shoots next to fruits pinched at two leaves; *d*, replacement shoot growing freely; *e*, fruiting shoot will be severed here after harvest; *f*, last year's fruiting shoot was cut here.

shoots that are sprouting, except this basal one and also one near the tip, a little beyond the last blossom. Allow the one near the tip to start and then pinch it beyond its fourth leaf, the purpose being to draw sap through the whole branch in order to ripen the fruit. When fruiting is over cut the whole of the old shoot back to the point where the replacement shoot begins. That is all there is to it.

In early years the tip shoot can be retained, and the whole member allowed to grow on to become part of the permanent framework. Shoots sprouting in awkward places can be stopped at two leaves.

The fruit also must be thinned. Allow no more than two peaches per shoot—one only on a short growth. Thin first to

A sturdy, wind-resistant annual mallow, *Lavatera trimestris*

A sea-holly, the white-collared *Eryngium alpinum*

Hypericum olympicum in the author's rock garden

One of the herbaceous borders

The Canary ivy at the front door

Below: the multiple sprays of the Canadian lilac '*Virgilia*'

Right: *Verbascum broussa*, completely clad in white felt

The author displays his cordon redcurrants

four per shoot when the size of a pea, and then to two when the size of a walnut.

Winter tar-oil. Also (*very important*) spray against the leaf-curl disease with Orthocide or lime-sulphur just before autumn leaf-fall and again in mid-February before the leaf buds open. Derris against observed insect pests.

Varieties

Easily the best is Peregrine; alternatively Hale's Early.

PEAR (Pyrus communis)

Sister to the apple, the pear is a trifle less hardy. In the colder counties, according to variety, it needs the protection of a wall, and the more *recherché* varieties are best on a wall in many districts.

Most pears readily and obediently adopt the spurring habit —a great blessing, allowing them to be shaped as espaliers and as single or multiple cordons. A few, however, are tip-bearers. Most are self-fertile or partially so, but the same care should be taken in the choice of varieties as with apples.

Special rooting stocks also are available. They are Quince stocks, and the one usually most recommended now is that which is known as Quince A. Some of the best varieties, however, known as 'incompatible', do not marry well with quince, and, taking two husbands as it were, have to be 'double worked'. The favourite 'Williams' is an example. Your safeguard is to avoid cheapjack nurseries.

Cultivation is in all respects virtually the same as for the apple. On the spurring varieties summer-prune to five leaves near the end of July, and winter-prune further to 3 in. Do not summer-prune leaders on bushes and standards, and winter-prune according to vigour and habit—cut upright varieties such as Doyenné du Comice by a third to outward buds, drooping varieties to upward buds, tip-bearers scarcely at all. Don't give any lime to pears unless the soil is definitely acid.

Trickier than apples, pears need an atmosphere slightly warmer and slightly drier. Handle very tenderly. Do not wrap. They must not touch each other. Examine from time to time, as they go 'sleepy' in the centre and rot rapidly.

SPRAYS

Winter tar-oil. Lime-sulphur at 1 pint to 5 gallons against scab at 'white-bud' (end April); at petal-fall, liquid copper or lime-sulphur at $\frac{1}{4}$ pint to 3 gallons and again three weeks later, except on those sulphur-shy. Watch for fire-blight.

VARIETIES

There is little point in growing a cooking pear, unless it be *Catillac*; for bottling, the dessert varieties are superior. Of these, the following are prime choices:

Doyenné du Comice, the queen of pears, large, sweet, melting, prolific, but not for cold places. Pick early Oct.

Conference. Distinctive elongated shape. Prolific and scab-resistant. Pick late Sept. for Oct.–Nov. Fine as a cordon. Very easy and beginner's first choice.

Dr Jules Guyot. Resembles a Williams. Pick Sept. just before ripe. Non-keeper. Incompatible. Easy.

Josephine de Malines. Delicious late pear. Pick Oct. for Dec.–Feb. Tip-bearing and best as a dwarf bush.

Beurré Superfin. Melting, sweet and aromatic. Pollinated by Conference. Pick early Sept.

Louise Bonne de Jersey. Rich, melting, and exuberant. Pick late Sept. for Oct. Easy but needs thinning.

Williams's Bon Chrétien (the Bartlett of America). Most widely known pear. Ready Sept.; *pick when green*. Very disease-prone. Incompatible.

PLUM (Prunus domestica)

The plum is a very hardy fellow. The greengage is simply a celestial version of it, slightly less hardy, and vying with the nectarine as the most seductive of fruits. The damson, bullace, and sloe are also plums.

The standard and the bush are the usual forms, taking up much room; they *can* be grown as fans, but need a large wall and a bit of skill. There is much 'incompatibility' of stocks (*see under* Pears). There is now a good semi-dwarfing stock known as St Julien A, but it is well to consult a specialist nurseryman. Plant at 15-ft spacing.

Plums are often self-fertile, but it is best to consult the nurseryman. On the other hand, they flower so early that the bee often funks its job of pollination. If so, you must hand-pollinate.

Save as mentioned, planting distances are 30 ft for standards, about 18 ft for bushes, and the same for fans.

Pruning

The plum fruits on one- and two-year-old wood, spurring freely. As for peaches, the less pruning the better. It therefore pays to buy three-year-old trees, with the basic framework already built. What pruning may be necessary (e.g. crossing and rubbing branches) should be done in late May or after cropping and in dry weather (which reduces the risk of silver leaf).

Plums often over-crop heavily. Thin the fruit to about 3 in. apart, and prop up heavily laden boughs.

Sprays

Tar-oil in winter. Derris against sawfly a week after petal-fall. Liquid copper may be needed about the end of May against bacterial canker, which attacks the main stem. Watch for silver leaf.

Varieties

Reine Claude, the true original greengage, is most delicious of all, but very capricious in fruiting; best on a wall. A very good substitute is the more dependable Cambridge Green Gage. Other choice ones are: Coe's Golden Drop, a jewel, but needs a wall in the north, self-sterile but mates with Cambridge Gage; Early Transparent Gage, Denniston's Superb, Late Transparent Gage, Jefferson's Gage.

The best all-purpose plum—for cooking, bottling, or dessert —is Victoria; self-fertile but disease-prone. Of cookers and jammers, Early Rivers and Pershore (or Yellow Egg) are much better than the usual Czar.

Likewise of damsons, the Shropshire Prune has a much better flavour than the more usual Merryweather.

RASPBERRY (Rubus Idæus)

Easy enough, but, like other cane fruits, immensely improved by enrichment of the soil with animal or vegetable manure. They do well in partial shade but prefer sun. Liberal watering and generous mulching (manure, leaves, etc.) greatly improve the crop and the quality. A neat and sturdy framework is needed for their support, one wire 2 ft from the ground and another about 5 ft. Run the rows North–South if possible.

Plant 2 ft apart, at least 6 ft between rows. Cover the top roots by about 3 in. and cut the canes down to 9 in. They fruit only on canes of the previous season's growth. So the first year you will get no fruit, but a row of nice new canes to fruit next year.

Thereafter, as soon as fruiting is over, cut the old canes that have fruited, and any weakly new ones, down to the ground. If the new canes are very long, shorten to 5 ft 6 in. in February. Autumn-fruiting varieties, if grown, are cut down in February.

Stock is readily multiplied by digging up a new cane with its roots in autumn. When hoeing, merely skim the surface.

SPRAYS

Lime-sulphur at 1 pint to 2½ gallons, just before the flower-buds open against 'cane spot' (q.v. Part IV). Derris in late June as the fruit begins to colour against the maggot of the raspberry beetle. A yellow mottling of leaves, which often curl downwards, suggests the 'mosaic' virus; burn all affected plants, complete with roots and suckers.

VARIETIES

I consider Lloyd George to be quite the best; it fruits both summer and autumn. But you must get certified disease-free

New Zealand stock from a top nursery. Malling Jewel, Malling Promise, and the old, late Norfolk Giant are also good. For autumn, Hailsham or September. Of the delicious yellow varieties, Yellow Antwerp.

RED AND WHITE CURRANT (Ribes rubrum)

Another easy one, either as a natural bush or in the artificial forms which I have mentioned and which I strongly commend. Fruits largely on two-year-old wood, and partly on one-year-old, and forms spurs readily. The white currant is merely a colour variation of the red, often of finer flavour.

Cultivate, propagate, and space as for the gooseberry (*not* as for the black currant). Whatever the shape, prune as for cordons, with summer pinching and winter cutting-back of spurring laterals. Leave leaders unpruned in summer but reduce by a half in winter. Keep the centre fairly open.

SPRAYS

Tar-oil in winter. Derris or a proprietary against summer aphis. Look out for coral spot, rust, and leaf spot.

VARIETIES

Laxton's No. 1 is easily the best early red, and Red Lake for later. White Versailles is a sweet and delicious white.

STRAWBERRY (Fragaria)

Merely from the economic point of view, strawberries, like asparagus, are not worth growing in the very small place. For the limited amount of fruit they provide, all so quickly gobbled up, they take up a disproportionate amount of ground. They are best grown in the kitchen garden, forming part of the vegetable rotation.

A warm position in full sun and a rich humus content in the soil are essential. Good crops cannot be had without a heavy manurial dressing of some sort. Add bonemeal at 3 oz. per square yard, and sulphate of potash at 1 oz.

Plant in August or September for preference; alternatively March, but if so allow no fruit to form that season. Space the plants 15 in. apart in rows a good 2 ft apart. Be most watchful not to bury the crown of the plant, but to set it level with the soil. Cloches are a great help in repulsing spring frosts and bringing the crop on early.

As the fruits come on, lay some straw, or special strawberry mats, beneath them to save the fruit from soiling. You must also net the bed, unless you want the birds to have them all. Arrange the nets, well off the ground, in a manner that will allow them to be easily thrown off and replaced.

PROPAGATION

A strawberry plant is not much use after three years. To renew itself it throws out 'runners' that take root. Remove these until you are ready to make a new planting. Then allow

A strawberry runner has taken root.

only one rooting per runner, and only one or two runners per plant in the fruiting bed; but if a few plants are kept specially for propagation, five runners may be rooted. There is no special merit in rooting the runners in pots in the ground. Let them root naturally.

When rooted (in about six weeks) sever the youngsters from their parents, lift a week later and plant in the new bed. They will fruit next year, and thus form one stage in the annual programme of renewal, which has a three-year cycle. Discard the three-year-olds, planning your space accordingly.

SPRAYS

A nicotine spray or dust just before flowering or when observed against strawberry aphis (malformed leaves and stunted growth). Flowers of sulphur for mildew. DDT if fruits are eaten by the otherwise friendly ground beetle.

A flattened, stunted, sickly appearance, with leaves often edged bright yellow, denotes a serious virus. Burn the whole plant and its near neighbours.

VARIETIES

Royal Sovereign is the best for flavour, but not a heavy cropper. Cambridge Favourite crops more heavily. Cambridge Rival and Cambridge Vigour are good for soils poor in humus and are early. Talisman is a good late variety.

Many people discern a delicate flavour in the little Alpine strawberries, which go on and on and are best in partial shade. Baron Solemacher is the usual (no runners).

The recent introductions of 'perpetual' strawberries, which extend the season till the autumn, are very interesting. They make large bushes, and the best known so far are San Rivale, St Claude, Triomphe, and the Rollerberry; but the nurseryman should be consulted for varieties most suitable to your district.

For all strawberries, indeed, you *must* go to a first-class grower, for there is a great deal of weak, disease-prone stuff about the country.

CHAPTER XXI

SIMPLE VEGETABLES AND HERBS

GENERAL CULTIVATION—SPECIAL FAMILY NEEDS— ROTATION OF CROPS—LAY-OUT—FRAMES AND CLOCHES— SELECTIONS

To grow good vegetables requires a higher standard of gardening and much more constant attention than is needed for acceptable flowers; but the economics of today, if not a natural predilection, impel many of us to grow them. A careful consideration of the space factor is first necessary.

If space is small, the kinds of vegetables which should have first priority—on economic grounds only and disregarding personal choice—are the easy salads of summer and the more difficult vegetables of winter that are often so expensive: celery, leeks, parsnips, endive, and winter greens generally. Next in importance I would place those that ripen in summer but keep through the winter: onions, haricot beans, and such root crops as you care for. The long range of summer vegetables you will certainly grow if you have the room, particularly peas and beans, which are so delicious straight out of the garden, but generally they are an uneconomic crop for the room they take up. A row of peas, for example, is gone in no time, and the proper way to treat them is to grow them in succession —relatively small sowings at intervals of about three weeks, so that there is a continuous supply until autumn—for which you need a good deal of room.

The last things to be grown in the small garden, economically speaking, are potatoes. To sow enough for a family takes up a great deal of space. If a half-way course is decided on, then go in for early potatoes, but not main-croppers.

The average British housewife, I regret to say, is lamentably conservative in her choice of vegetables. She shies away from anything with which she is not familiar and is at the mercy of the farmer, who is not interested in the flavour of his crops but only in how many tons per acre they will yield.

So, whatever is the general plan, grow whenever you can those varieties which are a little out of the common rut. Flavour is the thing. All the varieties I suggest in the following notes are chosen, other things being equal, for the excellence of their table qualities. The mangetout, the golden waxpod bean, the calabrese broccoli, the flageolet bean, salsify, sweet corn, and the turnip grown especially for its top—these are the tasty things that make vegetable-growing worth-while, and few of them are obtainable in the average shop. For the same reason pick your marrows, your beans, your carrots and turnips and radishes, I urge you, while they are young and tender. Vegetables are for eating, not for pride of display. Look out also for some of the dwarf varieties I mention, such as the delicious dwarf French Brussels sprout, the dwarf broad bean, the dwarf lettuce; all these will save space.

General Cultivation

The prime secret of vegetable gardening is good digging, accompanied by the generous use of organic manure of some sort for those crops that need it; not all do, and the experienced gardener plans his digging and manuring to suit his crop rotations or sequences. Each year a part of the kitchen garden should be trenched or bastard-trenched and dressed with rotted animal manure or an equivalent. The best time to do this is in November, but any time up to the end of February will do nearly as well. In years when plots are not due for manuring they are dug over one spit.

Lime is very important in vegetable gardens, except for potatoes. Again, by good planning, you do it to a part of the garden each year, preferably to plots intended for the cabbage tribe. Autumn liming is best on heavy soils, early spring on light ones, but you will remember that liming should be at least a month before or three months after manuring. Bear in mind that the amount of lime any soil may need depends on its acidity factor, but the rule of thumb given at the end of Chapter III may be adopted. Wherever I say in the following notes that lime must be supplied, it is subject to the natural lime content of the soil and to the rotation you are following in your soil management.

Vegetables benefit greatly from chemical fertilisers also, and the amateur's best plan is to buy a good all-purposes fertiliser, such as National Growmore, and follow directions. For all the usual vegetables give 1½ oz. of Growmore per square yard two to three days before sowing. Bonemeal is also valuable, especially on light soils, and especially for potatoes. Well-preserved old soot and fresh wood ashes are also boons, especially for the onion tribe.

The way in which a vegetable is started off in life affects its whole future. Be sure to sow only when the weather is suitable, and to reduce the seed-bed to a fine, loose, well-aerated tilth by raking and treading, whether the seed is sown direct into permanent quarters, as in onions, carrots, spinach, etc., or into the nursery seed-bed, as for cabbages, leeks, etc. Sow always in straight lines, running always north and south if possible. Sow very sparsely (except parsnips) and thin the seedlings as soon as you possibly can. Thinnings of cabbages, onions, lettuces, and others can be transplanted, but not those of root crops; these are commonly thinned first to half their final distances, and a second thinning follows.

For economy of labour and of seed, the practice of sowing 'at stations' (Chapter VI) is very much to be recommended when sowing direct into permanent quarters.

In the vegetable garden, as in the orchard, it is quite vital to protect one's crops against pests and fungal disease. Part IV deals specially with the gardener's usual enemies, and references to them in this chapter are accordingly of a summary nature. But one may say that the afflictions one should specially guard against are the pests of the soil, the little flies whose grubs attack the onion, the carrot, and the cabbage, the serious club-root disease of cabbages, the weevil that attacks the foliage of peas and beans, and the special maladies of the tomatoes and potatoes.

Special Family Needs

For gardening purposes it is convenient to classify vegetables according to the portion of it that we generally eat; e.g. Brassicas (cabbage, cauliflowers, etc.); root crops (carrots, parsnips, beets, etc); legumes or pulses (peas and beans); tubers (potatoes and Jerusalem artichokes); salads; and bulb crops (onions, shallots, leeks). In order to avoid constant repetition in the following cultural notes, I give here, for some of these groups, some general notes which must be followed for all members of their families.

BRASSICAS

For spring plantings, dig the ground deeply in autumn. Early digging allows the soil to settle, and it is essential for all Brassicas to have a firm, well-consolidated bed. The ground should have been dressed in the previous or current year with manure or other organic food. It should contain ample lime. Before planting out, the rows should be well trodden down by foot, but the top inch or two hoed to prevent caking. Finally the seedlings should be *firmly* planted. Where greens are put out at times other than the spring the same rules apply—a deep bed rich in nitrogen, dug well ahead of planting-out time, a firm, consolidated bed, the presence of available lime, firm planting.

Brassicas are usually sown in a nursery seed-bed and pricked off. Sow sparsely, and, if the permanent quarters are not ready, prick off into a nursery bed 6 in. apart as early as possible, otherwise the seedlings will be leggy and weak. If planting out has to be done in dry weather, 'puddle' the roots in a thickish mixture of clay and water. Pick off any leaves that turn yellow in autumn and consign at once to the compost bin.

331

About the beginning of November earth up the stalks of winter-standing greens several inches, except the cauliflower type of broccoli.

Dress all seed-beds with Growmore a few days before sowing. After transplanting give each plant $\frac{1}{4}$ oz., and repeat a month later. Moreover, though I generally avoid particularist advice, Brassicas do benefit tremendously from $\frac{1}{4}$ oz. of nitrochalk per square yard once or twice when the plants have been growing-on strongly for two months or so; but don't use it on broccoli or kale.

Root Crops

These prefer a light or medium soil, reasonably stone-free. Heavy soils should be lightened with sand. Root crops must *not* be sown in ground recently manured; this causes the roots to split into distorted fangs. Therefore use a piece of ground which was manured for a *previous* crop; e.g. leeks or Brassicas, which they may follow. Beetroot, however, will benefit from a special manuring with seaweed (being a seaside native), deeply dug in. Do not neglect, however, to treat the seed-rows with Growmore before sowing; give another dressing at 1 oz. per 6-ft run after thinning, and repeat a month later.

Root crops are almost invariably sown *in situ*, as they do not transplant, and the easiest method is to sow at stations. Parsnip seed does not germinate well, and should accordingly be sown fairly thickly. For carrots and beets you can sow at half-stations, pulling every other one for the table when small and tender.

After picking for current use, those crops which cannot stay in the ground all winter are lifted and stored before the frosts. Lift with a fork carefully so as not to cause damage, especially beetroot. Clean off clods of earth. Store in a frost-proof place between layers of slightly damped sand. Do not store any diseased, damaged or pest-bitten plants.

Legumes

Peas and beans have long roots, and therefore need deeply dug soil. They are also greedy feeders, and so need plenty of

Sowing—

Peas

Beans

Parsnips or Carrots
in Heavy Soil

Planting Celery in
Trench Spinach on ridges

Celery earthed-up
(Single Row)

Next
row

Planting a Leek

Onion - right

Onion - wrong

→ N

Heeling Broccoli over to the North

VEGETABLES: Sowing, planting, etc.

organic manure, and should have the first feed of it, for preference, before the Brassicas, for which, moreover, they will supply the nitrogen Brassicas need so much. They also like lime. They are potash eaters, and should have abundant wood ash dug into the soil. Treat the rows with Growmore before sowing, and dress with it again at 2 oz per 6-ft run when the plants are well away.

Legumes are generally sown direct *in situ*, and usually in broad drills made by the draw-hoe or spade. In these broad drills the seed is sown staggered in a double row, thus: . · . · . · Distances vary, but don't crowd them. Water thoroughly in dry seasons. Weekly feeds of liquid manure greatly improve crops. Mulch with lawn mowings, stable manure, etc., after a good rain or watering.

When a crop of peas or beans is finished, cut off the stems at ground level, but leave the roots with their present of nitrogen for the next crop. The tops, or haulms, are valuable for the compost if cut up and moistened.

Rotation of Crops

It is a general agricultural rule over all the instructed world that the same crop, or one too nearly related to it in genus, must not continually be planted in the same piece of ground. Expressed in simple terms, the main reason is that one genus of plants takes out of the soil more of one of its constituent qualities than another. Another reason is that continued cultivation of one crop on the same piece of ground encourages the pests and diseases particular to that crop. It is from neglect of these principles that so many allotments today are riddled with club-root through over-planting of Brassicas. For some odd reason, onions seem to be an exception to what is a general rule, and many old gardeners, having found a spot that onions like, grow onions there always.

Some method of crop rotation also saves the gardener labour, in that he digs in manure only in those parts needed, year by year; and the same with lime. These workings of the soil may indeed be called 'soil rotations', to be matched to crop rotations. Thus it may be taken as a useful rule of thumb that in any one season you manure only those plots needed for potatoes, legumes, celery, and bulb crops. These crops are followed by the Brassica family, which specially like the nitrogen left in the soil by the roots of legumes, and the Brassicas are then followed by root crops, which need no manure.

Crop rotation is a scientific subject, but all that the small gardener need concern himself with is the general principle of sowing each kind of crop in a different part of the garden each year, and a rotation on the broad lines of the previous paragraph will do well. For this purpose the ground should be divided up into approximately equal portions, either three or four.

Lay-out

The site of the kitchen garden should be in full sun as far as possible, though some shade is valuable for summer lettuce, turnips, and mint.

Ease of working is the next consideration. All plots should be rectangular, or some other straight-edged shape. Avoid a lot of fussy little beds. Paths should be laid out on strictly utilitarian lines, going from A to B directly in a straight line.

Then broadly apportion the uses of each part of the garden. The most precious site—the wall or fence facing south—will be for tomatoes and the more tender fruits. Next site the permanent crops—those that do not have to be sown every year, such as rhubarb, seakale, asparagus, Jerusalem artichokes if you grow them. Rhubarb, being a tough fellow, can go in an east border, artichokes in the coldest NE corner; but asparagus must have full sun in the centre. So also must strawberries if grown, for, though a fruit, they are best fitted into the vegetable rotations. Spinach sowings can alternate between sun and shade. Scarlet runners, if you like, can climb a fence or trellis at the sides, somewhere in the sun. The rest of the central space can be apportioned as you like for easy management on broad rotational principles in three or four roughly equal plots.

Remember a little space for the herbs, and site them if possible close to the kitchen; but all must be in full sun, though mint does not mind some shade.

It will be seen, therefore, that a certain amount of fore-thought and management is needed to get good results out of a small space. Work out well in advance what is to follow early potatoes and peas when they are lifted, what space shall be reserved for celery trenches and what for marrows, where you will work in your successional sowings of lettuces and peas, what you will be able to pop in as inter-crops and catch-crops. If some such general planning is not done ahead, you are likely to find either that large pieces of ground are lying idle for long periods, or that you have got masses of seedlings on your hands for which you have no room.

Frames and Cloches

A greenhouse enables you to raise from seed plants you would otherwise have to buy, and to grow tomatoes with suc-cess; and a frame is also a good stand-by for many jobs, such as over-wintering young onions and lettuce. But the great thing in the vegetable garden is the cloche (*see* Chapter IX). Even a very few are a godsend. Cloche gardening is now a specialised subject, but the apprentice may employ them in general terms to ensure the success of early spring sowings and to prolong the growing season into the autumn, especially for early and late lettuces, peas, sweet corn, French beans, and so on.

Selections

I propose to give only a very few, being the one or two generally found to be the best. It is always sound to take the local advice of an old hand. Too many nurserymen have the exasperating habit of giving their own fancy name to a variety that scarcely differs from the standard; but as a rule good catalogues will give, if not exactly the names used, some-thing recognisable as the same.

¶ *In reading the cultural Notes that follow, remember in each case to refer to the 'Special Family Needs' for all Brassicas, Legumes, and Roots in pages 331–4.*

NOTE.—Sowing times are given as for the South and Midlands; for Northern gardens times should generally be some three weeks later for spring sowings and three weeks earlier for autumn sowings. All timings given are subject to conditions of weather and soil. Depth of sowings are as for medium loam. Sow a fraction deeper on light, sandy soils, less deeply on heavy clays.

Artichoke. There are the Jerusalem and the Globe. The former is the tuber resembling a deformed potato considered by a few misguided people to be edible. If you really do like these things, they come in usefully in a cold NE corner, when their tall growth (they are Sunflowers) will hide an unsightly spot. Plant 6 in. deep and 15 in. apart. Lift the tubers as required.

The Globe or true artichoke, which you nibble delicately in expensive restaurants, is part of the floral adornment of a large ornamental plant; not suitable for small gardens.

Asparagus. In a garden of half an acre, room can be spared for this special delight, but 100 plants is about the minimum to give you a good feast. It is perennial and lasts many years. It prefers a light soil, and cold, ill-drained clays are useless.

Trench deeply and dress lavishly with well-decayed manure or compost. Make built-up beds, 4 ft wide and about 9 in. high, using the top spit between each pair of beds for the building-up; the space between each bed constitutes a path, say, 18 in. wide. Buy three-year-old plants for preference, and have the beds ready in good time. Insist on male plants. Plant the crowns (early April) quickly the moment they arrive in three rows 15 in. apart and 15 in. between plants in the row. Make holes of ample size, shape the soil into a ridge or saddle, and plant the spidery roots astride it, with the crown at least 4 in. below the surface. The part you eat is a young stem shooting up from the soil. Take nothing from two-year-old plants till the second season after planting, but a light cutting may be taken from the three-year-olds the year next after planting. Cut the shoots when about 3–4 in. above ground about the end of April; use a sharp knife and cut just below the surface. Don't cut after mid-June, but leave the remaining shoots to develop. Cut these down when they turn yellow in autumn. Dress the beds in January or February with seaweed if you can get it, or with manure or compost early in March. Rake the beds clean in autumn and spring, but never dig them, nor the paths between.

The standard variety in this country is Connover's Colossal.

Bean, Broad (Legume). In all except the coldest counties it is most profitable to sow in October, leaving the plants to stand through the winter for an early crop. Other sowings can be made in January and again in April. Sow 3 in. deep in double ranks, 6 in. apart and 9 in. between ranks, with a space of 3 ft to the next double row. A position sheltered from winds is best, to avoid staking. Earth-up autumn sowings about 6 in.

When nearing maximum height pinch out the tips of the plants to make them less attractive to blackfly; the right moment is when the lowest flowers have begun to set into pods. If any fly appears, attack at once, preferably with derris. If fly is really bad in your district, give up growing broad beans.

Varieties. Try the excellent dwarf varieties The Midget or Sutton's Dwarf, 1 ft high, noted for being hardy and fast; good for autumn sowing or any time up till July. Of the taller types, sow a white-seeded Longpod in autumn or winter, and a green-seeded Windsor in spring.

Bean, Flageolet (Legume). These delicious beans, very popular in France but almost unknown here, are eaten in the green stage, shelled, just like peas. Culture is easy and exactly as for Dwarf French Beans. Pick when the beans within the pod are swollen but the pods still green.

Varieties. Roi des Verts or Chevrier Vert.

Bean, French or **Kidney** (Legume). Nothing else gives such good returns for a small space as this delectable and easily grown dwarf bean. Sow outdoors in full sun in mid-May, in drills 2 in. deep, 4 in. between seeds, 2 ft between rows. Thin to 8 in. apart in the rows. Pick early and pick often. Make successional sowings in the third week of May and the first or second week of June.

Varieties. The Prince, Phœnix Claudia, and Golden Butter.

Bean, Haricot (Legume). Is simply a French bean, of which certain varieties have been specially developed for drying for winter use, though they can also be eaten green. Sow early in May and treat exactly as for the ordinary Frenchman, except as to harvesting. Leave the pods on the plant till they turn brown, then pull up the plants whole, tie them into loose bundles, and hang them up in a dry, airy shed until the pods are ready to be shelled, which is when they come away easily with a light twist. Then spread out the shelled beans on a clean paper to complete drying. If ripening is late for any reason, cover with cloches late August or pull the plants while still green and they will ripen in the shed. Harvesting must take place before frost, say, end of September.

Varieties. Contesse de Chambord or Brown Dutch.

Bean, Scarlet Runner (Legume). Following normal amateur practice, sow 3 in. deep in May in double rows, 9 in. between seeds, and 6 ft from the next double row. Plant tall bean poles, 7–8 ft long in two rows 18 in. apart, up which the plants will climb. *Pick while small and tender*. Further sowings can be made fortnightly till late June.

Varieties. Prizewinner or Scarlet Emperor. The rarer Blue Coco, however, has even better table qualities—tender, velvety, and stringless if picked young.

Beetroot (Root). An easy vegetable but required by the family only in small quantities. Omit from very small gardens, and buy the few needed from the shops, ready cooked.

If convenient, use ground that was manured the previous season. Sow mid-April onwards in permanent quarters in drills or at stations 1 in. deep and in rows 1 ft apart. Thin out to 8 in. apart in the row. For current use, make limited sowings only, and make successional sowings every three weeks up till the end of June. For winter storage, make a maincrop sowing in June or late May.

Lift for the table as required, using great care not to break or bruise either the skin or the roots, else the beet will 'bleed'. For the same reason use care when hoeing—merely shave the surface. For storage, lift before frost; twist off the leaves (do not *cut*) 2 or 3 in. above the crown, using two hands.

Varieties. For summer use Crimson Globe; for storing, Cheltenham Green Top (does not bleed).

Borecole. *See* Kale.

Broccoli (Brassica). There are two groups: the sprouting, and the cauliflower-headed. Both very hardy, especially the former. Better than cauliflower for the amateur, and do well on heavy soils. Stand outdoors all winter in the South and favoured districts elsewhere, and there are varieties which provide fare for autumn, winter, and spring. The sprouting types—purple-sprouting and white-sprouting—throw out a lot of small shoots, tender and rich in vitamins.

Sow seed for all types late April. Plant out finally into permanent beds from late May to July—2 ft apart for the cauliflower types and 6 in. more for the sprouters. When frosts are likely to become hard, snap a couple of the large leaves over the heads of the cauliflower sorts for protection, and in November heel them over to the north—loosen with a fork, push the plant well over, gently, take out a shallow trench on the north and heap the soil over the disturbed roots on the south side.

Cauliflower Varieties. For autumn, Veitch's Self-protecting, which protects its own head; for winter, Snow's Winter White; for spring, Late Queen and Methven's June.

Sprouting Varieties. Calabrese, or Green Sprouting (after taking the central head pick the delicious side shoots before they flower and treat like asparagus) for late summer and autumn, a most desirable vegetable; for winter the very hardy Purple Sprouting.

Brussels Sprouts (Brassica). Sow towards the end of March. Plant seedlings into permanent quarters firmly and as deep as the first pair of leaves, a good 2 ft apart and the same between rows; a little less for dwarfs. When ready, gather the sprouts from the bottom upwards. When the stalk is cleared, the tuft of leaves at the top—known as 'Brussels tops' —makes excellent eating.

Varieties. Local advice is most important. Subject thereto, use—Dwarf Gem, Jade Cross (F₁ hybrid), Fillbasket; Early Button for the small, French–style sprout.

Cabbage (Brassica). The numerous varieties available will provide cabbages nearly all the year round if wanted.

Sow in March or April for summer and autumn sorts; late April for winter sorts, including Savoys; and at the end of July in Northern gardens and early August in Southern gardens for spring cabbage the following year. Spring varieties are liable to bolt if sown too early.

Planting distances depend on the ultimate size of the plants, but in general put them 2 ft each way; where space is limited, they may be put closer, and every alternate one cut for use as required. Take precautions against cabbage-root fly, club-root, the caterpillar of the 'cabbage-white' butterfly, etc. (Chapter XXIII). Where there are wood-pigeons the cabbages will be ruined unless protected by nets.

Varieties. The following are the pick of a very large range. For summer: Velocity. For autumn: Greyhound (18-in. spacing only). For winter: Christmas Drumhead, January King, and all the 'Savoys' (especially the dwarf varieties for small places). For spring: Flower of Spring.

Carrots (Root). The proper way to grow carrots is to make small sowings every three or four weeks from the end of March till July. In this way there will be a constant supply of tender young roots. For winter storage a maincrop variety is sown in early June.

Sow direct into permanent quarters, preferably at stations or half-stations, in dry weather on a surface reduced to a fine tilth; sow only ¼ in. deep in rows 9 in. apart. Thin out as necessary. Final distances apart should be from 4 to 8 in., according to variety. Beware the carrot-fly. Apply gamma-BHC, before sowing; do any thinning out and pulling when the soil is moist if possible and firm the soil afterwards, or else water the soil well; do not leave any thinnings lying about.

Soils that are on the heavy side should be lightened by liberal dressings of sand and wood ash. On very heavy or stony soils, make a wide-mouthed hole 10 in. deep with a long dibber, fill up with prepared sifted soil gently rammed in, sow two or three seeds at each station, and when they germinate thin out to one strong seedling.

Varieties. Early Nantes for successional use in summer; St Valery; James's Intermediate for winter storage (sow early June).

Cauliflower (Brassica). Not advised. The true cauliflowers are not hardy, need a very rich soil, are quite unsuitable for dry soils and hot summers, and tend to ripen all together, so that there is a sudden glut and then no more. Cauliflower-headed broccoli is to be preferred. If grown, get a couple of dozen seedlings from a good nurseryman in May, or sow the variety All the Year Round outdoors under cloches, making three or four sowings at about ten-day intervals from mid-March, and plant out in May 2 ft apart, 2½ ft between rows. A lavishly manured soil is needed, and fertiliser ten days after planting out.

Celeriac. Very useful for soils that are too hot and dry for celery. Is a bulbous root plant, closely resembling celery in flavour. Good for soups, or grated or sliced for salads, or boiled like beetroot. The leaves, if hung upside down and dried, are good in stews and soups. Raise seed exactly as for celery, but plant out late May into a heavily-manured flat bed, not a trench. No earthing-up. Space 1 ft apart and 18 in. between rows.

Variety. Globus (Dobie's).

Celery. It is not much use attempting to grow good celery unless you give it rich, deeply-dug, heavily-manured soil, and take a bit of trouble over it. Seed is best raised in heat, but in mild districts can be sown very shallow under cloches or in a frame in March; or young plants can be bought from a nurseryman.

Dig a trench in late winter about 18 in. deep, taking out all the soil and breaking up the bottom with a fork, and leave it open for some weeks for the elements to work on it. On heavy soils something shallower suits. For a single row of plants the trench should be 15 in. wide, for a double row 18 in. Throw the soil out on each side and spread it out as a flat raised bed between each pair of trenches; on this bed can be grown 'inter-

Sprouting a Spud.

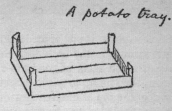

A potato tray.

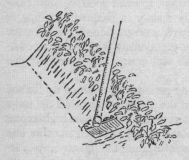

Earthing - up
Potatoes.

marrow.   Cucumber.

Female flowers

Marrow.   Cucumber.

Males.

Potatoes, Marrows, Cucumbers.

343

crops' of lettuce, summer spinach, radishes, etc., before the soil is used for the subsequent earthing up. Trenches should be 3 ft apart.

Before planting out, spread a thick layer, 6 in. deep, of farm-yard manure in the bottom of the trench, mix it with about half as much again of good top-spit soil, and tread it lightly down; then fill up to within about 3 in. (or, say, 6 in. on light soils) of the top of the trench with good friable top soil. Plant out the seedlings late May or early June, 10 in. apart. If in a double row, plant side by side, not staggered. Water in each plant as you go, or give the whole trench a good soaking. Subsequent cultivation consists mainly in frequent flooding of the trench in dry weather; removal of side-shoots from the base of the plant; spraying occasionally with Volck or dusting weekly and lightly with soot against the celery fly; and blanching.

To blanch. This is done by periodically earthing up the soil on to the plant. Do it when the plants are dry, but the soil a little moist and crumbly. Start when they are 6 in. high, repeat at 1 ft and finally at 18 in. Rake the soil between trenches into a fine, crumbly tilth. Remove from the plants any side-shoots, suckers, and small outer leaves. Hold each plant bunched up with one hand, and with the other draw the soil up loosely round the plant, taking care that no soil trickles down into the heart of the plant you are holding. Repeat at least twice at fortnightly intervals. Finally, tie up the topknot of leaves and give a *gentle* patting with the spade (never beat it hard) to the now steep sides of the ridge, to help shed winter rain. Give a dusting of lime at each earthing up. The practice of using paper collars for blanching does not give as good results as earthing up, nor is the 'self-blanching' celery as good as the usual sorts.

Varieties. The red and pink sorts are hardier and easier than the white, and dwarf varieties are much better than mammoths. E.g. Webb's Perfection Pink, or Sandringham Dwarf White.

Chives (Herb). Of the onion family, producing tufts of neat foliage which is of mild flavour and excellent for omelettes, soups, and stews. Buy a dozen or so bulbs from the nurseryman. Plant out about 6 in. apart, and use as an edging. The leaves are snipped off with scissors or shears as required. Lift, divide, and replant the clumps every three or four years in autumn or spring. They multiply rapidly.

Courgettes are simply immature marrows. A variety favoured by some is Zucchini, but English marrows are tastier.

Cucumber. Another vegetable that can be omitted with little loss. One wants only one at a time, and the greengrocer will oblige. However, for those who like to grow their own, the 'ridge' or prickly type of cucumber is quite easy. A few young plants may be bought for putting out the first week in June, or the seed may be raised as for marrows at the end of April. Prepare the bed also as for marrows in full sun, but a low mound or flat-topped ridge is an advantage in colder places. Plant out the seedlings 2 ft 6 in. apart. When about seven leaves have formed, nip out the tops of the plants. Later all shoots which form may also be so stopped if desired after one fruit has formed on each. Water abundantly, give liquid manure every week after the first fruits are 3 in. long, and mulch with lawn mowings, etc. Cut as soon as fruits are of usable size, and keep on cutting.

Varieties. Stockwood Ridge or King of the Ridge.

Endive. A valuable winter salading much neglected in this country. There are two sorts—the Batavian, with broadish leaves rather like cos lettuce, and the 'mossy' or curly, with lacy leaves. Any soil in good heart and well tilled should do. Sow $\frac{1}{2}$ in. deep in late May in the nursery seed-bed, and transplant 9 in. apart and 1 ft between rows; or sow *in situ* and thin out. Germination is slow. Where there is room, make successional sowings at monthly intervals till August.

The plants have to be blanched, being otherwise too bitter. The usual method is to cover them with an inverted soup plate when about three-quarters grown. Leaves of the Batavian should be tied up while dry, like cos.

Varieties. Green Curled and Batavian.

Flageolet. *See under* Beans.

Haricot. *See under* Beans.

Horse Radish. Simple enough to grow, but seldom grown well. Straight thick roots are to be aimed at, not thin and fangy ones. The roots go a long way down, so dig very deep and give what soil food you can spare, especially in lower spits. It is really best to build up a mound, about 2 ft high. Buy or cadge some thick roots about 6 in. long in March, make a very deep hole with a dibber, and plant the roots with their crowns 5 in. below surface. In November lift the whole of the crop and store in sand, etc. Some will be used in the house and some kept for planting out again next March.

Kale (Brassica). Also called Borecole. Very easily grown in poor soils, kale is a winter vegetable and one of the very hardiest. Good for very cold places and of high nutritional value. For a maincrop sow late April in the seed-bed, rather thin and shallow. Except for the dwarf sort, transplant a good 2 ft apart, and $2\frac{1}{2}$ ft between rows. Avoid nitrogenous fertilisers. On Scotch kale the leaves are eaten; on others, after the top has been used, side-shoots sprout from the stem, and these should be eaten while young and tender

Varieties. The best are—Extra Curled Scotch, of which you eat the top. Asparagus Kale has tasty side-shoots in spring to be cooked as asparagus. Hungry Gap Kale, cropped in April and May, should be sown *in situ* in June.

Kohl Rabi. This rather queer-looking vegetable is a cabbage with a bulbous stem, turnip-flavoured, and a useful substitute for turnips in very dry soils. The secret is to eat it when it is no bigger than a tennis-ball, when it is tender. Sow in April in rows 2 ft apart, and thin to 1 ft apart in the rows. Early White is perhaps the best variety.

Leek. Member of the onion family, very hardy and subject to few diseases. One of the best winter vegetables. Southern gardeners are backward in its cultivation as compared with Northerners and Scotsmen.

The tastiest leeks are small ones, not whoppers. Even so, they are greedy, and you must dig quantities of manure deep into the soil; they also like bonemeal. There are many ways of growing them. The simplest is to treat them just like onions, sowing *in situ* in very shallow drills and thinning to a few inches apart, without any earthing up. The eating results are excellent. The next easiest, and most usual, is this: About 1st April sow seed very sparsely in a nursery bed. About 1st June make holes 6 in. deep and 2 in. wide and 8 in. apart in the permanent bed with a blunt dibber, drop in the nurseling plant and fill the hole with water—that is all. Don't firm the plant; as it grows it swells to fill up the hole and is automatically blanched.

The only other point is to snip an inch or two off the tips of the longest leaves from time to time.

Varieties. Giant Musselburgh and The Lyon.

Lettuce. Though very long-suffering, lettuces benefit enormously from a little manure or compost, not only as food but also as a check to their bolting to seed in hot weather. The way to grow them is to sow very small quantities of seed in succession at about three-week intervals, being careful to choose a variety suitable to the season. Even without heat they can be grown over a very long period.

Start early March with May Queen (or May King), or in February under cloches. For the main season summer crops, begin early April with Sutton's Unrivalled or Trocadero, or, if you prefer a cos lettuce, Lobjoit's Green (no tying up). Cloches hasten all early sowings. In August change to May Queen for autumn use. In October sow May Queen again, under cloches. In most districts Imperial and Arctic King can also be sown in October in the open to overwinter and mature in early spring. If you want to stick to one variety only for spring, summer, and early autumn cutting, use All the Year Round. The 'crisphead' lettuces, such as Webb's Wonderful, need hot weather.

Make the sowings of earliest spring and those after June at stations *in situ*; those of the main season in tiny drills (a foot long is quite enough) and transplant. Transplant the moment three or four leaves show. Do not plant too deeply. When grown under cloches, watch for fungal diseases; ventilate freely and don't over-water. Normal spacing is 10 in., but 8 in. for autumn sowings and for dwarfs. A splendid little dwarf for continuous spring and summer sowings is Tom Thumb—

good for small spaces, and for growing on the ridges between celery.

In prolonged dry summer spells water lettuces copiously, but not at other seasons.

Marrow. Only three or four are needed by the average family. Buy seedlings from a nurseryman the first week of June, or sow seed (on edge) singly in small pots in mid-April in the greenhouse or frame and plant out in June; they are not hardy.

Choosing a sunny position, dig a trench in May two spits deep and 18 in. wide, and enrich the soil with lavish quantities of animal or hop manure or compost, and with lawn mowings or other vegetable matter. Build a low ridge round the bed so that it can be flooded. Don't grow marrows on a mound.

Plant out a yard apart. Water copiously at all stages. On the trailing sorts nip off the tip of the main shoot before it is 3 ft long; nip off the resultant side-shoots also at seven leaves if too rampant. Fertilise each female flower (recognisable by a bulbous swelling at the base) by stripping a male blossom of its petals and thrusting the pollen-bearing core into the female. Don't attempt to grow large marrows. Small ones are far more succulent. Cut them when about 6 in. long, cook whole, and keep on cutting. These are 'courgettes'. Use no chemical fertiliser. The best variety is Table Dainty. Bush marrows are less satisfactory than runners.

Mint (Herb). A few roots will suffice. Spreads rapidly, and invades other crops unless planted in an isolated bed. Prospers in sun or partial shade, but should not lack moisture. Plant roots in March or autumn $1\frac{1}{2}$ in. deep. Pick leaves as required. For winter use dry off the stalks (well spread out) in an airy, dry, warmish place. When dry, strip off the leaves, powder through a sieve and store in an air-tight bottle.

Mint rust (tiny orange spores) is a great nuisance. If it appears, pluck out the whole stem from the ground and burn. In October lay straw on the ground and burn off the whole crop; the roots will sprout afresh.

The most commonly grown type is spearmint, but by epicures the apple-mint (mentha rotundifolia) is much more valued; for herb fans there are several other mints.

Mushroom. These are outside the scope of this small book. It would be a disservice to pretend that mushrooms are easy; they are very much a specialist's job. If you do want to have a go, get a proprietary mushroom compost, such as Stoner's, and follow directions. Don't attempt to grow them in manure.

Onion. This is is not really an easy vegetable. Experienced people sometimes fail, but the onion is far too valuable to omit. It needs plenty of hot sun, a light, rich, preferably alluvial soil, and a really firm bed. Undoubtedly the easiest way to grow them nowadays is from 'sets', which are tiny bulbs raised under crowded conditions. A pound (at about 4s.) is enough for a small family.

Bastard-trench and thoroughly manure the soil in November to ensure settlement and consolidation. In March make a seed-bed which is very firm, but with a fine tilth by repeated treading and raking in dry weather. Work in wood ashes, bonemeal and soot. Plant the bulblets at 6-in. spacing, in rows 12–15 in. apart, by pressing them into the soil so that their tips just show and watch for any that jump out.

In August bend the stalks down to the ground, towards the north, to hasten ripening. Harvest in September by lifting the bulbs with a fork and leaving them on the ground a few days to dry in the sun (under glass if wet) before roping and storing. Use early any with thick, soft necks.

By seed. Sow when the soil is dry in early March very sparsely in drills only $\frac{1}{4}$ in. deep. Thin out finally to 6 in. apart, using the thinnings as 'spring onions'. Dust with BHC dust, and after thinning and weeding firm the soil to discourage the onion fly (*see* Chapter XXIII). Don't leave any thinnings lying about. The fly does not attack sets. Snap off any seed-heads that form.

In the North it is often preferred to sow in boxes in the greenhouse or frame, or under cloches, and to plant out seedlings rather late in April. Plant very firmly but *not* deeply—the soil level should come only half-way up the little bulb.

Tree Onions bear a cluster of small bulbs at the top of the stem; good for pickling or general use. Give good treatment, and plant the mother bulbs in rows 18 in. apart. The basal bulb can also be eaten.

Varieties. For amateur main crop use James's Long Keeping or Bedfordshire Champion. For pickling, Pearl Pickler or Silverskin; no manure or other food for picklers.

Parsley (Herb). Sow as an edging and give it good, fine soil. Sow very sparsely $\frac{1}{4}$ in. deep and thin to 5 in. apart. Slow in germination. Don't sow a lot at a time, but thinnings may be transplanted. In most districts stands the winter but in others cloches are needed. Champion Moss Curled is an old favourite. Lack of lime often causes failure; so do root aphis (p. 371).

Parsnip (Root). Sow very early—in February in the South if the ground allows—in drills 15 in. apart. Sow fairly thickly, as the seed is uncertain (and slow) in germination. Thin out to 9 in. apart. There are few troubles with parsnips. They can be left in the ground all winter and lifted as wanted. On hard, heavy, and stony soils it is necessary to make holes 2 ft deep with a crowbar, fill with fine soil, sow two or three seeds in each and thin out when necessary.

Varieties. The Student and Tender and True.

Pea (Legume). Peas like bonemeal, a dressing with an all-round fertiliser, just before sowing, and a soil with lime in it. Sow in two staggered rows 3 in. apart in a broad drill 2 in. deep made with a draw hoe or spade. Distances between rows of dwarf varieties should be 2 ft or more, and for taller sorts the distance should be the same as the height of the variety. To protect against mice or birds dip seeds in a mixture of paraffin and red lead before sowing—it often works. Before the seedlings show their noses protect against birds with wire netting pea-guards or a few tripwires of black thread strained between sticks, though later on pigeons will strip all the pods. Except for the dwarf sorts, plant pea-sticks generously when seedlings are about 5 in. high. Guard against mildew and thrip.

The following is a good programme for successful sowings: Early March, sow an early variety. Early April, another sowing of earlies, and first sowing of maincrop. End April, second sowing of maincrop. End May, final sowing of maincrop. End June, sow an early variety for September cropping.

Varieties. Of ordinary peas there is a bewildering multitude. Note that the round-seeded varieties are the more hardy, but that the wrinkled seeds are the sweet and delicious marrowfats. These are my pick: Early dwarfs—Kelvedon Wonder and Little Marvel, both quite outstanding; Meteor for cold districts. Early maincrop—Alderman or Giant Stride. Maincrop—Onward or Alderman. All are marrowfats except Meteor.

I commend also the Mangetout or sugar pea. You pick them young, before the peas have swollen in the pod, top and tail the pods and boil whole, serving with a spot of melted butter. They need staking.

Potato. Order 'seed potatoes' early and from first-rate suppliers only, preferably from Scotland or Ireland, for delivery January or February. In districts where the wart disease is prevalent you are bound by law to grow only those varieties certified as 'immune'.

Unpack immediately on arrival and stack in shallow boxes or trays in a light, frost-proof place, such as a brick garage or light attic. Stand them with their 'eyes', or 'rose' end, upwards—the end opposite to the little scar where the potato was attached to its root. This will induce early sprouting. Only two shoots are wanted at the rose end, but if others appear elsewhere the tuber can be cut in two at planting time and each part planted separately. Rub out excess sprouts.

Dig the soil at least 10 in. deep in autumn, laying in manure at one full barrow load per 10 sq yd and adding bonemeal to the top spit. Do not lime unless the ground is definitely sour, and if so, not till early spring. Weather permitting, plant the early varieties any time after mid-March, maincrop a month later. Allow 2 ft between rows for early varieties, 28 in. for second earlies, and a good 2 ft 6 in. for maincrops. Dress with National Growmore at 3 oz per 10 ft a few days before planting. Plant in drills at least 5 in. deep made with a spade at these distances apart—10 in. between earlies, 12 in. for second

351

earlies, and 15 in. maincrop. Some people spread a layer of lawn mowings on the bottom of the trench before planting. Alternatively, instead of drawing a deep drill, plant with a trowel, ensuring there is no air pocket beneath the spud.

As soon as the first leaves show, cover them with straw or bracken against frost, or draw some soil lightly over them progressively, allowing a wee tuft of leaves to see daylight. When the haulms are 8 in. high, begin the process of 'earthing up', the main purpose of which is to prevent the potatoes from coming to the surface and turning green and bitter. You do this by straddling the rows and drawing the soil between the rows up to the plant with a draw-hoe, so that a trench appears between each row. Earth up again three weeks later. Carry the soil up to the lowest leaves, leaving not less than 6 in. of foliage above soil level, and making the ridge broad, not pointed. Give a second dressing of Growmore at $2\frac{1}{2}$ oz per 10-ft run at the first earthing.

Spraying, with Bordeaux Mixture or an equivalent, is a most desirable preventive measure against potato blight. In the SW, spray at the end of June, in the South the first week of July, in the Midlands and East the second week of July, in the North and West at the end of July.

The earlies can be lifted for the table as wanted when adequately grown, say in July when the blossom is over. Use a broad-tined potato-fork. Others, to ensure full maturity, should be left till the haulms have died down, and then lifted and stored. Dig up on a dry day and leave the tubers on the ground for a few hours to dry. Big crops go into an outdoor clamp, but for small gardens storage can be done in any shed, attic, or cellar that is dry, cool but frost-proof and dark. Clean off any clods of earth and spread the potatoes out loosely. They may also be put into sacks. Look them over occasionally for signs of disease. If saving one's own potatoes for next year's seed choose the medium-sized ones, not the large.

Varieties. Of the innumerable varieties the following is my pick for flavour, always subject to local advice: Earlies— Arran Pilot, Sharpe's Express, Duke of York, Epicure. Second Earlies—Great Scot, Arran Banner, Redskin (very

Tomatoes.

Remove Axillary Shoots —

But not this growing tips.

A watering dodge.

Asparagus

Path

Path

Note the "saddles"

What they look like—

Kohl-rabi.

Celeriac

Salsify.

Top: Pinching and watering Tomatoes. *Centre:* Planting Asparagus.
Bottom: A gallery of oddments.

dry and floury, popular in Scotland). Maincrop—Kerr's Pink, Majestic, Arran Victory (floury), King Edward. For epicurean palates—Golden Wonder (rich soil, small crop).

Radish. Choose a patch in partial shade that was well manured for previous crops. Add some leaf-mould and hoe to a very fine tilth. Broadcast a pinch or two of seeds, very sparsely indeed, and cover with a sprinkling of fine soil Thin to 3 in. apart. Use when young and tender. Ample moisture is needed. For a continuous supply, sow at fortnightly intervals from early March till July. Use the plain 'French Breakfast', without any prefix.

Rhubarb. Can be grown on most soils, but to produce big juicy stems should have deeply-dug, well-drained, and manured soil. Is a perennial.

Buy unforced crown from a nurseryman—only a few are wanted—and plant out in March a good 3 ft apart, with the tops barely covered. Plant firmly and dress with basic slag at 6 oz per square yard. Do not pick stalks at all the first year, and very few the second. Picking can start April but must stop at midsummer. The stalks should always be *pulled* when gathering. If any flower stalks form, break off at ground level.

To Force. The simplest method is to put a box or tub over the crown in December, and encase it with strawy manure and leaves to generate heat. Don't attempt to force young plants, nor weakly ones. The best variety is Champagne.

Sage (Herb). Buy one or two plants, specifying broad-leafed sage, and plant out 18 in. apart. When established, one good plant is enough, and it is decorative enough to go anywhere.

Salsify (Root). A hardy root vegetable, with very distinctive flavour which many enjoy but others don't. Pronounce the y as in 'Rugby'. Dress with an all-purposes fertiliser before sowing. Sow late April $\frac{1}{2}$ in. deep in rows 12 in. apart; or in heavyish soils make a 10-in.-deep hole as for carrots or parsnips. Thin to 10 in. apart. Hoe and lift carefully, for, if damaged, they 'bleed' like beetroot. Roots become usable late October. Lift as required, and the remainder can stay in the ground. It is not my business to tell you how to cook them.

If left till spring they throw up flowering shoots called 'chards'. Cut these when 5–6 in. long and eat them like asparagus.

Scorzonera is a similar vegetable, but not quite so good.

Savoy. *See* Cabbage.

Scarlet Runners. *See under* Beans.

Shallots. Will succeed in almost any soil, but do best in a firm bed on an old manured plot. Buy a few dozen bulbs (small ones are best) and plant them just before Christmas in the South, early March in the North. Space 8 in. apart with 12 in. between rows. Plant the bulb with one-third of it above soil level. From each bulb will grow a cluster of new ones. When the leaves wither at the end of June, lift the clusters in dry weather, break them up, dry them outdoors or in an airy shed, and store in a cool, dry place. Keep a few for next year's planting.

Varieties. The old 'true' red and yellow shallots are better than the Russian, Dutch, etc.

Spinach. Of the several breeds of spinach, I shall deal only with the annual summer round-seeded, the winter prickly-seeded, and the 'perpetual' or beet spinach, which is the least trouble and the most useful. All are sown *in situ*.

Summer Spinach. Very ephemeral, but succulent. Sow early March 1 in. deep in drills 1 ft apart. Thin to 4 in. between plants. Make additional sowings every three weeks up till June, the later sowings in partial shade. Use the variety Long Standing Round. You need to sow a lot to make Summer Spinach worth-while, but it makes a good catch-crop, and you pick a whole row at a time.

Winter Spinach. Sow from August to September in sun in drills 1 in. deep. Thin to 4 in. In colder districts it may be necessary to use cloches. Do *not* pick winter spinach too hard, but take the large leaves first. Use Long Standing Prickly or Standwell.

Perpetual Spinach (or Spinach Beet). A form of beetroot, easy and good. Less trouble than the frequent sowings of summer spinach, easier to pick and to cook, but a thought less succulent. For all-the-year crops, sow early April, and again mid-August, in rows 15 in. apart, and thin to 8 in. between

355

plants. Pick regularly, but lightly, as soon as ready, taking the larger leaves first. It lasts a year or so.

Swedes. Those who care for this vegetable should treat it just the same as maincrop turnips. Sow in May, good varieties being Purple Top and Bronze Top.

Sweet Corn. Indian corn or maize is not really a crop for the small garden, but I have known people with only a quarter of an acre or so grow a useful patch. It likes ample rain, yet long hours of sun-basking. Therefore a risky crop in our climate but frequently successful in the South. Should not be ventured in very dry, sandy soils, nor in heavy clays. Cloches are a great help.

Bastard-trench the soil in autumn, winter, or spring, putting in ample organic food. Into the top spit work in some damped horticultural peat and an all-round fertiliser just before sowing.

Seed may be sown direct outdoors in the middle of May 8 in. apart and 1 in. deep, with the rows 2 ft 6 in. apart. Thin to 16 in. in the rows, using thinnings to fill up any gaps. If grown in small quantities it should be arranged in a block or clump, rather than in one or two straight lines, in order to assist pollination, which is effected by the pollen from the male 'tassels' at the top of the plant falling on the female 'ears' below. In drought, water thoroughly evening or morning and apply a mulch. Feed with liquid manure.

To test when the cobs are ready for use, strip back the tip of the sheath and press one of the grains with the thumb-nail. If a creamy substance squirts out the cob is ready. An indication will be when the silky tassels turn brown and wither. Pop them into boiling water as soon as they are picked, and cook for ten minutes only. Cobs allowed to go hard can be fed to chickens.

Variety. Kelvedon Glory.

Thyme (Herb). Must have full sun and prefers a light soil; in heavy ones work in sand or road grit. Buy two or three plants and put out a foot apart. Easy and decorative.

Tomato. The tomato is a native of hot climates, and, as with sweet corn, the outdoor grower is a good deal in the hands of the weather. It likes heaps of sun, and regular rain, but not too much of it.

Outdoor Cultivation. As a dozen or two plants are usually enough for a small household, it is common to buy young plants. They should not be planted outside, even in the South, before the first week of June. People who have a little heat can sow seed, 2 in. apart, in a J. I. Compost in mid-March, very thinly covered, and transplant deeply into 3-in. pots.

Undoubtedly the best site for planting out is close to a wall or fence facing south. Dig the site in autumn or winter, using no animal manure unless old and thoroughly rotted. Compost is excellent but there is nothing better than old turves roughly chopped or broken up. Leaf-mould is also good. Apply Tomorite at 3 oz per square yard 7–10 days before planting—or some other good tomato fertiliser to maker's instructions.

Plant out the young tomatoes about 18 in. apart, firmly, but not too deep; it is sufficient if the pot-soil level is barely covered. Plant the supporting stakes, which must be stout and 4 ft out of the ground, before planting the tomatoes.

Tie-up loosely, as the plant grows, with soft string. Persistently cut out the side-shoots which grow in the leaf-axils. Be careful not to mistake other growing parts for these side-shoots—it is the growth in an angle or elbow to look for. (*See* illustration.) However, the main stem itself is also pinched-out or 'stopped' two leaves above the fourth truss of flowers (the third truss in Northern gardens). The purposes of this treatment and of taking out side-shoots is to centre the plant's energies on ripening a few good trusses in our short and uncertain summer.

Water well in dry spells and apply a mulch. Begin dressings of a tomato fertiliser when the first fruits begin to set. Spray with a copper fungicide against blight. If any leaves turn yellow, remove them. Do not remove healthy lower leaves, as sometimes advised, but tie them back so that the sun reaches the fruits.

Pick the fruits as soon as they are ripe. At the end of the season (in September, before frost) the remainder of the fruit should be harvested. Pull the whole plant (or the trusses only if space is limited) and hang up in a sunny place indoors to ripen. Any that are obstinate can be sentenced to the chutney jar. Alternatively, the plants can be untied and (without root disturbance) laid down on a bed of straw or bracken and covered with cloches.

Indoor Cultivation. In a greenhouse or glass porch more certain results can be obtained, but they need a good deal of attention, and, in small houses, some skill. So if you plan to take more than a week's holiday in summer, especially after midsummer, don't grow tomatoes indoors.

Common causes of failure are irregular watering, insufficient ventilation, too stuffy an atmosphere, and starting without enough heat. It is therefore best, in the absence of heat, not to raise one's own plants. Buy good stock late in April, and for planting out in the greenhouse prepare some boxes or very large pots. Any clean box will do which has ample bottom drainage. One foot is sufficient depth, with a surface area of about 1 sq ft per plant, or a little less. After crocking, nearly fill with a rich friable loam, with plenty of chopped turf or top spit, bonemeal, fresh wood ash, and a little mortar rubble. Treat this soil mixture with 1 lb of Tomorite per barrow-load a few days before planting.

Give ample day ventilation to the house, but close up at night until June. Subsequent culture is much as for outdoors, but five or more sprays of blossom may be allowed. Tap or lightly shake each plant daily when in flower to disperse the pollen, or use one of the new fruit-setting 'hormones'. From June onwards ventilate day and night according to the weather. Water the soil *regularly*—rather sparingly at first, more when the fruits begin to set, and, come August, a good half-gallon per plant per day. But regularity is the thing—a spell of drought followed by a flooding will cause the fruit to split. Apply a fertiliser as for outdoors; fine rootlets are likely to appear soon afterwards on the surface of the soil of indoor tomatoes, and if so cover with an inch of leaf-mould.

Next year make up entirely fresh soil for the boxes; never use the same soil twice. *See* Part IV for various tomato ailments.

A more modern indoor method is the 'ring culture' system. At ground level or on the greenhouse bench make a bed of washed gravel or weathered ashes, 5 in. deep. On top of this bed place bottomless pots of about 9 in. diameter (now in the shops). Fill with John Innes No. 3 compost. Plant the tomato seedlings in the pots, firmly. Water very thoroughly. Thereafter never water the pots, but keep the gravel base always wetted; the roots spread down into this water bed. Feeding, however, is through the pot only, using a liquid fertiliser. It is now being said, however, that you should feed the gravel base also.

Varieties. The most popular is Moneymaker, because it is easy and crops heavily. For sheer flavour, however, Ailsa Craig is far better and is the one to have if you grow from seed. For outdoors: Outdoor Girl.

Turnip (a Brassica, but treated as a root). The turnip is a cabbage with a swollen root. The most profitable varieties for small gardens are those which are grown especially for their excellent leaves or 'turnip tops' as a winter vegetable, notably the variety Greentop Stone; its root is also good. Sow sparsely in early September in rows 15 in. apart, thinning to 8 in. between plants. Pick off leaves as wanted (cook as cabbage), or take the roots as well.

To be acceptable as a summer vegetable, turnips must be eaten while young and tender. Therefore summer varieties should be sown in small quantities at a time from April till July. Sow in rows 1 ft apart, and thin to 4 in. apart in the row. Make the later sowings in a moist and shady bed.

Varieties. Early White Milan or Snowball for summer; Greentop Stone for winter.

PART IV: KNOW YOUR ENEMY

Not many amateur gardeners are likely to be carried away by the lure of bug-hunting or to have any interest in distinguishing one sort of mildew from another. All they care about is how to get rid of the brutes. But, since one doesn't treat measles in the same way as toothache, one does need to be able to recognise broadly between one group of ailments and another—particularly between the bite of an insect and the growth of a fungus. This is not difficult as a rule, and, fortunately for the non-expert, we can reduce the problem to fairly simple terms and evolve a system of mass or group treatment; moreover, to quite an appreciable extent, we are able to apply the principles of preventive medicine instead of waiting for the attack to fall upon us.

In the arrangement of this part, therefore, we shall first consider the enemy in general terms, and the most simplified possible routine method of dealing with him. Then we shall see how to deal with him *seriatim*, and finally the last chapter will show, where necessary, how to apply the treatments.

In my restricted space I am able to give no more than a few potted notes on these matters. Readers who feel the need for something more extensive are strongly recommended to read *Garden Pests and Diseases*, by A. G. L. Hellyer (Collingridge).

CHAPTER XXII

FRIEND AND FOE

OUR friends are all too few, so that it is a pity that so many are needlessly slaughtered by the gardener who goes on the principle of killing 'every kind of bug'. No doubt this practice is partly due to the fact that many of our natural friends are a long way from conforming to our conventional ideas of beauty. On the one hand, we consider the most villainous butterflies and moths as pretty creatures, and, on the other, even Shakespeare brands the beneficent toad as 'ugly and venomous'.

Friends

Our most valuable, and indispensable, friend is, of course, the bee. Less obviously, the wasp is also an ally in early summer, preying on the greenfly and carrying pollen, but by August he becomes a despoiler of the orchard. The hedgehog, the toad, the frog, and the 'devil's coach horse' beetle are excellent handymen in killing slugs and other hostile creatures. The tortoise, by the way, is entirely an enemy. Birds have today become a serious problem. The earthworm, though a pest in lawns, is valuable elsewhere for aerating the soil. Of our other friends to be noted, two are soil-dwellers and four are winged in their adult phase. The soil-dwellers are:

The **centipedes,** to be carefully distinguished from the quite different and destructive millipede. Note two kinds of centipede, both rather flat and very fast-moving and brisk. One is long, thin, yellow, or light-brown, intensely wriggly, with legs rather splayed out; the other shorter, dark-brown, fatter, a runner rather than a wriggler, with a pair of swept-back 'whiskers' in front and another pair at the tail. The destructive *millipede*, by contrast, has a round rather than flat body, dark, slatey-brown, shiny, shell-like skin, innumerable very small legs, and is slow moving and often found coiled up like a little snake. When worried he gives off a slightly obnoxious and bitter smell from his stink-glands.

The friendly **ground-beetle** larva is rather like a caterpillar; dull, dark-brown, light under-body, three pairs of legs in front, and two very pronounced whiskers or horns at the tail. Very nimble. Unfortunately it is very like the evil *wireworm*, but the wireworm is thinner, deep yellow, glossy, and has only tiny tail whiskers, and is less nimble. The adult ground-beetle may damage strawberries.

Those that fly in the adult phase all prey on the greenfly. They are:

The familiar **ladybird.** The larva, less well-known, is black or near-black, agile, torpedo-shaped or resembling a minute crocodile. The pupa or chrysalis is a small blackish blob that adheres to stems.

The **hover** or **serphid fly.** Wasp-like markings; hangs almost motionless in the air in between quick darts. The larva is an unpleasant leech-like creature, green, grey, or brown.

The **ichneumon fly.** An elongated creature whose plump abdomen is separated from its thorax by a thread-like tissue. Diaphanous wings. Pupa lives in a small yellow cocoon.

The **lacewing.** Thin pale-green body and two pairs of diaphanous wings, like a small dragon-fly. Larva is a fierce-looking little chap, very active, yellow, flushed brown, three pairs of legs, pointed tail, and a useful pair of nippers. A peculiarity of the lacewing is that it lays its eggs in a little bunch or cluster at the end of a long thin stalk attached to a leaf.

Notice how many of these friendly little chaps are nimble and lively. When in doubt, it is quite a good general rule, especially in the soil-dwellers, to take the agile creatures as friends and the sluggish ones as foes.

Enemies in General

The worst of garden pests is certainly Man, as long as he remains ignorant or lazy. The remedies for this widespread evil are knowledge and patient attention. Good husbandry is the first of garden commandments—not only good drainage and deep digging and liberal manuring, but also the annihilation of weeds which act as hosts for disease carriers, the cleaning out from hedge bottoms and odd corners of rubbish under which insects and fungi hibernate, the burning of waste wood and of leaves from trees that have carried disease and the scarifying of lawns. Overcrowding, stagnation, dirt, lack of light—these in particular may lead to one particular class of ailment known as physiological diseases, which are caused by some fault in what I have called the social science of plant life. Admittedly these diseases are sometimes obscure, as for instance those caused by the lack of some essential food in the soil such as potash or boron. Thus a leaf with brown, burnt-looking edges suggests lack of potash; a pale, sickly, yellowish one lack of nitrogen; bronze tips or patches lack of phosphates. But good cultivation and balanced feeding will see us through most of such problems, and will create conditions unfavourable to many insects and fungi.

In addition to physiological diseases, we can array garden nuisances into four categories, having in mind our intention of treating them as easily recognised classes or groups, rather than by identification *seriatim*. First there is the very distinct category called Pests; these are creatures of *animal* creation— caterpillars, grubs, slugs, beetles, earwigs, flying insects, and so on. Birds are in a special category.

The remaining three are classed as Diseases and consist of

fungi
bacteria
viruses

Bacterial and virus diseases are subjects fit for the expert only, but we may usefully note that any kind of malformation in a plant, any stunted growth, any unnatural streaking or mottling of foliage are probably due to some virus, and that the only way to arrest it is to burn the whole plant with its roots. Viruses are largely carried by aphids.

Thus the amateur is left to deal only with pests and fungi—and quite enough too. He must now distinguish between them. Fungi, or blights, manifest themselves in

mildews and fluffy moulds (but note the so-called 'American Blight');
rusty discolorations of foliage;
spots of black or brown on leaf or stem; together with less obvious ones such as the damping-off disease common in greenhouses.

Pests, for our purposes, are of three sorts: soil pests, a relatively small class, most of which feed on roots; and plant pests, of which one sort are biters, and the other suckers. The distinction is extremely important.

The biters are betrayed by the eating away of leaf, stem, fruit, or flower. The culprits are generally to be found in the plant, though sometimes hidden. The more obvious ones are caterpillars, all of which the gardener must treat as predatory, whether the creeping sort, the looping caterpillars that move with comical archings of the back, or the harlequin or tufted caterpillars. We attack these biters by poisoning their food, and we can do so before the pest comes.

The suckers go to work on foliage with a fine proboscis, with which they minutely pierce the leaf or young stem-tip and suck out the sap, not the leaf-surface. The best-known are the aphids—greenfly, blackfly, cuckoo-spit, etc. For these one has hitherto used a contact poison, but the modern 'systemic' insecticides (e.g. Abol X and Murphy's) introduce a poison into the sap of the plant itself, so that most insects, whether suckers or nibblers, are killed. Observe makers' instructions for all edible crops.

Some creatures create special problems.

Chafers, for instance, are soil pests when they are grubs and plant pests when adult. Once loose in the air they are free, so we shall attack them in the ground. Others are difficult to tackle unless you get them at just the right moment, as for instance the apple sawfly and codlin moth, who will be safely inside the heart of the fruit if you are too early or too late. Likewise it is unpractical to attack the 'flies' whose maggots ravage onion and carrot-root, and their damage is done before you see the result of it, so all we can do is to repel the fly from laying its eggs in those places.

Remedies in General

The remedies to be applied are mainly chemical, either insecticides or fungicides, the majority applied either in liquid form through a syringe or sprayer or else in powder (or 'dust') form through a bellows or blower.

Whether it be liquid or powder, make sure to cover the whole plant thoroughly, especially the under-surfaces of leaves by means of a curved nozzle which should be on every syringe. A fine mist or cloud should be delivered. Spraying is best done on a calm day in mild, dry weather, never in hot sun. When using the contact sprays, such as nicotine or derris, drive the poison well into the heart of clusters of buds or fruitlets. The 'systemics', however, you use much more casually. For dusting, the air should be still, and the foliage slightly damp, so the best times are early morning, evening, or after showers. They are possibly less effective than liquids.

The gardener need not be fussed by the exaggerated propaganda against chemical pesticides. All those normally sold in shops are of low density and approved by Government, but there are a few caveats in the next chapter.

The broad and simple classification of nuisances in the last sections leads us to a similar simplification of remedies, which we can summarise thus:

Soil Pests. Dress the soil with gamma-BHC.

Plant Pests—Biters. Systemic or derris.

Plant Pests—Suckers. Systemic or nicotine (or a proprietary containing nicotine), alternatively derris (which is both a contact and a stomach poison).

Fungi. A useful all-round deterrent for the garden generally is Tulisan, used early and often; spray both soil and plant. On actual appearance of any disease: *Mildews:* use Karathane; lime-sulphur is an alternative for some outdoor fruits and flowers of sulphur for more delicate foliage. '*Spots*' and '*Rusts*': use a non-caustic copper solution, of which there are several trade makes (*see* p. 379); specifically for Black Spot on roses, scab on apples and pears and various 'rots', use Orthocide, Maneb, or Zineb.

Fungi, being rooted in the tissues of a plant, can seldom be 'cured' once they have started, but they can be arrested; the whole crop, and not only the affected plant, must therefore be treated.

Besides these chemical means, there is no better advice in tackling insect pests than that of a wise rosarian who urged 'plenty of finger and thumb work'. A pinch of the fingers for caterpillar or greenfly, a snip of the nails for millipedes, the weight of the foot for slugs—these are swift and effective methods. Anyone who cannot overcome squeamishness should collect the creatures and give them a quick mass death in boiling water or a concentrated insecticide.

The simplified system above will not, of course, deal with everything, but the busy amateur may have time to do little more. Special measures are necessary for fruits and some other crops. Moreover, though I often mention only primary remedies, it should be remembered throughout this Part that there are many excellent proprietary remedies which combine two or more toxins capable of dealing with both biters and suckers, such as the preparations of Plant Protection, Shell, Boots, Murphy, I.T.P., P.B.I., Synchemicals, and other good manufacturers. Examine the specifications or analysis on the labels to see if they meet your needs.

An outstanding insecticide is that known shortly as BHC, of which there are several good brands, but it must not be used on certain plants (*see* Chapter XXIV). Moreover, neither this nor any other insecticide likely to kill bees, such as DDT, should be used when blossoms are fully open. Derris is safe at this period.

Combined Sprays. Insecticides and fungicides can sometimes be mixed together and applied as a two-in-one spray. Examples for general use are:

Tulisan mixed with Sybol, if caution is used in spraying when blossoms are fully open.

Karathane (for mildew) with gamma-BHC or malathion.

Karathane with Orthocide against both mildew and black spot on roses.

Systemics with both the above.

When making these cocktails, mix one ingredient with the required quantity of water, then add the second ingredient in the same water.

Beware, however, of advertised 'cure-alls'. Personally, I never buy a garden medicine of fancy name unless its main ingredients are disclosed or unless its manufacturers are of the highest standing.

CHAPTER XXIII

THE ENEMY IN DETAIL

SOIL AND GENERAL PESTS—PLANT PESTS—FUNGUS
DISEASES—PHYSIOLOGICAL AILMENTS

THE following are some epitomised notes on how to negotiate
and deal with the commoner garden enemies *seriatim*. Descriptions and usages of the various medicines are given in the next
chapter.

Soil and General Pests

Ants. BHC or 'Nippon'.

Birds. Certain species, most of all bullfinches, wood
pigeons and house sparrows (but not the quiet little hedge
sparrows), are 100 per cent pestiferous to fruit, vegetables and
flowers. Others have some virtues to balance their vices. I
know of only two effective deterrents. For small plants a few
strands of black thread stretched between twigs makes the
birds suspect a snare as their feet touch them and they will
keep away. For larger trees, such as fruiting and flowering
cherries, a nylon net thrown right over protects most of the
buds and fruit. For bush and cane fruits and strawberries the
best thing is a complete cage of any sort of small-mesh netting.

Earwig. Make traps of hollow broad bean stalks or partially
open match-boxes stuffed with hay or dry grass and suspended
high in the foliage; less unsightly than the flower-pot method.
Shake out the pests into a cup of paraffin or into boiling water.

Slugs and Snails. Aluminium sulphate watered on in
winter *when plants are leafless* at 1 lb in 3 gallons, or dusted on
dry at 1 lb to 25 sq yd, kills by contact and dissolves eggs. It
makes soil acid. In the growing season, use powdered metal-

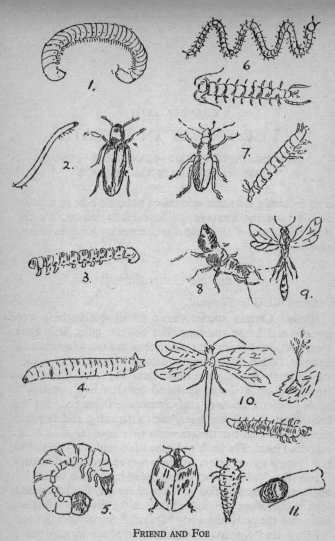

FRIEND AND FOE

Foes: 1, millipede; 2, wireworm with adult click-beetle; 3, cutworm; 4, leatherjacket; 5, chafer-grub.

Friends: 6, centipedes; 7, ground beetle and larva; 8, devil's coach-horse; 9, ichneumon fly (one type); 10, lacewing with larva and egg-cluster; 11, ladybird with larva and pupa (adhering to stem).

dehyde mixed with bran in little heaps or a proprietary liquid (e.g., Slugit) or the pellets made by various people; all, however, get washed out by rain and need frequent renewal.

For the following, use BHC in one of its forms:

Millipede (*see under* centipede, earlier); **Wireworm** (compare ground-beetle); **Chafer grubs,** bloated, dirty white, swollen purple-black tail, horny head, also half-coiled; **Leatherjacket** (larva of the daddy-long-legs), fat, dark-grey, *no legs*, looks like a dirty little worm and wriggles like one, most destructive; **Cutworm.** Caterpillar-like, with a tucked-in tail, sluggish, a menace to small plants, which it attacks at ground level, distinguish from ground-beetle larva.

Plant Pests

American Blight. An aphis that protects itself with a familiar covering like cotton-wool on branches. Impenetrable to sprays. Apply methylated spirit with stiff brush.

Aphis (greenfly, blackfly, etc.). Suckers. Use a systemic or else malathion, nicotine, derris, or BHC. A breed of aphis sometimes attacks roots; try malathion or BHC, but not on edible plants.

Big Bud, on black currants. Distinctive globular swelling of a dormant bud caused by mites in winter. Pick off and burn swollen buds and spray with lime-sulphur as on page 312.

Cabbage Gall Weevil. Small round swellings on the roots caused by tiny white maggot. Not serious. Break open and crush maggot. Burn galled roots. Cf. club root.

Capsid Bug. Sucker. Resembles large greenfly, but nimble. Distorted flowers, leaves, or stems. On apples a rough brown patch. Systemic, nicotine, or BHC on most plants.

Caterpillars. Biters. Use a systemic or spray or dust with derris; on cabbage tribe with DDT; on fruit trees, apply grease-bands and winter washes.

Codlin Moth, on apples. Biter. The maggot usually enters the fruit at the eye about midsummer. The point of entry has a dry 'frass'. Lead arsenate is best but dangerous. In default, spray with DDT or derris at midsummer, and repeat thrice at

371

weekly intervals; also tie bands of hay or sacking very lightly round the trunk in July (in which caterpillars may pupate) and burn in autumn.

Cuckoo-spit, or **Spittle Bug,** or **Froghopper.** Sucker. Inside a mass of frothy spittle is a curious soft creature which on disturbance will attempt to escape by weak hops. Hand-pick or use a systemic.

Eelworm. Microscopic creatures that attack chrysanthe-mums, phloxes, bulbs, onions, tomatoes, each genus having its own worm. Curable only by experts. Lift and burn the plants and do not plant the same genus on that site for five years.

Flea Beetle. Bites tiny holes in Brassica seedlings. Dust the ground with derris.

'Flies'—Cabbage-root fly, onion fly, carrot fly. These small creatures, seen only by the keen eye, are very widespread and destructive. Their maggots eat into the bulb of the young onion, into the carrot or into the roots of the cabbage. A wilting of the plant, especially noticeable in onions, is evidence of them. Those of the onion and the carrot are attracted by the smell of the plant, especially when thinning is done. Infected plants must be pulled up and burnt. Remove seedling onions and carrots when thinning. Dress the ground with gamma-BHC before sowing or planting.

Greenfly. *See* **Aphis.**

Leaf Hopper or **Frog Fly.** Sucker. Pale yellow creature the size of greenfly on the underside of leaves. Leaf becomes mottled with yellow patches, later turning white. Spray undersides of leaves with a systemic, nicotine, or derris.

Leaf Miner. Wriggly channellings within the tissue of a leaf, or, on celery, irregular blisters. The maggot is at the extremity of the channelling. Pinch it and spray with a systemic, gamma-BHC, or malathion.

Mealy Bug. Sucker. Tiny bug protected by coat of white mealy wax on hard-wooded greenhouse plants, especially vines. Spray tar-oil wash in winter (after rubbing off bark on vines) and spray or fumigate with nicotine after growth starts.

Raspberry Beetle. The maggot eats out the hearts of

raspberries, loganberries. Spray or dust forcefully with derris at the earliest flush of pink on the fruits as a preventative.

Red Spider. Sucker. Very difficult customer. A mere dot of red or rust scarcely visible to the naked eye. Encouraged by hot, dry conditions, especially in greenhouse. Often disclosed by grey mottling of leaf. Outdoors spray malathion or derris, indoors fumigate with azobenzine.

Sawfly, Apple. The maggot makes characteristic ribbon scars of rough skin, and its point of entry into the fruit is wet and rank. Spray with BHC at 3 oz per gallon, or with nicotine spray or possibly derris, just after blossom-fall and again seven days later.

Sawfly, Leaf-rolling. Rose leaves are rolled up like paper spills, and the grey-green grub is inside. Handpick, and spray with nicotine or derris.

Slugworm. Biter. Its sign-manual is a leaf eaten to a papery skeleton. Use a systemic insecticide or derris.

Spittle Bug. *See* **Cuckoo-spit.**

Thrip. Sucker. Tiny, slightly hairy, louse-like, nimble; adults winged. Encouraged by hot, dry conditions, especially in greenhouse. Pea and bean pods distorted, with mottled, silvery streaks. Rose petals speckled. In the greenhouse white patches on leaves, dark secretions on under-surfaces, blossoms distorted. *Dust* rose buds with BHC, food crops with derris; indoors fumigate with nicotine shreds twice.

Weevils (long-snouted beetles). Biters and borers. Ragged holes in foliage, especially roses; scolloped edges of bean and pea leaves; on apples, blossom turns brown and fails to open. Spray or dust DDT; on apples not later than green-cluster stage; roses, dust the soil. Caveat in next chapter.

White Fly. Sucker. Clouds of minute white flies in the greenhouse. Fumigate with DDT or BHC smoke. The little chalcid wasp preys on them and will survive fumigation but not a winter without heat.

Woolly Aphis. *See* **American Blight.**

Black Spot. Black or purple-brown patches on rose leaves, sometimes on stems also. A menacing disease. Spray with Orthocide, Maneb, Trispot, or Dithane. *See* Chapter XIV.

Botrytis, or **Grey Mould.** A fluffy mould, affected parts going soft and black. A difficult disease, flourishing in damp, cold conditions. Spray with liquid copper or Orthocide. Burn all infected parts.

Brown Rot. Apples, pears, and some other fruit go brown, putrid and mummified on the tree, often dotted with small white pustules in concentric rings. Burn all infected fruit.

Cane Spot. Purplish patches on raspberry and loganberry canes, later turning grey. Burn all infected canes, and spray with lime-sulphur as in Chapter XX.

Canker. Deep oval wound, typically on apples, pears, and roses, with gnarled, corky edge, exposing smoother wood below. Starts with a number of small depressions. Cut off and burn diseased twigs, and treat the amputation with Arbrex.

Club Root. Grotesque and evil-smelling swellings on the roots of the cabbage family. A serious disease. Thrives on soil deficient in lime. Cf. Cabbage Gall Weevil. Burn all diseased plants, dress the ground heavily with lime and do not use it for any Brassica for four years.

Coral Spot. A speckling of bright coral pustules on branches, especially dead wood. Burn all infected wood.

Damping-off. Kills small seedlings at ground level, especially in the greenhouse. Treat the soil with Cheshunt Compound when sowing seed or when pricking out.

Fire-blight. May attack apples, pears, cotoneasters, and pyracanthas. See page 306.

Leaf Curl. The leaves of peaches, nectarines, and almonds are twisted and distorted, with red or yellow blisters. Burn all infected leaves. Spray with lime-sulphur or Orthocide in February and just before leaf-fall in autumn.

Mildews. White, powdery growth on leaves and stems, sometimes on fruit, as on gooseberries. Encouraged by lack of ventilation. Dust or spray with sulphur, Karathane or Tulisan.

Rose-leaf Scorch. Starts with small yellow patches which turn brown and dry and drop out. Dust with sulphur. Dress the soil with potash in autumn.

Rots. Various rots attack celery, lettuces, onions (wet rot), and others. Plants go soft and slimy, sometimes covered with fungus. May not appear till crop is in store. Burn them all and add potash to the soil. Orthocide controls storage rots.

Rusts. A rusty speckling on the undersides of leaves (brighter orange on roses). Burn infected leaves. On roses spray with Dithane; on other plants, with a liquid copper fungicide.

Scab, of apples and pears. Small, black, hard, dry patches develop with deep cracks and distortions of fruit, rough and broken surface on twigs; black spots under leaves. Very prevalent. Spray with lime-sulphur at winter strength before blossoms open, and at summer strength when they have fallen; on sulphur-shy sorts use Orthocide. Prune out and burn infected twigs and burn all fallen leaves of infected trees.

Silver Leaf. If a dull, metallic silvering (not mere whitening) occurs on the leaves of stone fruits, better get in an expert, If it is silver leaf you are liable to prosecution if the infected bough is not removed. Cut cleanly back to the parent limb with no snag, and paint with Arbrex; burn all infected parts.

Tomato-leaf Mould. Patches of brown-grey mould on undersides of leaves with yellow blotches on surface. Encouraged by lack of ventilation. Spray with liquid copper and burn infected leaves. Same treatment for **Blight**— brown patches on leaf, stem, and fruit.

Wart Disease of potatoes. Large wart-like growth, the whole tuber becoming an evil mass. A notifiable disease, avoided by buying immune varieties.

Physiological Ailments

Blossom-end Rot of tomatoes. A sunken dark patch at the blossom end of the fruit spreads and blackens. Due to lack of

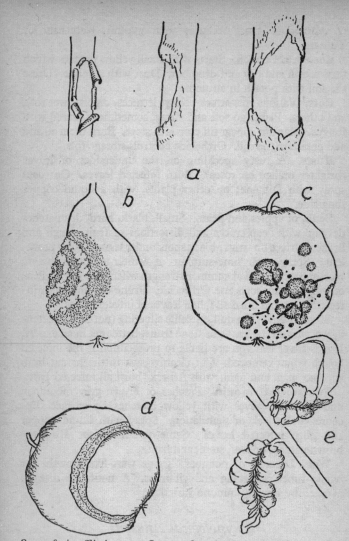

Some fruit afflictions: *a*, Stages of canker—the peeling bark, the gaping wound, death; *b*, brown rot; *c*, the cracks and dry, round scars of scab; *d*, the ribbon scar of the apple sawfly; *e*, peach-leaf curl.

water, or a root disease. Burn affected fruits, correct watering, dress soil 4 oz lime per sq yd.

Chlorosis. A yellowing of foliage caused by lack of chlorophyll. Due to shortage of iron in the soil, which may in turn be due to excess lime. Water with 'iron sequestrene'.

Greenback on tomatoes. A band of hard green or yellow flesh round the stalk refuses to ripen. Due either to lack of potash or excessive hot sun. Use a tomato fertiliser.

Gumming (Bacterial Canker) of plums, cherries, and other stone fruits. Is an excretion of resinous gum. Not usually serious, but if branches begin to die, cut back to healthy wood and dress the wound with Arbrex.

Reversion of black currants. If a new sort of leaf appears—smaller and more elongated than the cultivated leaf, with unserrated edge—burn the whole bush. No cure.

CHAPTER XXIV

THE MEDICINE CUPBOARD

IN this chapter is some outline information on insecticides and fungicides of the more usual sorts only. The more complicated ones and those requiring the use of protective clothing are omitted. Readers who have no chemical knowledge are advised to buy proprietary articles; not, for example, nicotine and pyrethrum in their pure chemical forms.

Very few of these concoctions are 'dangerous', but it is common sense to keep then out of the way of children and pets. A few affect tender skins and noses. Some (DDT, BHC, malathion) will taint vegetables and fruit if used too soon before picking. Captan, malathion, DDT, and derris kill fish. ALWAYS READ WHAT THE LABEL SAYS.

Obviously, small gardeners will not keep a stock of everything mentioned here, but the medicines that will be useful to keep always at hand for use at short notice are:

Cheshunt Compound, for seedlings,
Derris, dust or liquid, a safe general-purpose insecticide,
Powdered sulphur, as a general fungicide,
A modern slug-killer.

As we have seen on page 368, insecticides and fungicides can sometimes be mixed and put on together, but care is necessary. For example, the insecticide nicotine and the fungicide lime-sulphur can be married at the 'pink-bud' stage in apples, but if so the nicotine must not have a soapy spreader, for it is cardinal not to mix lime-sulphur with soap.

Those who have sensitive skins may wish to protect themselves with lanoline or Vaseline and goggles when spraying with lime-sulphur, which is just a little caustic.

BHC (benzene-hexachloride). A valuable toxin for many plant and soil pests. If used for soil pests in the kitchen garden it may taint the vegetables, and the new formulation called 'gamma-BHC' should be used instead. Several proprietary brands available, e.g. Sybol and Lindex. Not to be used on hydrangeas, potatoes, black currants, marrows, nor on grapes or any soft fruit after blossom stage, *nor on any vegetable crops within 14 days of eating*.

Captan, marketed under the trade name **Orthocide,** is a valuable fungicide, especially for Black Spot on roses, peach-leaf curl, apple and pear scab, etc. Not for mildew, but it can be blended with Karathane, or with insecticides.

Copper Fungicides. For spots, rusts, botrytis, peach-leaf curl, potato and tomato blight, etc. There are now various improvements on the traditional Bordeaux Mixture, in liquid and dust forms, made by several firms, such as Murphy, Pan Britannica, and Shell. 'Copper-lime dust' is also often recommended for some uses.

Do not put copper preparations in any iron or tin vessel—use glass, earthenware, plastic, or copper.

Cheshunt Compound. Fungicide for protecting seedlings against damping-off disease. Apply to the soil before sowing and when pricking out at $\frac{1}{2}$ oz per gallon of water. Use no iron or tin vessel, as it contains copper sulphate.

DDT. Contact insecticide in powder and liquid forms. For weevils, caterpillars, capsid, woodlice. No good against greenfly. Also kills bees and other friends. Do not use while nearby flowers are in open blossom; nor for fourteen days before picking any vegetable or twenty-one days for fruit. Is often incorporated in proprietary mixtures.

Derris. Safest all-round insecticide, for both biters and suckers. Great stand-by for general use. Obtainable as powder or liquid. If applied at same time as lime-sulphur (q.v.) use in powder form only. Poisonous to fish.

Dinocap. Valuable specific for mildew. Best known under

379

the proprietary names Karathane, Toprose Mildew Spray, etc. Can be mixed with Captan, or with insecticides, e.g. BHC, derris and malathion.

Lime-sulphur. See under **Sulphur.**

Lindane. The American name for 'gamma-BHC'.

Malathion. Strong contact poison for suckers—aphids, thrips, mealy bug, outdoor red spider. Poisonous to man and other animals, and to bees. Crops should not be eaten for a week afterwards. Avoid getting it on your hands. Read what the packet says.

Nicotine. A telling insecticide, especially for aphis and apple sawfly. Alkaloid poison; same warnings as for malathion. Get it ready mixed with a spreader. Often included in proprietary mixtures. Available also as greenhouse fumigant.

Pyrethrum. Insecticide for suckers often incorporated in proprietaries, e.g. Pyrethrex; harmless to man and his friends.

Sulphur. Essential fungicide available in several forms. Flowers of sulphur is for dusting against mildews, harmless to the most tender plants and fruits; available in a green tint. Colloidal sulphur is a liquid, sometimes preferred to lime-sulphur for scab on apples and pears; may scorch foliage. *Thiram* and *Tulisan* are sulphur derivatives. *Lime-sulphur*, liquid, is for fruit trees for scab and other infections, but on sulphur-shy apples and pears use Orthocide. Do not store in metal containers. Never use it at the same time as any soapy sprays. Appropriate strengths are given under each fruit—apple, pear, black currant, gooseberry and raspberry.

Sulphurs, like coppers, are preventatives and 'controls' for mildews, etc., rather than cures.

Tar-oil Winter Wash. Standard winter spray for fruit trees, better for beginners than DNC. Seals up eggs of aphis and many caterpillars and cleanses bark. Will injure any leaf crops it may drift on to, so don't grow vegetables beneath fruit trees.

Zineb (e.g. PBI's Dithane and Shell Zineb). Valuable fungicide, liquid or dust, for rose black-spot, rust, tomato leaf-mould, etc. Non-poisonous, but read the label.

PART V: THE YEAR'S WORK

THE following notes are intended to serve as reminders—and reminders only—of work that should be done month by month, so that the gardener may always be thinking a little ahead. The programme is based on a normal season, and on the assumption that weather and soil conditions are satisfactory. If in fact they are not, then delay the operation till they are. Thus seed-sowing outdoors must wait until the surface of the soil is tolerably dry, and planting out till it is tolerably wet (though this can be corrected by watering). Likewise spraying cannot be done on a windy day, but pruning may.

In the mildest climates operations scheduled for spring and early summer can be advanced a week or two, and those for late summer and autumn delayed a little; but in hard climates the opposite applies in both instances.

Only the more usual sorts of operations are dealt with, and a programme of this sort cannot, of course, be all-embracing. Out-of-season jobs and those needing heat are generally excluded. So also are reminders of the obvious that the gardener ought to see for himself, such as pricking off and planting seedlings and cuttings as they come ready. Usually the first normal date for an operation is given (e.g. planting Clematis), and if not done at the time stated it should be done soon afterwards, or otherwise as stated in the appropriate cultural notes.

In many instances, as in January, I have given reminders of matters on which the gardener should take thought in advance; but it is always best to read the calendar a month in advance, so as to be ready for the job due, whether it be preparing the ground or buying seed, fertilisers, etc.

JANUARY

General. Digging and planting ought to have been completed by now, but may still be done in open weather.

Write your orders for seeds of vegetables and flowers, including seed potatoes if not already done; also Gladioli,

Montbretia, Begonia, and Dahlia for spring plantings. Make vegetable cropping plan in conjunction with seed order.

Overhaul tools and send mowers and sharp-edged tools to a good grinder.

Flowers. Sow Schizanthus in greenhouse. Except in the North, begin pruning roses.

Vegetables. In the South and Midlands make a sowing of broad beans (e.g. Royal Dwarf Gem) and plant shallots if not done in December.

Force a few selected crowns of rhubarb.

Dress asparagus with seaweed if obtainable now or February.

Towards the end of the month set out potatoes for sprouting.

Fruit. Prune all fruit trees and spray with tar-oil wash if not done last month—apples last.

Root-prune overgrown trees if necessary.

FEBRUARY

General. Dress light soils with lime if needed, and any soils that were manured in autumn. Don't get behindhand with anything this month, as March is going to be a busy time.

Flowers. Early in the month prune Clematis. Late in the month, or early March, prune Buddleia Davidii, Hypericums, Wisteria, Winter Jasmine. Remove old wood and thin branches of deciduous berry shrubs.

Give top-dressing of loam, leaf-mould and sand to rock gardens.

In a greenhouse with some heat, sow Antirrhinum, and start Dahlias into growth for cuttings in boxes of soil.

Vegetables. Fork over and level ground that was rough-dug in autumn, and prepare seed-beds for first outdoor sowings, working in bonemeal, soot and wood ashes.

Sow parsnips.

In districts unfavourable to early outdoor sowing, sow Brussels, onions and leeks in boxes or frames or under cloches.

Prepare celery and leek trenches at the end of the month or early March.

Fruit. Shorten tips of summer-fruiting raspberries. Cut

late-fruiting ones, and all newly-planted canes, down to 6 in. of the ground. Spray peaches, etc., against leaf-curl. Top-dress fruits with manure if needed or with bonemeal and compost; or dress with lime as appropriate.

MARCH

General. Complete forking over of soil and preparation of seed-beds.

Flowers. Plant out (or transplant) all herbaceous perennials if not done in autumn. Also plant now those that dislike autumn planting—Pyrethrum, Scabious, Gallardia, etc. Plant Gladiolus, Montbretia, Caen and other hybrid Anemones, Kaffir Lily, water-loving Iris; or early April.

Take Delphinium, Chrysanthemum and Lupin cuttings.

Where required, top-dress at the end of the month with manure, etc., all beds of *established* roses (after pruning), flowering shrubs and climbers and herbaceous borders. Top-dress Peonies and Lily-of-the-Valley.

Prune Passion-flower. Late in the month, or early April, prune Hydrangea paniculata (not others), late-flowering Ceanothus (e.g. Gloire de Versailles), Ceratostigma, Indigofera.

Sow Sweet Peas and other hardy annuals in the open late in the month, or early April.

In the greenhouse sow China Asters and summer Stocks; also Clarkia and other annuals for greenhouse decoration. Plant Scarborough Lily.

Sow new lawns at the end of the month (or, better, prepare it now for August sowing). Begin work on old lawns by raking and brushing. Rake and re-sow any bare patches. Begin mowing, according to growth.

Vegetables. Having prepared proper seed-beds in both nursery and main gardens, make the following sowings:

In permanent quarters: lettuce May Queen (first week), onion, early potatoes (end of month), summer carrots (short or stump-rooted), parsley, early dwarf peas (early in month and in sheltered place), summer spinach. From now onwards spinach, carrot and radish can be sown in succession. Under glass sow celery, and, if there is heat, tomato.

In nursery beds late in the month: summer lettuce (then in succession), Brussels, leek, summer cabbage (e.g. Velocity or Greyhound).

Late in the month plant out seedlings (after proper hardening off) of varieties previously raised under glass, including autumn-sown onions.

Plant onion sets (early), rhubarb, seakale thongs, horseradish roots. Divide clumps of chives. Plant shallots in the North.

Fruit. Prune *new* black currants down to three buds above ground level. Plant greenhouse grapes.

From now until the end of May carefully watch the bud development of apples and pears (Green Cluster, Pink, or White Bud, and Petal Fall), and spray with lime-sulphur at the appropriate times and strengths.

APRIL

General. Attack young weeds everywhere and as early as possible. Don't get behindhand with thinning and transplanting.

Flowers. Plant out Sweet Peas raised in pots. Plant or transplant evergreen shrubs in the middle of the month.

Sow Delphinium, Lupin and other hardy perennials. Continue sowing annuals.

Apply lawn sand, etc., to old lawns in a dry spell if required. Prune Forsythia, Flowering Currant and other early-flowering shrubs as soon as blossom is over (cut back generally to within three buds of the old wood). Trim winter heathers. Pick off seed-pods of bulb plants and Hydrangea heads (late).

In the greenhouse, 'start' Begonias, 'stop' Chrysanthemums, and sow seed of Zinnia, and African and French Marigold. Start Dahlia tubers for division if not done earlier under heat.

Vegetables. Plant new asparagus beds. Finish planting potatoes.

Celery and leek trenches must be completed by now. Prepare marrow and cucumber beds.

Sowing for this month: Leeks and perpetual spinach early in the month; broccoli for all seasons, winter cabbage and Savoys, salsify, kale, kohl-rabi, pickling onion, late in the month; limited sowings of globe beetroot, summer turnip, swede (and afterwards in succession); a further sowing of broad beans; first sowings of cos lettuce, and perpetual spinach (end month); continue successional sowings of summer cabbage, summer lettuce, summer spinach, stump-rooted carrot. Sow a few seeds of vegetable marrow and ridge cucumber in pots under glass.

Peas: make a second sowing of earlies and the first sowing of maincrop variety early in the month, and a second sowing of maincrop at the end of the month.

Tomatoes: if not raising your own seed, order plants late in the month for the greenhouse (not for outdoors yet).

Begin picking rhubarb on established plants.

Fruit. Plant strawberries if not done in August.

Continue the spraying of apples and pears with lime-sulphur at appropriate bud stages. Spray black currants when the leaves are the size of a shilling, and gooseberries just before the blossoms open if necessary.

Watch for attacks of aphis on all fruit trees and spray with nicotine or derris.

MAY

General. Be specially on the lookout for the treacherous late frosts, which may occur at night right up to the last week. Give night protection to anything not hardy, and replace losses by fresh sowings. Hoe. Spray early against fungus diseases, aphis, etc.

Flowers. Begin hardening-off half-hardy plants (Antirrhinum, etc.) of your own raising. If not raising your own, order plants for putting out end of month or first week of June.

Plant out Early Chrysanthemums about the second week and pinch tops end-May. Stand greenhouse sorts outdoors in the last week. Plant Dahlia tubers (not growing plants) mid-month in mild places where it has not been possible to start them earlier under glass. Bed out any hardy annuals started in boxes.

Sow Primula malacoides for the greenhouse now or June.

Prune early-flowering shrubs as they cease to bloom. Trim back rock plants that have finished flowering.

Evergreens may still be transplanted.

Vegetables. Outdoor sowings for this month:

Dwarf French beans, early in month; sweet corn, scarlet runners, haricot bean, flageolet, all mid-May; first sowing of endive and final sowing of maincrop peas, end of month. A second sowing of French beans in the third week.

Earth-up potatoes.

Plant out early sowings of Brassicas; also leeks, celeriac and celery (end of month or earliest June).

Tomatoes: if not raising your own, order plants for outdoors for planting first week of June. The same for marrows, cucumbers and celery.

Pinch tips of broad beans as soon as lowest pods begin to set. Dress onions, cabbages, and carrots with gamma-BHC against their 'flies'. Repeat when thinning or transplanting.

Fruit. Continue spraying apples and pears with lime-sulphur. Add BHC to the petal-fall spray against sawfly. Spray gooseberries and currants with derris, etc., if caterpillars invade.

Thin fruits of peach, nectarine, apricot when the size of a pea. Mulch raspberries.

JUNE

Flowers. The big job of the first week is to clear out the early flowering, non-perennial stuff (Wallflowers, etc.,) to fork over and feed the beds, and to plant out their successors. Lift Tulips, if necessary, with a ball of soil and heel-in. Lift, divide and transplant in a shady border Primrose, Polyanthus, Pansy. Plant out Antirrhinum, Stock, Zinnia, scarlet Salvia, etc.; also Begonia and Dahlia.

Plant Bearded Flag Irises at the end of the month (the best time). Plant Belladonna Lily.

Pick off dead blossom everywhere. Prune early-flowering shrubs as they cease blooming, e.g. Broom (very hard), Lilac, Laburnum, Rhododendron. Do second 'stopping' of indoor Chrysanths if desired.

Begin feeds of liquid manure, soot-water, etc., as appropriate. Mulch Sweet Peas, Rhododendrons, Roses. Begin staking in the herbaceous border.

Late in the month sow biennials—Wallflower, Sweet William, Canterbury Bell, Polyanthus, Pansy, etc.—for next year.

Place orders now or very shortly for autumn plantings—roses, fruits, shrubs, herbaceous plants, bulbs. Order Madonna Lilies for next month.

Carefully watch ventilation and watering in greenhouse.

Vegetables. Plant out tomatoes, marrows, ridge cucumbers in the first week. Transplant Brassicas as ready; Brussels should be in final quarters by third week.

Sowings: maincrop beetroot and carrot for storing; final sowings of French beans and scarlet runner; sowing of dwarf early pea for September (end of month); successional sowings of lettuce (*in situ* now), endive, summer spinach to be made now in partial shade with some peat.

Stop cutting asparagus mid-June. Harvest shallots end of month. Dress onions, carrots and cabbages again with fumigants. Mulch early sowings of pea and bean. Earth-up potatoes as necessary, and spray against potato blight in the SW (other areas in succession).

Fruit. Root strawberry runners, and prepare new bed for their planting in August.

Spray apples against codlin moth mid-month. Collect apple

and pear droppings. Anticipate the 'June drop' by thinning heavy-cropping trees.

Begin summer pinching on stone fruits and select the new shoots on wall-trained peaches, nectarines and cherries to be tied in for next year. Summer-prune gooseberries and red currants.

Lay straw under strawberries, and spread nets when fruits set.

JULY

General. Watering will need special care in a dry year. Hoe. Look out for pests and fungi.

Flowers. Prick out into a nursery bed the nurselings of Wallflower, etc., sown earlier.

Plant: Madonna Lily, Snowdrop, autumn- and winter-flowering Crocuses, Meadow Saffron and Sternbergia.

Layer Border Carnations late in month. Take cuttings of Fuchsia for insertion in a moist atmosphere under glass (or early August).

Lift any Tulips and Ranunculus still in ground, dry off and store.

Prune early-flowering shrubs and climbers, e.g. Philadelphus. Summer-prune Wisteria and Japanese Quince early. Feed roses after first blooming.

Clip non-flowering evergreen hedges in the last week or early August.

Sow Cineraria seed end of month.

Vegetables. Some early potatoes may be lifted for the table as required. Sow spring cabbage late this month in Northern gardens (early August elsewhere). Sow winter prickly-seeded spinach at the same time.

Fruit. Summer-prune apples and pears if required—pears about the middle of the month, apples at the end. Tie sacking-bands round apple trunks to trap codlin moth.

AUGUST

Flowers. Plant Daffodils. Sow new lawns late in the month. Cut back and top-dress Violas. Cut down the foliage of Bearded Flag Irises by about a half. Disbud Chrysanths as necessary. As Gladioli fade cut off the stalks, not lower than the lowest blossom, or pluck off buds. Cut out feeble new stems of rambler roses.

Take cuttings or make layerings late in the month (or early next) of early flowering shrubs, e.g. Ceanothus, Berberis stenophylla, Cotoneaster, Flowering Currant, Laurustinus, Escallonia, Diervilla.

In the greenhouse: Begin planting Freezias in pots (Chapter IX). Take Pelargonium ('Geranium') cuttings. Sow Schizanthus, and Clarkia, Antirrhinum, etc., for spring display.

Vegetables. Keep celery and leeks copiously watered and earth-up. Mulch peas and beans.

Sow: Lettuce May Queen *in situ* for late autumn use (early in month); spring cabbage in Southern gardens; pickling cabbage; winter (prickly) spinach or perpetual spinach.

Towards the end of the month bend over onion tops to hasten ripening. Watch out for cabbage-white butterfly on Brassicas and spray with derris.

All winter greens should have been planted out by now.

Fruit. Cut down all canes of raspberry and loganberry that have finished fruiting this summer to within 6 in. of the ground, and cut out weakly new shoots (late-fruiting raspberries wait till February). Prune black currants when fruit has been picked.

Plant out rooted runners of strawberries in their new beds soonest.

Pick early varieties of apple and pear, and remember that they will not keep.

SEPTEMBER

General. This is like May in reverse, and early frosts have to be guarded against late in the month in the North. It is also the beginning of the digging, harvesting, and bulb seasons. Special attention to compost bins. Order new fruit trees, roses, shrubs, herbaceous plants, etc., if not already done. Order manure, lime, etc.

Flowers. If a new herbaceous border is planned, dig it now; the like for new rose-beds, and for spring bedding.

Prune rambler roses early. Take cuttings of roses; and of Violas from those cut down last month.

Plant bulbs of Hyacinth (late), spring Crocus, Muscari, bulbous Iris, Scilla, Chionodoxa, Anemone species, hybrid Anemones if not done in March, etc. (*not* Tulips yet). Plant bulbs in bowls and pots for the house. Plant Peonies, Red-hot Pokers, and Clematis; and Flag Irises if not done in the summer.

Late in the month bring pot-grown Chrysanths into the greenhouse.

Vegetables. Harvest: Tomatoes (end of month), potatoes, onions, haricot beans, marrows.

Sow turnip Greentop Stone. Plant out spring cabbage.

Cloche late-sown peas and French beans third week.

Begin to blanch endives late in month.

Fruit. Prepare ground for any new fruit trees ordered. Grease-band all tree-fruits. Harvest apples and pears as they become ready, leaving late varieties till next month.

OCTOBER

General. Frost-sensitive plants must now all be out of the ground unless protected.

Flowers. Lose no time in completing preparation of new rose-beds, herbaceous borders and sites for trees and shrubs.

Lift, dry and store Dahlias and Begonias at the first touch of frost.

Plantings: Clematis, Lilies, spring bedding plants (Wall-flowers, Sweet William, Polyanthus, Canterbury Bell, etc.); sever Carnation layers early in month and plant out a week or two later; begin planting deciduous trees and shrubs, and conifers; complete bulb plantings, but not Tulips till end of month or early November.

Bring Cinerarias into the greenhouse (early).

Vegetables. If the digging programme is going to be a big one, start towards end of this month. Clear all decaying crops, cabbage leaves and rubbish.

Harvest: Carrots, beet, turnips (except sorts to stand out in the winter).

Sow: Broad beans to stand the winter; lettuce May Queen under cloches.

Give celery final earthing-up. Cut down asparagus when foliage turns yellow.

At the end of month cut down spearmint and dry off; top-dress bed with loam.

Fruit. Cut fruited canes of blackberry to the ground.

Complete preparation of sites for new fruit trees.

NOVEMBER

General. This is the big digging and planting month; the ideal time for planting all deciduous trees and shrubs including fruits and roses—plant early. Begin to withhold water in greenhouse and frame.

Flowers. Dig all unoccupied ground. Be sure Sweet Pea bed is done early.

Plant (or transplant): Roses, hardy deciduous shrubs and trees, climbers and hedges, Tulips, turban Ranunculus, Lily-of-the-Valley; divide and re-plant old overcrowded stock of the last.

Herbaceous and mixed borders: clean up old borders, cutting down any decayed herbaceous stems. Plant out new borders, and new stock in old borders. Lift, divide and transplant old overgrown clumps, *except* those that resent autumn shifting (Scabious, Pyrethrum, Gaillardia, the Amellus group of Asters, Delphinium and Kniphofia in heavy soils, etc.).

Lift stock plants of Early Chrysanthemum and plant under glass. Lift, dry and store Gladioli.

Mulch shrub and herbaceous borders with leaves (not manure).

Vegetables. DIG. Trench or bastard-trench and apply manure to those plots whose turn it is. Plain-dig other plots, applying bonemeal or basic slag as necessary. Make sure of early completion of beds for next year's Brassicas, onions, and potatoes.

Begin forcing rhubarb and seakale if grown, and continue forcing endives.

Heel 'heading' broccoli over to north in exposed regions and earth-up all other winter greens. Lift horse radish.

Fruit. Plant all species of fruit.

Take cuttings of gooseberry and red and black currant.

Take down and burn sacking bands on apples.

Begin pruning apple, pear, gooseberry and red currant, and outdoor grapes towards end of month if there are many to do.

Lower rods of greenhouse grapes; clean bark if necessary.

DECEMBER

Flowers. Roses, deciduous trees, climbers, etc., and herbaceous plants may still be planted if the weather is open.

Aerate damp lawns with a fork or special spiked tool.

Dress trees, shrubs and hedges with bonemeal; dress also with lime any borders in need of it if not recently manured.

Vegetables. DIG.

Protect celery heads towards end of month with loose straw, etc.

Plant shallots just before Christmas in Southern gardens.

Examine vegetables in store for signs of disease.

Fruit. Prune apples, pears, etc. Grapes, indoors or out, *must* be done before end of month.

Spray plum, cherry, gooseberry, red and black currant and peach with tar-oil wash; spray pear and apple at end of month or early January.

APPENDICES

1. *SOME MEMORANDA*

A linear rod, pole or perch = 5½ yd.

A square rod, pole or perch = 30¼ sq yd; 160 sq rods to the English acre (4,840 sq yd); the Scottish acre is 6,150 sq yd.

2 tablespoons = 1 fluid oz; 20 fluid oz (480 minims) = 1 pint.

One shallow or near-filled dessert spoon = 1 oz of fertiliser, etc., in powder form.

1 oz per gallon = 60 minims per pint.

1 bushel of J. I. Compost fills 12 2-in seed boxes or 48 pots size 48.

2. *FLOWER-POT SIZES*

Flower-pots are made in 'casts'. Sixty 3-in. pots go to the cast, and are therefore called Sixties or 60's.

English Sizes

No.	Top diameter in inches
Thimbles	2
Thumbs	2½
60's	3
48's	4½
32's	6
24's	8½
16's	9½
12's	11½
8's	12

Scottish Sizes

No.	Diameter	No.	Diameter
60	2	12	7
48	2¼–2¾	8	8
42	3¼	6	9
36	4		
30	4¾	4	10
24	5½	3	11
18	6	2	12½

3. SEED AND POTTING COMPOSTS

John Innes Seed Compost

> 2 parts by bulk sterilised loam
> 1 part „ peat (moss or sedge)
> 1 „ „ sharp lime-free sand

To these are added, per bushel, 1½ oz superphosphate of lime and ¾ oz ground chalk or limestone.

John Innes Potting Compost

> 7 parts by bulk medium loam
> 3 „ „ moss peat
> 2 „ „ coarse silver sand

To this is added a special fertiliser compounded of 2 parts by weight of hoof-and-horn meal, 2 parts superphosphate of lime, and 1 part sulphate of potash. For pots up to 4½ in. size, 4 oz of this fertiliser is added per bushel of compost; for pots from 4½ to 8 in., 8 oz; over 8 in., 12 oz.

John Innes Compost for Cuttings

> 1 part by bulk medium loam
> 2 parts by bulk peat
> 1 part by bulk sharp sand

No fertiliser.

4. THE NORTH WALL AND BORDER

The following is a short selection of plants that succeed on the shady north side of a wall, fence or hedge.

For the wall or fence itself (according to height), provided there are no overhanging trees—

Morello cherry, Kentish Red cherry, and some sweet cherries; red currants and gooseberries, either trained or as bushes; loganberries and blackberries on fences.

Pyracantha. Cotoneaster. Hydrangea petiolaris. Virginia Creeper. Winter Jasmine. Forsythia suspensa. Flowering quince.

Clematis: especially Nelly Moser and Barbara Jackman.

Climbing Roses: Mermaid, Mme Alfred Carrière, Mme Grégoire Stæchlin, Gloire de Dijon.

For the border—

Lilies: regale, Henryi, Crow's Hybrids, Hansonii, monadelphum, and many others.

Campanula (border varieties). Woodland Anemones and Anemone japonica. Foxgloves. Lily-of-the-Valley (extra good). Snake's-head Fritillary and any small bulbs of early spring.

Cyclamen. Peony. Mossy Saxifrage. Lupins. Columbine. Primrose and Auricula. Dicentra. Solomon's Seal (Polygonatum multiflorum). Forget-me-not, and other shade-lovers.

Some shrubs other than wall-climbers: Mahonias, Elaeagnus. Camellias. Daphne Mezereum and Burkwoodii. Forsythias. Flowering Currant. The flowering bramble, Rubus deliciosus (easy and useful). Rose of Sharon as an edging. Periwinkle.

5. SOME PLANTS FOR DRY SOILS

Shrubs and Trees

Gorse (for dry, arid banks).
Brooms (Cytisus, Genista, Spartium).
Cistus (mild counties).
Helianthemum.
Lavender.
Heathers, except the Dorset Heath and the Cross-leaved Heath.
Potentilla.
Laburnum.
Syrian Hibiscus.
Tree Lupin.
Olearia Haastii.
Buddleias.
Senecio laxifolius.
Ceanothus, evergreen varieties, if not over-dry and the climate not too severe.

Border and Rock Plants

Stonecrops and House Leeks.
Everlasting Pea (Lathyrus rotundifolius), 4 ft, pink flowers at mid-summer, good for an arid bank.
Valerian (Centranthus).
Cranesbill (true Geranium).
Catananche.
Thymes.
Arabis.
Several Dianthus, such as the Cheddar Pink and the Maiden Pink.
Anchusa (if not over-dry).
Baptisia australis (as substitute for Lupins).
Belladonna Lily and Nerine Bowdenii in warm spots.
Soapwort.
Alyssum saxatile.

6. SOME PLANTS FOR MOIST SOILS

Shrubs and Trees

Willows, Alders and Bamboos.
Hydrangea.
Some Spiræas.
Diervilla.
Deutzia.
Nearly all lime-hating shrubs if the moisture is not excessive
and the drainage good—Rhododendron, Eucryphia, the
little Kalmia polifolia, Azalea, etc.—but not Heathers other
than the Dorset and the Cross-leaved.
Cornus alba, a waterside Dogwood grown for its brilliant bark.
Thujas.

Border Plants

Astilbe and most of the herbaceous Spiræas.
Iris Kæmpferi, if you can! Iris lævigatus (standing in water).
Siberian Iris.
Rodgersia pinnata (plumes of deep pink, 3 ft, resembling
Astilbes and the popular notion of Spiræa).
Marsh Marigold (Caltha palustris), standing in water.
Loosestrife (Lysimachia) and Purple Loosestrife (Lythrum).
Forget-me-not.
Bergamot (Monarda).
Ranunculus.
Mimulus (shallow water, water-side or bog).
Monkshood (Aconitum).
Phlox, up to a point.
Many Primulas, generally the 'difficult' ones, such as Florindæ,
japonica, pulverulenta, etc.
Day Lily (Hemerocallis).
Trollius.
Lychnis chalcedonica, good also for water-side and bog.
Salvia uliginosa.

7. TOWN GARDENS

The following is a selection of some plants that, subject to soil
conditions, are generally found to succeed even in the atmosphere of large towns. Give them plenty of space and spray or
hose them overhead occasionally with water. In old town garden
soils lime dressings are often called for.

Trees and Shrubs

Catalpa bignonioides, extra good.
Daphne Mezereum, extra good.

Hawthorns of all sorts.
Flowering Almonds, Peaches and Cherries.
Sumachs.
Senecio laxifolius.
Buddleias.
The Bladder Senna (Colutea arborescens), very useful.
Barberries, nearly all
Hypericams, especially 'Elstead'.
Forsythia.
Diervilla.
Syrian Hibiscus.
Philadelphus (Mock Orange).
Spindle Tree (Euonymus europæus).
Kerria japonica.
Pyracantha.

Climbers

Virginia Creeper, Vitis coignetiæ.
Some Honeysuckles, as Lonicera japonica Halleana.
Wisteria.
Clematis.
Hydrangea petiolaris.
Ivy.
Polygonum baldschuanicum.

Roses

A great many succeed in towns and in the industrial ones
escape the black-spot disease.

Some Border Plants

Most bulbs, especially the small ones.
Chrysanthemum.
Hellebores.
Thrift.
Michaelmas Daisy.
Bergamot (Monarda).
Catananche.
Anchusa.
Catmint.
Viola.
Hollyhocks.
Lavender.
Lily-of-the-Valley (dense shade).
Solomon's Seal (dense shade).

8. *SOME GOOD NURSERIES*

The following is a small selection of some of the leading nurseries in the country, to serve as an introduction, not arranged in any significant order.

GENERAL

Hillier and Sons, Winchester.

R. C. Notcutt, Ltd., Woodbridge, Suffolk.

George Jackman and Sons, Woking.

John Scott and Co., The Royal Nurseries, Merriott, Somerset.

L. R. Russell, Ltd., Richmond Nurseries, Windlesham, Surrey.

John Waterer, Son and Crisp, The Floral Mile, Twyford, Berkshire.

Bakers, Albrighton, Wolverhampton; especially for Russell Lupins and Bishop Delphiniums.

Reginald Kaye, Silverdale, Carnforth, Lancs.

Sunningdale Nurseries, Windlesham, Surrey; especially for 'old' roses.

Dobbie and Co., Edinburgh, 7.

Bees, Ltd., Sealand Nurseries, Chester.

TREES and SHRUBS (in addition to several of the above)

D. Stewart and Son, Ferndown, Dorset.

Burkwood and Skipwith, Lane End Nursery, Elstead, nr. Godalming, Surrey.

Donard Nursery Co., Newcastle, County Down, Northern Ireland.

Walter Slocock, Goldsworth Nurseries, Woking (chiefly Rhododendrons, etc.).

HERBACEOUS and ROCK PLANTS

Blackmore and Langdon, Bath; specialists in Delphiniums, Polyanthus and Begonias.

Gayborder Nurseries, Melbourne, Derbyshire.

Bressingham Gardens, Diss, Norfolk.

Burleydam Nurseries, Little Sutton, Wirral, Cheshire.

Thomas Carlile, Twyford, Reading.

Perry's Plant Farm, Enfield, Middlesex; Herbaceous and water-side plants.

Robinson's Hardy Plants, Sidcup, Kent.

Kelway and Son, Langport, Somerset; especially for Peonies.

ROCK PLANT SPECIALISTS

W. E. Th. Ingwersen, Ltd., Birch Farm Nurseries, Gravetye, East Grinstead, Sussex.

J. R. Ponton, The Gardens, Kirknewton, Scotland.
Jack Drake, Inshriach Nursery, Aviemore, Inverness-shire.
Joe Elliott, Broadwell Nursery, Moreton-in-Marsh, Glos.
H. Davenport-Jones, Washfield Nursery, Hawkhurst, Kent.

ROSES

R. Harkness and Co., Hitchin, Hertfordshire.
Dicksons of Hawlmark, Newtonards, near Belfast.
McGredy and Son, Portadown, Northern Ireland.
E. B. Le Grice, Roseland Nurseries, North Walsham, Norfolk.
Edwin Murrell, Shrewsbury; especially for 'old' roses.
John Cocker and Sons, Aberdeen.
Cant's of Colchester, Colchester.
C. Gregory and Son, Stapleford, Nottingham.
John Mattock, Nuneham Courtney, Oxford.
Harry Wheatcroft and Sons, Edwalton, Nottingham.

BULBS, etc.

Walter Blom and Sons, Leavesden, Watford.
Wallace and Barr, Marden, Kent (also seeds and herbaceous).
For miniatures: Broadleigh Gardens, Sampford Arundel,
    Wellington, Somerset.

SEEDS (Flower and Vegetable)

Thomas Butcher, Shirley, Croydon, Surrey.
Samuel Dobie and Son, Chester.
Carter's Tested Seeds, Raynes Park, London, S.W.20.
Thompson and Morgan, Ipswich; including unusual sorts.
Sutton and Sons, Reading, Berkshire.
Geo. B. Roberts, Faversham, Kent; some good specialities.
J. L. Clucas, Ormskirk, Lancs.

CARNATIONS and PINKS

Allwood Brothers, Ltd., Haywards Heath, Sussex.
Lindabruce Nurseries, Lancing, Sussex.
Napiers, Stepswater Nurseries, Taunton.
Stewart Low Co., Bush Hill Park, Enfield, Middlesex.

FRUIT TREES

Lord Wolmer's Nurseries, Blackmore, Liss, Hampshire.
Bunyards and Laxtons, Huntingdon.
Thomas Rivers and Sons, Ltd., Sawbridgeworth, Herts.
W. Seabrook & Sons, Boreham, Chelmsford.
Justin Brooke, Ltd., Wickhambrook, near Newmarket.

W. J. Unwin, Ltd., Histon, Cambridgeshire. Sweet Peas; also general seedsmen.

R. Bolton, Ltd., Birdbrook, near Halstead, Essex; the like.

John Crutchfield, Snow Hill, Copthorne, Sussex; Dahlias.

Anthony Ayton, Ltd., Kibble Lane, Southborough, Tunbridge Wells; Pelargoniums.

H. Woolman, Ltd., Shirley, Birmingham; Chrysanthemums.

Rileys, Alfreton Nurseries, Woolley Moor, Derbyshire; Chrysanthemums.

Orpington Nurseries, Orpington, Kent: especially Irises.

Maxwell and Beale, Ltd., Broadstone, Dorset; Heathers.

John F. Letts, Foxhollow, Westwood Rd., Windlesham, Surrey; Heathers.

INDEX

In most instances plants are entered under both their botanical names and (where there are any in normal or recommended use) their vernacular; if the entry is a short one, page references are given in both.

Where there is more than one page reference in an entry the main paragraph on cultivation and selection of varieties is shown in **bold** figures, unless otherwise indicated. References of no significance are omitted.

Page references of line drawings are preceded by an italic *d*.

AARON'S ROD, *see* Mullein

Abelia Schumanii, 255

Abutilons, 255

Acæna microphylla, 178

Acer (Maple), 222, **227**

Achillea (Yarrow): border sorts, 139, **140**; rock, 139, **176**

Acid soil, 13, 33, 48–9; shrubs for, 237–40

Aconite, Winter (Eranthis hyemalis), 182, 202

Aconitum (Monkshood), **150**

Acre, 393

Æthionema, **169**, 178

African Marigold (Tagetes erecta), **127**, 384

Ageratum, 121, **122**, 166

Agricultural salt, 47

Alkaline soil, 13, 33

Allium, 167, 186, **187**

Almond, flowering, 224, 225

Alstrœmeria, 136, 137, **140–1**

Althea rosea (Hollyhock), 148

Alyssum: annual, **122**, 166; A. saxatile, **176**, 178

Amanogawa, 221, 224

Amaranthus caudatus (Love-lies-bleeding), **126**

Amaryllis Belladonna (Belladonna Lily), 183, **189**, 387

American Blight (Woolly aphis), 365, 371

Ampelopsis, 250

Anagallis (Pimpernel), 166

Anchusa, 86, **141**

Androsace, 166

Anemone: tuberous species and hybrids, 33, 137, 166, 167, 168, 169, 180, 182, 183, 184, **187–8**, 383, 390; in rock gardens, 166,

167, 168; herbaceous species (A. japonica and A. Pulsatilla), 140, **141**, 394

Angels' Fishing Rods (Dierama pulcherrimum), 157

Annuals: definition, 35; seed-sowing, 74 *et seq.*; in greenhouse, 107, 383, 384, 386; in hotbed, 114; general cult., Ch. X; for rock garden, 166; 'winter annual', 120

Anthemis, *see* Camomile

Anther, 33, 34

Antirrhinum (Snapdragon), **122**; in greenhouse, 107; cuttings, 81; other refs., 23, 34, 35, 69, 75, 81, 91, 118, 119, 121, **122**, 123, 166, 184, 382, 385, 387, 389

Ants, 369

Aphis, 215, 365; treatment, 371; carriers of virus, 365

Apple, 26, 33, 34, 89, 93; general cult., 301–7; as cordons and espaliers, 297, *d* 296, 301–2, *d* 302; root stocks, 302; planting distances, 302–3; picking, 303; storing, 303; thinning, 305; spraying, 306, refs. to, 384, 385, 386, 388, 389, 390; bud stages (for spraying), *d* 306, 384, 385; pruning, 303–5, *d* 304; refs. to, 93, 392; summer pruning, 298–9; *d* 304, 388; buds and spurs, *d* 304; varieties, 306–9

Apricot: flowering, 225; fruiting, **309**, 386

April, work during, 384–5

Aquilegia (Columbine), 21, **79**, **144**

Arabis albida, 176

Arbor vitæ, *see* Thuya
Arbrex, 94
Arbutus Unedo, 242
Arenaria (Sandwort), **170**, 178
Armeria (Thrift), **178**, 179
Artemesia, 139
Artichoke, **337**
Artificial fertilisers, *see* Inorganic Foods
Ashes, for garden use: wood, 45; coal, 47
Asparagus, 72, 335, **337–8**, 382, 385, 387, 391; planting, *d* 353
Aspect, factor in planning, 27–8
Asphalt, paths, 100
Aster: annual species, **123**, 383; perennial species, 136, 138, 140, **141–2**, 391; A. luteus (Solid-aster), 136, 138, **142**; for rock garden, 176, 179; Michaelmas Daisy, 141
Astilbe, 109, **142**
Aubrieta, 139, 165, 168, 169, **170**, 178, 179; cuttings, 84
Aucuba, 263
August, work during, 388–9
Auricula, 122, 152, 166, 168, 174, 395
Azalea, 109, **239**

BACTERIA, of soil, 36
Bacterial diseases, 365; bacterial canker, 377
Bamboo, 82
Banks, 164–5
Baptisia, 156
Barberry (Berberis), 23, 93, 222, **228**, 389; hedging, 260, **262**
Bartonia aurea, 107, 120, **123**
Basic slag, 46–7
Bastard-trenching, 62
Bean, generally, under Legumes, 332–4; sowing, 76, *d* 333
  Broad, **338**, 382, 385, 386, 391
  Flageolet, **338**, 386
  French or Kidney, **338–9**, 386, 387, 390
  Haricot, **339**, 390
  Scarlet Runner, 335, **339**, 386, 387
Bedding, spring and summer, 121–2, 387, 390, 391
Bee, leaf-cutting, 215
Beech (Fagus) as hedge, 260, **262**; renovation, 264
Beetroot, **339**, 385, 387; *see also under* Roots, 332
Begonia, 74, 106, 121, 181, 183, 184, **188–9**, 387, 390; in greenhouse, 106, 107, 384; fibrous-rooted, 86

Belladonna Lily (Amaryllis bella-donna), 183, **189**, 387
Bellows, for insect powders, 55, 366
Berberis, *see* Barberry
Bergamot (Monarda species), 140, **142**
Besom, 55
BHC, 368; use, **379**
Biennials: definition, 35; seed-sow-ing, 74 *et seq.*; pricking out, 79, **121**; and Ch. X generally
Big Bud (of Black Currants), 371, *d* 311
Bignonia (Campsis) radicans, 249, **251**
Bindweed, 66
Birch (Betula), weeping, 222
Birds, 301, 364, 369
Black Currant, **311–12**; pruning and propagation, *d* 311; big bud, *d* 311; treatment of, 371; rever-sion, 377; refs., 84, 385, 386, 389, 392
Black Fly, *see* Aphis
Black Spot, 216, **374**
Blackberry, 73, 294, **310**, *d* 310, 391, 394
Bladder Senna (Colutea arbores-cens), 397
Bleeding Heart (Dicentra specta-bilis), **109–10**, 140, **143**; in greenhouse, 109–10
Blood, dried, 41
Blossom: parts of, 33, *d* 33; male and female, 33; illustrated, *d* 343
Blossom-end rot, **375–6**
Bluebell, 21, 200
Blue-eyed Mary (Omphalodes verna), **172**
Bonemeal, 40, **41** and *passim*
Bordeaux Mixture, *see under* Copper Fungicides
Borecole (Kale), **346**, 385
Botrytis, 374
Box (Buxus sempervirens), 259, **262**
Bract, 33
Brassicas, general cult., 331–2, and in Part V *passim*
Bricks, for paving, 99
Broadcasting seed, 78, 80
Broccoli, **340**; *see also under* Brassi-cas, 332; heeling-over, *d* 333; refs., 385, 392
Broom (Cytisus), 23, 29, 30, 32, 74, 92, 93, 160, 165, 167, 178, **230–1**, 247, 285, 387; hedging, 261; renewal, 265
  for rock garden, 165, 167, 178
  Genista, 178, 231; in greenhouse, 110

Brown rot, 374, *d* 376
Brussels Sprouts, **340–1**, 382, 384, 387; *see also* Brassicas, 331–2
Bud stages, for spraying (apple and pear), *d* 306
Buddleia, 74, 91, 92, 95, 227, **228–9**, 247, 382
Buds, *d* 13, 33; fruit and growth, 293; of apple and pear, *d* 304
Bulbs: nature of, 180; where to plant, 181–2; manuring, 181; lime for, 181; among roses, 182, 218; among shrubs, 182; planting, 182–3; naturalising, 182; after-care, 183; lifting and drying, 183–4; heeling-in, 183; propagation, 184; in bowls and pots, 184–6, *d* 185, 390; in greenhouse, 108; for rock garden, 167; list of, 186–202
Bullace, 322
Bush fruits, definition, 293; general treatment, 295–301
Butterfly Flower (Schizanthus), 107, 382, 389
Busy Lizzie, 110

CABBAGE, 330, 331, **341**, and Part V *passim; see also* Brassicas, 331–2
Cabbage fly, 372
Cabbage gall weevil, 371
Cactus, 32
Calabrese, 329, 340
Calceolaria, 121
Calcifuges, 39
Calcium, soil element, 39, 47
Californian Poppy (Eschscholzia californica), 119, **123**
Calliopsis (Coreopsis), 156–7
Calluna (Ling), *see under* Heaths
Caltha palustris (Marsh Marigold), 396
Calyx, 33–4
Camellia, 32, 86, **240**; on walls, 249, 255
Camomile (Anthemis): in borders, 139, 140, **143**; for small paths, 177
Campanula: border sorts, 139, **143**; rock sorts, 139, 168, **170**, 178, 179. *And see* Canterbury Bell
Campsis radicans, 249, **251**
Candytuft (Iberis): annual, **123**, 166, 169; dwarf shrub, **176–7**, 178, 179; edging, 262
Cane fruits, definition, 293; general treatment, 295
Cane spot, **374**
Canker, **374**, 376
Canterbury Bell (Campanula

Medium), 22, 35, 79, 119, 121, **124**, 387, 390
Cape Gooseberry (properly Physalis peruviana), 21
Capsid bug, **371**
Captan, **379**
Carnation, Border: general cult., 266–9; planting, 267; layering, 74, 267–8, *d* 268, 388; disbudding, 267; from seed, 268–9; cottage and picotee, 269; refs., 74, 82, 87
Carrot, 31, 75, **341–2**, 383, 385, 387
Carrot fly, 341, 372
Caryopteris clandonensis, 245
Catalpa bignonioides, **226**
Catananche cœrulea, **143**
Caterpillar, **371**, 379
Catmint ('Nepeta Mussinii'), **143–4**
Cauliflower, **342**; *see also* Brassicas, 331–2
Ceanothus, 27, 74, 92, 95, **228**, **247**, 248, 249, 383, 389; on walls, 248, 249, 254
Celastrus orbiculatus, 249, **253**
Celeriac, **342**, *d* 353, 386
Celery, **342–4**; planting and earthing-up, *d* 333; and Part V *passim*
Celery fly, 344
Centaurea cyanus (Cornflower), 107, **124**
Centipede, **362–3**, *d* 370
Centranthus ruber (Valerian), 158
Ceratostigma Willmottianum, 139, **230**, 383
Chænomeles, *see* Quince
Chafers, 215, 366, **371**, *d* 370
Chalk, 49
Chamæcyparis (False or Dwarf Cypress, sometimes included under Cupressus), 167, 246–7; hedging, 258, 260, **262**, 265; renovation, 265
Cheiranthus, *see* Wallflower
Chemical fertilisers, *see* Inorganic Foods
Cherry, flowering, 26, 222, 224; cult. and selection, **224–5**
Cherry, fruiting, 34, **312–13**, 388, 392; as wall plant, 249
'Cherry Pie' (Heliotrope), **110–11**, 121
Cherry Plum or Myrobalan (Prunus cerasifera), 263
Cheshunt Compound, 77, 80, 81, 122, 378, **379**
Chimonanthus fragrans (Winter Sweet), 237
Chionodoxa, 167, 182, 184, 186, **189**

403

Chive, 344–5, 384
Chlorophyll, 14, 31
Chlorosis, 14, 377
Choisya ternata, 245
Christmas Rose (Helleborus niger), **144**
Chrysanthemum: general cult., **274**–9; annual, **124**; maximum, 21, **279**; Early Flowering, **275**, 386, 391; rubellum, 140, **276**; Korean and Windsors, 276; outdoors, 274–6; indoor, **276**–7, 386, 387, 390; stopping and disbudding, 277–8, d 277, 386, 387, 389; propagation, 278–9, 383; 'Marguerite', 111; refs., 22, 35, 69, 82, 91, 106, 118, 119
Chrysogonum virginianum, 177
Cineraria, 106, 110, 388, 390
Cistus, 21, **242**
Clarkia, 35, 118, 120, **124**, 126; in greenhouse, 107, 383, 389
Clay, 37, 38, 49
Clematis: general cult., 248, 249, 252, 270–4; wilt, 271; pruning, 272–3; selections, 273–4; propagation, 274
Climate, 29
Climbing plants: generally, Ch. XVI; clinging, 250–1; twining, 251–3; wall-hugging, 253–5; selections by aspect, 249; in greenhouse, 108–9
Clinkers, 159–60
Clivia, 108
Cloches, 75, 113–14, d 103; in vegetable garden, 336 and under several vegetables separately
Club-root, 47, 334; treatment, **374**
Cobbles, 99
Cobaea scandens, 109
Cockspur Thorn (Cratægus Crusgalli), 226
Codlin moth, 300, 306, 366; treatment, 371, 387
Colchicum autumnale (Meadow Saffron), 22, **197**, 388
Columbine (Aquilegia), 21, 79, **144**
Colutea arborescens (Bladder Senna), 397
Compost: definitions, 14
  as potting mixture, 79–80, 85, 106; John Innes prescriptions, 394
  as soil food, method of making, 42–3
Concrete: paths, 100; to mix, 100–1
Conifers: in rock garden, 167; planting time, 223, 390; selection of, 246–7

Convollaria majalis, *see* Lily-of-the-valley
Convolvulus (including Ipomæa), **124**
Copper fungicides: for roses, 216; for group treatment, 367–8; forms and uses, **379**
Coral Spot, **374**
Cordons, as fruit-tree forms, 294, 296–7, d 296, d 302; *see also in* Apple, Pear, Gooseberry, Red Currant
Coreopsis (Calliopsis), 156–7
Corm, 180
Cornelian Cherry (Cornus Mas), 226, 237
Cornflower (Centaurea Cyanus), 107, **124**
Cornus (Dogwood), **226**, 237, 396
Corolla, d 33, 34
Coronilla, 255
Cosmos (Cosmea), **124**–5
Cotinns, 248
Cotoneaster, 222, 228, **230**, 389; dwarfs, 244; on walls, 249, 254; hedging, 260, **262**; renovation, 265
Cotton Lavender (Santolina Chamæcyparrisus or S. incana), 139, **243**–4, 261
Cotula squalida, 178
Courgettes, 345, 348
Crab Apple, flowering, 225
Cranesbill (true Geranium), 22, 23; border sorts, 139, **144**; rock, 169, **170**–1, 179
Cratægus (Hawthorn), 221, **226**
Crazy paving, 98–9
Crinum, 183, 187, **189**
Crocosmia, *see under* Montbretia
Crocus, 107, 180, 182, 183, 184, **189**–90, 388, 390; in bowls and pots, 184–5; Autumn C., so-called, *see* Meadow Saffron
Croxden compost, 79, 106
Cuckoo-spit, 372
Cucumber, 345, 385, 386, 387; blossoms of, d 343
Cultivation in general, 56–8
Cultivator, 54
Cupressus, 222, 223, 246, 258, 260, **262**; renewal, 265; *see also under* Chamæcyparis
Currant, Flowering (Ribes sanguineum), 245, 384, 389
Currant, fruiting, *see* Black and Red
Cuttings: generally, 81–6, d 83 atmosphere for, 32, 85–6; compost for, 85; hardwood and softwood, 82, 114; nodal and heel,

82–4; preparation, 84–5; root, 86; leaf, 86–7; of bush fruits, *d* 311; of chrysanthemum, *d* 277; of roses, 216–17, 390

Cutworm, **371**, *d* 370

Cyclamen, 182, 184, **190**

Cydonia, *see* Quince

Cypress, *see* Cupressus for true Cypress and Chamæcyparis for the False Cypress. Leyland's C., 223, 246, 260, 262

Cytisus, *see* Broom

DADDY-LONG-LEGS, 371

Daffodil, *see under* Narcissus

Dahlia, 22, 30, 35, 69, 82, 106, 139, 180, 183, **190–2**, 382, 384, 386, 387, 390

Daisy-grubber, 55

Damping-off disease, 77, 122, 123, etc., **374**

Damson, *see* Plum, **322–4**

Dandelion, 31, 66

Daphne, 74, 166, **167**, **231**, 247

Day Lily (Hemerocallis), 157

DDT, **379**, and Ch. XX and XXIII *passim*

Dead-heading, 14, 91, 137

December, work during, 392

Delphinium, 35, 47, 69, 74, 75, 79, 82, 125, 137, 139, **144–6**, 383, 384, 391; cuttings, 145–6; staking, 69, *d* 68, 145; var. Blue Butterfly, 120, **125**; in greenhouse, 107

Derris, 366, **379** and *passim*

Design, 28–9

Deutzia, 245

Devil's Coach-horse beetle, 264, 362, *d* 370

Devil-in-a-bush, 21

Dibber, 53, *d* 52, *d* 77

Dicentra spectabilis (Bleeding Heart), 140, **143**; in greenhouse, 109–10

Dierama ('Angels' Fishing Rods'), 157

Diervilla (Weigela), **231**, 389

Digging: generally, 56–8; methods of, 61–4, *d* 59, *d* 63; when not to dig, 57, 136–7, 183, 208, 295, 338

Digitalis (Foxglove), 30, 119, **125–6**

Dimorphotheca, 125

Dinocap, 379–80

Disbudding, 14; roses, 208–9; Chrysanthemum, 277–8, *d* 277; Carnation, 267

Dittany (Dictamnus Fraxinella), 140, **146**

Division of plants, 87–8

DNC, 380

Dog's-Tooth Violet (Erythronium), 192

Dogwood (Cornus), **226**, 237, 396

Doronicum ('Leopard's Bane'), **146**

'Double-digging', 62

Dracocephalum (Physostegia) virginianum, 157

Drainage, 58–61, *d* 59

Dried blood, 41

Drill, for seed, 76, *d* 77

Dry soil, plants for, 395

Dry wall, 160; construction and planting, 164–5, *d* 165, *d* 169; plants for, 178

Dryas octopetala, **177**, 178

EARWIG, **369**

East wall, climbers for, 249

Ecceremocarpus, 109

Echinacea, 140, **146**

Edging-iron, 55

Edgings, of paths, 101

Eelworm, 372

Eleagnus, 241

Elm, dwarf weeping, 224

Endive, **345**, 386, 387, 390, 392

Enemies of the gardener, 364–6

Eranthis (Winter Aconite), 202

Eremurus (Fox-Tail Lily), 157

Erica, 164, 167, 240; hedging, 261, **262**; general cult., **282–5**

Erigeron, 139, **146–7**, 178

Erinus alpinus, 177

Eryngium (Sea Holly), 154

Erythronium (Dog's-Tooth Violet), 192

Escallonia, **241–2**, 260, **262**; hedging, 260, 261, 262

Eschscholtzia (Californian Poppy), 119, **123**

Espalier, 296–7, *d* 296

Eucryphia, 240

Euonymus, 231; on walls, 254

Euryops acraeus, 167

Evening Primrose (Œnothera): biennial, 119, 125; perennial, **147**

Evergreens, *see under* Shrubs

Everlasting Pea (Lathyrus rotundifolius), 395

'Eye', 94, 95

F_1 Hybrid, 119

Fastigiate trees, 221

February, work during, 382–3

Fertilisers, *see* Inorganic Foods

Fig, 313

Fire Blight, 200, 306, 322, 374

Fish manure, 43

Flageolet, **338**, 386
Flags, *see under* Iris
Flame gun, 66
Flax (Linum), annual, 125, 139, 157
Flea Bane (Erigeron), 21
Flea Beetle, **372**
Fleur-de-Lys (Iris Pseudacorus), 279, 281
Flies, of carrot, cabbage, onion, **372**
Flower-pot sizes, 393
Flowering Currant, 245
Forget-me-not (Myosotis), 107, 121, **125**, 166
Forks, garden, 52
Forsythia, 84, 91, 92, 95–6, 227, **232**, 384; on walls, 249, 254; hedging, 261, **263**
Foxglove (Digitalis), 30, 119, **125–6**
Fox-Tail Lily (Eremurus), 157
Frames, *d* 103, 112–13, 336
Frankenia thymifolia, **177**, 178
Fraxinella (Dictamnus Fraxinella), 140, **146**
Freesia, 106, **108**, 389
Friends of gardener, 362–4, *d* 370
Fritillary (Fritillaria), 182, **192**
Frog, 362
Frog Fly, 372
Frog Hopper, 372
Fruit: in general lay-out, 26, 293–4; on walls, 251, 293, 297; shaping, 295–7, *d* 296, 298; pruning, 297–9; summer pruning, 289–9, *d* 304, 388; root pruning, 299–300, *d* 299, and *see also under* fruits separately; planting, 295; situation and soil, 294–5; spurs, 299, *d* 304; buds, definition, 293; spraying, 300; labelling, 301
Fuchsia, 82, 138, 139, **232**, 388; in greenhouse, 110; hedging, 261, **263**; renovation, 265
Fungicides, 55; group treatment, 367–8; specifically, 378–80; on roses, 216
Fungus diseases: generally, nature of, 365; group treatment, 367–8; specifically, 374–5; some illustrated, *d* 376

GAILLARDIA, 69, 86, 136, **147**, 383, 391; cuttings, 86
Galanthus, *see* Snowdrop
Garrya eliptica, 237, 245
Genista, 178, 231, 285; in greenhouse, 110
Gentian, 168, **171–2**

Geranium, 21–2, 23, 82
    true G. or Cranesbill, 21–2, **144**; rock vars., 169, **170–1**
    See also Pelargonium
Geum, 147
Gishurst Compound, 318
Gladden, 281
Gladiolus, 108, 180, 181, 183, 184, **192–3**, 381, 389, 391
Globe Flower (Trollius), 155
Godetia, 107, 120, 126
Golden Rod (Solidago), 87, 157
Gooseberry, 26, 84, 91, **314–15**, 385, 386, 388, 392; as cordons, etc., 26, 294; cuttings, *d* 311, 392
Gorse (Ulex), 32; hedging, 261, **263**
Grape, 106; general cult., **315–18**; outdoors, 316–17; indoors, 317–18, 384; pruning, 316–17, *d* 317, 392
Grape Hyacinth, *see* Muscari
Gravel paths, 99
Grease bands, 300–1
Greenback, **377**
Green-cluster of fruit buds, *d* 306
Green Fly, *see* Aphis
Greengage, under Plum, 322–3
Greenhouse: refs., 26, 32; generally, 102 *et seq.*; 'cold' house and 'cool' house, 102; heating, 102–4; cleanliness, 104–5; ventilation, 105; humidity, 105; plants for, 106–12. *See also under* Chrysanthemum, Grape, Tomato
Green manure, 44
Grey mould, 374
Ground Beetle, 363, *d* 370
Ground Elder, 66
Guelder Rose (Viburnum Opulus), 236
Gumming, of fruit trees, **377**
Gypsophila, 137; for border, **147**; for rock, 163, **172**, 178

HABERLEA rhodopensis, 177
Half-hardy plants: definition, 34; sowing and raising, 74; in greenhouse, 79–81; hot-bed, 114; h.h. annuals and biennials, 120 *et seq.*; bedding-out, 121
Halimium, 245
Hamamelis mollis (Witch Hazel), 237
Hardening-off, 120
Hardy plants: definition, 34–5; sowing and raising, 74–9; h. annuals and biennials, 118 *et seq.*, and in greenhouse, 108

Haricots, see Bean
Hawthorn (Cratægus), 221, **226**
Heaths or Heathers (Erica Calluna,
    and Dabœcia or Menziesia);
    general cult., **282–5**; for rock
    garden, 164, 167; hedging, **262**,
    refs., 237
Hebe, 176, 242, 255
Hedgehog, 362
Hedges: generally, 256–65; planting
    and spacing, 257; pruning and
    shaping, 258, d 258, 388; after-
    care, 258–9; selections, 262–4;
    renovations, 264–5
Hedge-trimmers, 55
Heeling-in, 14, 72
Helenium, 87, 138, **147–8**
Helianthemum, 21, 139, 167, 178,
    179, **243**, 247
Helianthus (perennial Sunflower),
    148
Heliotrope, 110–11, 121
Helleborus (Christmas and Lenten
    Roses), 144
Hemerocallis (Day Lily), 157
Herbaceous border: siting and pre-
    paration, general cult., 135–58;
    shade, 136, 394; shrubs for,
    139; rock plants in, 139
Herbaceous perennials, 35; dividing,
    87; general cult. and uses, 135–
    40; selections, 140–58; staking,
    68, d 68; silver-grey plants, 139
Herbs, generally, 27, 336
Heuchera, 140, **148**
Hibiscus syriacus, **232–3**
Hippophae, 264
Hoes and hoeing, 52–3, d 52, 57–8
Holly (Ilex Aquifolium), 34, 222,
    241; hedging, 258, 259, **263**;
    renovation, 264
Hollyhock (Althea rosea), 23, **148**
Holm Oak (Quercus Ilex), 263
Honeysuckle (Lonicera): climbers,
    248, 250, **252**; hedging, 258,
    263; renovation, 264
Hoof and horn meal, 44
Hop manure, 44
Hormones: root-forming, 85, 87;
    weed-killing, 290
Hornbeam (Carpinus Betulus), as
    hedge, 260, 263; renovation,
    264
Horse-radish, 86, **346**, 384, 392
Hose, garden, 54
Hosta, **148**
Hotbed, 112
House Leek (Sempervivum), 32,
    163, **172**, 178
Hover Fly, 363

Hoya, 109
Humus, 37, 38
Hyacinth, 107, 181, 184, **194–5**, 390;
    in bowls and pots, 184–6, d 185;
    'Plumed H.,' see Muscari
Hybrids, 119, 123
Hydrangea, 67, 73, 87, 93, **233–4**,
    248, 383; climbing (H. petio-
    laris), 249, 251, 384
Hypericum (St John's Wort), 87, 92,
    139, 167, **234**, 247, 382; rock
    garden, 167

IBERIS, see Candytuft
Ichneumon Fly, 363, d 370
Ilex, see Holly
Impatiens, 110
Indigofera Gerardiana, 245, 383
Inorganic foods: generally, 45–6;
    classified, 46–7; application, 65
Insect friends, 362–4, d 370
Insect pests: generally, 364–6; group
    treatment, 366–8; specifically,
    369–73; some in rose garden,
    215; some in veg. garden, 330–
    1; some illustrated, d 370, d
    376
Insecticides, 55, 215–16
Iris, general cult., **279–82**
    Bearded Flags, **279–81**; planting
    of, 72, d 280, 387, 389
    bulbous, 107, 281, 390; in bowls,
    etc., 184–6, 281, 282
    dwarf selections, 279–82
    rock garden, 172
    waterside, 281; winter, 281–2
Irishman's heel, d 83, 84
Ivy (Hedera), 248, 250
Ixia, **194**

JANUARY, work during, 381–2
'Japonica,' 22 and see Quince
Jasmine: generally, 32, 73, **253**;
    winter, 87, 92, 249, 253, 382;
    on walls, 253–4
John Innes composts, 79, 106, 119,
    and passim; prescriptions for,
    394
July, work during, 388
June, work during, 386–8
Juniper, 246, 247

KAFFIR LILY (Schizostylis coccinea),
    148–9, 383
Kale (or Borecole), **346**, 385; see also
    under Brassicas, 331–2
Kalmia, 239–40
Karathane, 216, 367, 368, 380
Kerria japonica, 92, 245
King Edward Daisy, 21

407

Kniphofia (Red Hot Poker), **153**, 391
Kochia, **126**, 166
Koelreuteria paniculata, 221, **226**
Kohl Rabi, **346**, d 353, 385
Kolkwitzia, 245

LABELLING, 117, 301
Laburnum, **226**, 247, 387
Lacewing, 363–4, d 370
Lachenalia, 108
Ladybird, 363, d 370
Lapageria rosea, 109
Larkspur, 35, 75, 118, 119, **126**
'Lateral' branch or growth, d 90, 95
Lathyrus rotundifolius, 395
Laurel, 31, 258, **263**
Laurustinus, see Viburnum
Lavatera, 126
Lavender, 93, **242**–3; hedging, 261, **263**; renewal, 265
Lawn: general cult., 286–91; from seed, 287–8; from turf, 288; mowing, 289; rolling, 289; worms in, 48, 289; aerating, 289, 383; moss, 290; feeding, 290; renovation of old, 290; pests and diseases, 291; watering, 289; weeds, 289–90
Layers: generally, 87, d 83; of Carnations, 74, 267–8, d 268, 388; of Clematis, 274; serpentine, d 83
Lay-out, 25–7, 293–4, 335–6
'Leader' (of branch or stem), d 90, 95; replacement leader, d 90
Leaf curl, **374**, d 376
Leaf cuttings, 86–7
Leaf hopper, **372**
Leaf miner, **372**
Leaf-mould, 44, 76
Leaf, nature and functions, 31
Leaf-scorch, of roses, 15–16
Leatherjacket, 371, d 370
Leek, 331, d 333, **346**–7, 382, 384, 385, 386
Legumes, general cult., 332–4
Lenten Rose (Helleborus orientalis), **144**
Leopard's Bane (Doronicum), 146
Leptosiphon, 166
Lettuce, **347**–8, 384, 385, 387, 391
Leucojum (Snowflake), 200
Levington compost, 79, 106
Liatris pycnostachya, 139, 140, **149**
Lilac (true Syringa), 22, 23, 94, 139, **168**, **234**, 387; dwarf, 168
Lily, 32, 108, 136, 137, 181, 183, **194**–7, d 195, 387, 388, 390
Lily-of-the-valley (Convallaria majalis), 135, **149**, 383, 391

Lime, 37, 38, 39; properties and uses, 47–50; tests for, 49; application, 49; forms of, 49–50; in border, 132; for fruit, 295; for vegetables, 329–30
Lime-mortar rubble, 49
Lime-sulphur, 300, 367, 374, 375, 378, 379, 380; and in chapter on fruit *passim*
Limnanthes Douglasii, 166
Limoneum, *see* Statice
Linaria, 178
Lindane, 380
Line, garden, 54
Ling (Calluna), *see* Heaths
Linum (Flax), 125, 139, 157
Liquid manure, 44–5
Lithospermum, 163, 168, **172**, 178
Loam, meaning of, 37; fibrous l., 39
Lobelia, 121, **126**; in rose beds, 217
Loganberry, 26, 73, 294, **319**, 389
London Pride (Saxifraga umbrosa), 174, 179
Lonicera, *see* Honeysuckle
Loosestrife, Purple (Lythrum Salicaria), **149**
Love-in-a-mist (Nigella damascena), 21, 120, **126**
Love-lies-bleeding   (Amaranthus caudatus), 126
Lungwort (Pulmonaria), 157
Lupin, 31, 35, 74, 75, 82, 136, 137, 139, **149–50**, 383, 384; Tree Lupin, 149–50
Lychnis, 138, 139, 140, **150**
Lythrum Salicaria (Purple Loosestrife), **149**

MAGNOLIA, **225**–6; on walls, 255
Mahonia, 228
Malathion, 371, 372, 373, 378, **380**
Mallow (Lavatera), annual, 120, **127**
Mangetout pea, 329, 351
Manure, animals, 36–7; generally, 40–1; poultry, 41; fish, 43; hop, 44; liquid, 44; green, 44; application, 64–5; as mulch, 69–70
Maple (Acer), 222, **227**
March, work during, 383–4
Marguerite (Chrysanthemum frutescens), 111
Marigold: English or Pot (Calendula officinalis); African (Tagetes erecta); French (Tagetes patula) and Mexican Striped (Tagetes signata pumila), 127 and 384 for French and African
Marl, 37

Marrow, Vegetable, **348**; blossoms, d 343, 385, 386, 387
Marsh Marigold, 396
Maurandya, 109
May, *see* Hawthorn
May, work during, 385–6
MCPA, 290
Meadow Rue (Thalictrum), 22, **157**
Meadow Saffron (Colchicum autumnale), 22, **197**, 388
Mealy Bug, **372**
Mentha Requienii, 178
Mesembreanthemum, 166
Michaelmas Daisy, 87, 123, 135, 141–2
Mildew, 215, 365, 367, **374–5**
Millipede, 367, d 370, 371
Mint (herb), 27, **348–9**
  flowering, for paving, etc., 178
Mock Orange, *see* Philadelphus
Moist soils, plants for, 396
Monarda didyma (Bergamot), 140, **142**
Monkshood (Aconitum), **150**
Montbretia, **197**, 383
Moraine, 166
Morning Glory, **127**
Mortar-rubble, 49
Moss, on lawns, 290
Mountain Ash or Rowan (Sorbus Aucuparia), 227
Mouse-ear, fruit-bud stage, d 306
Mowers, 55
Mulching, 58, 69–70, 133, d 195, 208; *also under* various plants
Mullein or Aaron's Rod (Verbascum), 22, 140, **150**; cuttings, 86
Murphy's rooting hormone, 85
Muscari botryoides, 181, 182, **197–8**, 390; in bowls, etc., 184–6; M. plumosum or comosum, 198
Mushroom, **349**
Myosotis palustris (Forget-me-not), 107, 121, **125**, 166
Myrobalan or Cherry Plum (Prunus cerasifera), as hedge, 263
Myrtles, 255

NARCISSUS (including Daffodil): general cult., **198–9**. In bowls and pots, 184–6; selections for, 198–9. Refs., 22, 34, 107, 180, 181, 182, 388, 391
Nasturtium or Indian Cress (Tropæolum majus), 21, 127–8
National Growmore, 46, 330
Nectarine, **319**, 386, 388
Nemesia, 121, 128
Nemophila, 128

Nepeta Mussinii (usual catalogue name for Catmint), **143–4**
'New wood', 91
Nicotiana (Flowering Tobacco), 75, 107, **128**
Nicotine, 367, 378; use, 380
Nigella damascena (Love-in-a-mist), 21, **126**
Nitrate of Soda, 46
Nitrogen, as soil element, 39; lack of, 364
North wall: climbers and shrubs for, 249, 394; other plants for, 394–5
November, work during, 391–2
Nursery bed, 74, 79

OCTOBER, work during, 390–1
Œnothera (Evening Primrose): biennial, 119, 125; perennial, **149**
'Old wood', 91
Olearia Haastii, 395
Omphalodes, **172**
Onion: cultivation, **349**; planting, d 333; refs., 180, 330, d 333, 334, 382, 384, 386, 387; onion sets, 349
Onion Fly, 349; treatment, 372
Organic foods, generally, 40–5
Orthocide, 306, 321, 367, 374, 375, **379**
Ovary, of flower, d 33

PANSY, **128**, 387, *see also under* Violas, **156**
Papaver, *see* Poppy
Parsley, **350**, 383
Parsnip, 75, 330, **350**, d 333, 382; *see also in* Roots, 332
Parthenocissus (Virginia Creeper), 248, **250**
Partridge Berry (Gaultheria procumbens), 244
Passion Flower (Passiflora Cœrulea), **252**, 383
Paths, construction and types, 97–101
Paving, types of, 98–9; plants for, 178
Pea, culinary, 39, 76, 328, **350–1**, d 333, and in Part V *passim*; Mangetout Pea, 351. *See also in* Legumes, 332–4
Peach, Flowering, 225
Peach, Fruiting, **319–21**, and in Part V *passim*; pruning, d 320
Peach leaf-curl, 374, d 376
Pear, **321–2** and Part V *passim*; illustrations—shapes, d 296, 302; pruning, d 304; buds, d

304, *d* 306; some diseases, *d* 376
Peat, properties of, 38–9
Pelargonium ('geranium' of popular usage), 22, 82, 111–12; bedding, 121; cuttings, 111, *d* 83, 389
Pentstemon, 82, 138, **150–1**
Peony, 70, 135, 137, **151**, 383, 390
Perennials, definition, 35; from seed, 74 *et seq.*; *see also* Herbaceous P.
Perianth, 15, 33, 34
Periwinkle (Vinca), 244
Permanganate of Potash, 290
Pernettya mucronata, **240**
Peruvian Lily, *see* Alstrœmeria
Pests, *see* Insects
Petal, 33, 34
Petunia, 107, 121, **128–9**
*p*H factor, 48
Phacelia campanularia, 120, **129**, 166
Philadelphus (Mock Orange), 22, 139, **235**, 247, 388; hedging, 261
Phlox: annual (P. Drummondii), 121, **129**
    border, 70, 135, 136, 138, 139, **151–2**; cuttings, 84, 86
    rock, 139, 168, **172–3**, 178, 179; cuttings, 84
Phosphates, 39; lack of, 364
Physalis Alkekengi ('Winter Cherry') and P. peruviana (Cape Gooseberry), 21
Physiological diseases, 39, 364–5; treatment of some, 375–7
Physostegia (Dracocephalum) virginianum, 157
Picotee, 269
Pieris, 240
Pimpernel (Anagallis), 166
Pinching-out, 91, *d* 119
Pink: general cult. and selections, 266–7, **269–70**; selections for rock garden, **173**, 179; for dry wall, 178
Pink bud, *d* 306
Pinus sylvestris pumila, 247
Pistil, 34
Plain digging, 61–2
Planting, generally, 70–2, *d* 71; of rose, *d* 210; *see also under* Dibber
Plum, Flowering, 225
Plum, Fruiting, **322–4**, 392
Plumbago capensis, 106, 109
'Plumed Hyacinth', 198
Poinsettia, 33
Pollen, 34
Polyanthus, 122, 139, **152**, 166, **174**, 390
Polygonatum multiflorum, 157–8

Polygonum: border, **152**; rock, 165, **173**, 178; climbing, 253
Poppy (Papaver): annual, 119, **129**; Iceland (P. nudicaule), 129, 152
Poppy, Oriental, 86, 152
Portuguese Laurel (Prunus lusitanica), 263
Portulacca, 166
Potash, soil element, 39; lack of, 364
Potato, 25, 328–9, 330, **351–4**, and Part V *passim*; illustration—sprouting and earthing-up, *d* 343
Potentilla: shrubs, 92, **234–5**; border, 139, **152**; rock, 165, 168, **174**, 178; hedging, 261
Poterium obtusum, 157
Potting, 106–7
Poultry manure, 41
Pressing boards, *d* 80
Pricking off, 81, 120
Pricking-out, 78, 81
Primrose (Primula vulgaris and hybrids), 139, 152, 174
Primula: border vars., 152–3; rock vars., 139, **174**, 179; in greenhouse, 112; waterside, 152, 174; Asiatic, 166; Florindæ, 174. *See also* Polyanthus and Primrose
Privet (Ligustrum ovalifolium), 258, 260, **263**; renovation, 264
Propagation, generally, Ch. VI
Pruning, generally, purposes of, 89–96; of early-flowering shrubs, 94–5, 383, 384, 386, 387, 388; of late-flowering shrubs, 95, 382, 383; root, 299, *d* 299; of hedges, 258 *et seq.*, *d* 258; of fruits generally, 297–300; summer (of fruits), 298–9, *d* 304. Illustrated examples, *d* 90, *d* 92, *d* 299; *and see under* Roses, Fruit, etc., collectively and individually
Prunus, flowering species and vars. selections, 224–5, 263; P. cerasifera (Myrobalan Plum), 263; P. lusitanica (Portuguese Laurel), 263
Pulmonaria (Lungwort), 157
Pulsatilla vulgaris (Anemone Pulsatilla), 140, **141**
Puschkinia, 186, **199**
Pyracantha, 32, 94, 241; on walls, 248, 249, 254; hedging, 259, 260, **263**
Pyrethrum, 135, 136, **153**, 383, 391
Pyrethrum (insecticide), 380
Pyrus Malus (Crab Apple), 222, 225

410

QUICKTHORN (Cratægus Oxyacan-
tha), **263–4**
Quince, Japanese Flowering (Chænomeles or Cydonia), 22, 23, 92,
235–6; on walls, 248, 249, 254;
hedging, 261, 265

RADISH, **354**, 384
Rakes, 53
Ramonda pyrenaica, 86, 177
Ranunculus, 183, **199**, 388, 391
Raspberry, 26, 92, **324–5**, 382–3,
386, 389
Raspberry Beetle, 372–3
Rectangular paving, 98
Red Currant, 26, **325**, 388, 392; as
fan or standard, 293, 297, 394
Red Hot Poker (Kniphofia), **153**,
390, 391
Red Spider, 373
Rhododendron, 22, 30, 31, 67, 74,
87, **238–9**, 387; pruning, 239,
387; rock garden, 168; hedging,
261
Rhizome, 15, 180
Rhubarb, 335, **354**, 382, 384, 385,
392
Rhus, 245
Ribes sanguineum (Flowering Cur-
rant), 245, 384, 389
Ridging, 64, *d* 59
Rock, types of, 159, 162
Rock garden: siting and designing,
160–1, *d* 161; construction,
162–3; how not to, *d* 165;
planting, 163–4; paths, 177–8;
plant selections, 166–77; an-
nuals for, 166; shrubs for, 168–
9; bulbs for, 167
Rock Rose or Sun Rose, **243**
Rod, measurement, 26, 393
Rodgersia pinnata, 259, 396
Rollers, 55
Romneya, 86, 140, **153–4**
Root, nature and functions, 31
Root cuttings, 86
Root pruning, 299–300, *d* 299
Root vegetables, general cult. 332
Rose: 23; general cultivation, 203–
20
after-care, 208–9; alpine, 169;
breeds, 204–6; bush or dwarf,
168, 203–4, 208, 211, 218 (selections); climbers, 108, 204, 214,
218–19 (selections); com-
panion plants, 217; cuttings,
216–17, 390; disbudding, 209–
10; 'floribunda', 139, 205, 218;
forms and shapes, 203–4;
greenhouse vars., 108; hedging,

261, 264; lay-out, etc., 217;
lime for, 206; manuring, 206,
207, 208; mulching, 208; pests
and diseases, 215–16; pillar
roses, 219; planting 70, 207–8,
d 210; polyantha and hybrids,
205, 211, 218; propagation,
216–17; pruning, 92, 209–15,
d 212, 213; ramblers, 204, 208,
214, 219; shrub, 204, 208, 220;
situation and soil, 206–7; standard, 204; 'species' and their
hybrids, 205, 208, 214, 219–20
(selections); stocks, 205; suckers, 210, *d* 210; for town gardens, 397; varieties, selections
of, 217–20; weeping standard,
204, 219; Wichuriana, 205
Rose Campion (Lychnis, or Agro-
stemma, Coronaria), 139
Rose-leaf scorch, treatment, **375**
Rose Mallow, 120, **127**
Rosemary, **242–3**, 265
Rose of Sharon (Hypericum calycinum), 167, **234**, 244, 247, 261
Rotation of Crops, 334–5
Rots, **375**
Rowan or Mountain Ash (Sorbus
Aucuparia), 227
Rubus deliciosus, 395
Rudbeckia, **154**
Rust, 215, **375**

SAGE: herb, **354**; flowering, *see under*
Salvia
Salpiglossis, 107, **129**
Salsify, 329, **354–5**, *d* 353, 385; *see
also in* Roots, 332
Salvia (Flowering Sage): generally,
20–1; border vars., 21, 139, 140,
154; bedding (S. splendens),
129–30, 387
Sand, as soil ingredient, 37
Sandwort (Arenaria), **170**, 178
Santolina Chamæcyparissus (S.
incana), 139, **243–4**, 261
Saponaria ocymoides (Soapwort),
169, **175**, 178
Savoys, *see in* Cabbage, 295
Sawfly: apple, 366, **373** (treatment),
d 376; leaf-rolling, 215, 373
(treatment)
Saxifrage, 168, 169, **174–5**, 178, 179
Scab, **375**, *d* 376
Scabious, 135, 136, **154**, 383, 391
Scarborough Lily, 108
Scarlet Runner, *see* Bean
Schizanthus, 75, 382, 389
Schizostylis coccinea (Kaffir Lily),
148–9, 383

411

Scilla, 167, 182, 184, **200**, 390
Scorzonera, 355
Scotch Fir, miniature, 247
Scree, 166
Sea Buckthorn, 264
Sea Holly (Eryngium), **154**
Sea Kale, 86, 384, 392
Seaweed, 45, 47
Secondary shoot, 293, 299
Sedum, see Stonecrop
Seed: raising plants from, 74–81;
    in boxes and pans, 79–81, d 80;
    sowing at stations, 78, d 77,
    d 333; in vegetable garden, 330;
    peas and beans, d 333; s.-drill,
    76, d 77
Sempervivum (House Leek), 32,
    163, **172**, 179
Senecio laxifolius, 139, **244**, 395
Sepal, 33, 34
September, work during, 389–90
Seradix, 85
Serphid Fly, 363
Shade, problem of, 31–2. See also
    N. Wall
Shallot, **355**
Shasta Daisy (Chrysanthemum
    maximum), 21
Shears, garden, 55
Shrubs and Trees: 221–47; Deci-
    duous flowering, 227–36; as
    small standards, 227
    cuttings, 81–6; seed, 247
    dwarf and carpeting, 243–4
    evergreen: planting, 72; pruning,
    94; list of, 241–3; loss of leaf,
    257; renovation, 264
    for herbaceous borders, 139; for
    rock gardens, 167–8; for acid
    soils, 237–40; winter-flowering,
    237
    planting, 70–2
    pruning: 89–96, and under each
    genus separately
Siberian Iris, 281
Sidalcea, **154**
Silver foliage plants, 139, 175
Silver leaf, **375**
Skirret, 54
Slugs and Snails, 77, 195, **369–71**
Slugworm, 215, 373
'Snag', d 90, 94, 95
Snapdragon, see Antirrhinum
Sneezewort, 21
Snowball Tree and 'Japanese Snow-
    ball', 236
Snowdrop (Galanthus), 167, 182,
    183, 184, **200**, 388; in bowls
    and pots, 184–6
Snowflake (Leucojum), 200

Soapwort (Saponaria), 169, **175**,
    178
Sodium chlorate, 66
Sodium chloride (Agricultural Salt),
    47
Soil: generally, 29, 32–3, 36–40, 85–
    6; heating, 114–15; indicator,
    49; top soil and sub-soil, 36–7;
    types of, 37–9; chemical ele-
    ments, 39–40
Solanum capsicastrum, 21; S. cris-
    pum, **253**
Solidago (Golden Rod), 87, 157
Solomon's Seal (Polygonatum multi-
    florum), 157–8, 395
Soot, 47, 49, 77
Sorbus Aucuparia (Rowan or Moun-
    tain Ash), 227
South wall: definition, 27; plants
    for, 249–50
South-east wall, 27
Sowing, see Seed
Spades, 51
Speedwell, see Veronica
Spinach, 335, 355–6, and Part V
    passim
Spindle Tree (Euonymus euro-
    pæus), 231, 254, 397
Spiræa: shrub, 139, **236**, 261, **264**;
    hedging, 261, 264; border,
    154–5
Spittle Bug, 215, 372
Spraying: generally, 366–8; of roses,
    215–16; of fruit trees, 300, and
    under each fruit
Spruce, 247
Squill, 200
Staking, 68–9, d 68, 195
Standpipes, 54–5
Statice, **155**
Stepping stones, 97
Sternbergia lutea, **190**, 388
Stigma (of flower), 34, d 33
St John's Wort, see Hypericum
Stocks, 75, 118, 121, 122, **130**, 383,
    387
Stolon, 73
Stonecrop (Sedum), 22, 32; border
    varieties, 139, **155**; rock, 163,
    165, 168, **175**, 178; paving, 175
Stone fruit, definition, 293
'Stopping', d 119
Strawberry, **325–7**, 335, 385, 387,
    388, 389; propagation, d 326;
    alpine, 327
Suckers, 16, 73, d 210
Sulphate of ammonia, 46, 49
Sulphate of potash, 46
Sulphur: generally, 380; flowers of
    (on roses), 367

412

Sumach, Stag's Horn (Rhus typh-
ina), 245
Summer pruning, 298–9, d 304
Sump-pit, 60
Sunflower, annual, 130–1. See also
Helianthus
'Sun Rose' and 'Rock Rose', 243
Superphosphate of lime, 46
Swedes, 356, 385
Sweet Corn, 356, 386
Sweet Pea, 22, 69, 120, 131–3, 383,
384, 387, 391; pruning, d 131
Sweet Sultan, 133
Sweet William, 22, 35, 75, 133, 387,
390
Sweet Wivelsfield, 133
Subol, 368 and elsewhere
Syringa (Lilac), 22, 23, 168, 234
Syringes, 55, 366
Systemic fungicide, 216
Systemic insecticide, 365–6

TAGETES, see Marigold
Tamarisk, 264
Tar-oil winter wash, use, 380; and
in Ch. XX passim
Taxus, see Yew
Tecoma (Campsis) radicans, 249,
251
Tender plants, 34
Terraces, 97
Thalictrum (Meadow Rue), 22, 157
Thinning-out, 78
Thrift (Armeria), 177, 178, 179
Thrip, 373
Thuja (Abor vitæ), 223, 246, 247,
260, 264; renovation, 265
Thyme, Flowering, 165, 168, 175–
6, 178; T. nitidus, 261
Thyme, herb, 356
Tigridia, 108
Toad, 362
Tomato, 26, 27, 113, 114, 356–9,
385, 386, 387; some diseases,
375; pruning and watering, d
353
Tools, 51–5, 70; pruning, 95–6
Top soil, 36–7
Top spit, old, as plant food, 45
Tortoise, 362
Tortrix moth, 215
Town gardens, 29; plants for, 396–7
Transpiration, of plants, 31
Trees, 28; fastigiate, 221; weeping,
222; selection, 223–7; in de-
sign, 222–3, d 222; see otherwise
under Shrubs
Trenching, 62–4, d 63
Trollius (Globe Flower), 155
Trowels, 53

Tuber, nature of, 180
Tulip, 107, 121, 181, 183, 184, 200–
2, 387, 388, 390, 391; lifting and
heeling-in, 183–4; for bowls
and pots, 184–6, 201–2
Tulisan, 367, 368, 380
Turf, laying, 288; as plant food, 45
Turfing-iron, 54
Turnips, 75, 359

ULEX see Gorse

VALERIAN (Centranthus ruber), 158
Vegetables generally: 328–59; in
garden planning, 25–7; what to
omit in small spaces, 25, 328;
lime for, 329–30; manure and
fertilisers, 330; sowing, d 77,
330, d 333; some pests, 330–1
and Part IV generally; rotation,
334–5; layout, 335–6; special
family needs, 331–4
Vegetative propagation, 73
Venus's Navelwort (Omphalodes
linifolia), 21
Verbascum, see Mullein
Verbena, 121
Veronica (Speedwell): border, 155–
6; rock, 176, 178, 179; shrub,
242; hedging, 264
Viburnum, 228, 236
Vinca (Periwinkle), 244
Viola: border, 135, 156, 169, 380; in
rose-beds, 217; rock, 179; cut-
tings, 82, d 83, 390. See also
Pansy
Virginia Creeper, 248, 250
Virus diseases, 365
Viscaria, see Lychnis
Vitis, 251

WALLFLOWER (Cheiranthus), 35, 75,
79, 91, 118, 121, 122, 134, 177,
179, 387, 390; Scotch Double
(C. Cheiri Harper Crewe), 177,
179
Walls, some plants for, 248–55
Wart disease, of potatoes, 375
Wasp, 362
Watering, 67–8, d 67; seed boxes and
pots, 80; in greenhouse, 105;
water-table, 58
Watering-cans, 54
Weeds and weeding, 65–7, 384; in
paths, 66–7; in lawns, 289–90
Weeping trees, 222
Weevils, 373, 379
Weigela (Diervilla), 231
West wall, climbers for, 249
Wheelbarrows, 54

413

White Currant, 325
White Fly, 373
Whorl, 33
Willow (Salix), 396
Winter Aconite (Eranthis), **202**
Winter annual, 120
'Winter Cherry', 21
Winter-flowering shrubs, 237
Winter Sweet (Chimonanthus fragrans), 237
Winter tar-oil wash, 300, 380; and under fruits individually
Wireworm, 363, 371, *d* 370
Wistaria, **251-2**, 382
Witch Hazel (Hamamelis mollis), 237

Wood ashes, 45
Woodbine, *see* Honeysuckle
Woolly Aphis (American Blight), 365, 371
Worms, 48; in lawn, 289

YARROW (Achillea): border, **140**; rock, 139, **176**
Yew (Taxus), 246, 247; hedging, 258, 259, **264**

ZINEB, 380
Zinnia, 75, 114, 121, 134, 384, 387
Zucchini, 345

2,4-D (weed-killer), 66, 290

THE WELL-KNOWN 'PAN PIPER'
SMALL GARDEN SERIES
inspired by the continuing popularity of the
famous paperback gardening manual

THE SMALL GARDEN (416 pages, 7/6)

by Brigadier C. E. Lucas Phillips

The other volumes in the series are fully
indexed and illustrated with photographs
and diagrams.

THE SMALL ROCK GARDEN
E. B. Anderson 5/-
DO-IT-YOURSELF IN THE GARDEN
Barry Bucknell 5/-
FRUIT FOR SMALL GARDENS
Howard H. Crane 5/-
GARDENING BY THE SEA
J. R. B. Evison 6/-
WINDOW-BOX GARDENING
Xenia Field 5/-
THE SMALL GREENHOUSE
H. G. Witham Fogg 5/-
THE KITCHEN GARDEN
Brian Furner 5/-
BULBS FOR SMALL GARDENS
E. C. M. Haes 5/-
FLOWERS FROM SEED
Denis Hardwicke 5/-
PERENNIAL FLOWERS FOR SMALL GARDENS
Peter Hunt 5/-
RHODODENDRONS FOR SMALL GARDENS
Eric Joy 6/-
GARDENING IN THE NORTH
Kenneth Lemmon 5/-
GARDENING ON CHALK AND LIME
Christopher Lloyd 6/-
DAHLIAS FOR SMALL GARDENS
James E. Rooke 5/-
CHRYSANTHEMUMS FOR SMALL GARDENS
James F. Smith 5/-
GARDENING FOR THE ELDERLY
AND HANDICAPPED
Leslie Snook 5/-